PAINTING
LUMINOUS
PORTRAITS
FOR ARTISTS

STEVE FORSTER

PAINTING LUMINOUS PORTRAITS
FOR ARTISTS

An Essential Guide to Painting Facial
Features, Flesh Tones, Light, and Form

FOREWORD BY STEPHEN BAUMAN

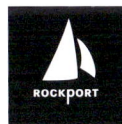

ROCKPORT

First published in 2025 by Rockport Publishers, an imprint of The Quarto Group,
100 Cummings Center, Suite 265-D, Beverly, MA 01915, USA.
T (978) 282-9590 F (978) 283-2742

EEA Representation, WTS Tax d.o.o.,
Žanova ulica 3, 4000 Kranj, Slovenia.
www.wts-tax.si

Rockport Publishers titles are also available at discount for retail, wholesale, promotional, and bulk purchase. For details, contact the Special Sales Manager by email at specialsales@quarto.com or by mail at The Quarto Group, Attn: Special Sales Manager, 100 Cummings Center, Suite 265-D, Beverly, MA 01915, USA.

10 9 8 7 6 5 4 3

ISBN: 978-0-7603-9562-2

Digital edition published in 2025
eISBN: 978-0-7603-9563-9

Library of Congress Cataloging-in-Publication Data available

Design and Page Layout: Megan Jones Design
Cover Image: Steve Forster, *Junyi*, oil on aluminum, 16" × 16" | 15.2 cm × 15.2 cm

Printed in Guangdong, China TT122025

For my mother, without whom none of this would have been possible. Drawing with you as a child changed my life forever. Thank you for all of the small sacrifices you made over many years to help me along my path.

CONTENTS

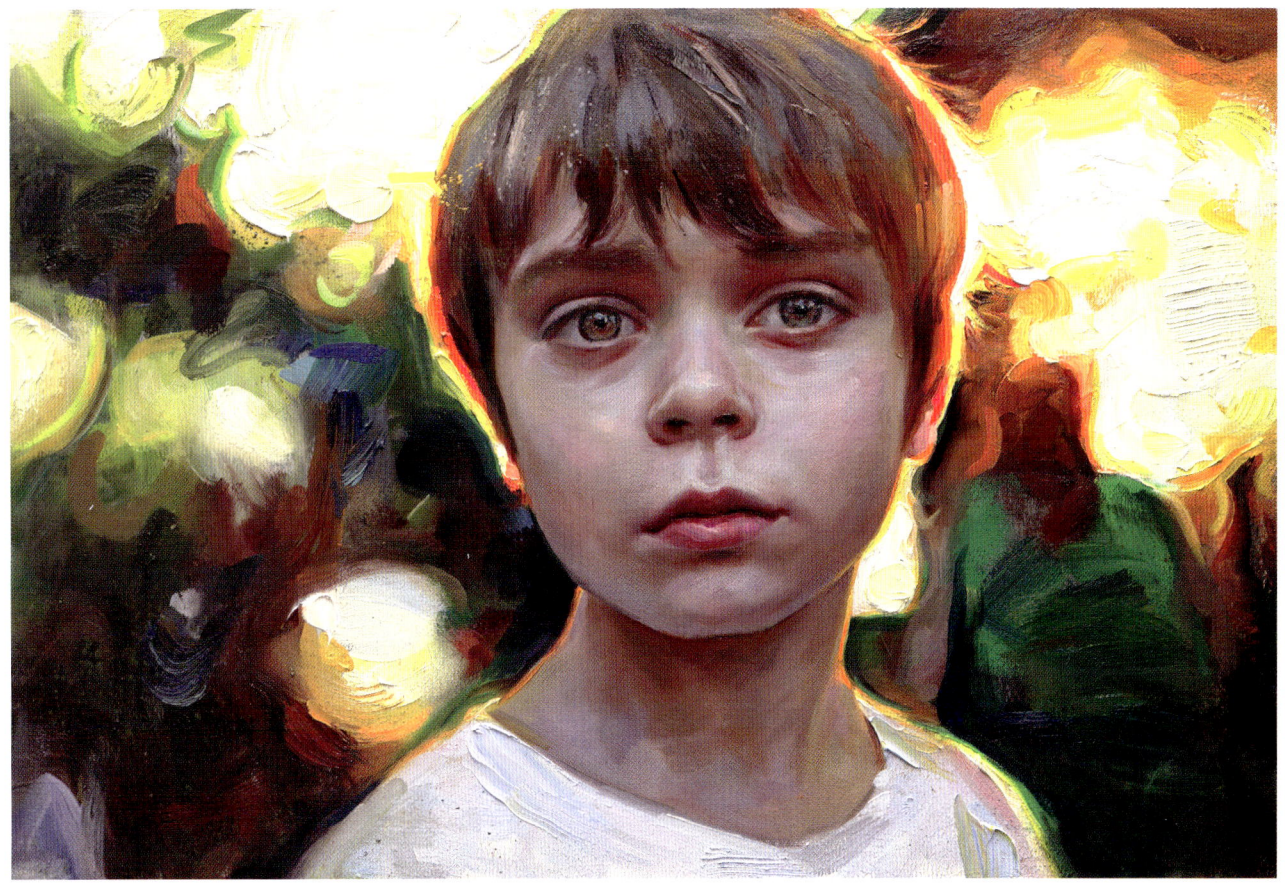

Steve Forster, *Detail of Elijah*, oil and charcoal on aluminum, 12" × 18" | 30.5 cm × 45.7 cm

FOREWORD

For more than twenty years, Steve Forster has dedicated himself to the art of portrait painting, mastering not only the technical demands of the craft but also the deeper challenge of telling human stories through this genre. I've had the privilege of working alongside him throughout this journey, and I can confidently say there's no one I'd advocate for more strongly in his capacity as a thoughtful and thorough instructor.

I first met Steve in 2002 while we were both studying at an art college in our home state of Florida. While many students were absorbed in creating experimental, often incomplete works, he devoted himself to classical drawing techniques, such as sight-size and perspective-endeavors, which were completely outside the curriculum. After completing his undergraduate studies, Steve pursued a two-year intensive program at the Florence Academy of Art in Italy, following closely the traditions of nineteenth-century figurative drawing and painting taught there. Recognizing the need to place representational art in a contemporary context, he later earned his master's degree in 2010 at the New York Academy of Art in New York City, rounding out his academic career with a modern perspective.

In this book, Forster distills his vast experience into a practical guide for artists eager to elevate their portraiture. He tackles the challenges all painters face—from developing a consistent painting process to capturing the subtleties of a model's expression—offering clear, actionable solutions to help artists overcome these hurdles. These lessons, drawn from years of experimentation, trial, and refinement, provide invaluable insight for artists at any stage of their development.

What sets this book apart from other technical manuals is its focus on the storytelling power of portraiture. For Forster, the craft isn't about mastering form or color for their own sake; it's about using those skills to reveal character, mood, and the essence of a person. Every technique and concept presented here is a tool for capturing the depth and

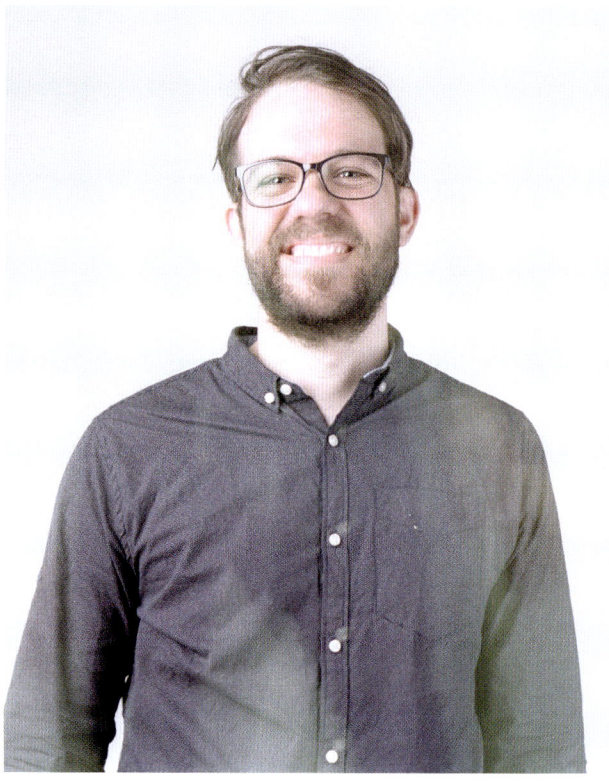

individuality of the subject. It's an invitation for you to elevate your work by using the fundamentals of oil painting to express the humanity in every face you paint.

While this book will undoubtedly teach you how to manufacture a superlative portrait painting, it offers much more than that. It's about understanding the opportunity artists have to bring their subjects to life through the language of oil painting. Under Steve Forster's guidance, readers will not only gain technical skills but also the inspiration to tell these stories with clarity, sensitivity, and, most importantly, heart.

—Stephen Bauman

▸ Stephen Bauman, *Ghost on the Highway*, graphite on paper, 18" × 24" | 45.7 × 61 cm

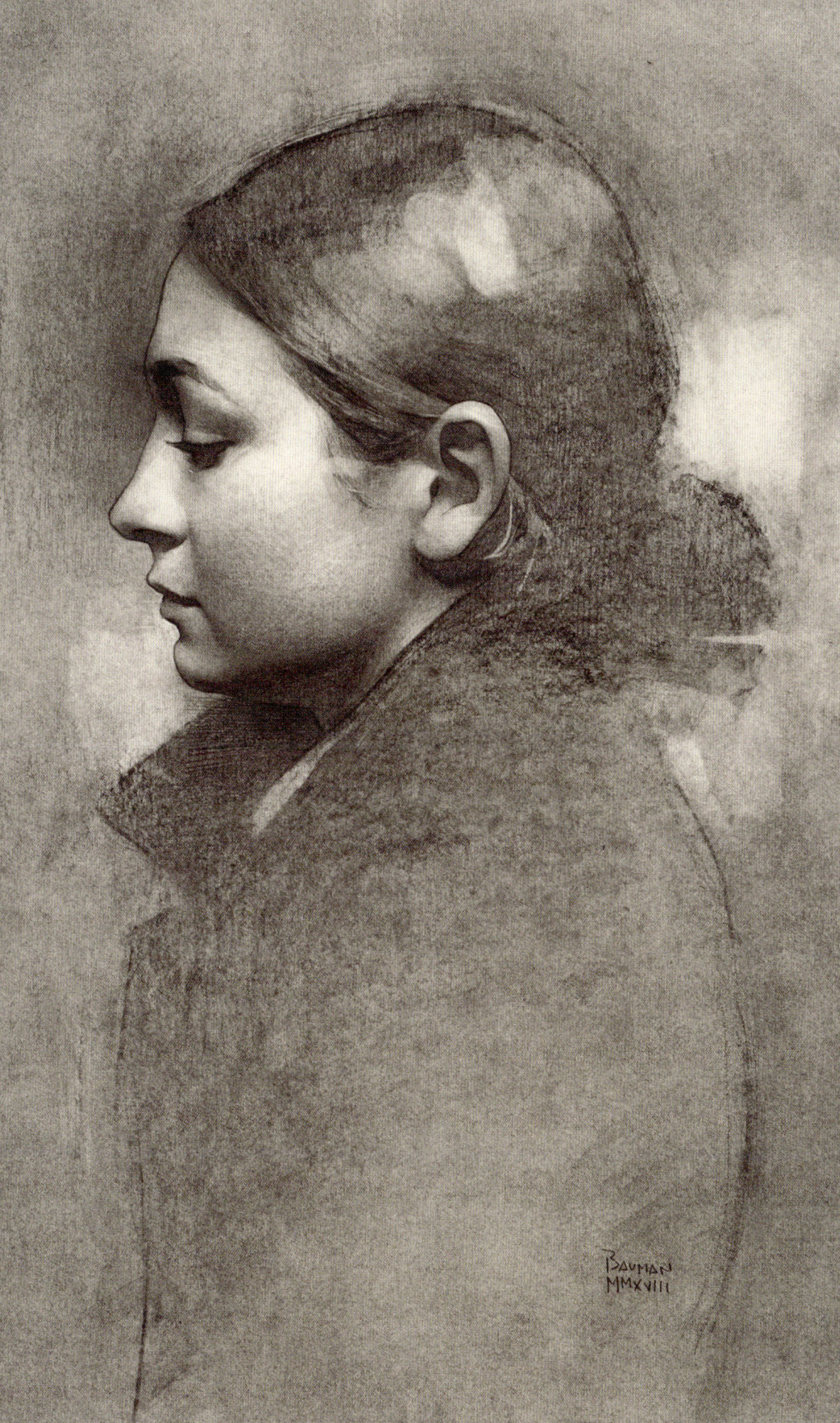

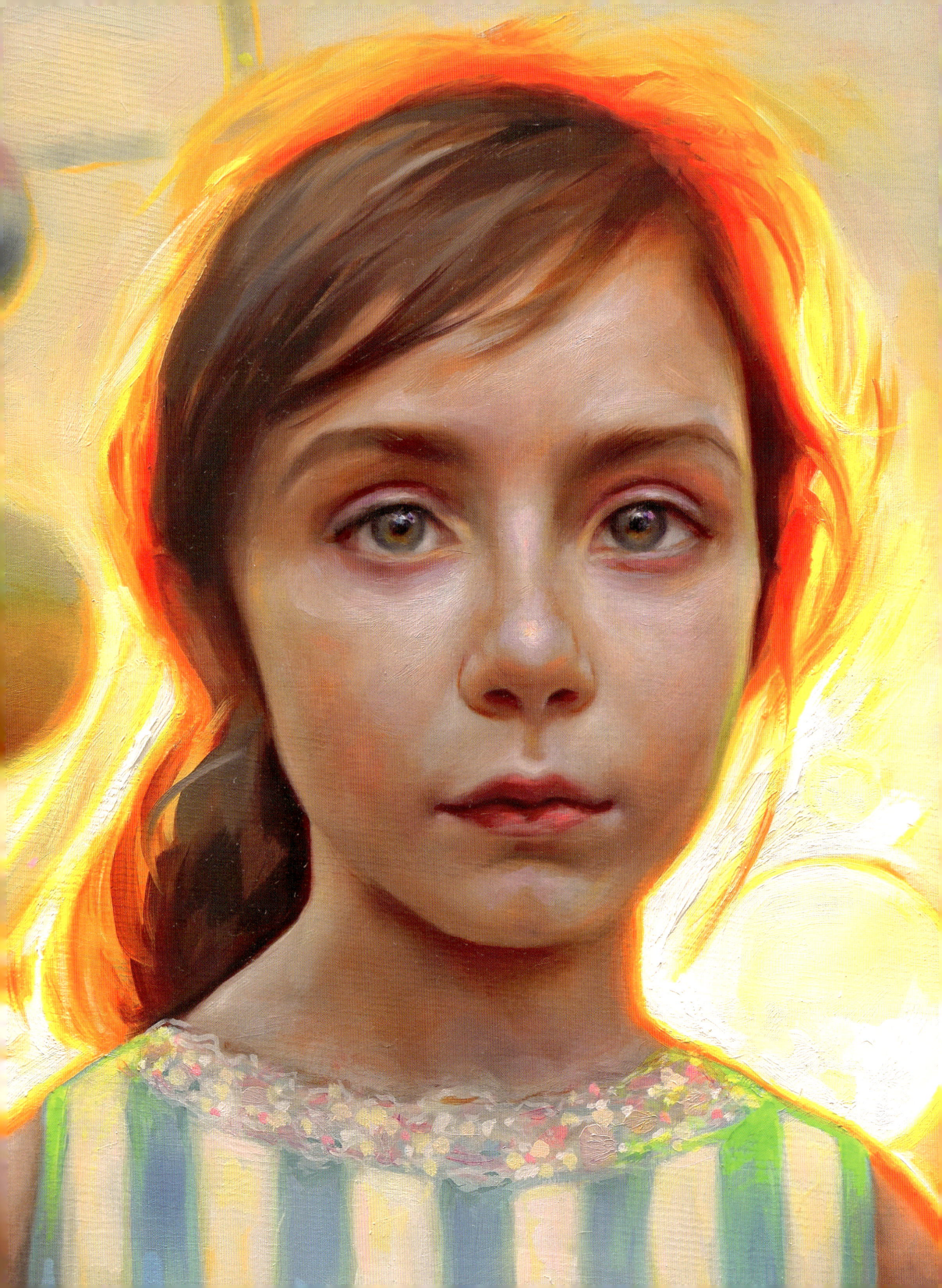

ABOUT THE AUTHOR

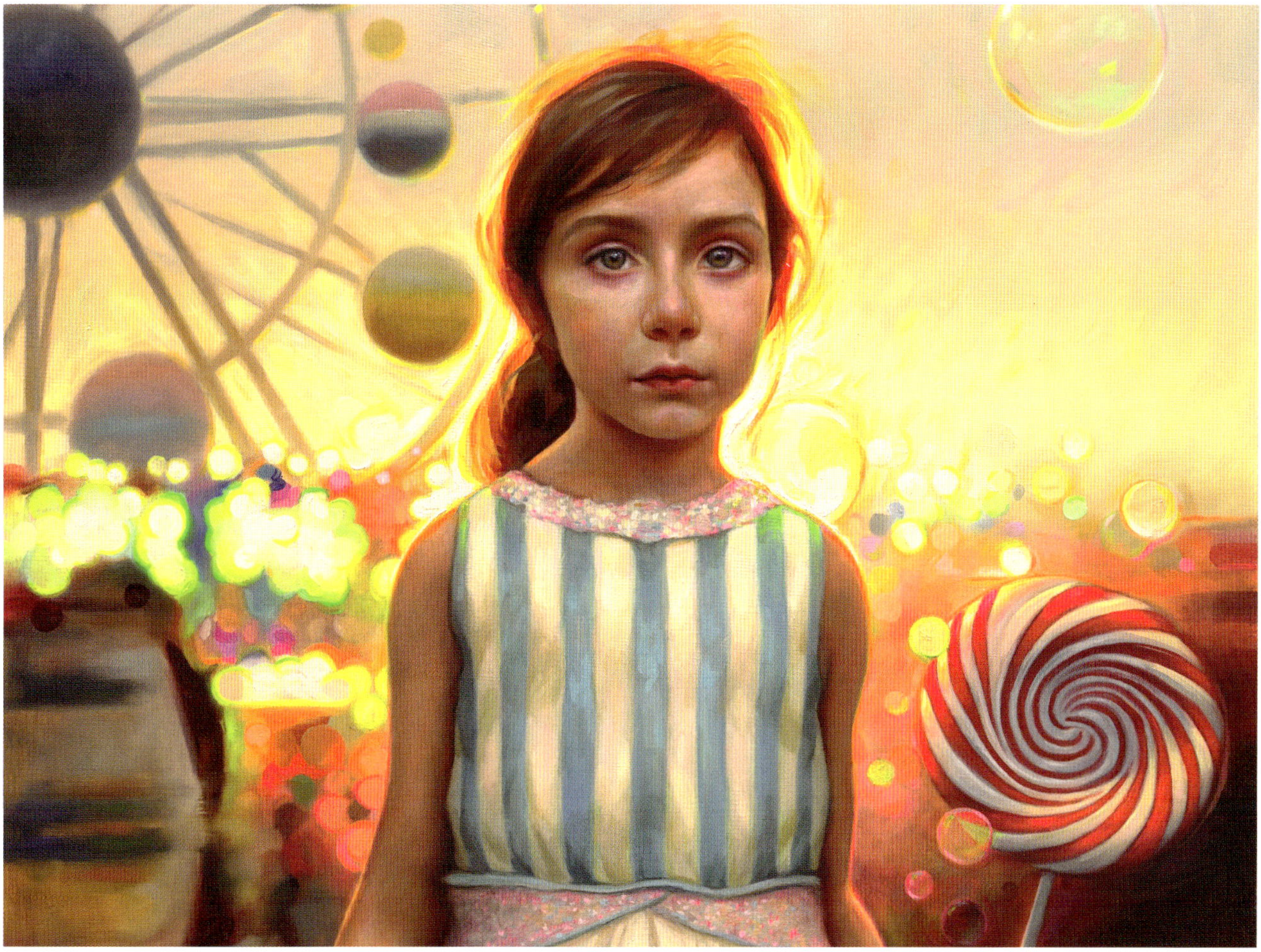

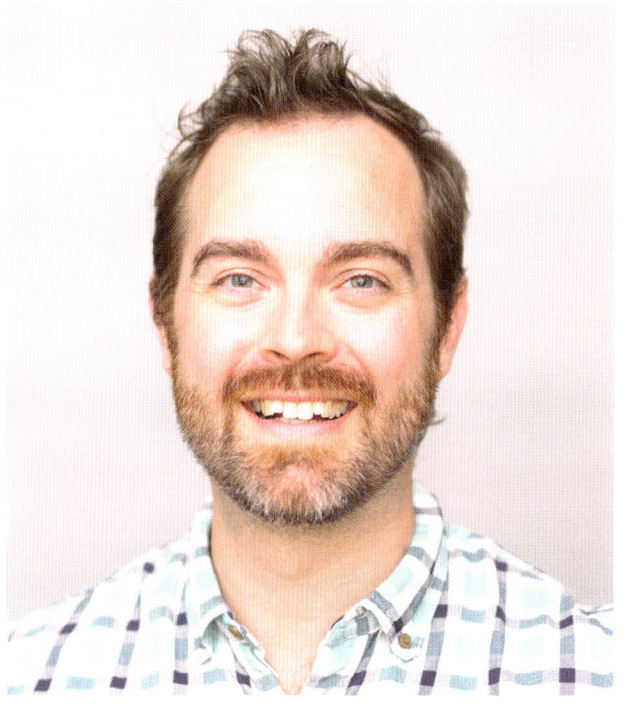

STEVE FORSTER was born in Boston, Massachusetts, and grew up in central Florida. He received his MFA in painting from the New York Academy of Art (NYAA) and also attended the Florence Academy of Art in Italy, where he met his wife, Rebecca. Since 2014, Steve and Rebecca have been co-directors of the Long Island Academy of Fine Art (LIAFA) in Glen Cove, New York. He currently teaches painting at LIAFA and previously also taught painting at NYAA for almost fifteen years. He blends digital painting and a love of traditional media to create unique contemporary portrait stories. His paintings are regularly exhibited in solo and group shows nationally. Steve and Rebecca have three kids—Elijah, Evie, and William.

◄ Steve Forster, *Detail of Evie at San Rocco's*, oil and charcoal on aluminum, 24" × 32" | 61 cm × 81.2 cm

INTRODUCTION

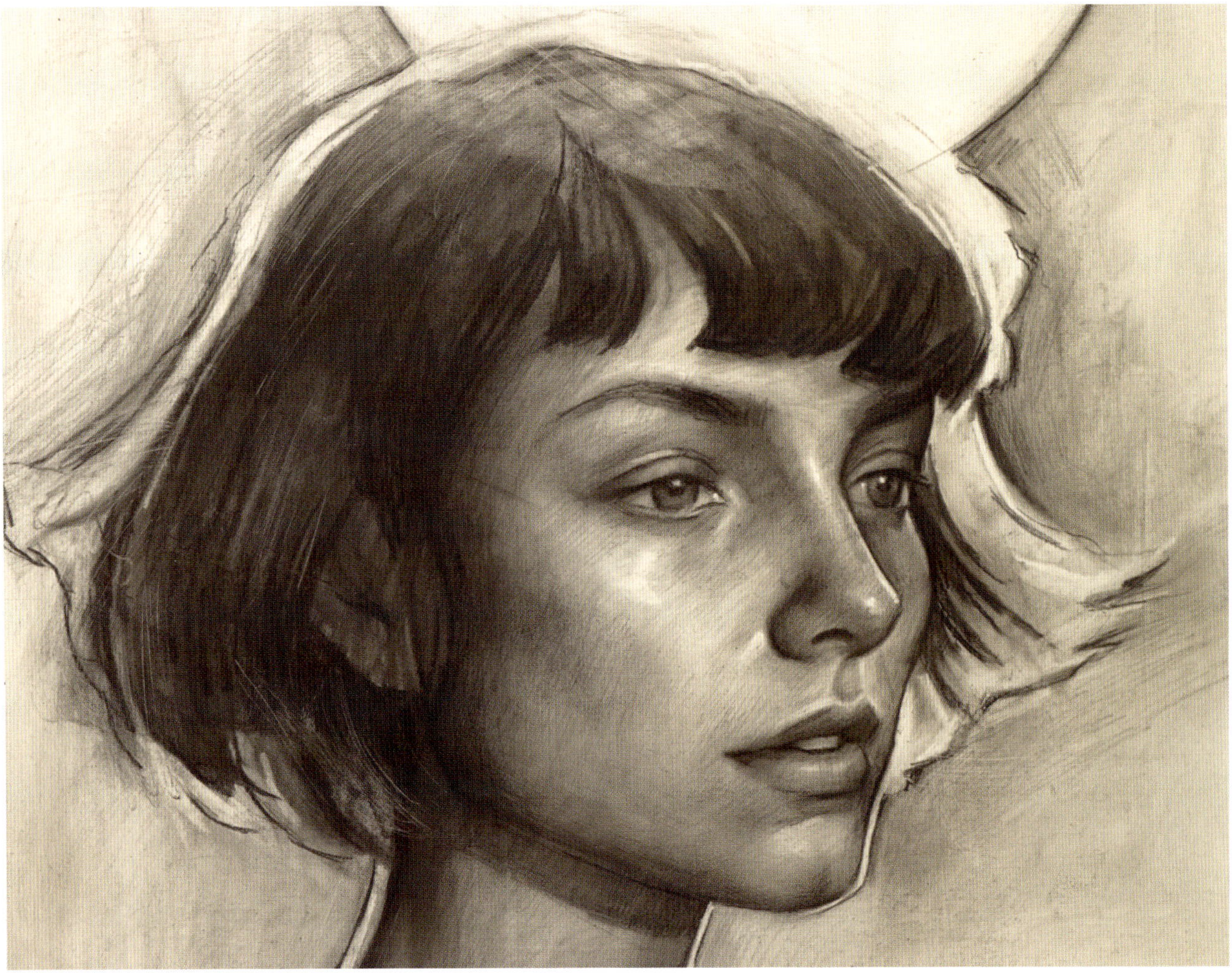

SEPARATING YOUR DRAWING PROBLEMS FROM YOUR COLOR PROBLEMS

When making a portrait, there are a lot of concepts to juggle, and that process can often become so convoluted that all the ideas we're juggling come crashing down.

One of the main objectives of this book is to establish a process in which you can separate drawing problems from painting (color) problems. When performing this complicated action such as building a portrait, I find it comforting to separate these problems into separate phases, so I can create a flow from one concept to the next and make steady progress. There's a long list of things that need to be done, and if you can check off these boxes, with each successive phase the portrait can slowly accumulate layers of success.

The main process put forth in this book is a unique one, in which the drawing is at least 80 percent resolved before the painting is ever really begun. That's not to say that the painting isn't redrawn at some point, and that drawing doesn't continue to be a serious function of painting, but it's great to have already achieved a likeness and be settled in the foundational work so you can deal with color and the alchemy of paint separately.

I've found that this approach allows me to loosen up and be more experimental, knowing that, with the drawing sealed underneath, if I run into a problem, I can always wipe the paint away in order to expose the drawing if I've

Scan to view a video tutorial

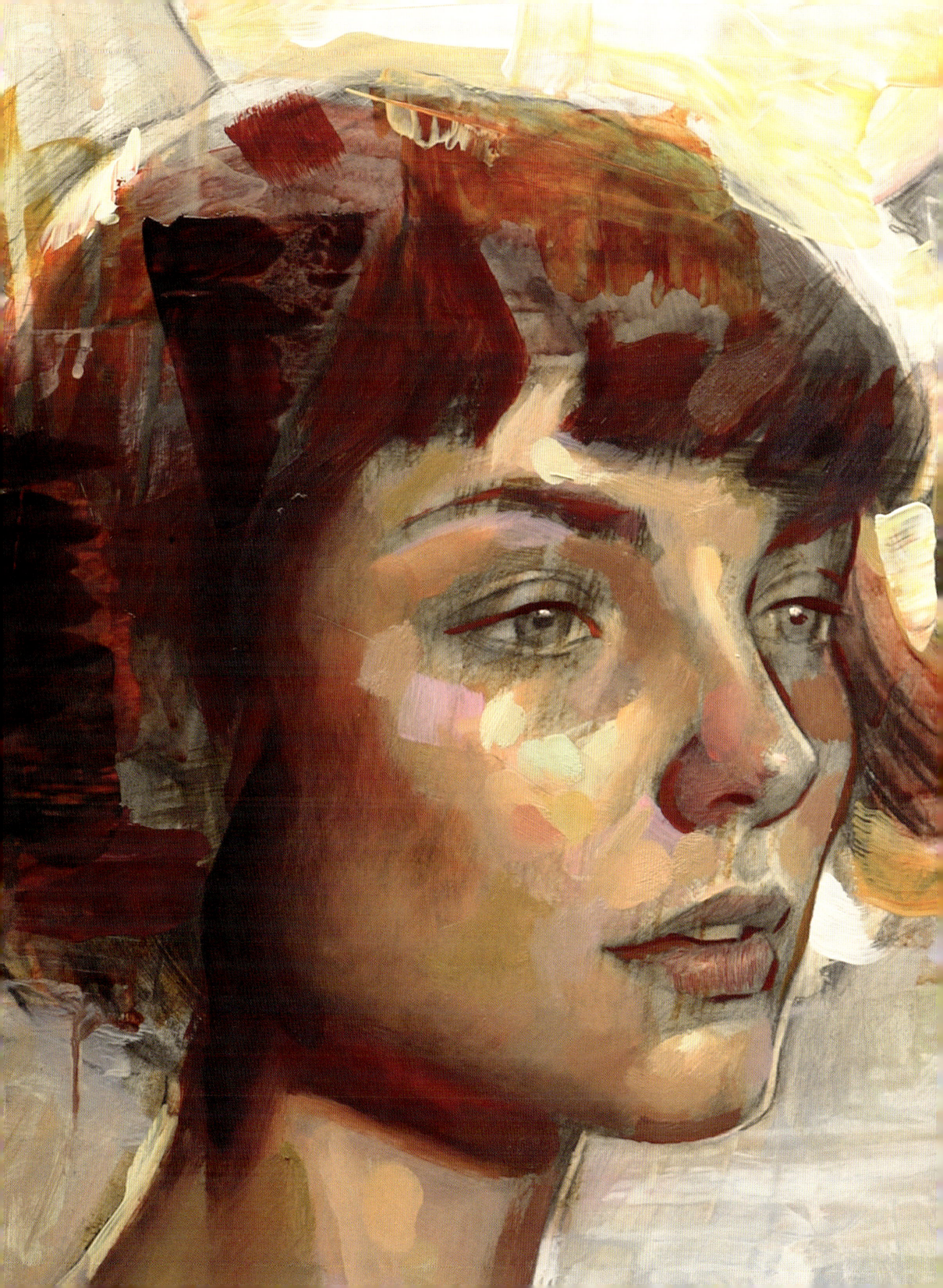

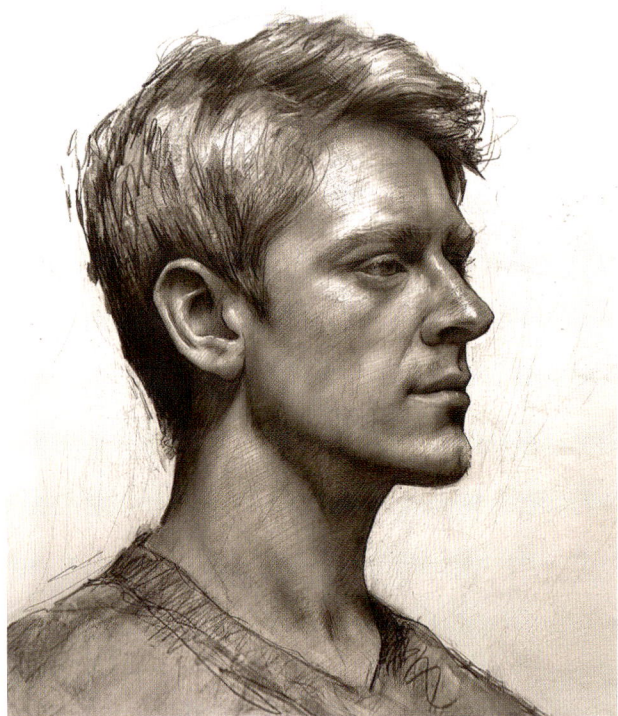

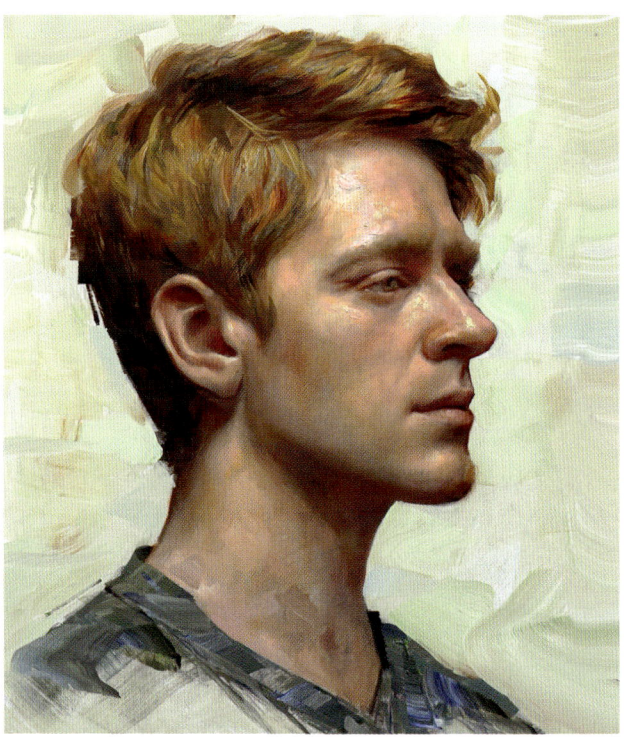

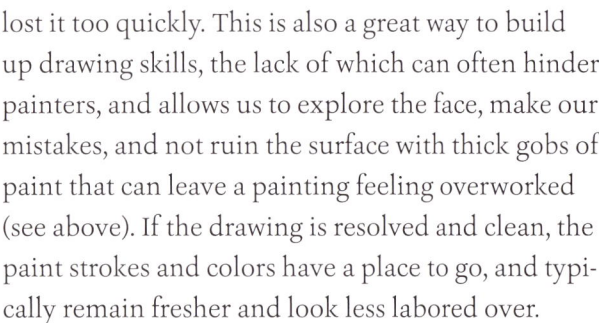

lost it too quickly. This is also a great way to build up drawing skills, the lack of which can often hinder painters, and allows us to explore the face, make our mistakes, and not ruin the surface with thick gobs of paint that can leave a painting feeling overworked (see above). If the drawing is resolved and clean, the paint strokes and colors have a place to go, and typically remain fresher and look less labored over.

As a teaching method, I find this to be quite effective to create the opportunity for students to become proficient at drawing and build on this success by painting over it. If someone is just starting out and wanting to paint portraits, and you hand them a paintbrush and a white canvas, it typically doesn't go well because there isn't a foundation of value and drawing that underpins the painting. Either the drawing, the application of color values, or the painting technique itself is failing, or at its worst, all three at the same time. This is frustrating to most people who start off with high hopes of achieving a beautiful creation, especially when they have seen the hands of a master dash off a portrait in a couple of hours in an alla prima style. But the accumulation of skill and experience is something that helps lay the groundwork for such an improvisational performance that an expert can make look so easy.

This book presents a clear structure for how to go through this process and includes thorough explanations of the thought process behind drawing, plus a few alternative methods that can add a little bit of variety to the painting experience. There are many different approaches, such as an alla prima approach or a brown underpainting approach with glazes over the top, but I find that this "underdrawing" approach is more effective for training people how to connect their drawing skills to their painting skills.

I believe in the concept of showing an idea rather than telling it, so I've made large diagrams to demonstrate what I aim to communicate. We're all visually inclined in this medium, and most artists prefer to look at just the pictures in books anyway, so the text is there as an aid to the visual diagrams, which are really the core of this book.

It's my hope that painters will be able to connect with a drawing approach that allows them to fully appreciate the act of painting unhindered by the act of drawing. But also, it's my hope that this book will help those who already know how to draw to transition into oil painting gracefully and have a method to bridge the gap between these two spheres of visual art.

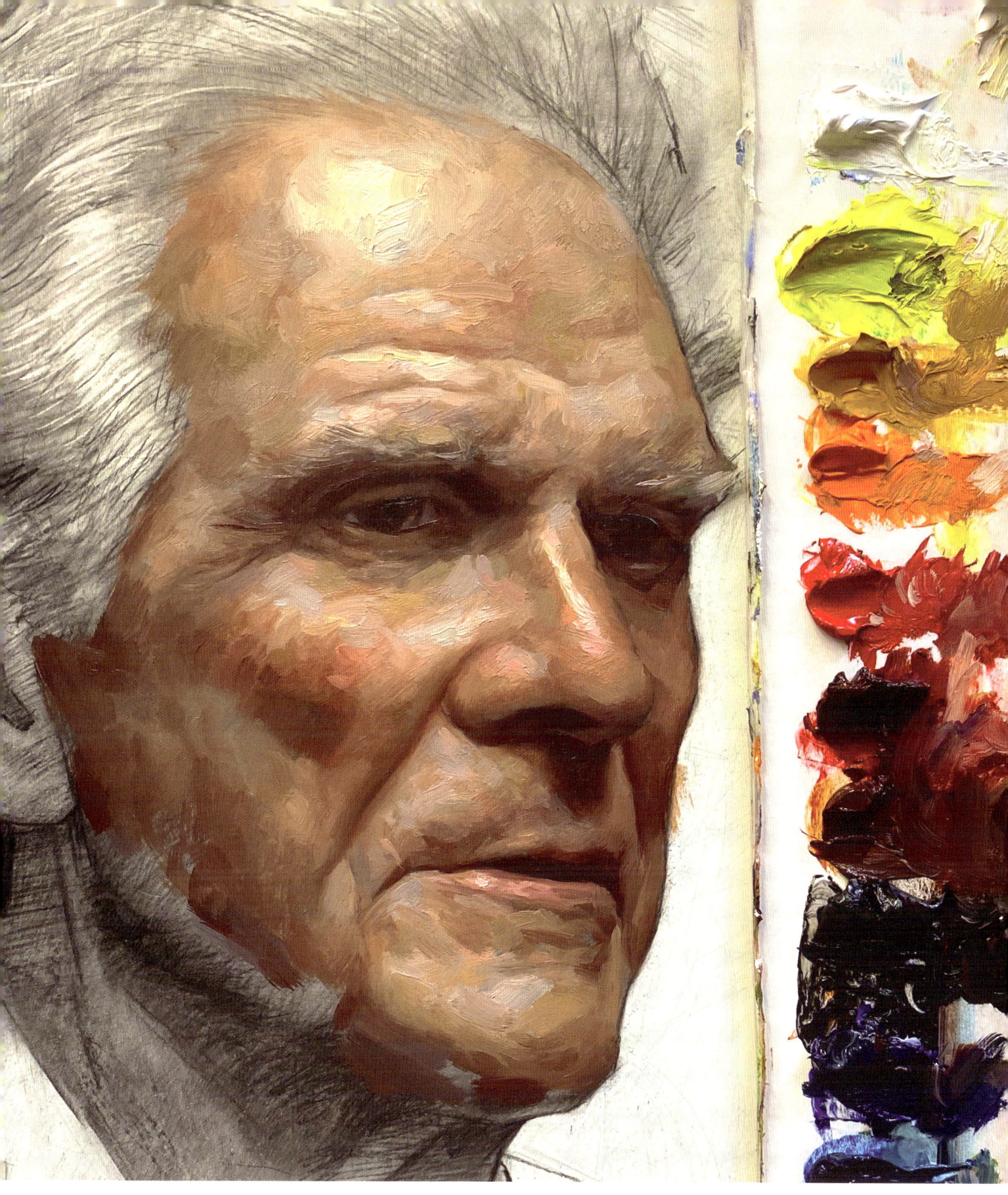

(pages 16–19)
Steve Forster, *Kevin*, oil on aluminum, 14" × 18" | 35.6 cm × 45.7 cm
Steve Forster, *Jean*, oil and charcoal on aluminum, 12" × 12" | 30.5 cm × 30.5 cm
Steve Forster, *Detail of Thais (Waiting for the Sun)*, oil and charcoal on aluminum, 36" × 36" | 91.4 cm × 91.4 cm
Steve Forster, *Junyi*, oil on aluminum, 16" × 16" | 15.2 cm × 15.2 cm

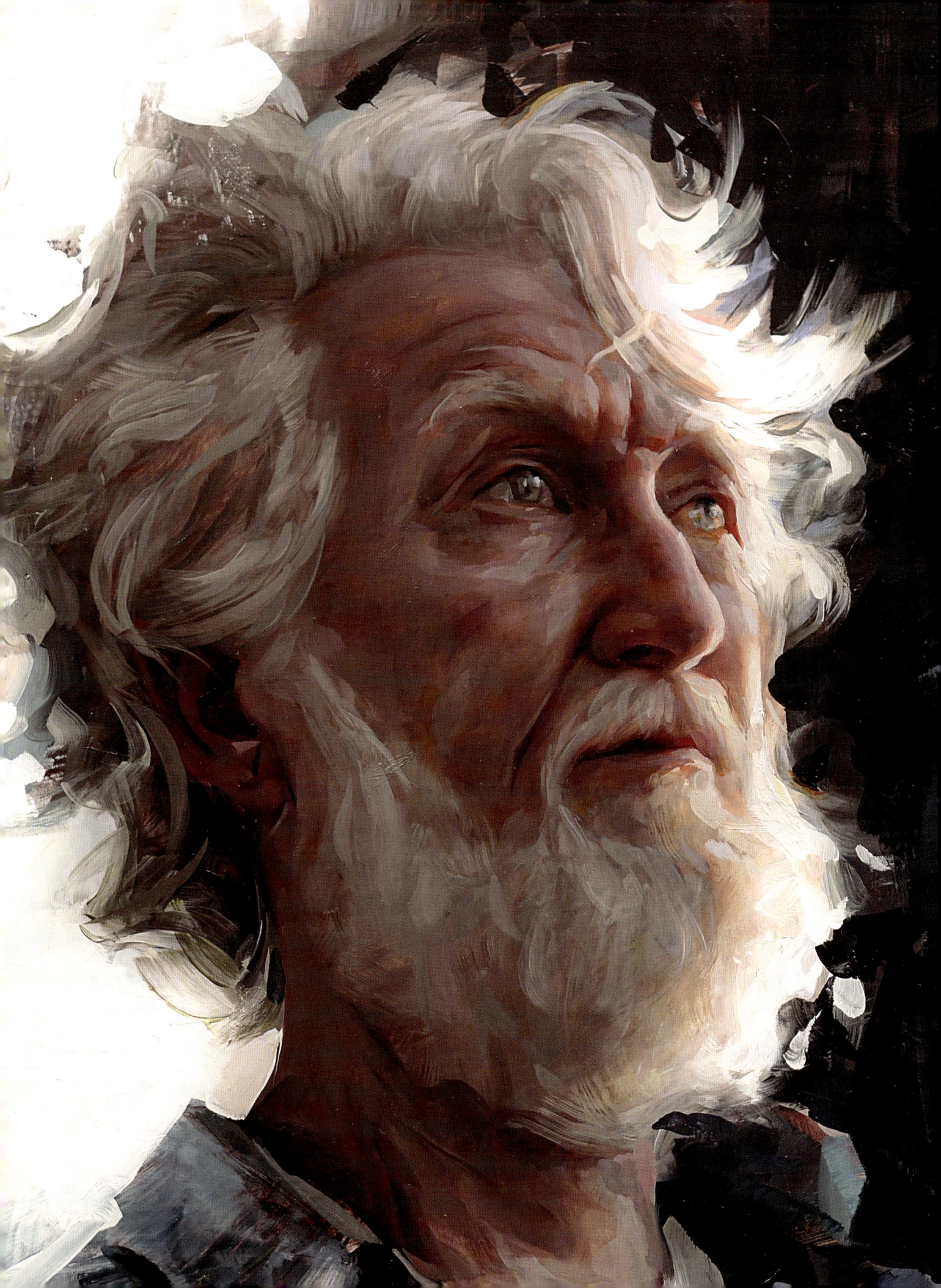

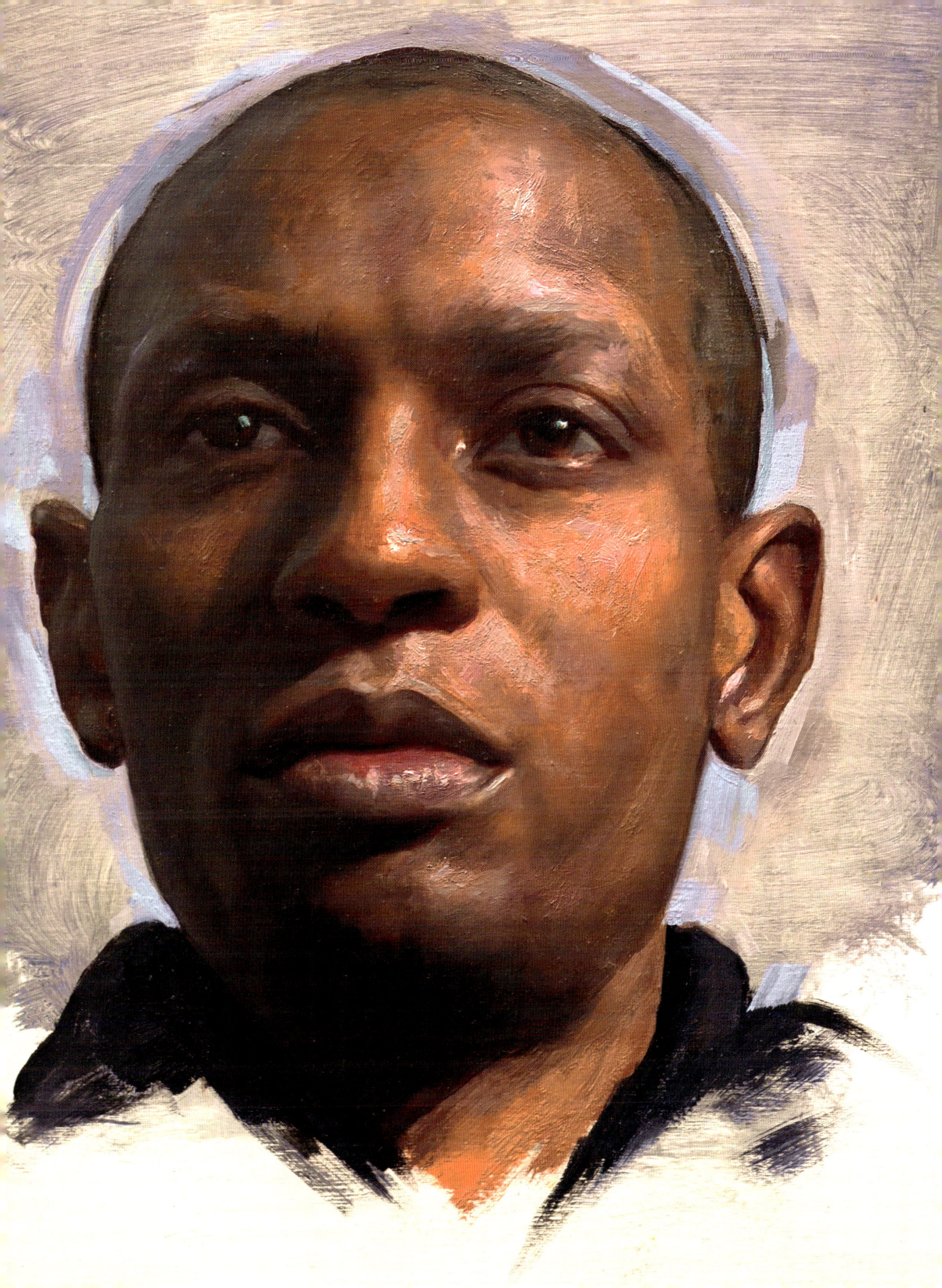

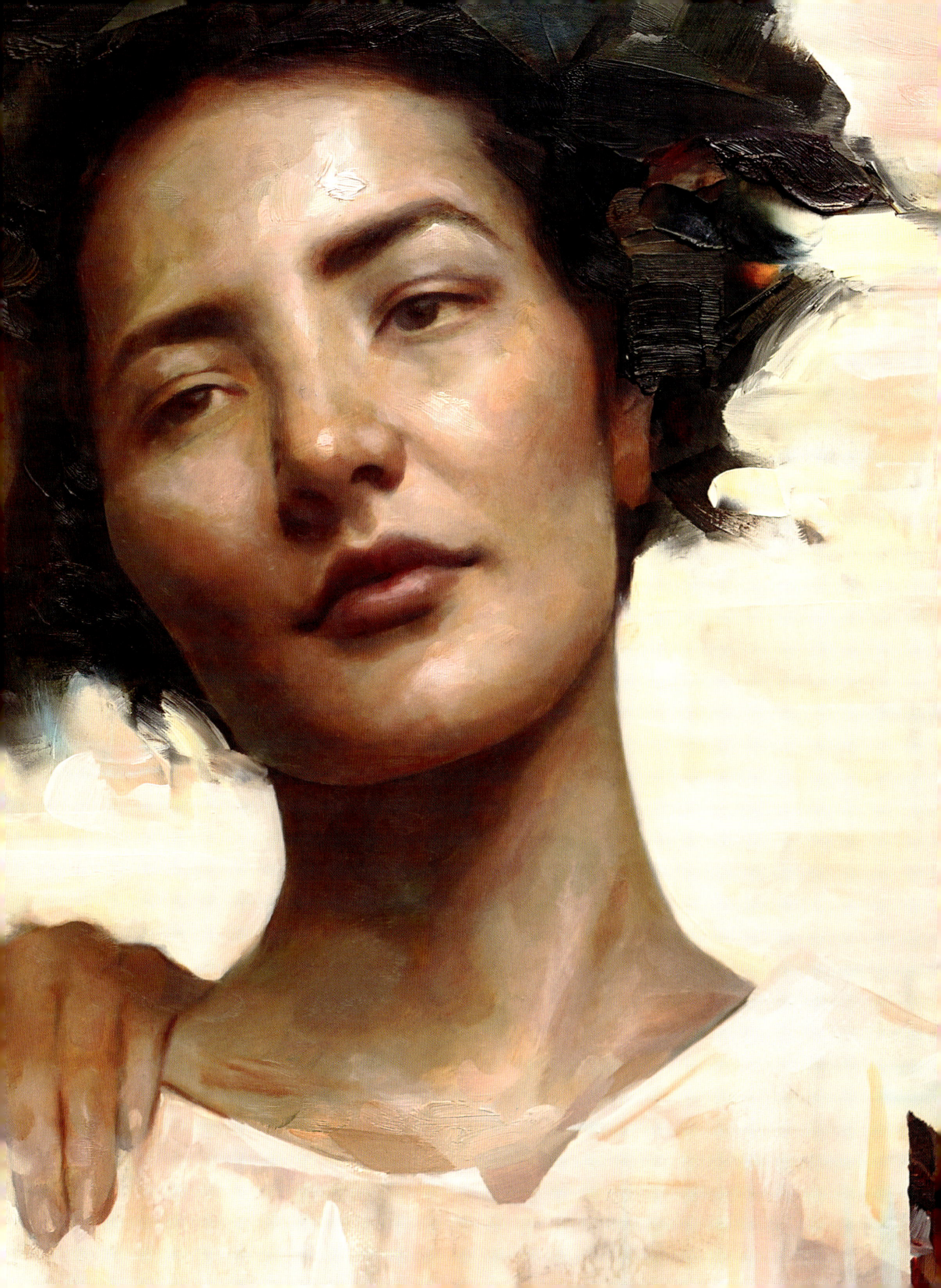

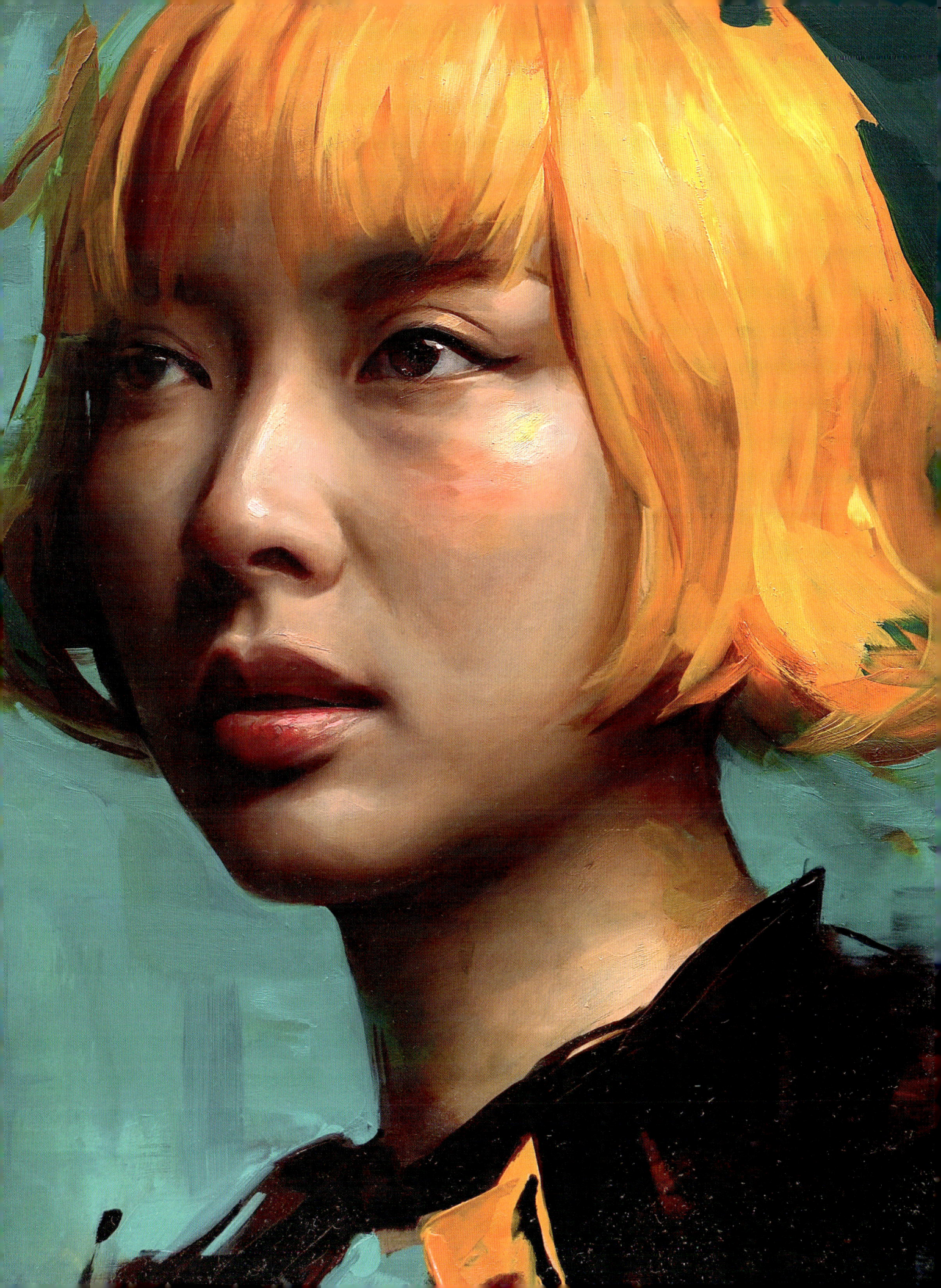

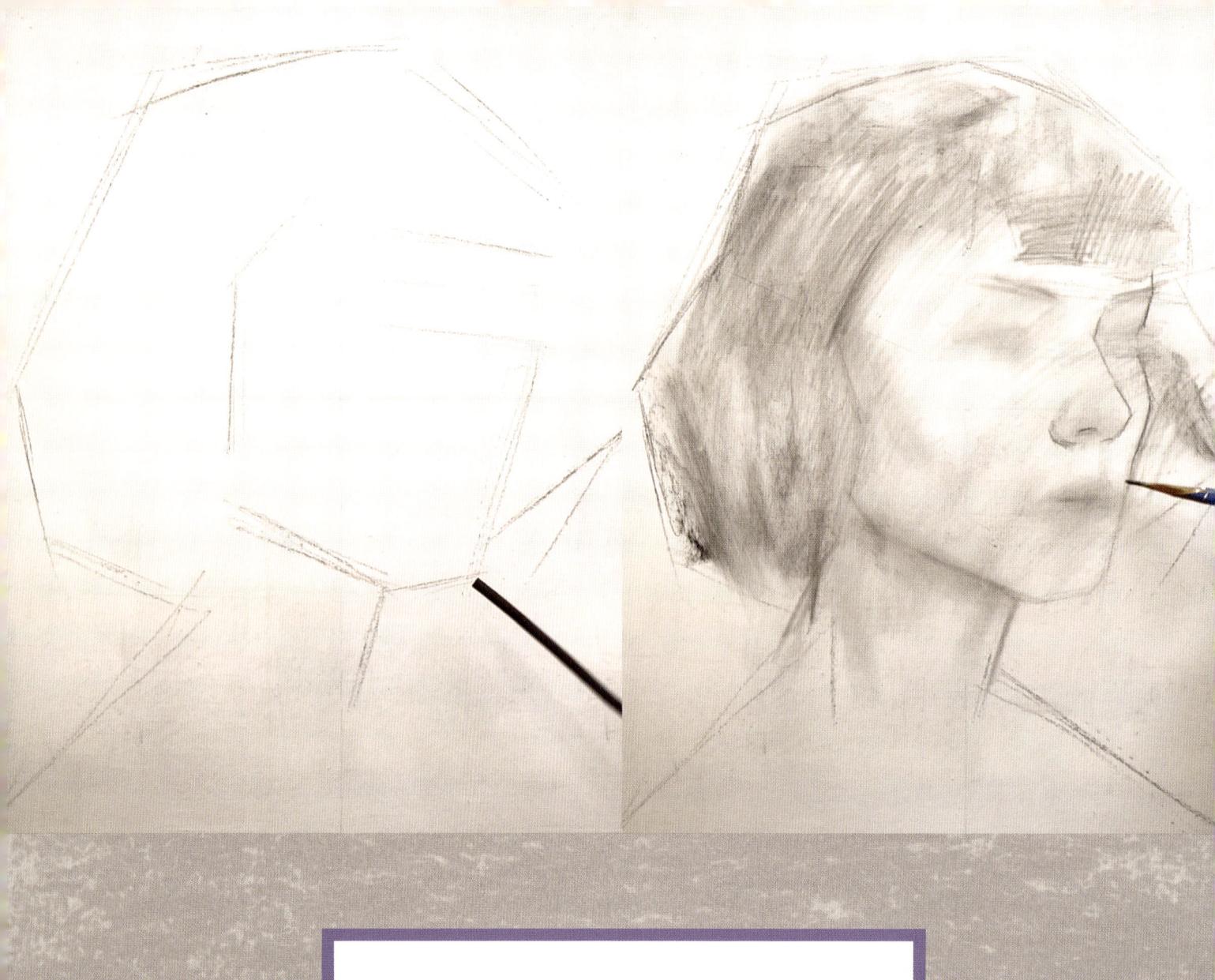

PART I

—

DRAWING AS
A FOUNDATION
FOR COLOR

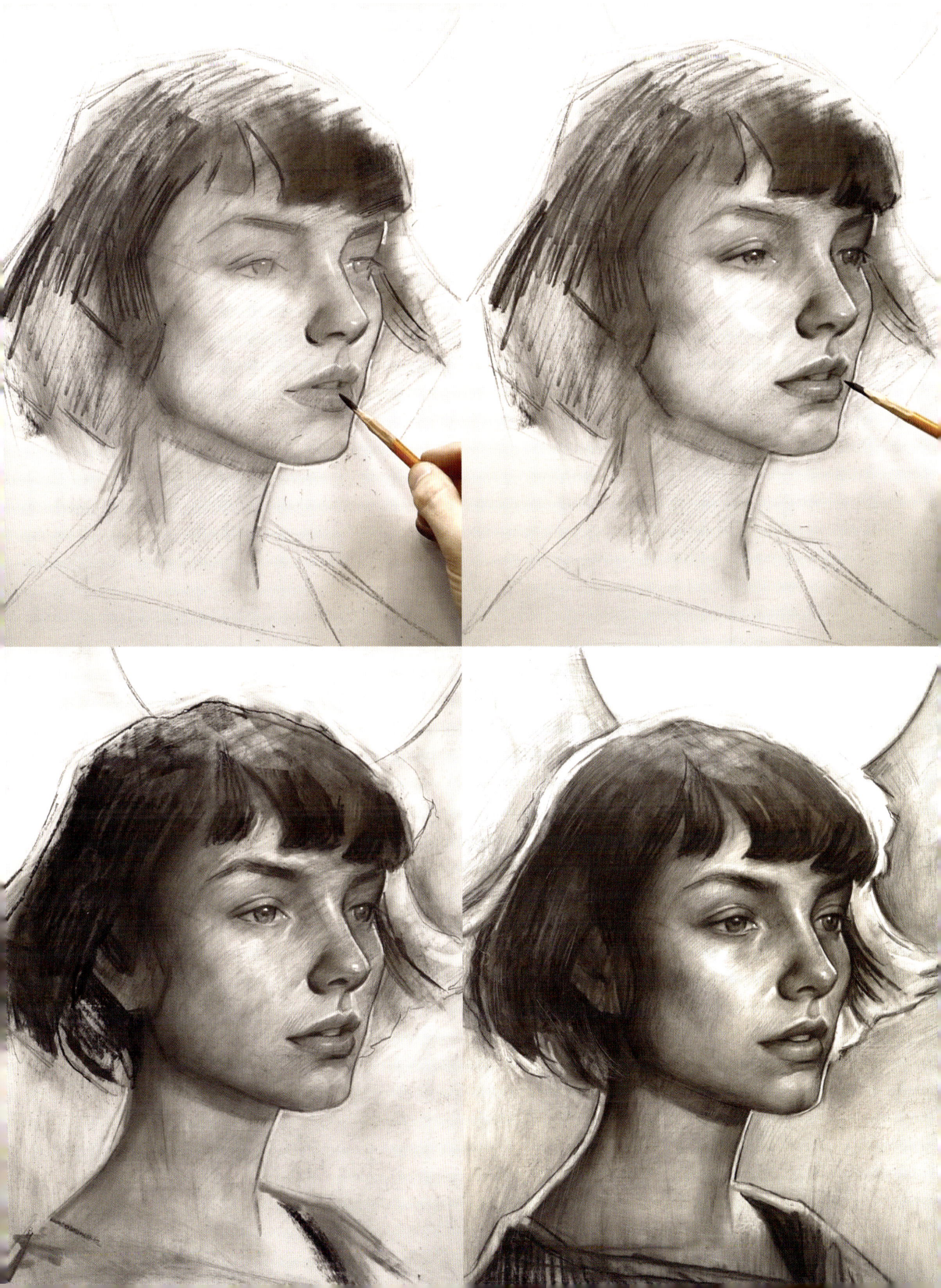

1 | GETTING STARTED WITH DRAWING

Before starting a drawing, which will eventually lead to a painting, it's crucial to not only understand your materials, but also to do a bit of photo editing. This could be cropping and gridding or perhaps something a bit more creative using digital programs. The following pages go over the basics of these concepts, with a section that focuses on Painting Materials as we get into painting in "Visualizing Color Concepts" (see page 90).

DRAWING MATERIALS

When I first started drawing, I was handed a No. 2 pencil and a nubby pink eraser that left a stain on my paper when I tried to erase with it. My understanding of drawing materials has definitely come a long way since that first encounter. The more tools and implements I acquired, the more I can communicate a wide array of textures and effects. This exploration has also helped me to learn to apply the right tool to the right situation. My first love is painting when it comes to art-making, but drawing became a lot more like painting with this wider, expressive range of materials. This includes a wide array of brushes, several types of smudgers and modifiers, graphite powder, water, electric erasers, sandpaper, and basically anything that might be considered somewhat non-traditional. Half of the fun with drawing materials is experimenting and trying new implements to really expand your personal range of expressive capability. With all that being said, I typically group any of these wildly different tools into four broad categories: Is it a pencil, eraser, powder, or a modifier?

SOFT VS. SHARP

Each one of these categories has a dynamic range of edges they can produce. For instance, I prefer to start with a dull pencil, when I'd like to be soft and light with my lines, versus using a sharp mechanical pencil, which is best for the refinement of details and precision when finishing. This is also the case with graphite powder, using a brush, which is softer, to achieve a range of soft edges on the face versus

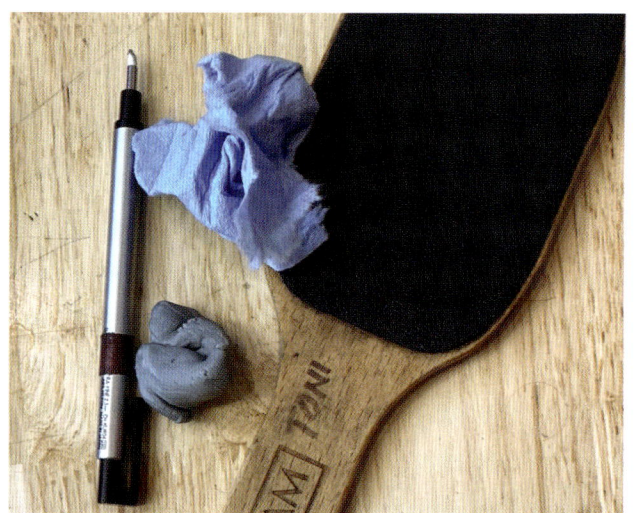

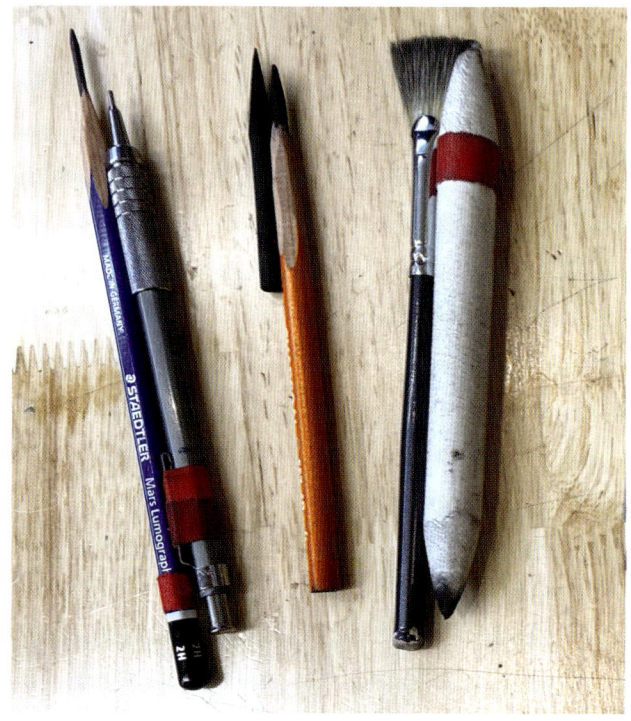

a smaller blending stump, which is sharper. Use a paper towel or a kneaded eraser to softly remove graphite or a round-tip eraser like a Tombow MONO Zero eraser to produce sharp, even hatching eraser marks. In the image above, you can see there are smaller groupings that show a sharp versus soft interpretation of each grouping. Sometimes, making this grouping obvious to yourself will help you to interpret your edges and use the right tool for the right situation when developing a drawing.

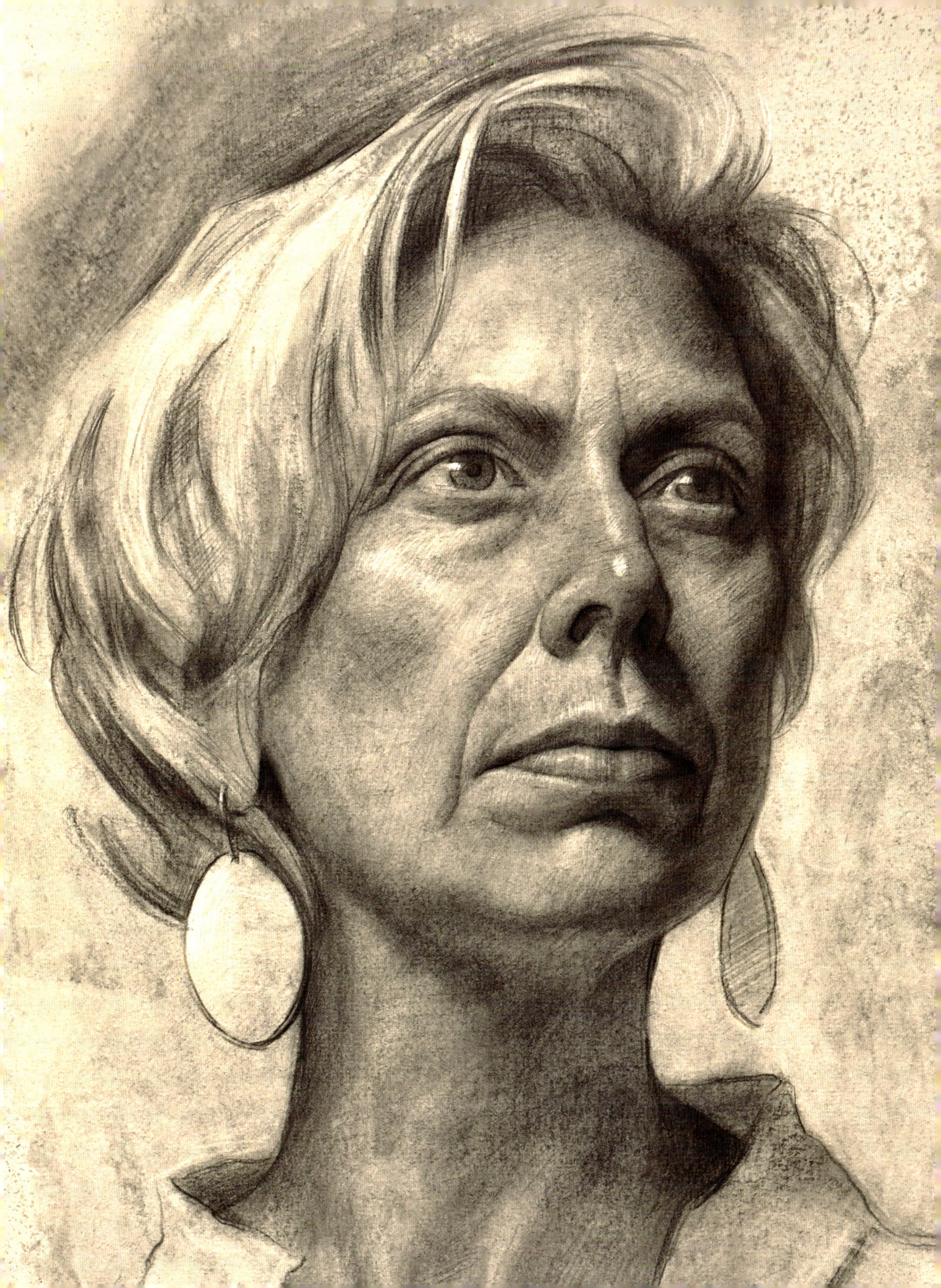

PENCILS AND CHARCOAL

The main pencils and charcoals that are used in my block-in drawing are a dull 2H pencil to initially block-in, followed by a 0.9 2B mechanical pencil for developing details and pushing a bit darker. When I really start committing to a drawing, I add a 6B Extra Soft General's Charcoal Pencil. The last one is made from willow charcoal; I often use it on its side to produce different texture effects that are hard to achieve any other way. The willow charcoal is also great for putting in a flat tone that's easily wiped away for highlights.

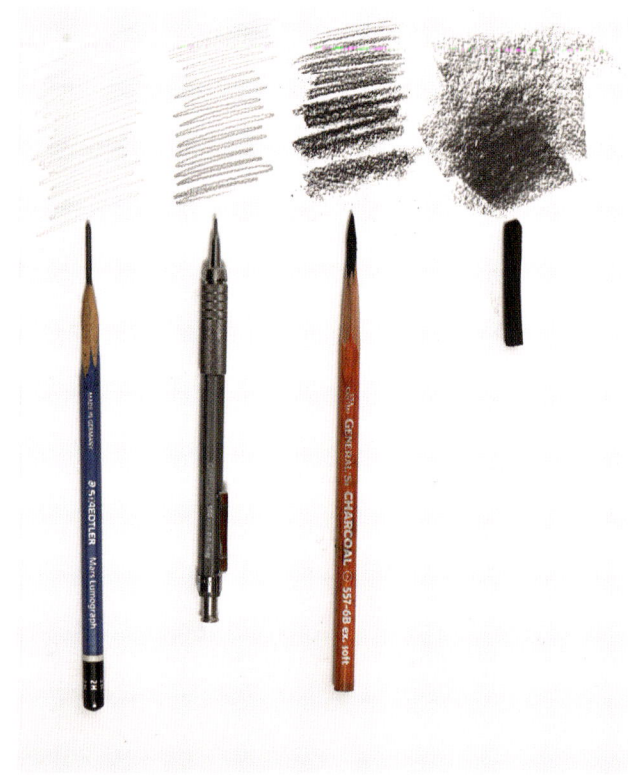

ERASERS

There's quite a range of erasers out there. I usually make use of three or four different kinds. The most gentle form of an eraser is a paper towel, followed by a kneaded eraser, then perhaps a sharpenable pencil-style eraser, and lastly a Tombow MONO Zero or electric eraser being the sharpest.

Each of these erasers has a unique quality about them, and it may seem overzealous to have so many, but I have them all for different applications. If I were to only pick two, they'd be the kneaded eraser and the Tombow MONO Zero eraser.

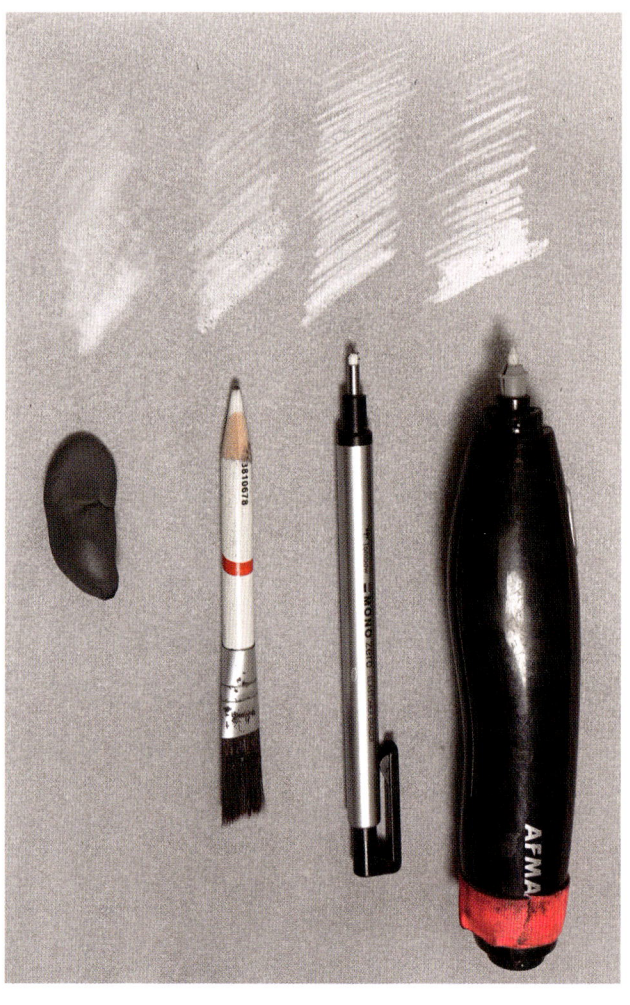

Previous page: Steve Forster, *Detail of Joni*, graphite and charcoal on paper, 18" × 24" | 45.7 cm × 61 cm

MODIFIERS

I'd put blending stumps, brushes, chamois, and paper towels in this category. They're my preferred tools to modify the material that's already on the drawing or to apply powder.

I usually use bristle brushes as my main modifier type of brush, but I've definitely explored some palette knife sponge covers and regularly make use of a squared off piece of paper towel.

But really, this lead list is by no means exhaustive. I often use sandpaper, razor blades, spray bottles—just about anything that would modify or give a slightly different texture to the drawing. These items are more for fun and experimentation, as I don't need all of these things to draw in a head for a foundation of a painting. They're just interesting ways to provide unique effects and edge work variety to the drawing.

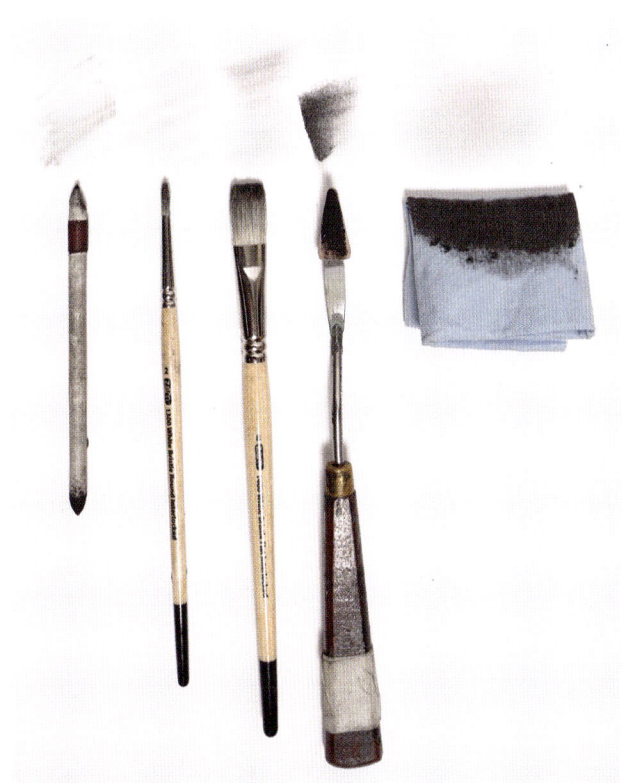

POWDERS

Graphite and charcoal powder make drawing much more painterly. While they can be overused and definitely can darken a drawing too fast, if used appropriately, they help speed up the process of toning your paper. They also can give you more expressive tools that have a variety of applications far beyond what a pencil can do alone.

Typically, the way that I use graphite powder is to pour it on a scrap sheet of paper, which becomes my palette of graphite. Then, I dip a dry brush or blending stump into it and test it out on that scrap sheet of paper to see how dark of a mark the brush will make.

In rare instances, I may use these powders mixed with a little water to create a variety of different expressive textures, but that's not the norm.

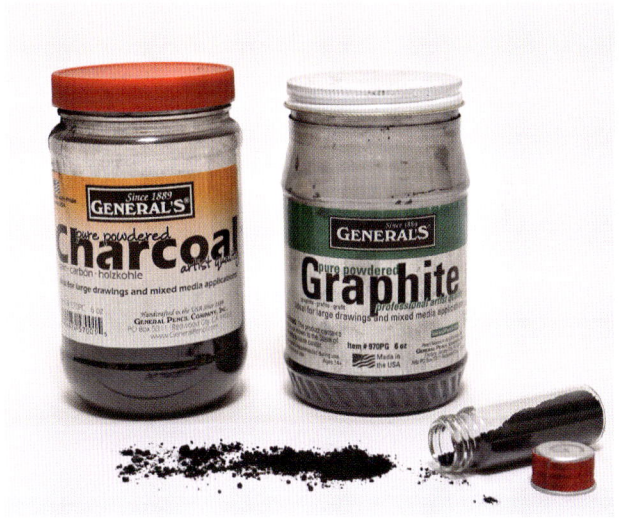

EDITING YOUR PHOTOS

CROPPING TO THE CANVAS SIZE

When editing your photos, crop the image to the same size as your canvas, cutting out any excess space that can diminish the overall presence of your model. Also, it's incredibly helpful when the aspect ratio of your canvas is the exact same ratio as your subject material; otherwise, you may be scaling up or scaling down or stretching the image to try to fit it into a box that doesn't work. If you have a printed photo, then you can put a piece of tape

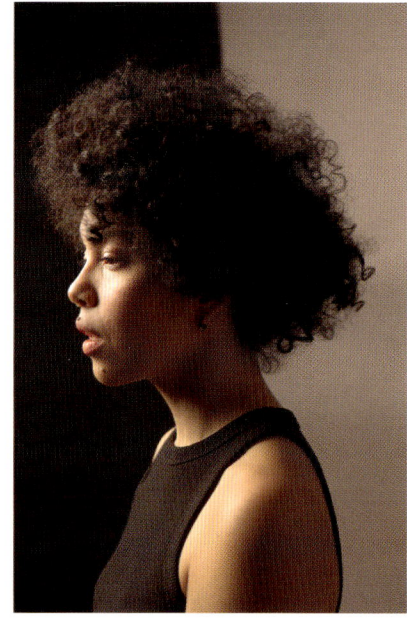
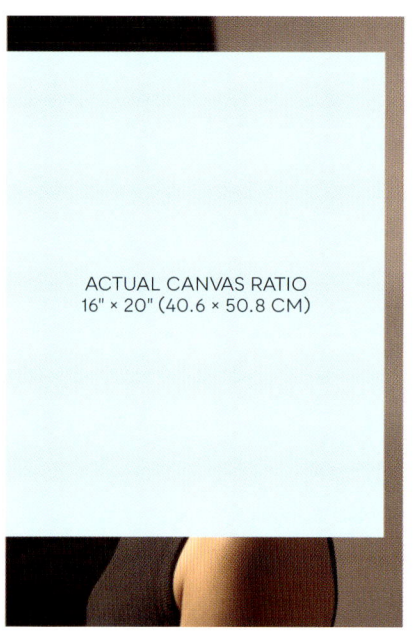

ACTUAL CANVAS RATIO
16" × 20" (40.6 × 50.8 CM)

around it to crop it to the same ratio, or if you're painting from a screen, you can crop it digitally. Whichever way you crop, it's a great preliminary idea to get both the image and the canvas in the same proportion.

SIMPLE GRID

Once you have established the right kind of crop for your picture and get it to match with the canvas ratio that you have chosen, establishing a simple grid will help you get the most basic things in the right place. On your reference material and your canvas, find the exact center going horizontally; mark that and do the same with your vertical center. I usually do this with a light 2H pencil as to not make it too dark. This establishes some basic reference points so that you have a successful block-in that's in proportion to your reference photo.

Doing this makes your life a whole lot easier, especially if your picture is quite large or if you have to scale up or down from your reference size.

Say your reference is 4 × 5 inches (10 × 12.7 cm) and you want to paint it 16 × 20 inches (40.6 × 50.8 cm). The scale difference between your reference material and your painting will be quite challenging, but if it's gridded, it makes it a little easier to see relationships. I try to avoid doing complicated grids with many lines because it can take a bit of the joy out of drawing and make it too mechanical.

Scan to view a
video tutorial

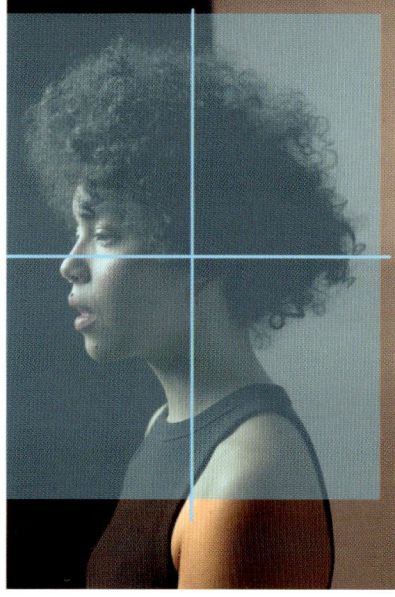

USING NEGATIVE SPACES

No matter how complicated your portrait may be, it's always a great opportunity when you can identify some major negative shapes that make drawing more objective. You don't have to use a grid to take advantage of the intuitive drawing method of copying negative shapes, but it definitely makes them more apparent, and the likelihood of getting their proportions correct goes up.

As you notice in the diagrams at the right, there's a clear negative shape (red) that has a certain relationship with that lower right-hand quadrant. It's much more easily drawn in when seen in a grid.

If we try to draw the shoulder, the shirt, the hair, and the neck without utilizing this negative shape, we'll probably get lost in all of the details along the way. In the beginning, ignore all of the little details of each deviant curl and particularity of each curve in order to see the big, general shape.

When looking at our model's hair in the original image (page 26), it might be somewhat difficult to try to observe a shape, but that's often the challenge. In finding shapes, sometimes the edges are very soft or there might be an excessive busyness that disguises them. Often in portraiture, the first thing that we notice are the details that make that model unique, but initially, we must zoom out and get the overall big picture to get the structure and big shapes correct (bottom right image), so that when the smaller details are expressed, they're not in the wrong spot.

Cropping to the canvas size and using the simple grid, along with observing negative shapes, achieves accuracy and a good layout for your portrait. These techniques help with two common problems—drawing too big and going off the page, or drawing too small. Proper usage of these ideas helps to maximize the overall effect of how the face sits on the canvas.

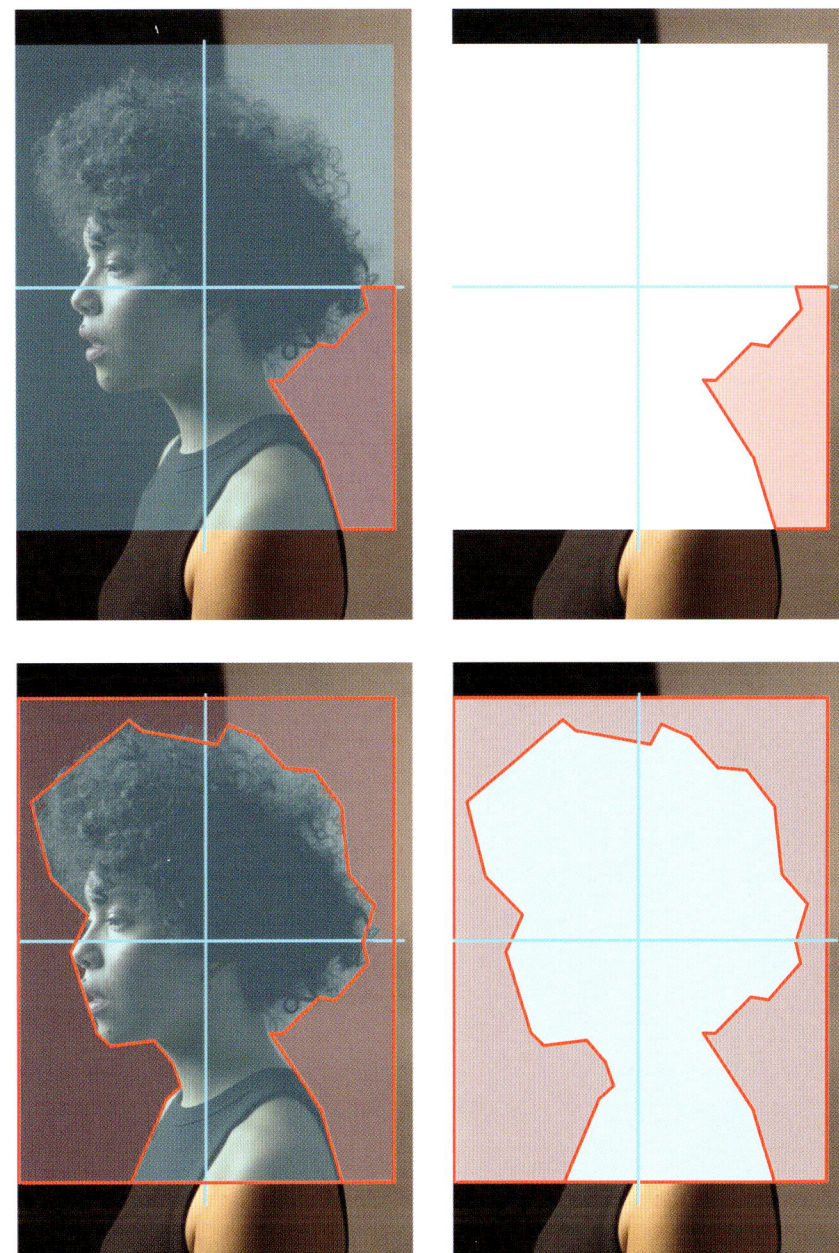

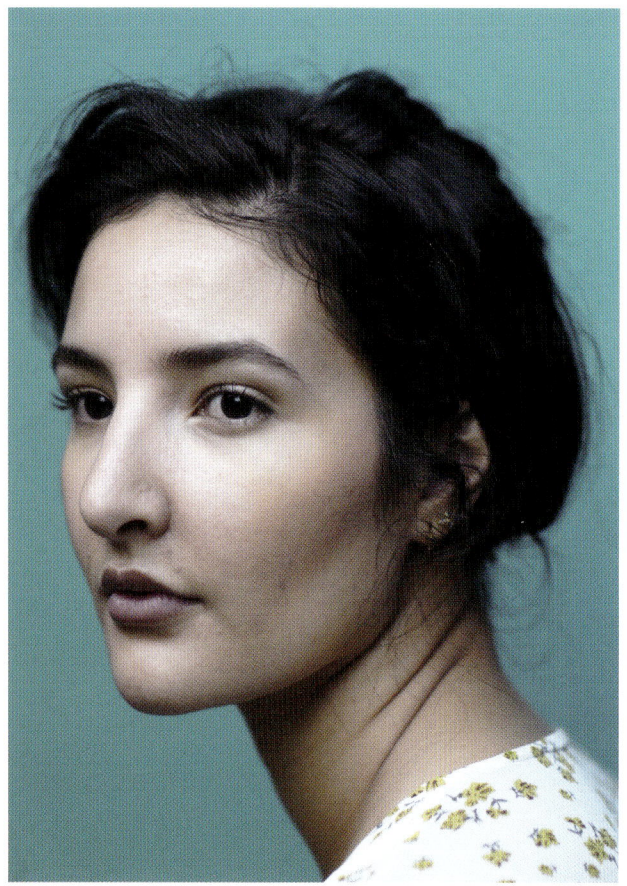
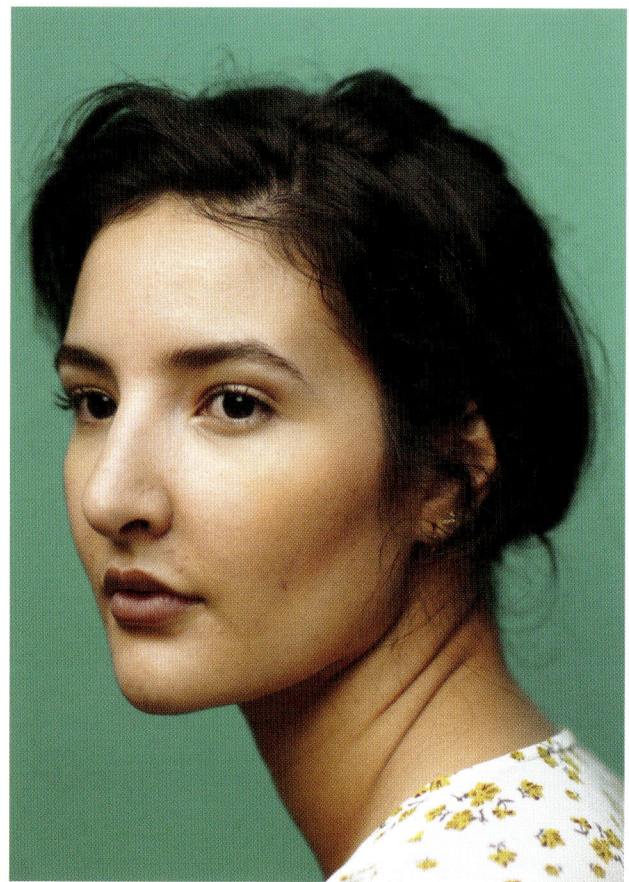

VIBRANCE AND COLOR

When taking your own photos, many things can go wrong in terms of color. A camera's lens and its digital way of processing the color, however advanced, may sometimes fall short and distort the image in an undesirable way.

You may find yourself in a situation where the colors just feel dead and homogenous. For example, with the image above left, the color balance of the camera was not set to amplify the differences of color between the background, the color of the light, and the color of the skin.

Using a basic photo editing program on your phone or computer, you can add more warmth and change the tint as well. If you like colorful images, you can also bump up the vibrance, which is a better modification than just setting the overall saturation too high. Experiment with adjusting the color balance, levels, and the vibrance/saturation features in whatever editing program you may be using. You can see the richness that photo editing can impart.

This is one of the advantages of painting from a screen, which is what *I* usually do. I paint from an iPad and do my digital modifications on a program called Artstudio Pro. If you are working from a printed image, it's yet another layer of distortion of color beyond the camera settings. This distortion could be due to the printer having less cyan tone in it, printing too light and washing out the image, or simply processing colors differently. All these problems are sidestepped by painting from a digital medium.

EXPOSING FOR MODELING IN THE LIGHT

Exposure can be one of the most frustrating things about photography. I think a camera is really good at exposing the light or exposing the shadow, but often seems not to expose both of them together correctly. This means that you tend to see either a great amount of drama and contrast, as in the example opposite above, or as in the example opposite bottom, you get much more definition and detail in the eyes, hair, and overall expression of the face when the shadows are lighter. Both versions are important to modeling in the lights and shadows, but it may require you to have two versions of the same image since it's difficult to see form in shadows and lights simultaneously in one image.

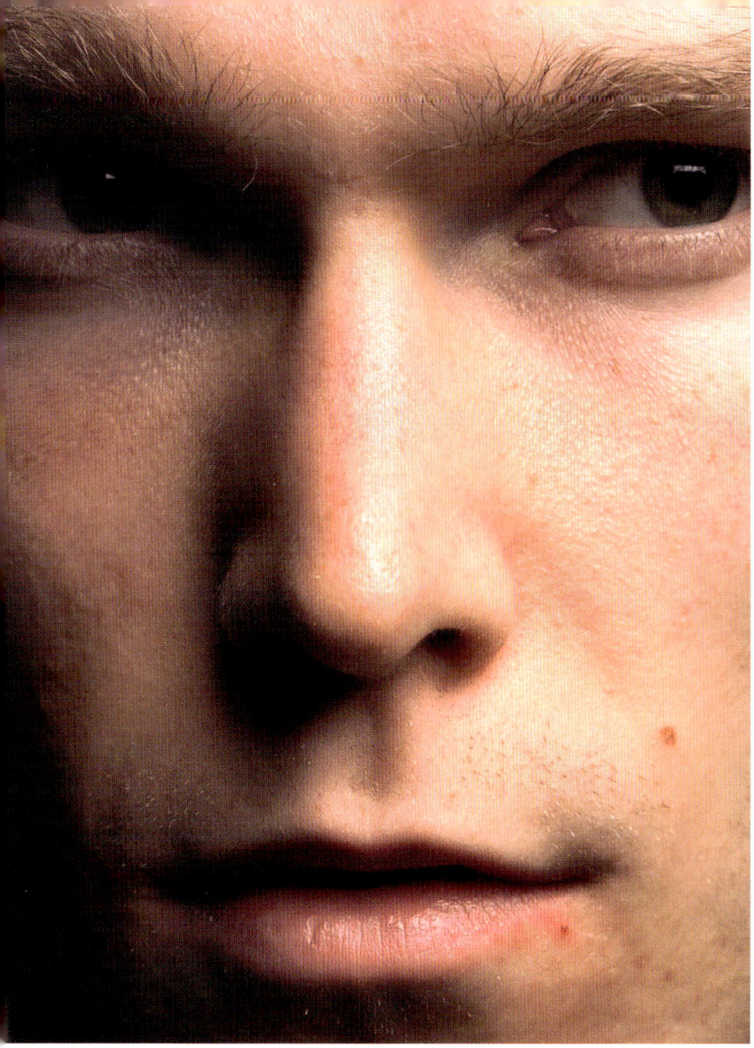

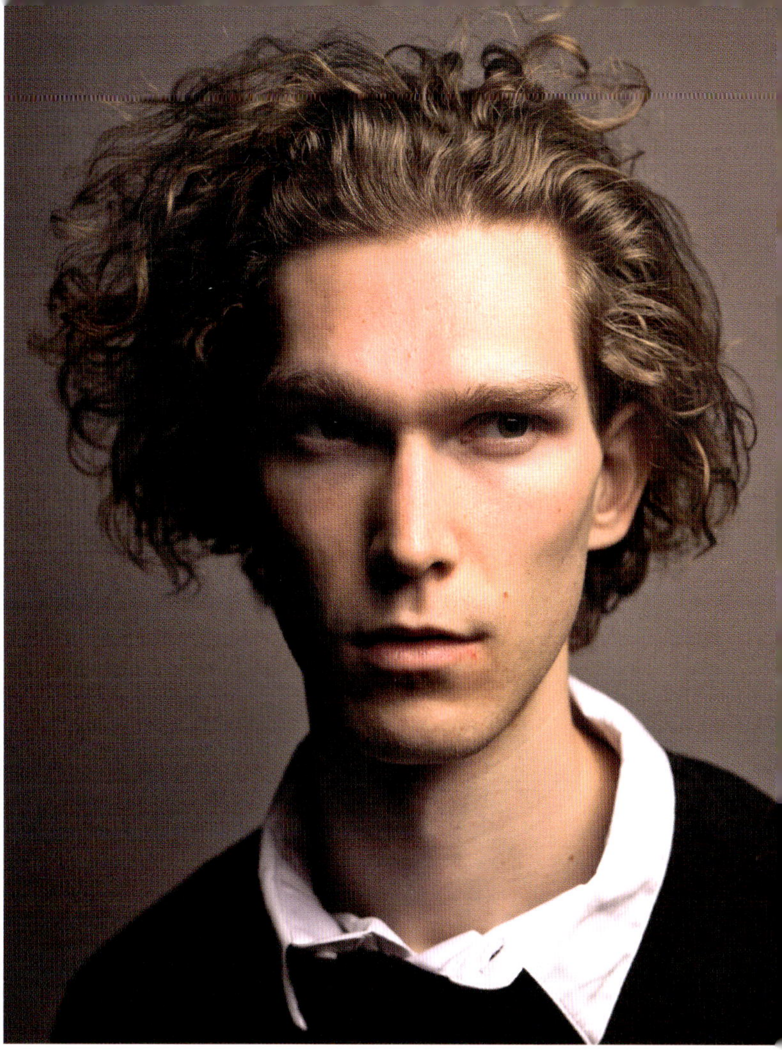

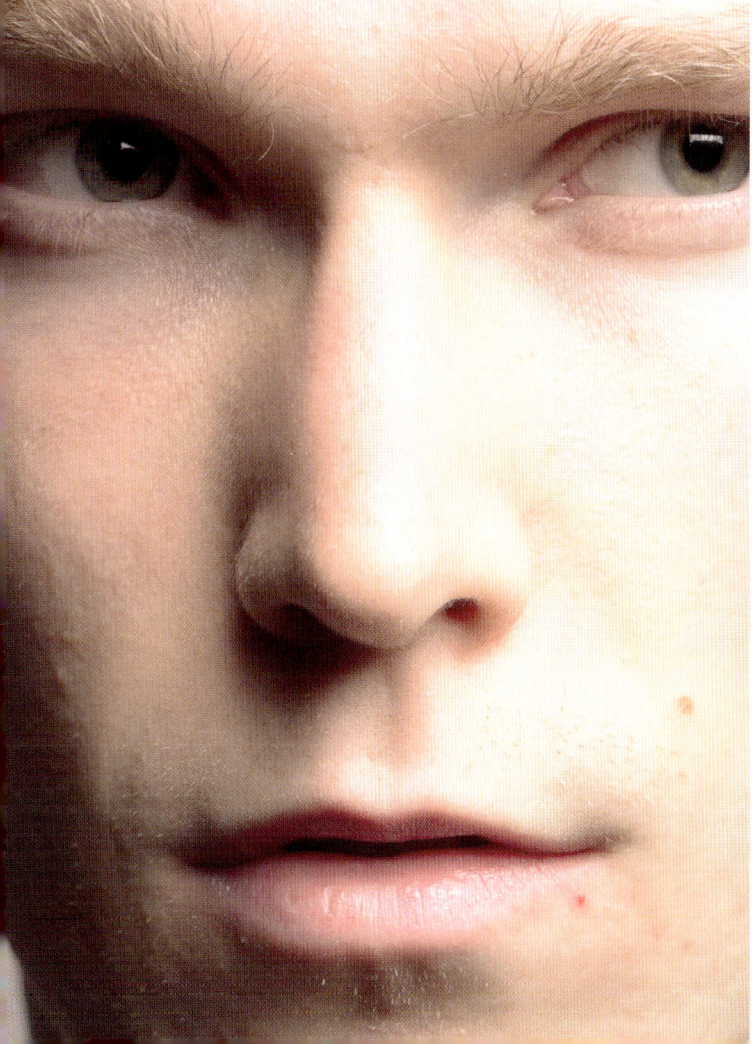
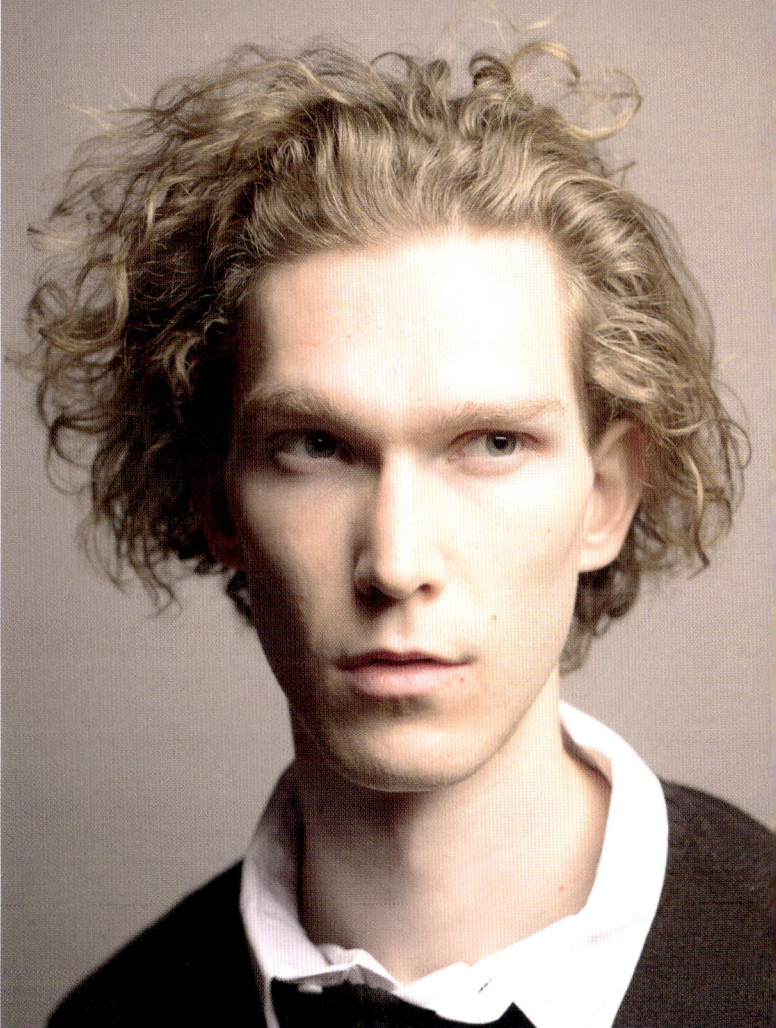

There are several benefits to exposing the image so it's easier to model the forms in the light. One is that you typically get more dramatic, dark shadows that appear vacant and empty and make grouping into visual shapes easier for drawing. As a painter, shapes are your best friend. They create a simplified, graphic expression of your subject that's powerful from across the room. You can figuratively "paint with a broader brush" in these areas, giving space for your paintbrush to roam, so you aren't chasing never-ending detail. Another benefit is that it gives quite a dynamic range from light to dark across the subject, creating the opportunity to describe a roundness of the form of the face and to sculpt the light.

By exposing your image with an eye towards modeling information in the lights (as in the p. 29 bottom example), the highlights are rather bright and the darker lights are rather dark. This creates depth and gives you information that may otherwise be washed out if the whole picture were too bright. Of course, if an image is overexposed and there's zero information because of the exposure setting on the camera, you can't recover this information with a simple editing adjustment; the information just isn't going to be there. But if the image is exposed properly and you can make some adjustments in your editing program in order to see this form in the light areas, it's extremely helpful when working from a photograph.

EXPOSING FOR MODELING IN THE SHADOW

For artistic effect, this darker version of our image described (p. 29 top) can be fantastic and fine on its own. You may notice that in this darker example, however, we really do lose one of the nostrils completely in the shadows, and if you'd like to find some of the detail there and in other areas such as the hair, you may have to do some more photo editing. If using Photoshop, the adjustment "Levels" is the quickest way correct the intensity of the shadows.

When exposing for modeling in the shadow, what happens as shown in the lighter example is that a lot of the structural information that was lost within these deep dark shadow shapes comes back, and you can put in details that had been missing. Of course, now we've lost most of the information in the lights, but this sacrifice allows us to see what's in the shadows that we can't see any other way. The jaw comes back, as well as the ear and information in the hair, there's greater clarity in the eyes and collar, and so on.

Great photo editing can sometimes combine these two experiences together and get the best of both worlds; however, most images that you'll work from probably won't have this type of sensitivity, and so toggling between these two different types of exposure can give you the information that you need. It perhaps isn't ideal to toggle back and forth between two reference images, but I find it sometimes necessary and useful when I want something that photography just can't give me, and I like to have the best of both worlds available in my reference images.

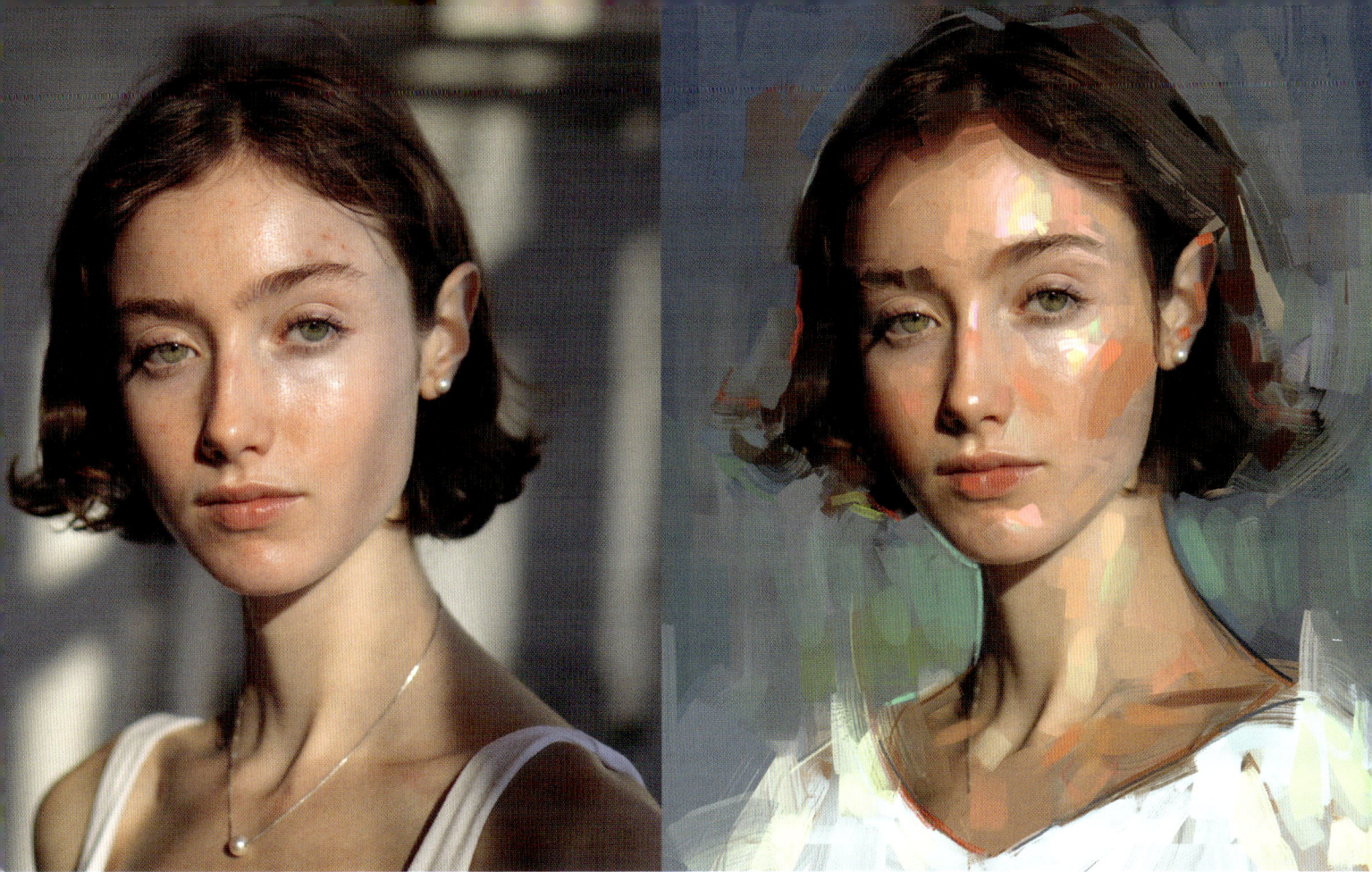

DIGITALLY ALTERED IMAGES

PAINTING DIGITALLY TO EXPLORE COLOR

In my personal quest to understand style as it relates to painting, I've explored many possibilities of altering images in order to aid my creative vision, such as photoshopping, collaging, digital painting, photobashing, and so on, anything to free myself from the tyranny of working from a photograph alone. There are perhaps so many ways of doing this that to just write a short entry about altering images in a portrait book that privileges the color of flesh is almost meaningless. But I think it's worthwhile to mention the simple fact that many of the images I work with have already been altered before I paint them. Sometimes, I use a program to amplify the color or to experiment with brushstrokes or textures, and this can be part of the creative process as a way to more easily become acquainted with the translation process. In a day and age when we're bombarded with so many images, sometimes sitting down and making a painting is either an act of rebellion against these images or an absolute faithful rendering of them.

I'm fascinated with the idea of seeing a portrait through many different stylistic lenses, especially with the innovations that are currently happening in the field of Artificial Intelligence (AI) and the many avenues we'll be faced with in the future. The possibilities of rendering a style in an effortless way are pretty overwhelming. The two images above represent the way that I often work. I usually have the unaltered reference image and a digitally altered "mood" image that deviates from the original, where I'll explore color or different brushstrokes and edge effects. The one on the right is a photo that has been painted over with a series of different types of digital brushes and has a unique color perspective that I find interesting.

I may explore different styles, but usually will use these two types of images to feed my creativity and also inform my vision of reality.

Scan to view a
video tutorial

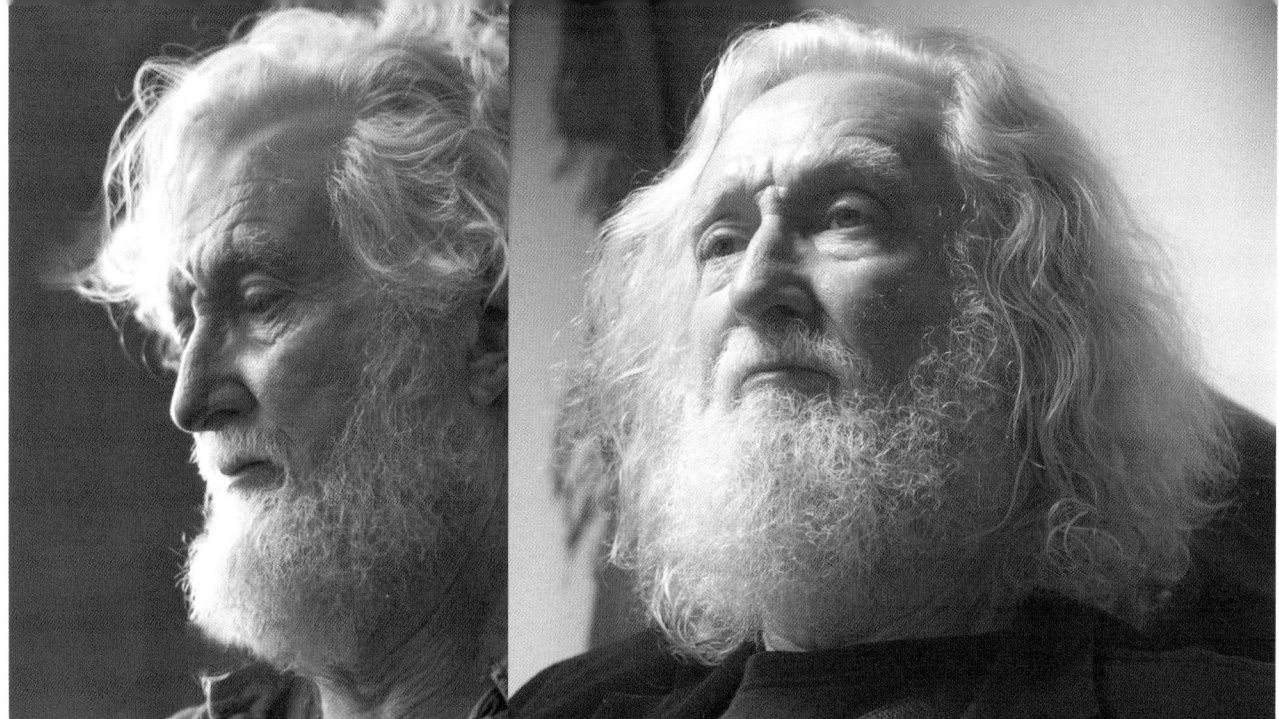

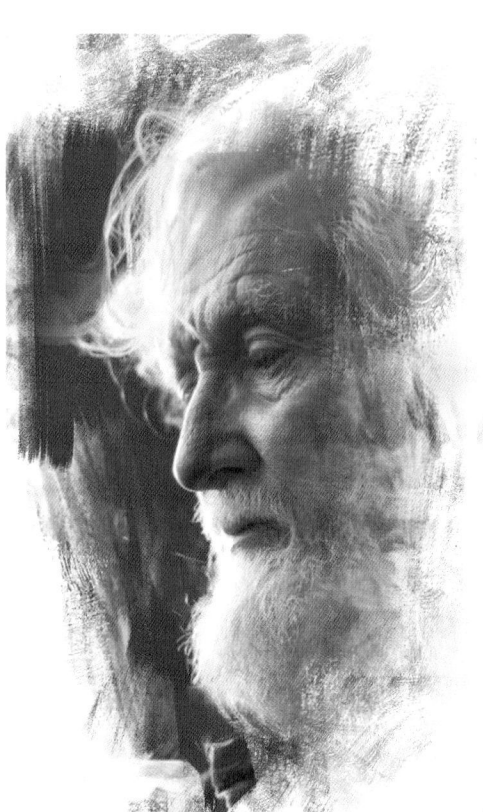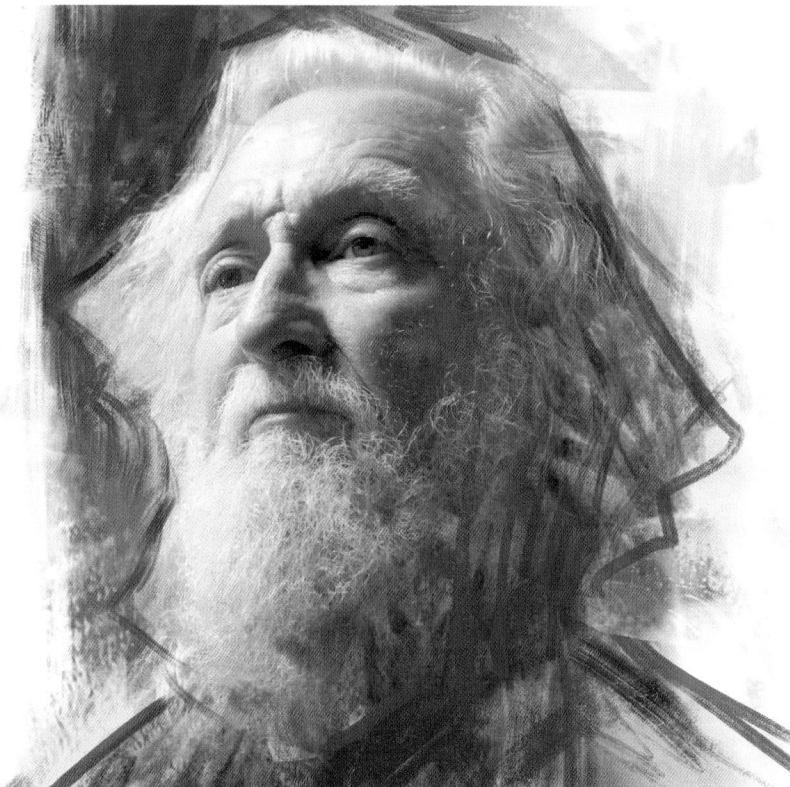

ADDING TEXTURES

With digitally altered images, style can be studied in a variety of ways, and one of my favorite things is to explore is texture. In the image above, I've taken these two portrait photographs and altered them in order to explore what they might begin to look like in charcoal. Often, I use this as a way to explore creating a vignette that simplifies a portrait and abstracts the surroundings. By doing this, it frees me from needing to paint every single detail and gives me a bit of a visual roadmap, helping me to understand where to end the drawing and fade away into the textures of the medium. Often, I collect photographs of different textures and things that stylistically interest me, and I overlay them in a digital art program like Photoshop through a variety of different blending modes, such as Lighten, Darken, Multiply, Overlay, Soft Light, and Hard Light.

MAKING A DIGITAL PALETTE TO EXPLORE COLOR

One of the coolest features of any digital painting program is that it allows you to sample colors from the picture and actually paint with them. You can use this concept to help establish a color palette. At right, we start off simple with a string of colors that go from light to dark and then incorporate some of the background blue colors. Simplifying all of the options into approximately ten colors can help you develop a palette for the flesh tones, giving you a head start to understanding the color of your subject.

Then, we're branching off of that main string and adding a lot of variation and diversity to that palette. No matter if you're creating a simple palette digitally or an advanced palette, it helps you to take the colors out of the soft context of your image and see them as hard color swatches.

COLOR DOTS TO EXPLORE COLOR

Taking it a step further and using colored dots to see all of the magnificent colors in your subject in context but unblended can help clear your mind from the blended reality color in the natural world.

As you'll see later, one of the most effective ways of understanding how to mix and apply color is to take blending out of the equation. I find that freeing yourself from the idea that it has to look smooth and believable and allowing yourself to explore color for color's sake with swatches is often a great tool for students to use if there's a digital painting program where they can sample each individual color from that location and put down a hard color dot. When you take the softness away, what you end up with is seeing the color for truly what it is and not for all of the transitions in and around it. Sometimes when I do this, I also bend the color slightly to a more saturated colorful place, while trying to not let that color stray too far from the original.

I believe it's easiest to see color in this context outside of the smoother blended state. It's so addicting and therapeutic to blend oil paint, but it softens away all of our beautiful colors. This homogenization of color frustrates many artists, so allow yourself the freedom to explore each individual color without the added difficulty of trying to make it look realistic.

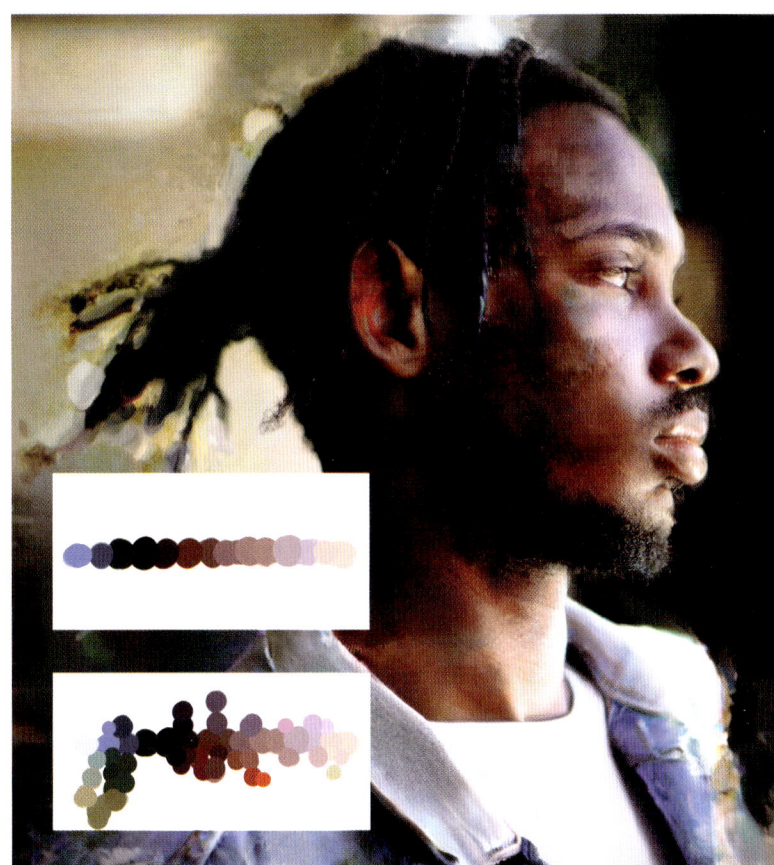

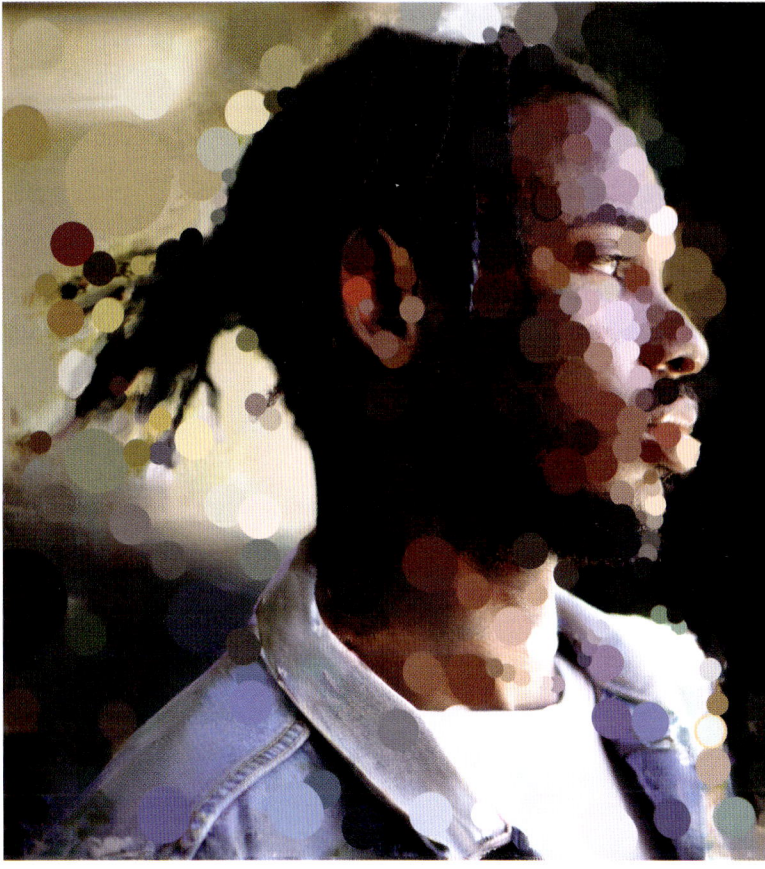

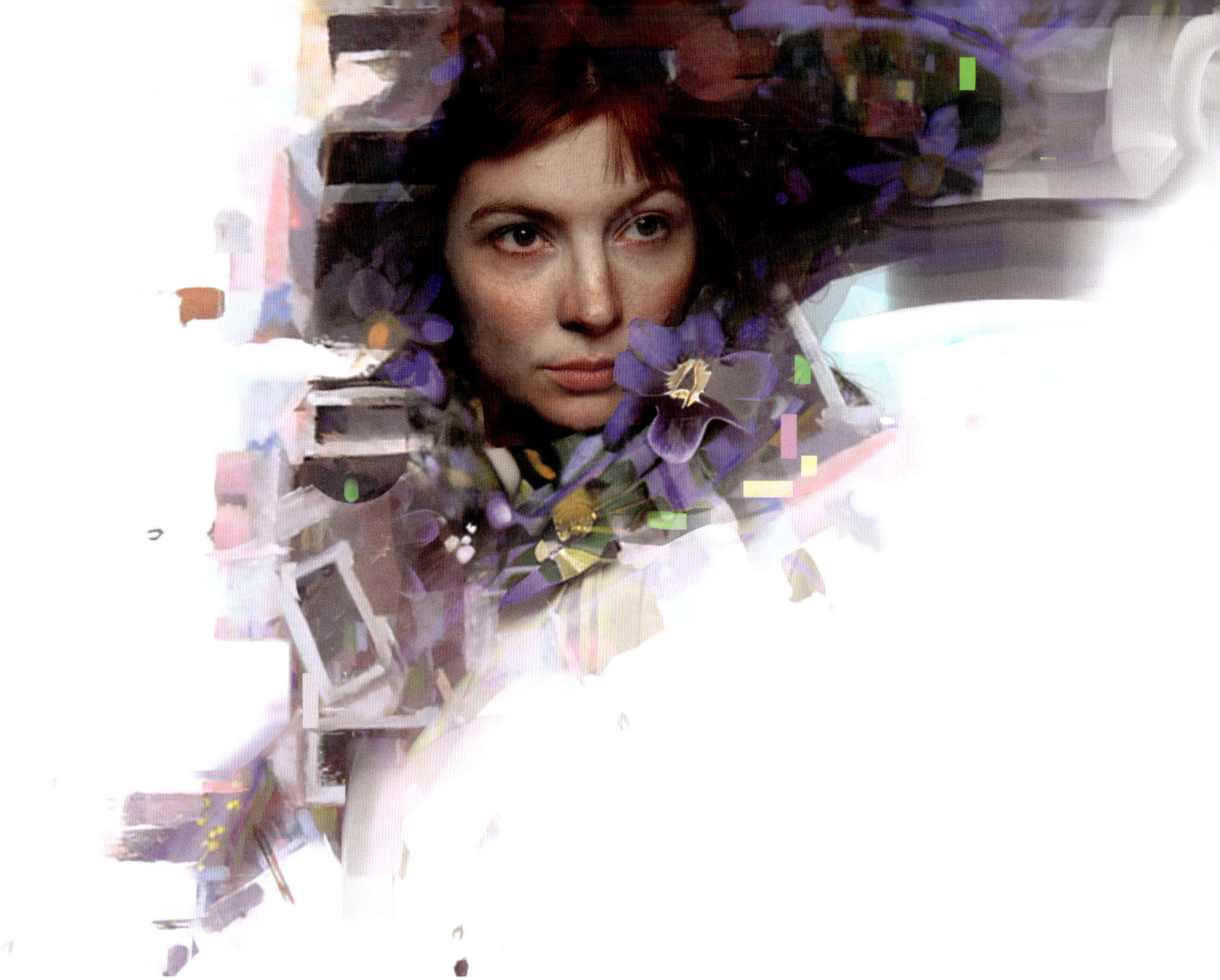

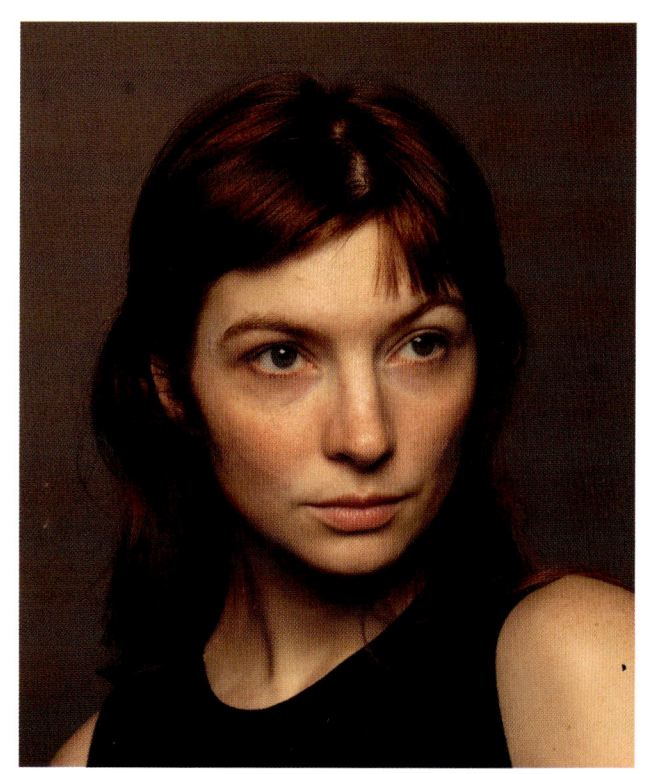

BACKGROUNDS, AI, AND STYLE

Changing the background or adding some kind of artistic environment to your portrait is definitely part of our responsibility as a portrait maker. There are many different programs that allow you to make these modifications, whether by hand, digitally, or collaging in a different background as in the image above. All of these methods provide a great artistic opportunity to pair some form of realism with some kind of artistic expression. There are also other avenues, such as using a program that uses AI.

AI in the artistic community is quite a controversial new thing that has not fully been explored. It feels like the Wild West of the art world as I'm currently writing this. It's a powerful tool that can make amazing things reality, but its seduction can also take away a certain kind of ownership and authorship to your artwork.

Spending years building your own personal aesthetic is a particularly important thing to develop and takes much time, exploration, and failure. AI can often make you feel that there's a shortcut through this development period; however, a true artist is guided through their thoughts, emotions, and feelings about the artistic world and not a random prompt and a button that is pressed.

That said, this tool can be used to explore and fill in the gaps of your own aesthetic vision in a productive way. That's an overall net positive, or at least that's the way that I feel about it. I use AI to explore different compositional possibilities as well as color and shape ideas.

In the image at top right, I've changed the hair into an overall more interesting shape to paint and also enhanced the color to reflect a sense of glowing in that warm atmosphere of being outside. I've spent many years photographing models, and it's pretty difficult for me to find a hairstylist or a makeup artist that has my perfect color aesthetic, and it's almost impossible to be able to shoot the model at just the right time of day with the sun shining through the trees in order to hit this perfect glowing rim of light. So, AI can be a terrific way to create more of an imaginative situation that wholly expresses what you *wanted* to see.

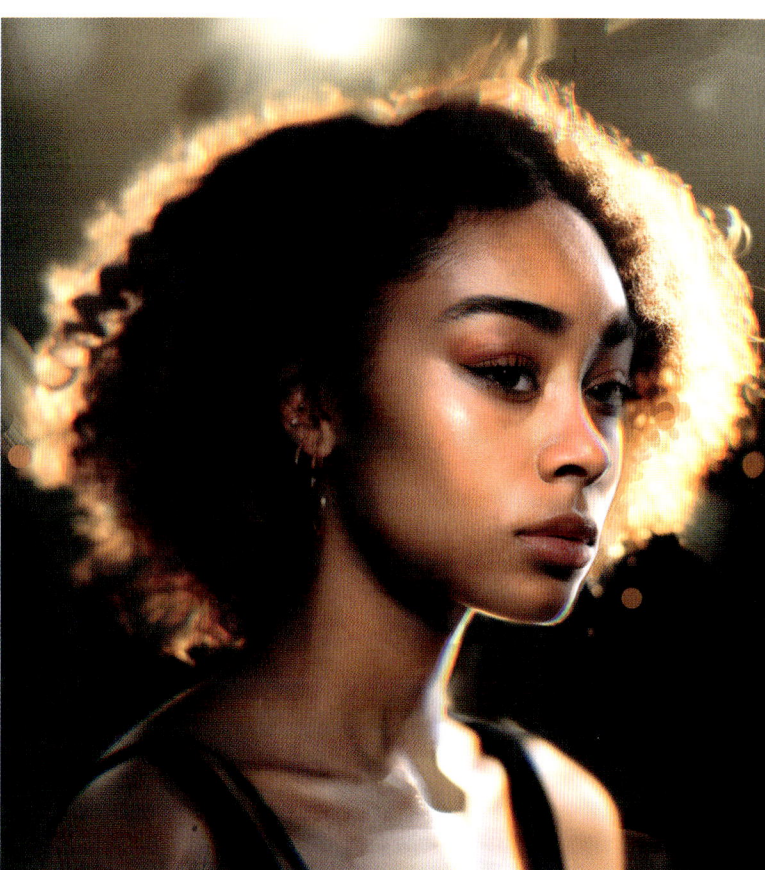

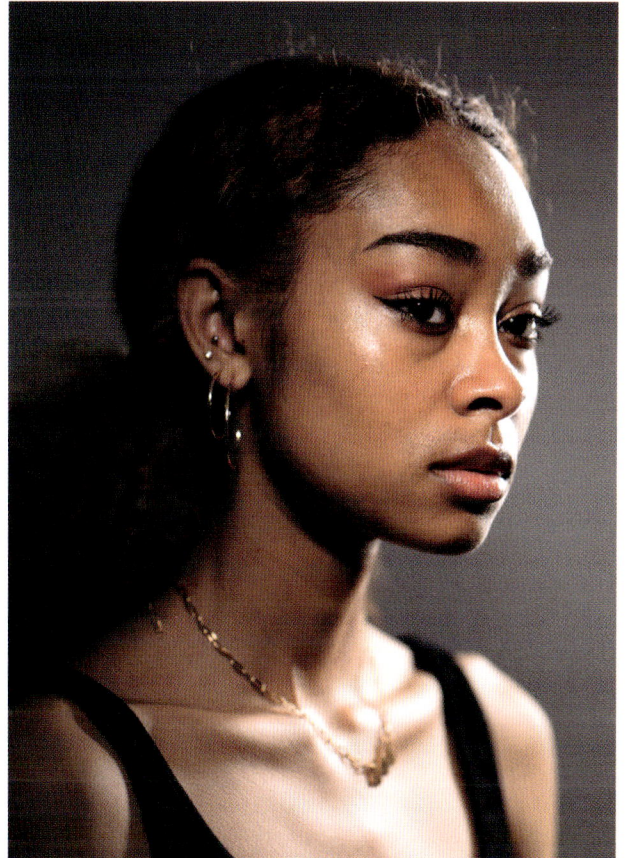

2 | PORTRAIT DRAWING CONCEPTS: WHAT TO DRAW

Drawing a portrait is complicated. In order for it to be done well and to create an authentic likeness of the model, there are different spheres of knowledge that you must slowly improve upon through repetition.

These next few pages represent some broad categories of thinking that will help you to construct a portrait. They'll be fleshed out in greater detail in the following sections, but here, you'll find all of the major concepts in one place to see how they might begin to fit together. I think of them as a set of checks and balances. For instance, proportion is essential, but unless you have a big shape on which to flesh out those measurements, you can get stuck in proportion purgatory, just measuring and plotting points ad nauseam that feel disjointed and unconnected. Another example is if your shapes and proportions are accurate but your internal structure of the facial armature is all wrong, so that when you draw in the features, everything is wobbly, crooked, and out of alignment.

Of course, there are many valid approaches to drawing a portrait, but this is a basic overview of the essentials so that we can make a decent drawing and then move on to the painting.

FACIAL ARMATURE

ENVELOPE SHAPE AND MAJOR SHAPES

The envelope shape in Figure **(A)** is perhaps the most intuitive concept of drawing out a portrait. It's not an overwhelming idea: simply enclose everything that's part of your subject within a series of straight lines to get a rough idea of the layout of the head. If you can minimize the number of these lines, even better! This envelope block-in will allow you to see the angles and simplicity of the pose, and you're much more likely to change what's wrong if it's first described in simple straight lines.

There's an art to simplifying your subject in this manner. As a student, our instructors would challenge us to make this envelope shape with fewer than twelve lines to force us to understand our subject in an extremely basic way. Once this simple envelope shape is drawn in lightly, take a step back and judge your angles to see if they're true. Usually, they're not and need some adjustment before continuing your block-in.

The next step is to find other major shapes (gray-blue lines, inside of the red envelope, to break it up into parts.

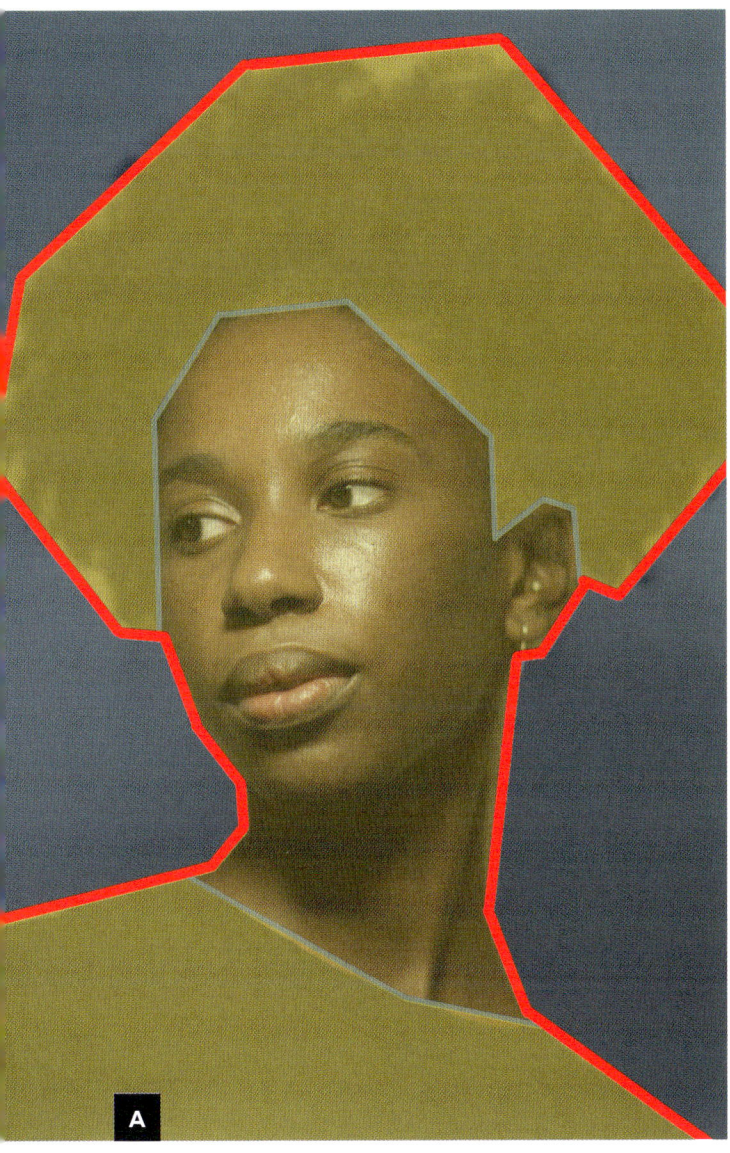

A

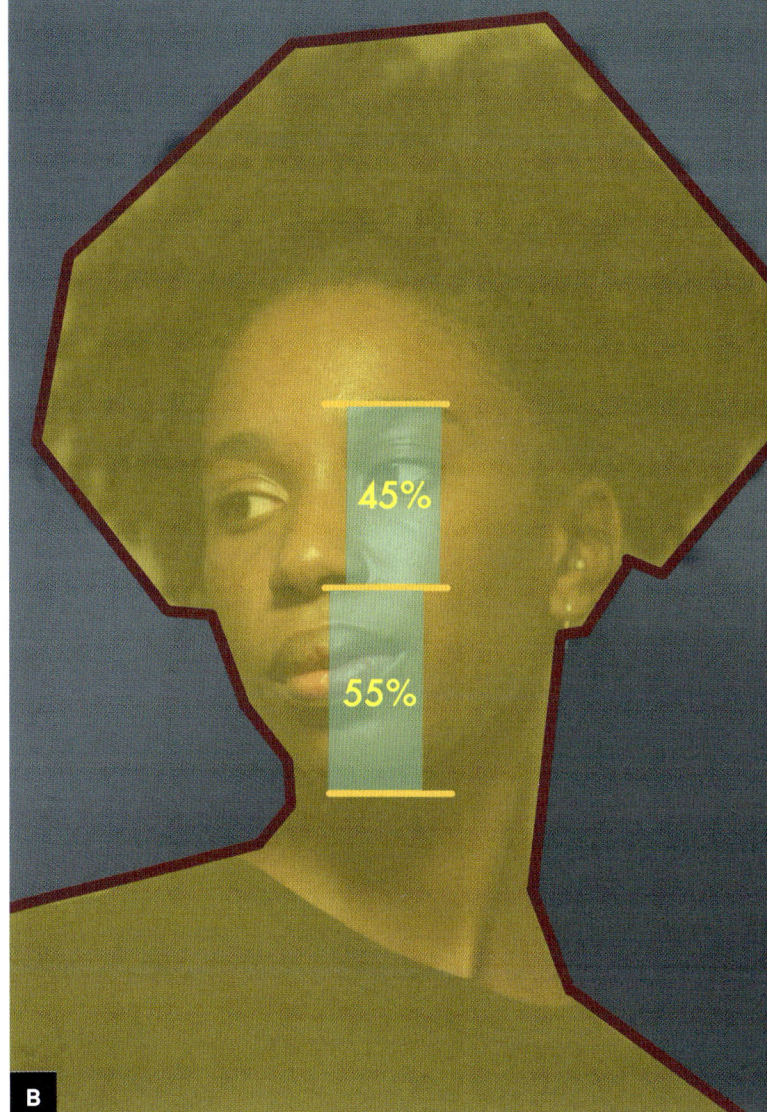

45%

55%

B

As you work through this block-in, remember the usefulness of negative shapes. In Figure **(B)**, if we look at the background by her head as a negative shape and we try to draw that, then turn our focus to seeing the same boundary line as the hair line (positive shape), there's a mental game of going back and forth, positive vs. negative, in which our brain can continue to refine the boundary line between head and background. You're working on the same line, but seeing it in two contexts, and this provides more checks and balances on your drawing accuracy.

PROPORTION

Proportion is a tool that allows you to dial in the spatial relationships that will help create a likeness. So many people are concerned with a likeness, but they can't quite achieve it and aren't sure why. While drawing in shapes is intuitive and can be very freeing, start to incorporate measuring as well and make sure that the relationships you're establishing are correct, rather than settling for whatever you happen to perceive with your eye.

CENTERLINE AND FACIAL ARMATURE

The centerline of the head and its proportional distance from the sides of the head, marked in thicker red lines **(C)**, set the proper angle that the head is tilted on and also quickly communicates which side of the face we see more of than the other. Of course, in a three-quarter view, this is of great importance because if this centerline is wrong and not in the right proportion to the sides of the face, everything else following will also be incorrect.

The centerline is easier to intuit when the model is facing us straight-on; we all gravitate naturally towards putting the centerline in the center of our drawing. It should be drawn anyway, so that you can measure to the sides, but the centerline is more important and impactful in a three-quarter view.

On that note, we almost always want to make the face appear more as if it's straight on. There's a tendency with humans when drawing to take a diagonal and straighten it up or take something that's asymmetrical and make it more symmetrical. Even when the model is in three-quarter view, we often want to straighten them out. Marking out the centerline and its proportion to the sides directs the orientation of the face before we ever draw in the features and will keep you in check.

Mostly oriented on perpendicular lines, the features transverse this centerline and begin to set order going side-to-side. I say mostly perpendicular because sometimes there's a bend in that centerline, which creates a slight deviation from perfectly perpendicular. These lines often wrap around the face in perspective and have a slight curve to them. Usually, they're set on a grid, and it's quite helpful to draw in the central axis and build a grid off of it, so there's a general structural symmetry to how we map out where the features will eventually be.

All of these lines working together I refer to as the *facial armature*. The facial armature is the foundation from which all subsequent decisions concerning the features in their relationships to each other and within the head will be based.

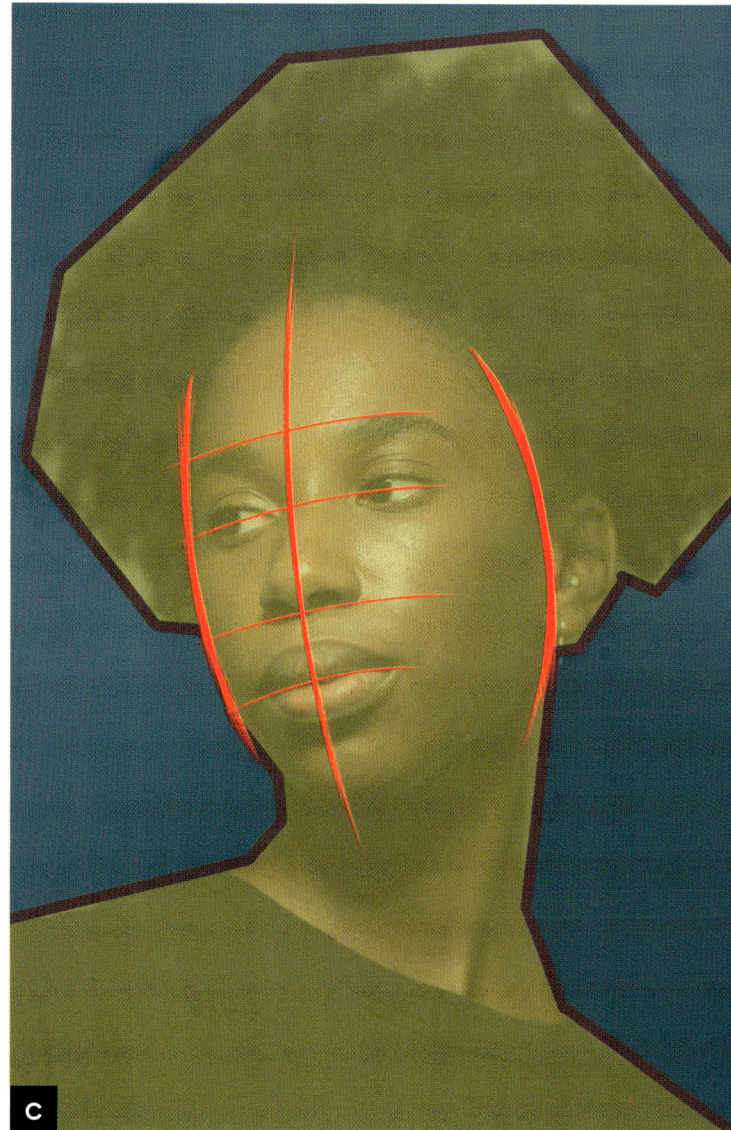

C

CONNECTING TO THE CENTER

In Figure **(D)**, we've dimmed down the presence of the facial armature, and you can see how the different points of the features will line up on these lines. By setting up the facial armature, you begin to anticipate symmetries that fall along these lines, so that even if you're drawing in an eye in great detail, you anticipate seeing its symmetrical counterpart on the other side of the centerline.

This is especially true on the lower portion of the centerline, where we see a smooth connection from the ball of the nose to the chin. The formation of the mouth and the lower part of the nose have a particularly direct connection to that centerline.

As you move up into the forehead and eyebrow area, this isn't as true because the angle of the nose dips in at that point, right under the brow.

Our centerline is deviating at that indentation. Remember that the centerline is really formed as a gentle arc that goes through the center of the forehead, through the center of the chin, and doesn't engage with the indentation just below the brow. This is because the centerline is really a simple approximation of the center, not the true center that bifurcates the face perfectly, running along the forms as they undulate.

If all of that was too technical, just remember this: the main point is to establish a center and then build out from this center. This central core will be the axis from which all of the features will build out from and relate back to.

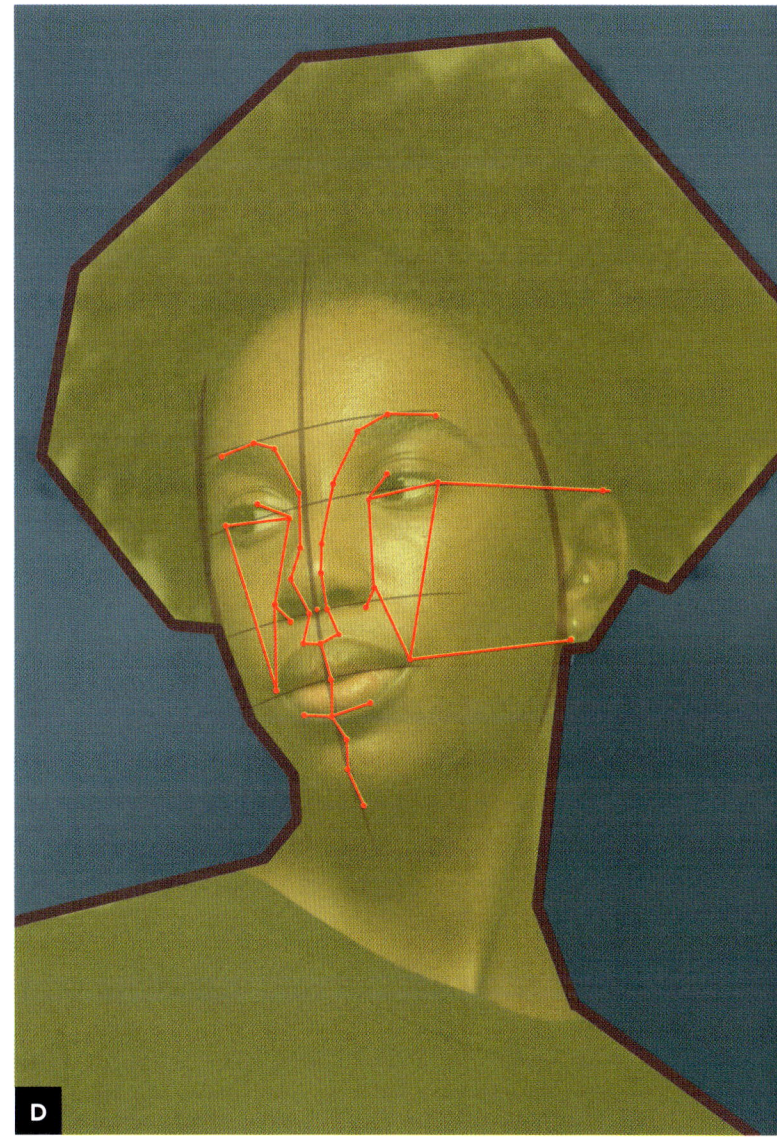

D

MEASURING AND PROPORTION

Measuring and proportion is one of the most overlooked steps in drawing. Whenever I try to explain it, my students' eyes glaze over and a tremendous amount of boredom descends upon them. It's the thing everybody knows that they should do, but perhaps don't have a system of how to do it. Plus, there a disambiguation that must happen in order to explain the type of proportion that I'm talking about.

Most students entering class think that proportion is predetermined or that there's a rule book we must follow containing all of the existing correct proportions. These written criteria are referred to as a "canon of proportion," or you could call them *averaged proportions*. These are proportions that are considered ideal or have been seen to be generally correct based on average human proportions. This has been understood since ancient times, and perhaps was truly codified with the Greek sculptures of antiquity.

What concerns me specifically in *this* book are the measured proportions of the specific model that we're looking at. And what that basically means is measuring a certain distance on the model, then comparing it to another distance on the model, and seeing the relationship between the two measurements. There are two primary ways that I choose to teach proportion: box proportion and span proportion.

BOX PROPORTION

When measuring the box proportion of the head, I create an invisible rectangular box around the head, including hair shape (red). In Figure **(A)**, the furthest ends of the head are quite easily seen (bright yellow) and define the edges of the box; when you connect these furthest ends together, it'll form a box. Our next job is to measure the proportion of this box. The way that I do it is to take the shorter side of this box and see how many times it fits into the longer side of the box. In the case of Figure **(B)**, it's a one to one and a quarter measurement.

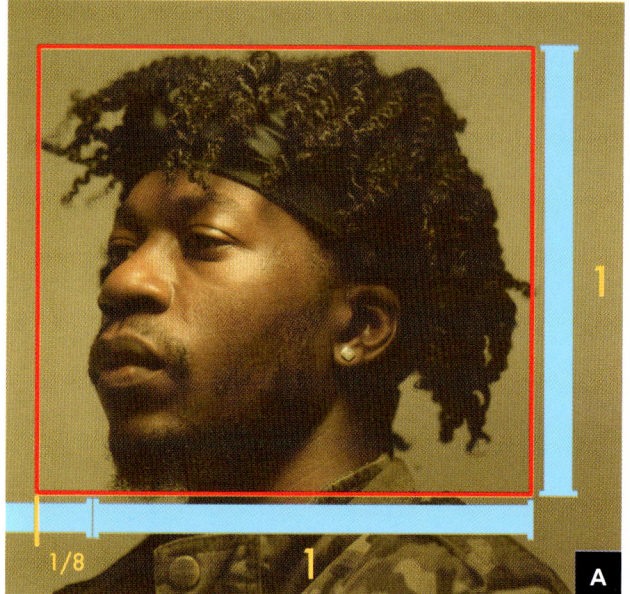

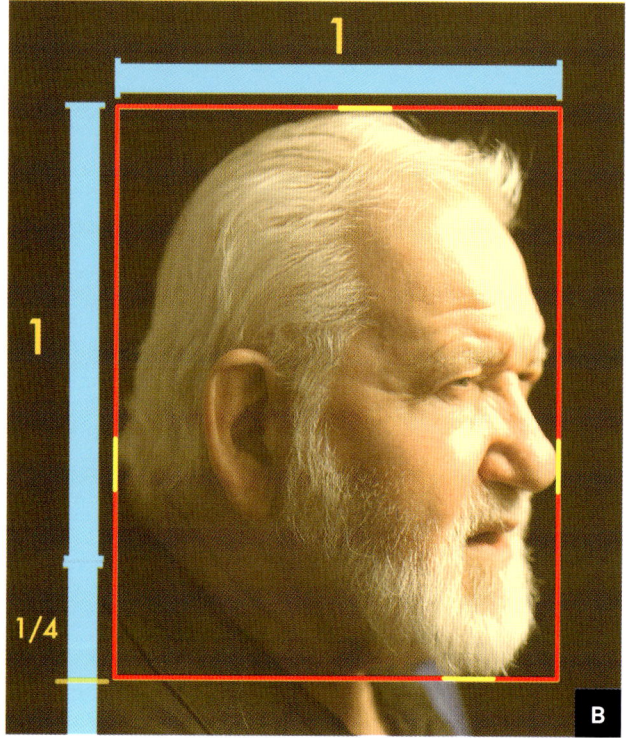

Scan to view a
video tutorial

As stated before, not every head is going to have the same measurement when seen from the profile view. This is not a canon of proportions. Some people will have more hair or they'll have a wider face. Everyone is different, and so this way of measuring allows you to understand the unique proportions of everyone's differently shaped head or different views of the head.

When defining the box, sometimes it can be slightly complicated as the hair might be moving or there's a beard, and it may be difficult to define where that box truly begins or ends, but try to pick landmarks that are easily seen and won't move. If you can define this box, it makes the proportional measurement of the head much easier to handle.

SPAN PROPORTION AND "EYEBALLING IT"

Span proportion is a slightly different way of measuring a specific spot that is on an overall length. For example, take the overall length (top of the head to the chin). If you want to understand the relationship between the top of the head to the brow, and the brow to the chin, span proportion is the correct way to measure. In span proportion, we're trying to understand the relationship between these two distances on the same length.

Again, the easiest way to understand a proportion and actually measure it is to take the shorter piece and see how many times it fits into the longer piece. As in Figure **(C)**, the distance from the top of the head to the brow is one length and then from brow to chin is that length and a quarter, making the relationship of this span one to one and a quarter.

All this measuring gets to be a bit too much for people, and they'd prefer to "eyeball it." I often do the exact same thing. When I choose to eyeball it, I use some simple proportions that help me clarify what I'm looking at.

The chart in Figure **(D)** shows regular measurements I often refer to when I'm eyeballing it or even when measuring. These measurements seem to me to fit within human error. I often use a visual measurement of 50/50 or 45/55 or 1/3 to 2/3 in order to have a simple, structured way of thinking about proportions.

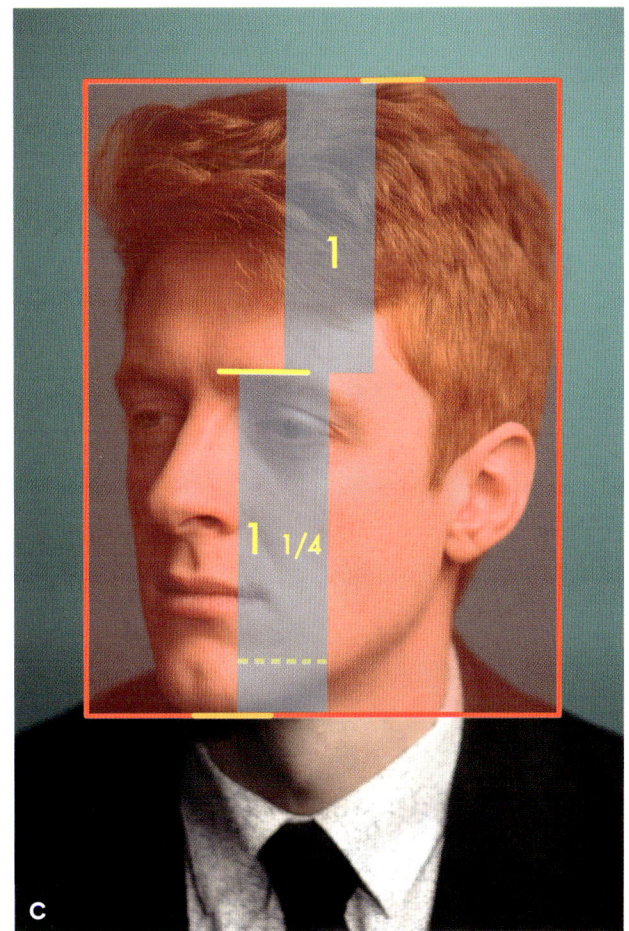

50		50	
45		55	
40		60	
1/3		2/3	
D 1/4		3/4	

Here are examples of simple proportions that I often use.

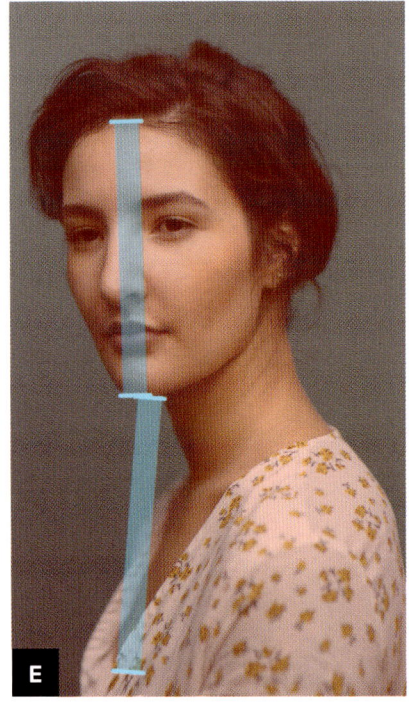
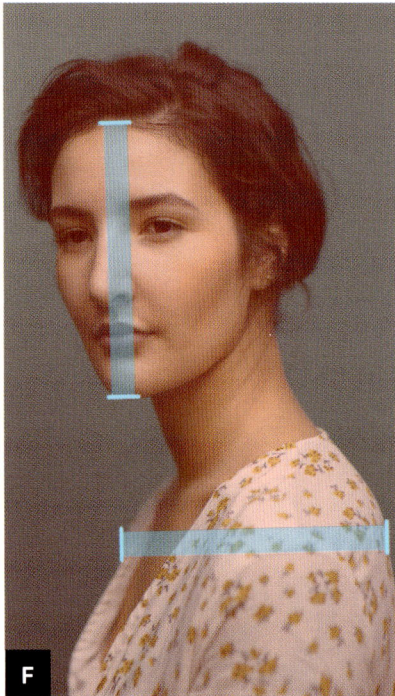
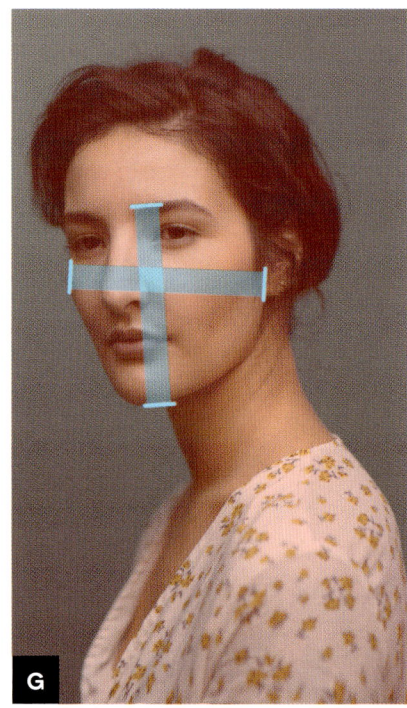

USING A UNIT OF MEASURE: LOOKING FOR COINCIDENCES

As you're measuring and looking for box proportions or span proportions, you may find that there are "coincidences" along the way. These coincidences can often be the most helpful and easily measured things that you observe. For instance, in looking for a good proportion between the head and the end of the neckline of the shirt, I found that the overall distance from the hairline to the chin was the exact same distance as from the chin to the end of the neckline **(E)**. These coincidences create easy relationships of one to one so that there are no fractional, complicated proportional relationships—just simple, easy comparisons that make proportion much more manageable, especially if you're painting from life.

This distance from the hairline to the chin could be considered a "unit of measure" and also used to measure other things and compare their distances with this same unit of measure. For instance, another coincidence that I found was that the distance from the hairline to the chin was also the exact same as the width of the shoulders **(F)**.

Yet another coincidence, but using a different unit of measure, was that the distance from brow to chin was the exact same distance as from the ear to the cheek **(G)**. These coincidences are much more common than one might think. Be on the lookout for them in your portraiture, so that you can use them to your advantage in measuring proportion the easiest way.

THE FOUR MOST IMPORTANT PROPORTIONS

Another thing I often see go wrong is that even after proportion is explained and someone makes their best effort at trying to use proportion, somehow it's still not correct. I often hear, "But I measured it!"

I don't think that everything should be measured. In fact, often I'm drawing first and measuring second when I get into trouble. There's a spirit and beauty in art that can't be measured, and it seems silly to be so uptight when talking about proportion, when the goal is making art. Nevertheless, when you need it, you need it! Then, it's important to define what the most important proportions are so that then you can stop measuring and start painting.

I've broken down what I believe to be the four most important measured proportions of the face. These proportions are calculable when working from life. Most dimensions that are smaller than these distances are just not worth measuring. Know what is measurable, get the most important things locked in, and let the rest develop in its own course.

THE BOX

We've already discussed box proportion, but on this page, I want you to view it as a foundation for every other decision that will be measured.

There are some decisions that should come first before others, and this is one of them. Establishing where the box is on the model and where it's going to fit on the canvas allows you to fit your model on the page correctly and gives a framework for the next most important proportions **(A)**.

When you choose to set up your image by using this box, what you're doing is giving yourself an x-axis and a y-axis to measure against. This takes away the confusing quality of measuring on an angle, which is subjective and prone to significant error. Measuring all of the other important areas becomes much easier because this overall proportion has been established, like having a small block of marble that you can measure and cut away from in order to shape your head **(B)**. I think this works better than just dropping in an egg for a head with a centerline. That egg-shaped void form is often used in blocking out a head, but it's not based upon the model's unique proportions.

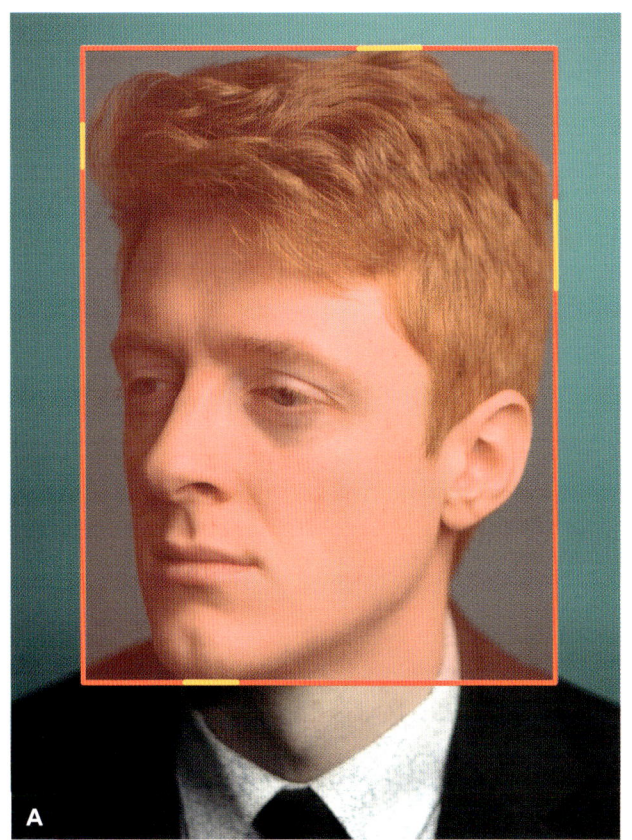

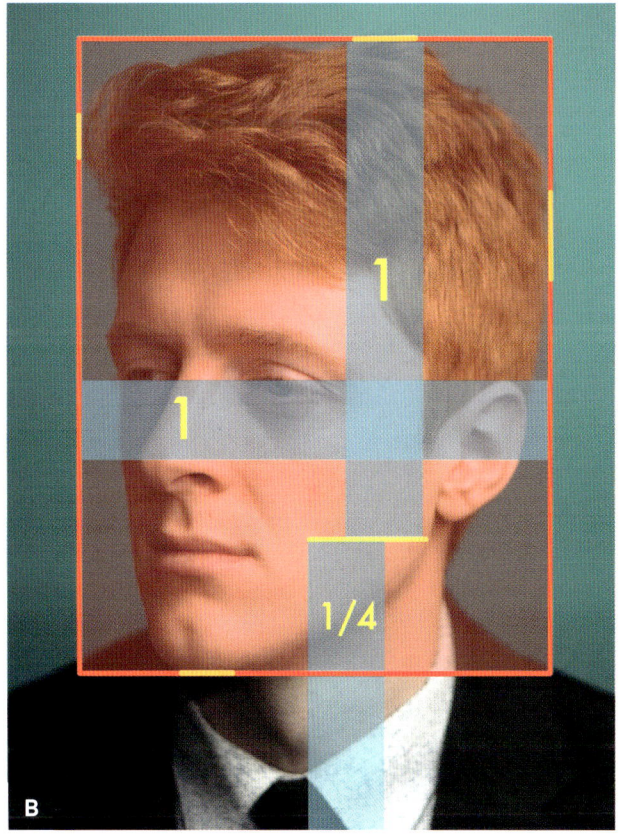

The box helps you to wrap your mind around the overall shape of the head and contain it. It's now under your control.

TOP, BROW, MIDDLE

After we establish the box, the next most important measurement is to use span proportion to find the relationship between the top, the brow, and the chin **(C)**. This measurement, top-brow-chin, will also affect the nose and mouth relationship. It sets up the brow as an anchor point, a landmark that makes sense with the box and sets up further measurements.

Typically, this relationship is either 45/55 or 40/60, but everything can be different, depending on the height of the model's hair and other various factors.

I choose the brow as a landmark because it's a central point of the face that's much more easily defined than the eye. Many people know that the eye is in the center of the head (typically), but using the eye as a landmark presents a question of where on the eye is the center? This creates too much ambiguity for me to use as a clear, reliable landmark.

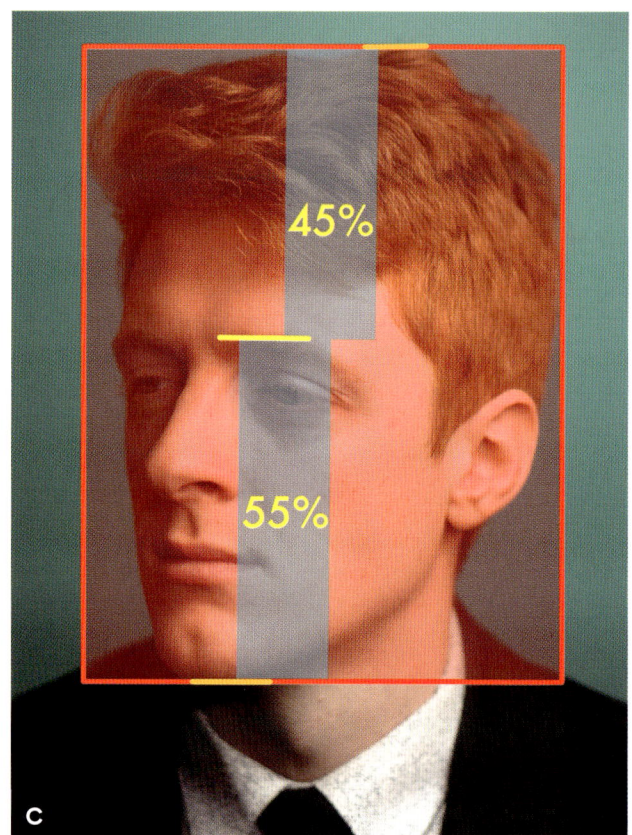

BROW, NOSE, CHIN

After the brow has been established and the chin has been decided by the box, we then measure the span proportion brow-nose-chin **(D)**. I'd say typically this relationship is 50/50 or 45/55, and in some cases it can become even more pronounced based on the model's proportions.

This proportion is critical for setting up the mouth properly and not having to redraw all the features later. I can't tell you how many times I've gotten the nose too long or the mouth area too big and then I end up trying to shrink or enlarge features to fit into the spaces that I've established incorrectly.

In fact, I rarely draw in the mouth until I've looked at this proportion many times, and usually, I just leave the mouth as a soft muzzle until I've secured this distance and feel good about it. I usually also don't define the eyes until this is looking pretty good. I treat the eyes as a soft, out-of-focus eye socket for a while because I don't want to have to redraw specific features later due to missed proportions.

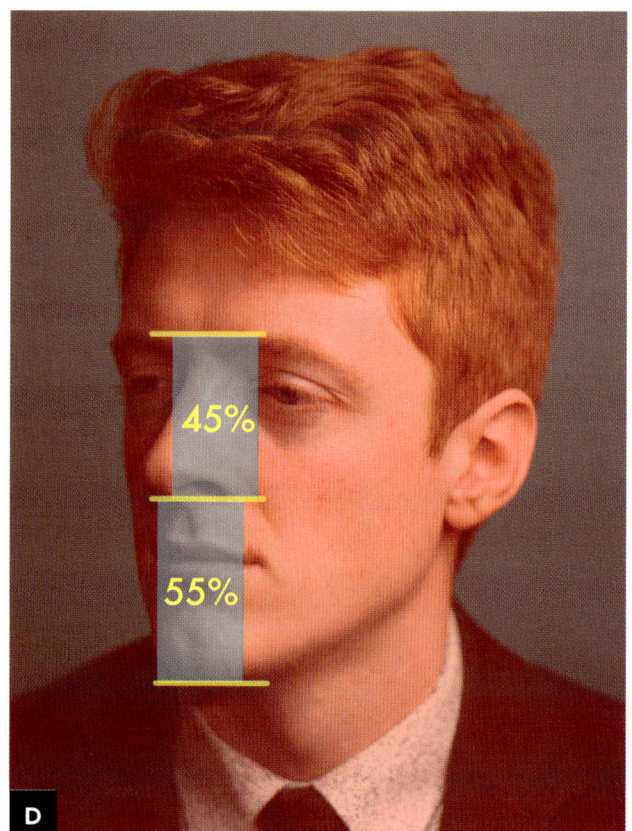

FRONT, SIDE, BACK

The last initial proportion to establish is the front-side-back proportion **(E)**. These proportions are the ones that directly deal with the orientation of the face moving from side to side. The centerline of the head is also an especially important proportion that deals with these factors, which we'll address next.

The most defining spatial proportions that go side to side on the face feel more difficult than the ones to go from top to bottom. These landmarks that help determine the side-to-side measurements are difficult to define.

The front-side-back proportion is defined by the edge of the eye socket or the cheekbone indentation of the zygomatic bone. However nebulous this proportion might seem, if we draw in the wrong place, we would wind up having to stretch or scrunch the eyes to fit!

I change the landmarks that I use for this proportion if the portrait is in profile or depending on the extent of the turn of the head. For a profile, I'll often use the sideburns or the beginning of the ear as a landmark; the key is to find a landmark towards the center of the face, according to how the face is turned.

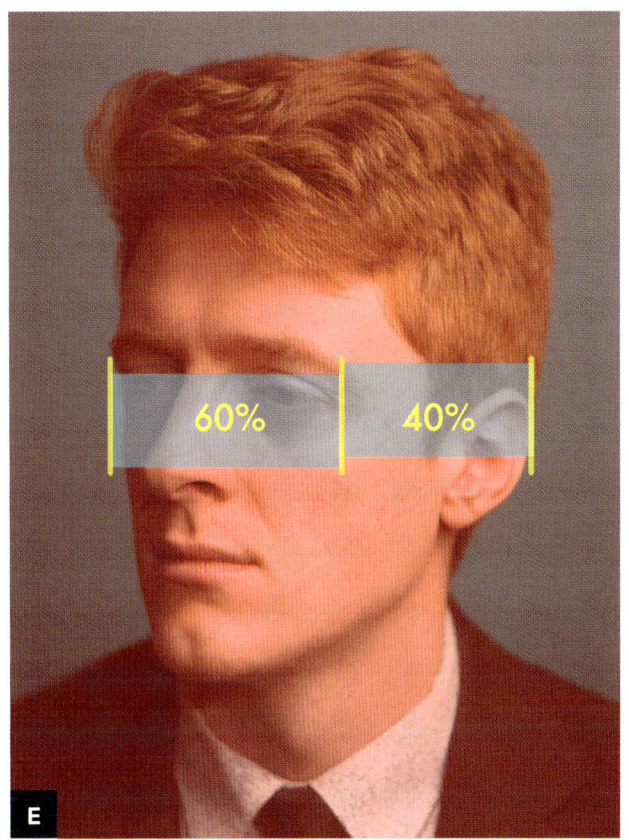

E

CENTERLINE OF THE HEAD

In this section, we're mostly talking about concepts that will help you in any situation when it comes to drawing the head. It's not necessarily a how-to book in which we go step-by-step on how to draw in a head in a linear way. These pages show theories that are meant to be tools for you to pick and choose from to apply the best option for your situation. Finding the centerline is one such option.

MIXING CONCEPTS

Sometimes, the box and measuring of all the proportions as previously described will fit easily with finding the centerline, and sometimes it doesn't so easily fit. As you can see in these dynamic poses from our model, the box may or may not work for you here, but perhaps finding the envelope shape will. Either way, the goal with these poses is to define the centerline of the head (red) and its relationship with the overall frame of the face (yellow).

This is a good reminder that some concepts in drawing are very rigid, clear, and logical; I call these Apollonian concepts. Other concepts in drawing are Dionysian, and in their expression, they're just a bit more intuitive—ideas that you feel out.

I've always struggled to try to understand the uniqueness of both Apollonian and Dionysian concepts and how they may fit together in art-making. The centerline of the head is one of those unique ideas where there is a marriage of these two kinds of thinking, which makes it, in my experience, to be one of the most difficult things to teach precisely.

Often in my portrait class, someone has drawn out an entire head and although it may look good in its parts, the centerline of the head is wrong, so it's impossible for the likeness to fall into place. Having to show them this is an incredibly sad proposition for a teacher because we all know the hard work that goes into making a portrait, and it's defeating to have someone come along and point out that because the centerline is off, everything must move! Being careful to get this right before developing the portrait further will save a lot of headache later.

FINDING THE CENTER

One can define this centerline in a more uninhibited, feel-it-out kind of way rather than just measuring alone. A good way to start is to just try! As in most cases, when you're trying something out in drawing,

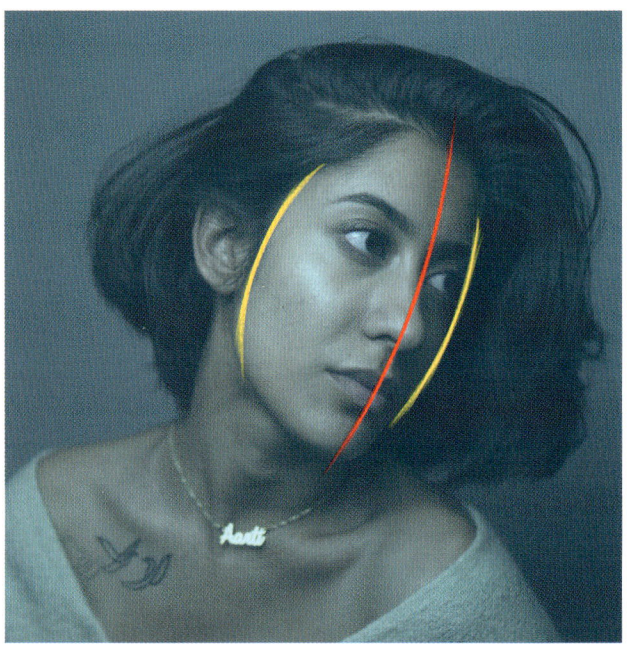

The goal is to define the centerline of the head (red) and its relationship with the overall frame of the face (yellow).

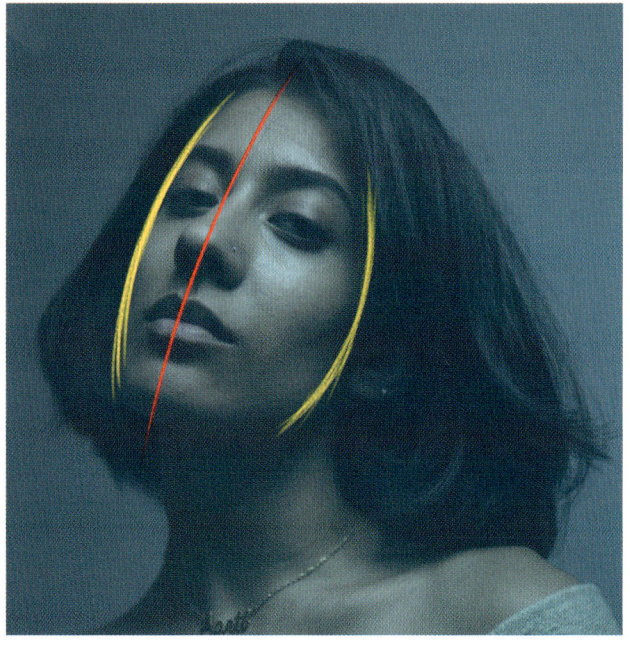

Seems like an 80/20 proportion

you should draw it lightly and sketchy so that you have some options on the page. The spirit of this red centerline is a line that runs from the middle of the forehead through the middle of the chin, while having a slow arc that defines the roundness of the head. In portraiture, this angle reflects the attitude and the gesture of the overall pose of the model.

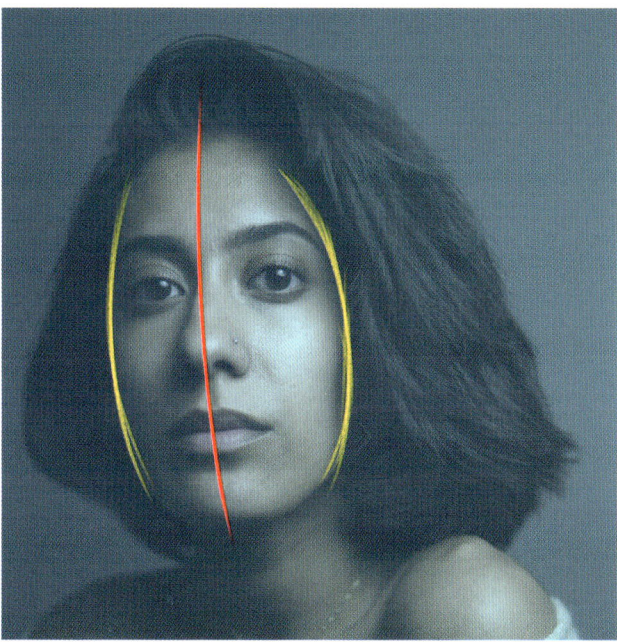

Perhaps a 40/60 proportion

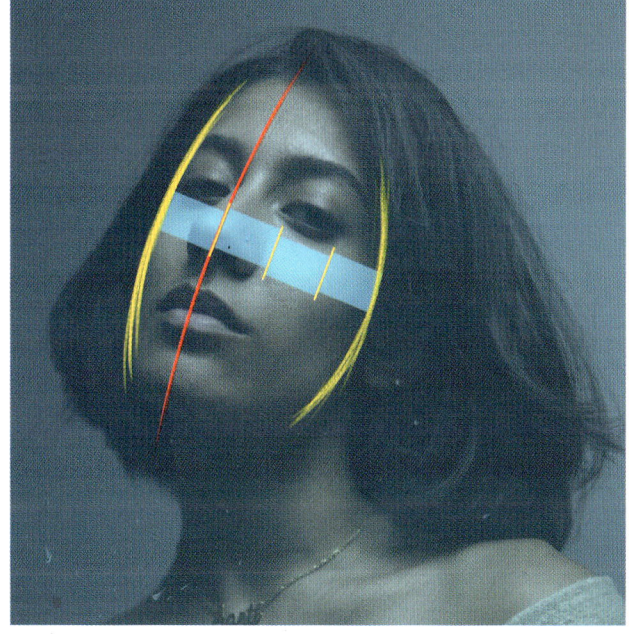

More carefully measured, this is a ¼ to ¾ proportion.

In most dynamic poses, this angle is quite askew. The more diagonal this line is, the more attitude and a sense of irregularity is conveyed. The straighter this line is up and down, the more static and restful the pose is.

The position of this red centerline is rarely perfectly in the center of the face. Yet, we subconsciously feel a pull to make this line in the middle of our head, which is unlikely to accurately represent the image we're working from.

PROPORTION OF THE CENTERLINE
Herein lies the mixing of Dionysian and Apollonian drawing approaches. Sometimes, the process of just "feeling it out" and intuitively drawing in this line renders an incorrect answer, so after quickly and lightly sketching in a head and getting a feel for its position, change gears and incorporate measuring.

It's better to lightly sketch the portrait out first and measure second so that we are not seized up with fear and afraid to make any incorrect decisions. Art is about problem-solving, and sometimes, you need a problem first (a light energetic sketch) and a method to solve it second (measuring).

Each one of these poses has a different proportion of the centerline (red) to the sides (yellow). And yet again, I may measure this in the very strict way, or I might use something like the simple proportion chart at the beginning of this section.

Sketching in and measuring can be awkward, but these are the foundational concepts that allow me to draw in the proportions of the features without having to move them later, and if I don't do this preliminary groundwork, which feels so abstract and technical, I'll have heartache later in my drawing.

Most of the ideas in the beginning of this section deal with laying the groundwork for where things will go before we ever draw them out, trying to get things in proper alignment so that we won't have to move them later. We can then set these ideas aside for a time and just draw and connect with our subject, but if things go wrong, we can always come back to this process in order to diagnose what's wrong and how to fix it.

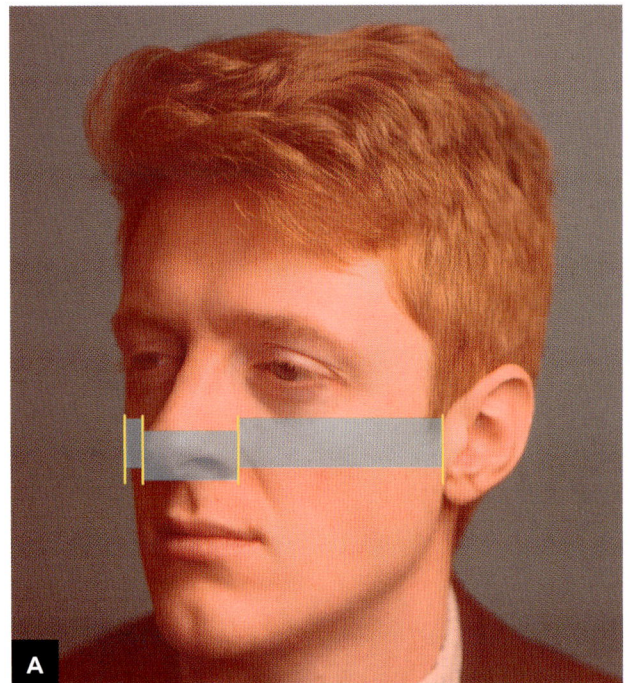

A

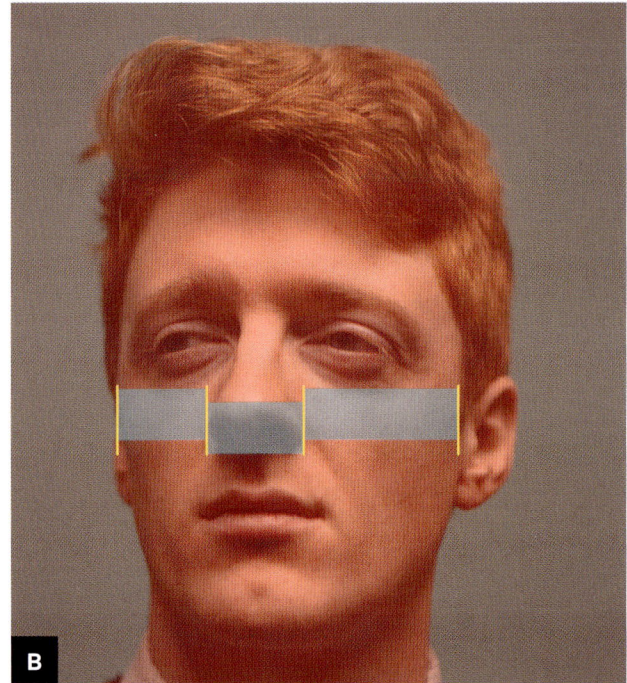

B

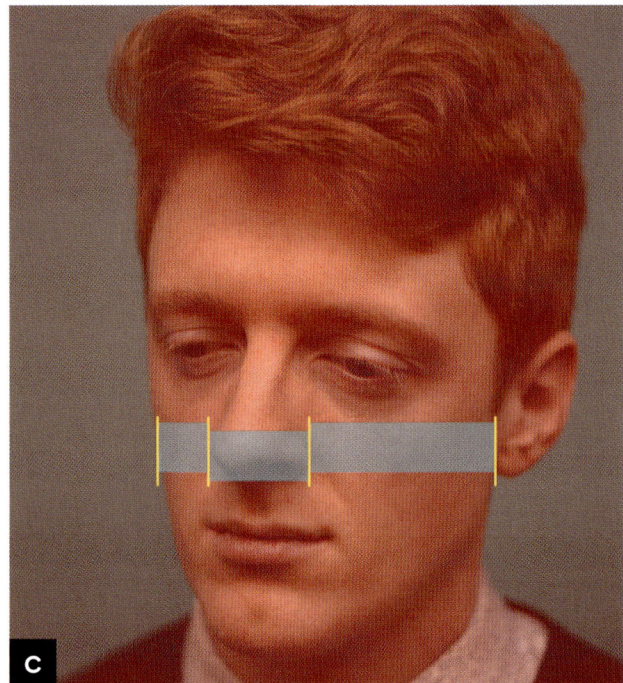

C

CONNECTING TO THE CENTER

SETTING THE NOSE

After the major portions are blocked out and/or the centerline is sketched in, the next most important step is to really make sure that the nose is set properly within this framework. It's so easy to get the nose out of alignment with the overall position of the head, and you must be mindful about the nose's proportion and relationship to the shorter side of the face. In Figure **(A)**, the shorter side of the face is so small it's barely worth measuring. And perhaps the more important proportion is the overall width from nose to far side of the face versus nose to the sideburns.

In Figure **(B)**, the shorter side of the face is just about the same exact width of the nose, and the longer side of the face is almost double this measurement.

In Figure **(C)**, the shorter side of the face is about half the width of the nose, and when these two widths are added together, they make up about 40 percent of the remainder of the face.

Some of these drawing concepts can get quite technical, but not everything needs to be measured out exactly with a caliper and some advanced proportional measuring system. However, it's helpful to acquaint yourself with the concept of being mindful of how these measurements fit together and create the right distances between the features for the correct pose.

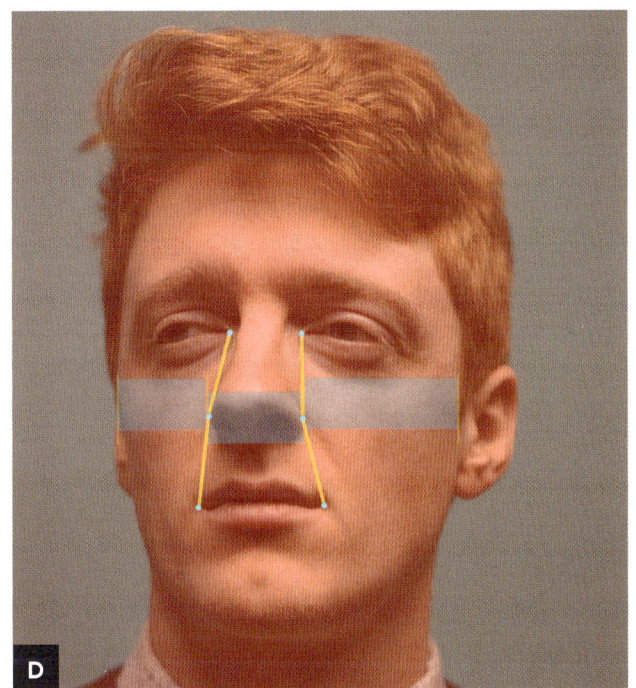

D

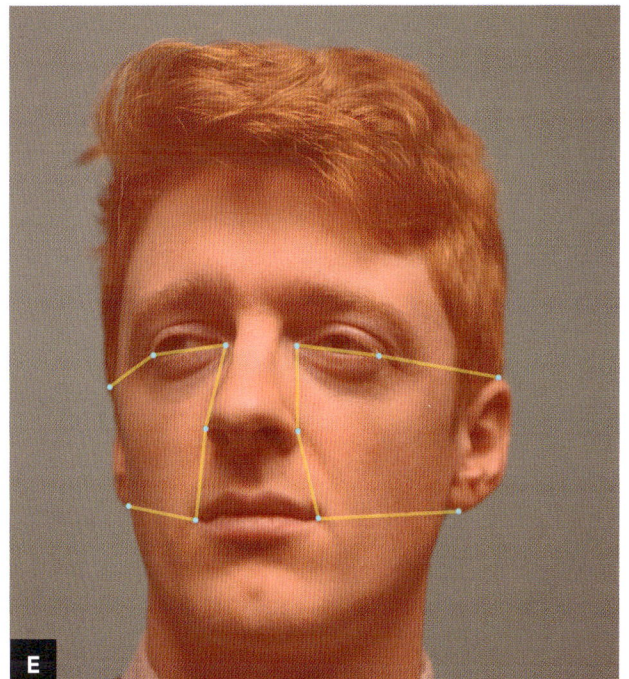

E

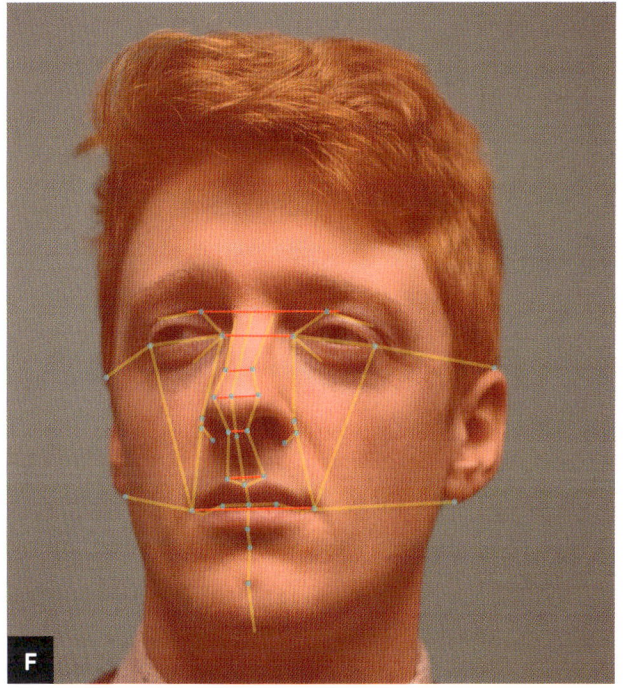

F

WORKING FROM THE HUB

If the nose has been set, then I move on to working out from this central area to plot out the major structural points of the features. I refer to the nose as the hub of the face in the same way as a bicycle wheel has a hub that spokes radiate from. If I establish the nose and then build out to the structural landmarks from that starting point, then I feel like there's not so much relativity and that I can really begin to build the portrait features.

In Figure **(D)**, the first moves that I make is to relate the edge of the nose to the tear ducts and the corners of the mouth. Usually, these are on some kind of angle, and the judgment of angles between these points becomes a critical tool.

In Figure **(E)**, we extend out from the central core and start thinking about how the corners of the mouth might relate to the bottom portion of the ears. We can also extend a line from the lateral corners of the eyes to the top portion of the ears, finding the relationship between these points.

In Figure **(F)**, we can see how to create a whole host of connection points based off of this simple structure and start triangulating the points in order to lock in our structural relationships. You can also see the central line that bifurcates the face—down the nose through the lips and the chin. This really helps to visualize a system of structural symmetry that anticipates an action on one side of this line being countered by the same and opposite action on the other side.

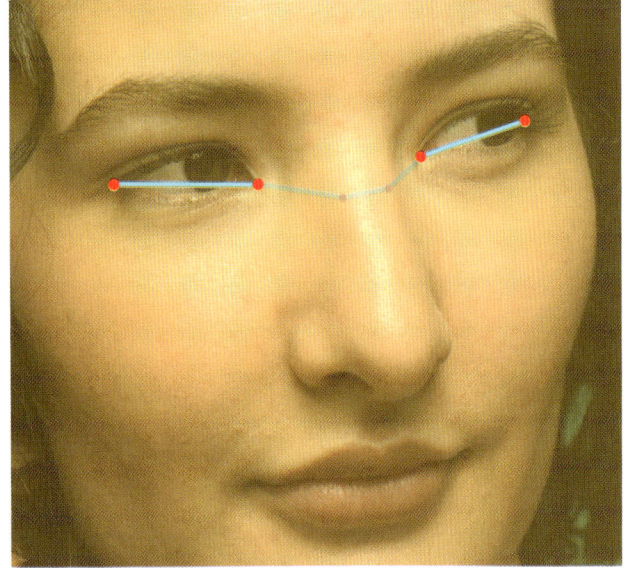
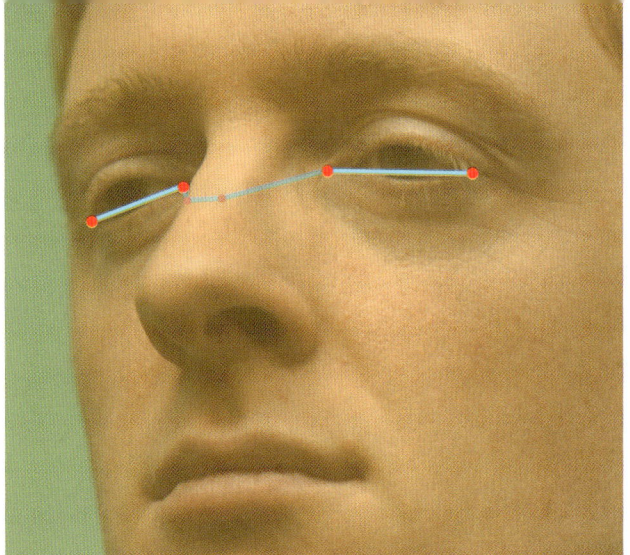

FEATURE CENTERS

HANDLEBARS: SEEING THE STRUCTURAL SYMMETRY OF THE EYES

One of our core concepts of drawing the face is this idea of connecting into the structural center of the face and building outward like veins on a leaf. When it comes to drawing eyes, it's so tempting to just go in there and render an eye, hoping for the best, and then draw the other one, praying that they line up with one another. Let me present a better way. From the beginning, see their relationship across the face. I often think of this relationship as looking for the handlebars of the eyes. This allows you to see the connection and structural symmetry that force them to be considered as a unit, rather than two separate objects.

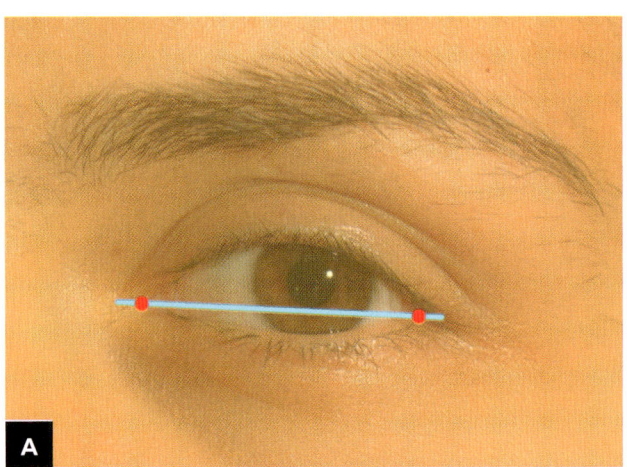

A

INNER AND OUTER CANTHUS

In order to assess the handlebar analogy correctly, you must also look at the angles created between the inner canthus (the tear duct) and the outer canthus (the outside corner) of your model's eyes.

Depending upon the model and the angle of the pose, this angle may tilt up or it may tilt downward. In Figures **(A)** and **(B)**, we have two left eyes, but they're from two different models. Notice that their eyes are at different angles. These angles can also shift if you're looking at the model from below or from above. But they'll be mirror images of each other when you look at the other eye across the head, as demonstrated in the handlebar diagrams above. Be on the lookout for whether your model has an angle to the inner and outer canthus of their eyes. It may even be straight.

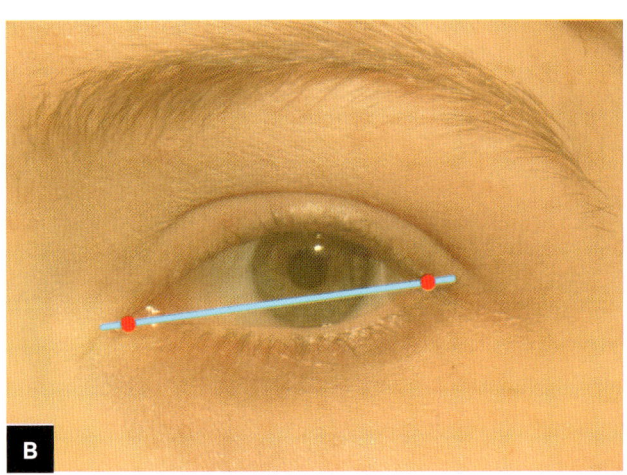

B

UP THE MOUNTAIN, DOWN THE MOUNTAIN

Let's say you now have the basic setup of structural symmetry, such as the handlebar analogy, and also other proportion measuring tools, like the hub concept of dotting out the corners of your features. Now, it's time to start shaping the opening of the eye. The eye is usually shaped like a leaf. It's called the *canthus* because the Romans likened eye shapes to Acanthus leaves.

One of the ideas that I use in shaping this "leaf" is that there's usually a gentle arc that defines the upper lid, and it climbs from the tear duct up to a point. It will be the highest point of the mountain, so to speak. Understanding where this point is in relationship with the colored part of the eye (iris), the eyeball (pupil), or other points on the face, will give you a landmark to help anchor this upper curve.

Likewise, the lower lid will have the same idea in reverse, where you'll be going down the mountain into a valley to the lowest point, and then it begins to arc upward. This spot has a specific relationship with other parts of the eye you may have drawn.

Understanding that when you're drawing the curves of this leaf shape there's a peak of the mountain and a valley helps to be more accurate and discern exactly what's happening with these lines **(C)**.

CENTERS OF THE EYE

Figures **(D)** through **(F)** will focus on a unique property that relates to the pupil and iris.

In Figure **(D)**, we see a yellow line that connects the inner and outer canthi. You may notice that most of the eye opening is above this angle line. This is true no matter the angle of the inner and outer canthus. This line that connects these two dots is also a terrific way to see where the pupil is in relation to them, the triangulation of these three spots.

Figure **(E)** shows how the upper eyelid usually covers a third of the iris circle. Typically, the upper lid will cover a third of the iris. When we start to see more of the upper portion of the iris, the effect is that the model looks intense, scared, or surprised, and your portrait may not yield the desired effect of an eye at rest. The upper lid covering so much of the iris makes it difficult to perceive the circular nature of it, as well as where to put the pupil inside of it. The

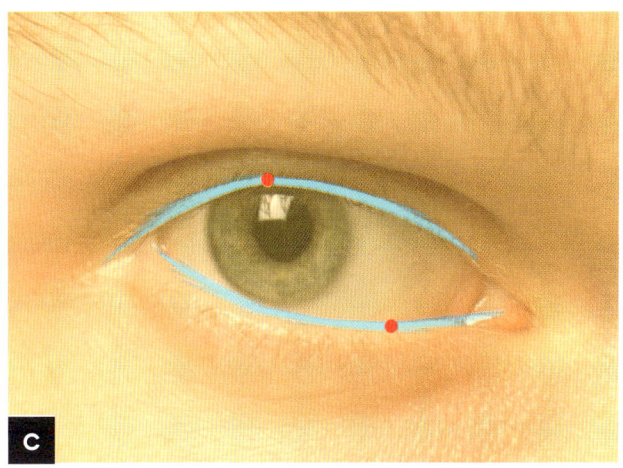

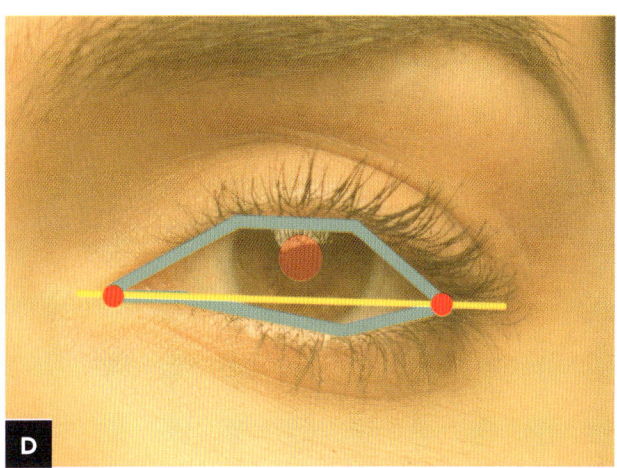

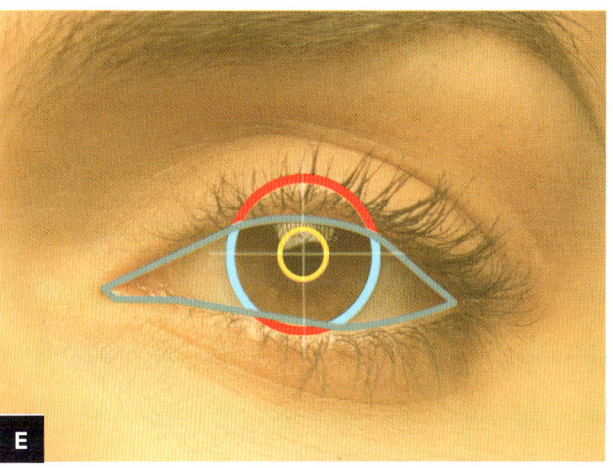

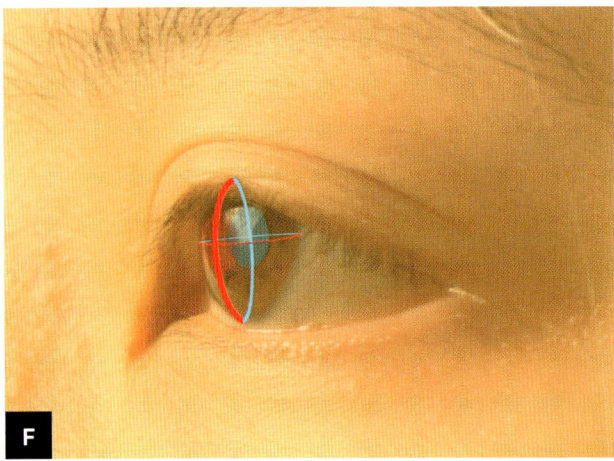

F

pupil will always be directly in the center of the iris when viewed from the front.

Often, when I'm working, I'll try my best to draw in all of this information, but then I'll soften and restate these marks with greater accuracy as the painting or drawing progresses. Since it's quite difficult to get all of these points in their perfect spot, be sure to stay flexible!

In Figure (F) we show what is actually happening anatomically with the pupil when you view the eye from the side. The pupil doesn't sit at the top of the lens of your eye. It's actually significantly set into the eye and creates a concave bowl shape. The blue lines show the depth beyond the front portion, moving inside the eye. The shape of the front, outward-facing layer of the eye is represented here by the red lines. Usually, this isn't something that needs to be dealt with, unless the eyes are in profile.

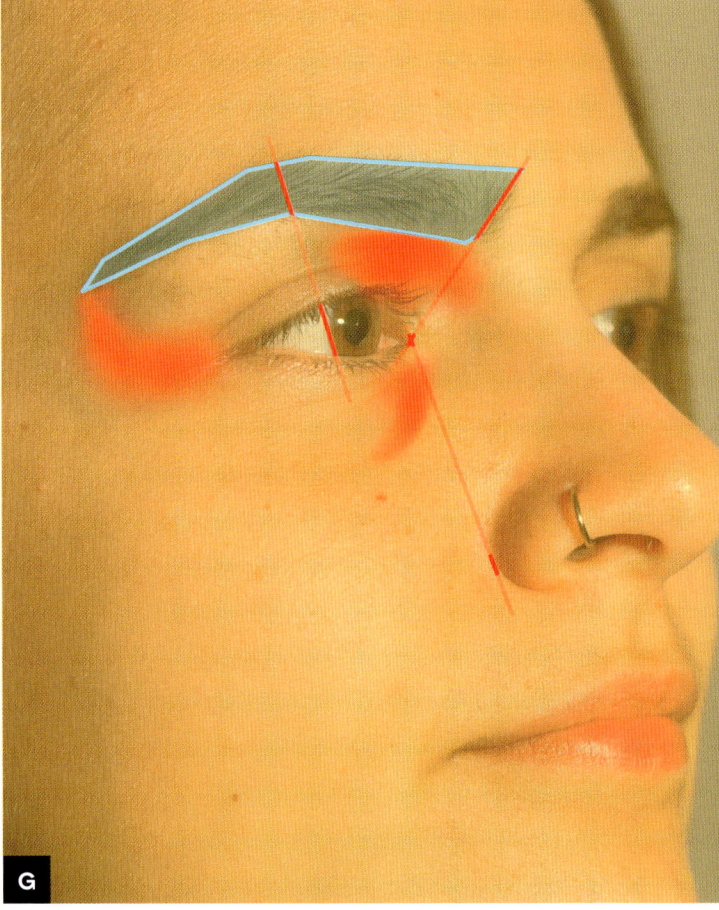

G

CONNECTING TO THE SURROUNDING AREAS

When the eye has been placed in symmetry to the center of the face and is in proportion, and all of these other aspects have been considered, there's still usually the problem of making the eye feel like it's connected to its surroundings. I often find that there are soft tones (represented by the red broad areas) that help us connect with the eye socket and even the eyebrow (G).

I also try to find points on the eyes that I can connect to other significant features, such as the band in the eyebrow relating to the side of the iris or the tear duct relating to the edge of the nose and beginning of the eyebrow.

CENTERS OF THE MOUTH

"A portrait painting is a painting of a person where there is something wrong with the mouth," said John Singer Sargent. Among the many difficult aspects of painting, foremost comes the expression of the mouth. You're trying to set yourself up for success, and often what this means is locating the center of the mouth and understanding its proportion to either side of the mouth out from the centerline.

As you see in Figure **(H)**, the view can be quite extreme where you may have a large portion of one side of the mouth and very little of the other side of the mouth showing. Of course, this is obvious when there's a diagram, but often when we're drawing a mouth, we may fail to realize how disparate the sides are.

In Figure **(I)**, you see how this centerline truly has an undulating contour, reflecting the centerline that runs down and bifurcates the entire face. All of these red points help plan out the unique expression of our model. See how the center of the division of the lips is set in deeper than the center point of the upper portion of the lip. We also see that both corners of the mouth dip down from the center point in the middle of the division of the lips. Use these points to your advantage, either to understand what has gone wrong with your drawing or in advance to plot out where your drawing should go.

Figure **(J)** shows that the corners of the mouth can also be above the center point of the division of the lips, very similar to the inner and outer canthus of the eye, depending upon your angle and your particular model. Whether the corners of the mouth are below or above the center point helps to get the expression of the model correct without having to chase contour lines.

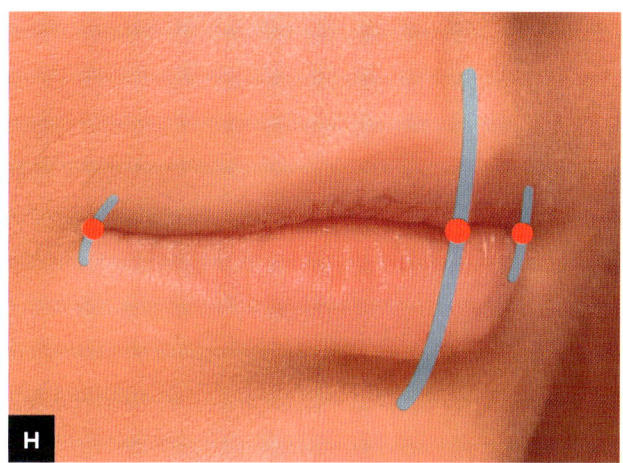

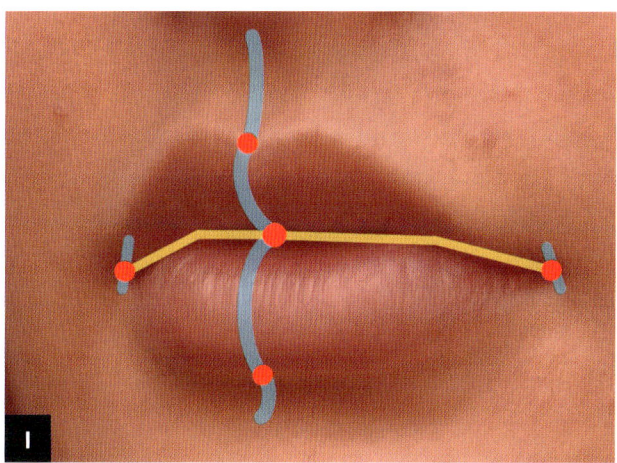

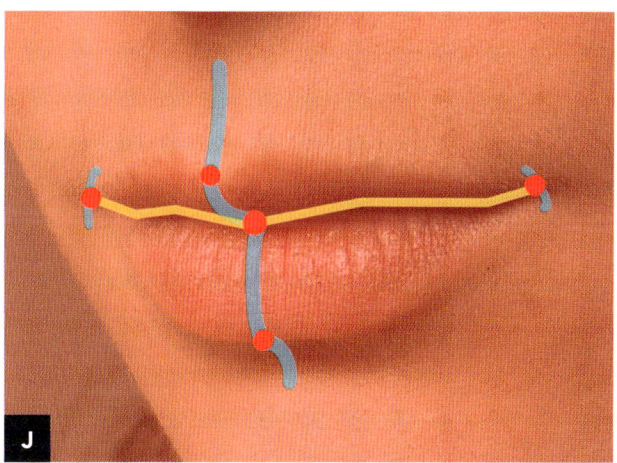

PROBLEM AREA: CORNERS OF THE MOUTH

So much about the model's expression is captured in the relationships that are happening in the corners of the mouth. In many portrait paintings, a neutral expression is desired. Something I've noticed is that in order to capture this neutral expression, the corners of the mouth have to turn down and they have to turn up.

First, the line of the division in the lips needs to slightly turn up at the last minute, preventing a look of displeasure; however, the soft indentation of the flesh around the mouth's corner simultaneously slightly turns downward, cutting short the upward movement. This is indicated by the blue lines and red dots in Figure (K). There's usually a soft, dark tone around this corner that needs to be blended into the crevice. This shadow is also going downward and creates a soft dimple in the corner of the mouth, visually attaching the mouth to the flesh around it (L).

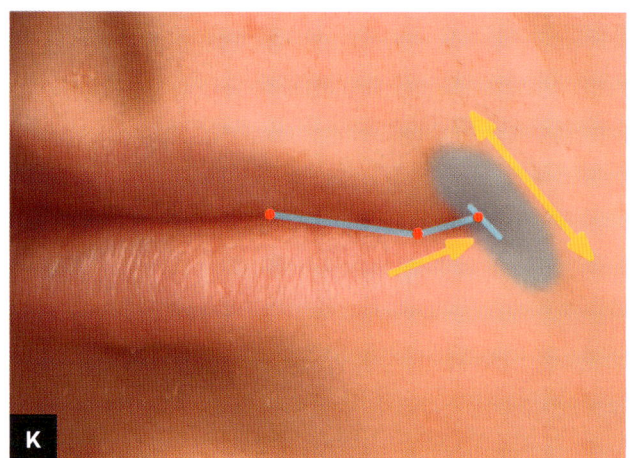

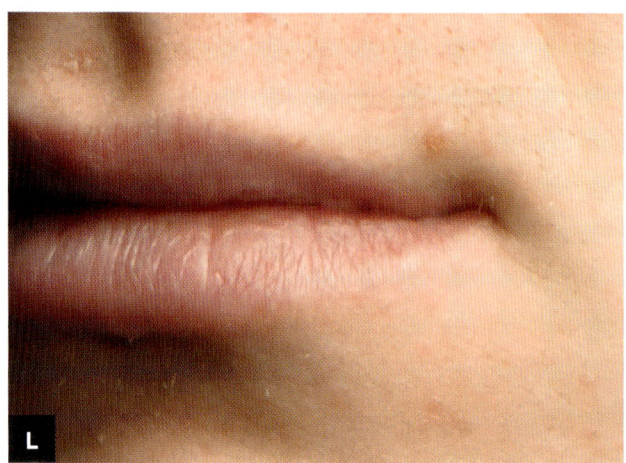

CENTERS OF THE NOSE

The nose is the keystone of the face from which all other features and shapes will be related. I use it as a central point to work out from.

The red dots in the images to the right indicate the origin points of the nostril wings and septum. Like the mouth, the nose also has a structural center that we must find in order to capture its character. As shown in Figure (**M**), the nose can feel like it tips down because the septum or the center point of the nose is lower than the nostril wings on the sides. Or a nose can feel like it's tipping upward if the septum is above the two origin points of the wings, as seen in Figure (**N**).

PROBLEM AREA: NOSTRILS

Nostrils are easily drawn in a manner that can make somebody very quickly look garish. My general advice to anybody drawing in nostrils is to ignore them in the beginning. Try to establish the soft tone that usually is around them, model the nose forms, and make the nose a round ball by creating a soft shadow shape. This will also prevent you from locking in too early. Remember, when we put in too much detail too early, we easily get attached to the position of the nose or whatever feature we're working on, not allowing it to change or modify based on updated information. After the nose is otherwise modeled and seems to be in the correct position, you can begin to lay the nostril in on top of this soft tone.

When you lay in your nostril, go easy. Draw in a gradient, not a solid, dark shape. The top edge of the nostril will be the sharpest line and darkest shade. Then, it gradually starts to fade gently into the light area below as it travels down.

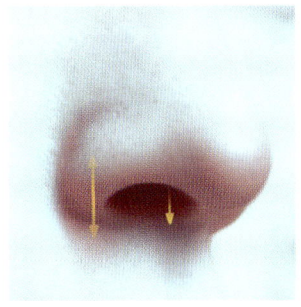
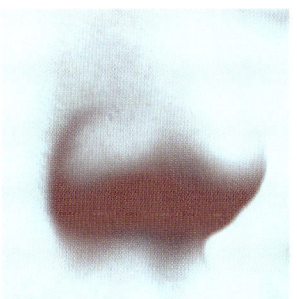

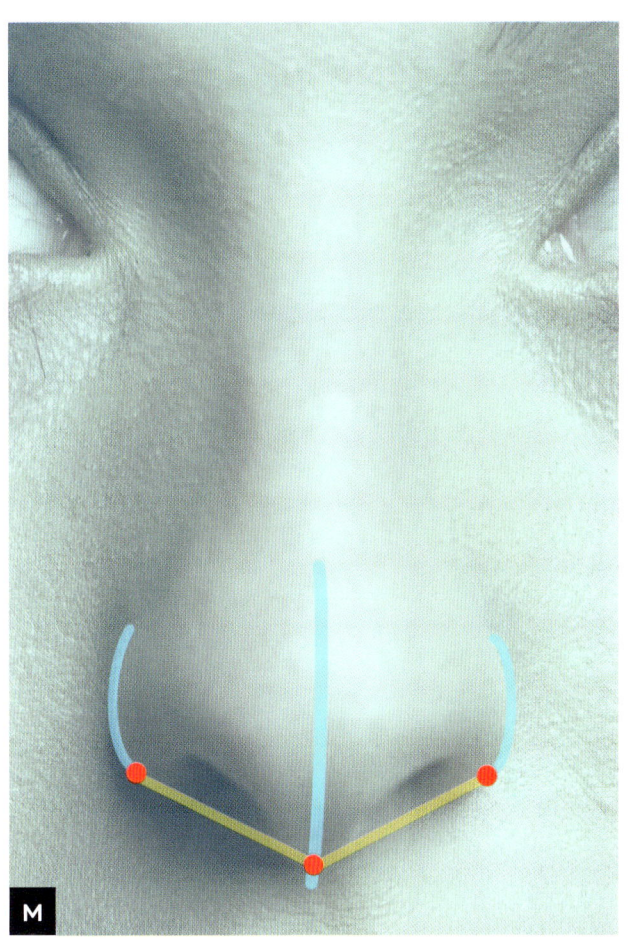

M

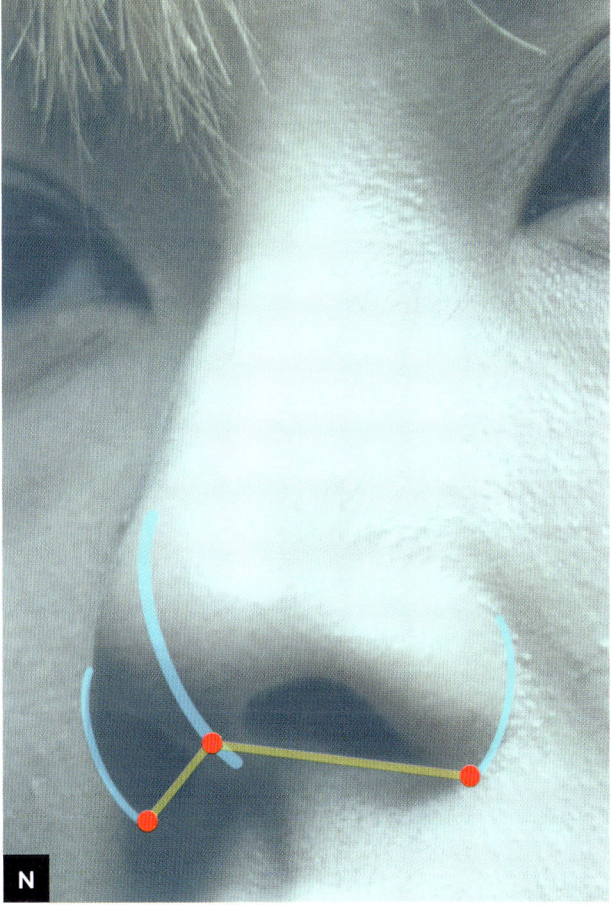

N

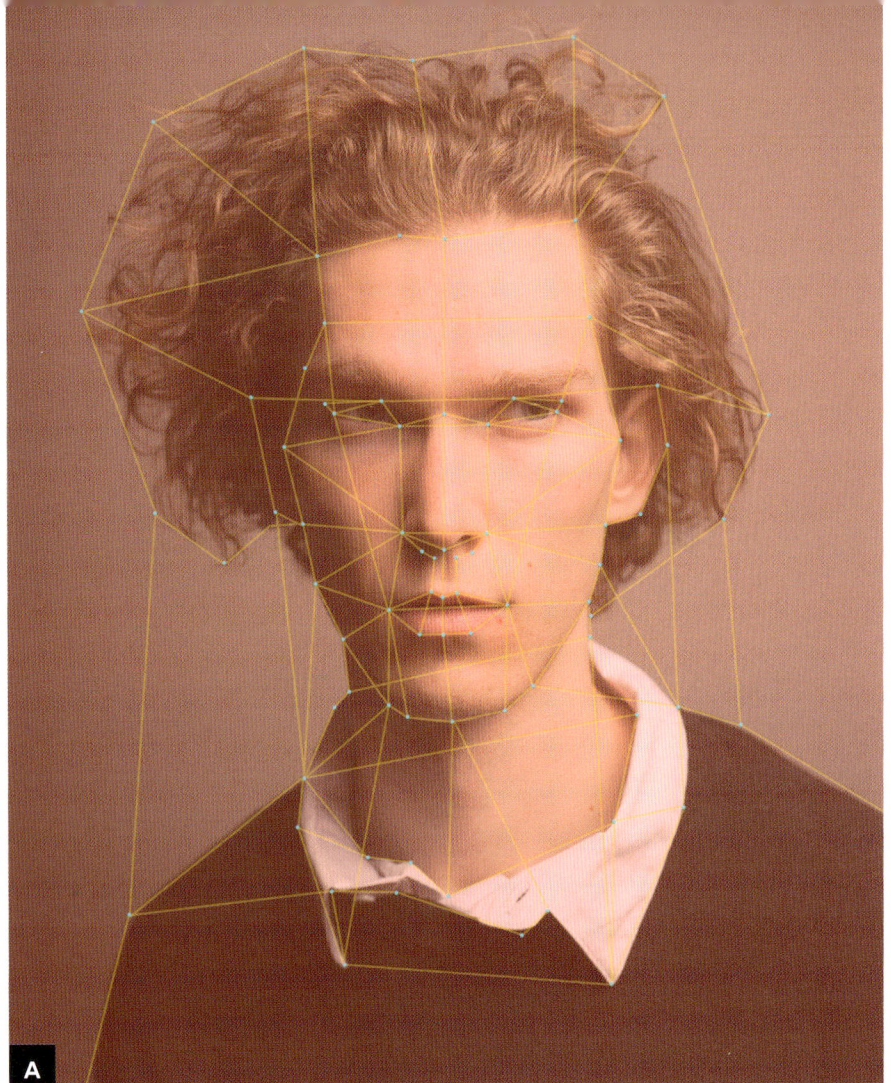

A

TRIANGULATION WIRE: AN INVISIBLE ROADMAP

I find explaining the importance of triangulation wire structure easy, but trying to illustrate it through a diagram rather difficult. Even in making Figure **(A)**, which looks absolutely insane, I feel it could seem intimidating and the importance of it could be lost. But this is probably the most important concept that I use to draw out the head. It creates a web of interlocking points in pieces that tend to self-correct the drawing, if there are enough of them. This web represents a visual way to create accuracy without always measuring, by seeing the angles between many points.

Let's start from the beginning. I first took a point on the side of the nose and followed this line to the tear duct, which is virtually a perfect vertical line. Then, I drew an angle from the tear duct to the top eyelid, then to the outer corner of the eye, and then back to the tear duct. This triangular relationship, based off of that origin point on the nose, creates a

sense of harmony and relationship that would be fairly accurate even without ever having to draw in any other features. Using triangulation alone would probably render one of the most ugly portraits you could ever imagine. Yet, in terms of drawing structure and understanding the relationship of the different pieces and proportions of the face, it illustrates best how one might go about creating these relationships. I call this *structural thinking*, where you're not dependent upon a unique shadow shape in order to map out your subject.

The real question is, do we draw in these lines or do we just think them? Usually, these yellow lines are just lines upon which my eyeball is traveling, looking at the angles in relationships between my subjects. If drawing with a light pencil, you can actually make very light lines that indicate these angles and some draft people do this. However, it's not necessary and may become a hindrance to you if you were to draw in these lines too dark.

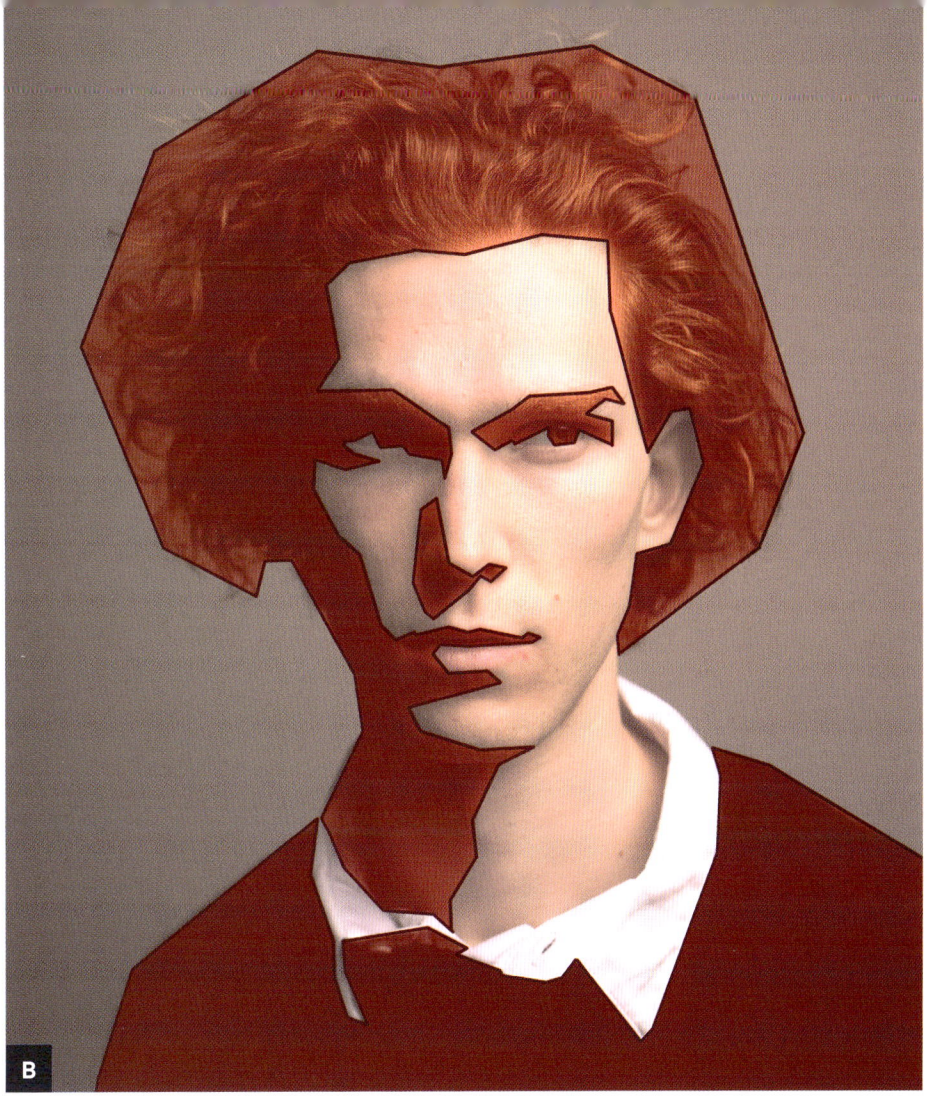

SHAPE DESIGN: AN INTUITIVE IMPRESSION

A more obvious and intuitive approach is to draw the major shapes of your subject. Design them so that each shape has character and also proportional relationships between the light and dark spaces. I think of it as designing two different types of puzzle pieces, light and dark, that interlock with one another in a special unique way that just happens to make a face.

While I do think it's intuitive to just draw and mark out shapes, it may not be intuitive to get the proportions and the spacing between them correct. For instance, if you mapped out this entire drawing **(B)**, and you didn't look at the proportional relationship of the height of the forehead versus the height of the hair, which is probably a one-to-one proportional relationship, you'll have missed an important part of shape design. Another example is the width of the dark shape on the nose is at one point the same width as the light shape of the cheek to the left of it. So when you design one shape, the next shape needs to be in proportion and designed with the previous shape in mind. Of course, not all images have a strong sense of shape, and you may have to work on your design skills in order to amplify this affect for impact.

3 | PORTRAIT DRAWING TECHNIQUES: HOW TO DRAW

USING GRAPHITE AND CHARCOAL TOGETHER

This drawing section is leading up to the point in which we're going to paint. The preferred method outlined in this book is to make an underdrawing, which we'll seal and paint over. When I use this method, I almost always combine graphite with charcoal. On page 59 you'll find a digital representation of my drawing process, how you might progressively draw out your subject. The first row of images represents a graphite sketch going from a rough, light, and energetic start and then progressing to a second draft, which is darker and more committed, hopefully learning from any mistakes of the previous draft and making corrections along the way. Then, I move on to a pseudo-final draft using a sharp 2B pencil to continue to hone the drawing and darken areas that need more clarity.

The second row of images represents developing values through ghosting, redrawing, ghosting, and erasing out the lights. The first image has been rubbed over with a paper towel to dim down the overall tone of the area being drawn, literally wiping out the drawing to soften and tone it. The second image in the series shows a reinforcing of our decisions and the gradual darkening yet again of the areas that need to be darkened, making it a more outlined and pronounced sketch. The last image shows this all softened yet again with a brush, but a little bit less aggressively, and then the highlights are lifted out with an eraser.

The last row of images represents the shift to charcoal. Generally speaking, the drawing is all there, and fairly accurate, then there's a shift to really push the values and the form of the ear. I used 6B Extra Soft General's Charcoal Pencils to put in dark accents in the right places. Not everything is going to get very dark. What we're trying to do is feed the darkest areas from which we'll brush out the darks to create a smooth, velvety transition. After applying the charcoal, the brush will also slightly lighten the charcoal so that it's not going to remain so black. The last image represents a repeat of this process as necessary, until it's resolved.

Graphite, Rough Draft, Light

Graphite, Second Draft, Medium

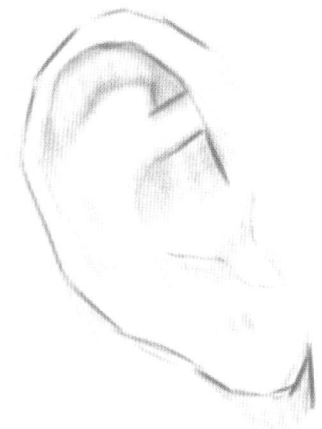

Graphite, Final Draft, Dark

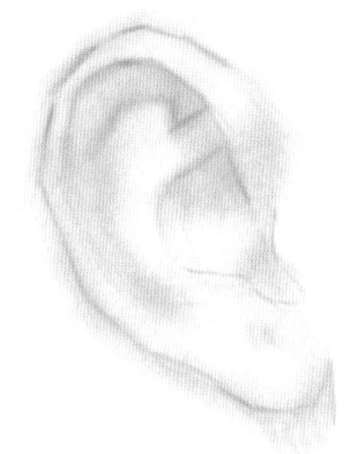

Graphite, Ghosting

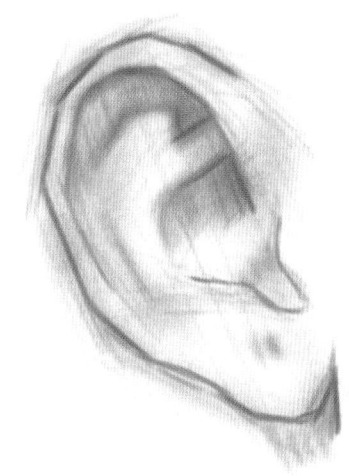

Graphite, Line Drawing

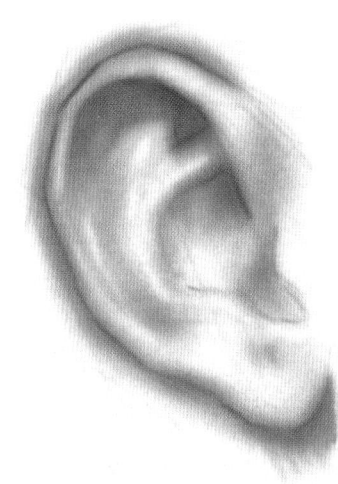

Graphite, Erase, and Darken

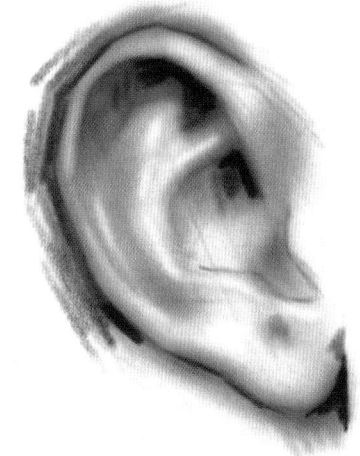

Charcoal Dark Accents

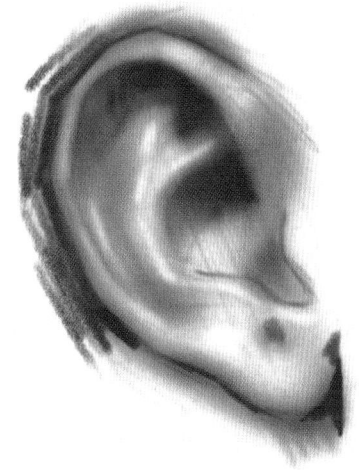

Charcoal Brush Form

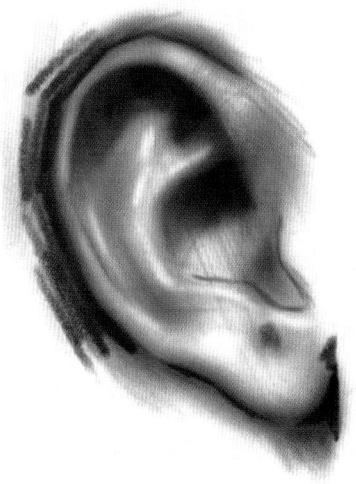

Charcoal Brush Form

3 | PORTRAIT DRAWING TECHNIQUES: HOW TO DRAW

59

CHARCOAL TECHNIQUE

This next progression is for those wanting to avoid using pencil and just use charcoal. I chose to insert the diagram at right to show the fastest way I know to model anything and form something from scratch that has a tremendous amount of depth and clarity.

1. Light Structure–Shadow Shapes. Typically, before I put down any paint or charcoal, I try to map out where this material will go with an outline. Often there's a chicken-and-egg situation: does the outline come first, or does the fill-in come first? Regardless, I almost always use some sort of outlining to pre-visualize where I'm going to put whatever material I'm working with so that I have some boundaries that are relatively noncommittal. Filling in with charcoal or paint is a level of commitment, so have some kind of plan, even if it's a bit wrong, because it's a starting place and it won't cost you anything.

Sometimes, it's difficult to visualize shadow shapes without actually filling them in, but I think it's a good practice to develop in order to at least have a rough draft of where the shapes will go before you fill in.

This outlining could be done with a hard piece of compressed charcoal or even a sharp small piece of willow charcoal.

2. Fill 2-D Shadow Shape—Flat, Crisp. Using a soft piece of willow charcoal, I fill in the shadow shapes flat, dark, and boldly, thinking about my image, as if it were a graphic logo. It's either in the dark, or it's in the light— nothing in-between. This helps me to identify the shape and forces me to make some strong editing decisions about where that shadow is.

This level of darkness may give you pause. You might say, "Am I sure enough about the shapes to make it this dark?" But willow charcoal is very low commitment and doesn't stick well. It's flexible and movable, and this is its strength. Feel free to go ahead and commit and make it dark, but also make it articulate and interesting as a shape. Don't make it a soft blob. Make it as particular as you can imagine. Often, I'm also just trying to make it look beautiful

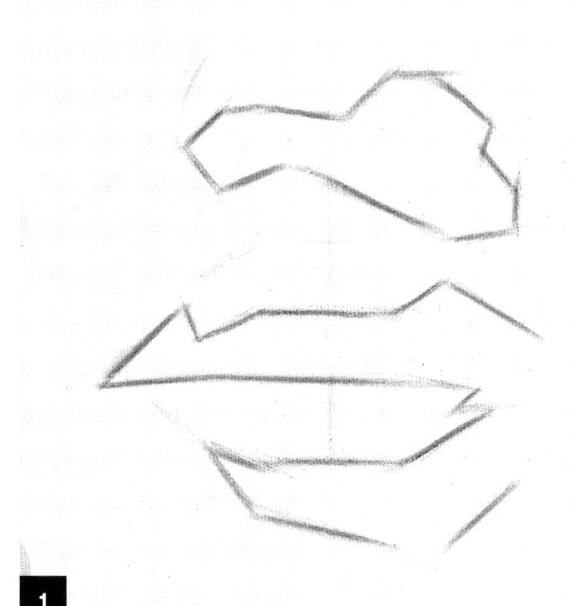

1

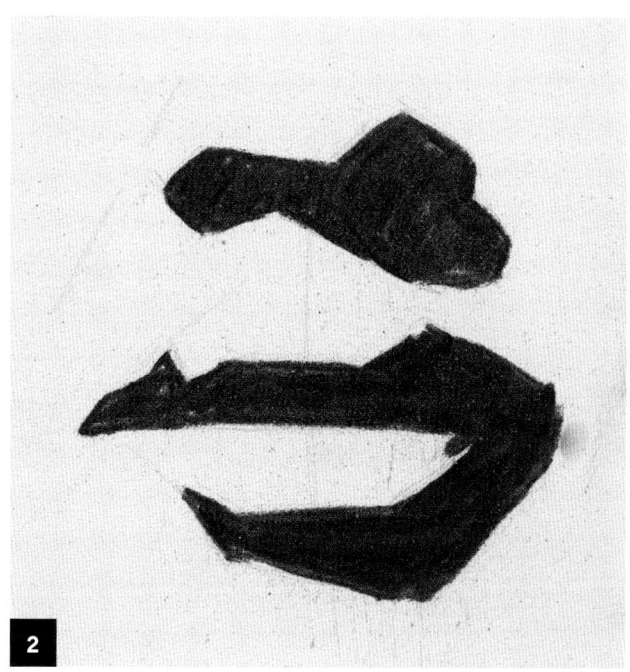

2

as an interesting shape while also thinking about the spacing and the proportions between the dark shapes and light shapes.

3. Create 3-D Pull with Brush—Direction of the Light. This is actually my favorite part of the entire process, the transition from a two-dimensional (2D) shape to a three-dimensional (3D) form through the act of pulling with a bristle brush. With a bristle brush, I begin pulling from the shadow shape towards the origin of the light. The origin of the light is your light source, wherever that's shining from.

By pulling your shadow shape edge towards this light source, it quickly softens and destroys one of the edges that is closer to the light source, leaving a sharper edge to the other side of the shape. I know this is complicated to verbally explain, but it's an especially important point to understand that one side of your shadow shape gets much softer than the other. This really gives a sense of roundness and softness to your shapes, pushing that three-dimensionality to your forms.

This softer edge of your shadow shape is usually called *the turning*. The sharper edge of your shadow shape is usually formed through a cast shadow or just a sharper edge to the form.

This three-step process so far has already yielded a quick visual impression that has movement, depth, and a variety of edges to rough out our drawing in a big way.

3

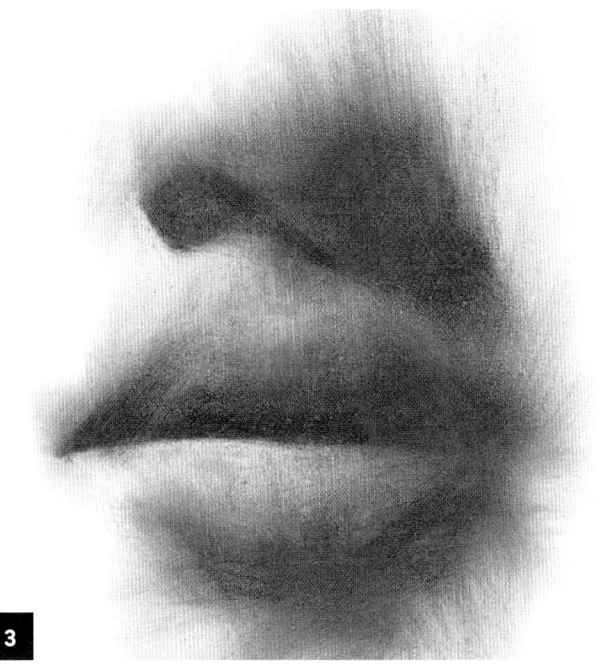

4. Lift Out Highlights—Different Kinds of Erasers.
Brushing the edges of your shapes can be a little
scary because if it's done too aggressively, the entire
drawing can be lost. With a little bit of practice, it's so
beautiful and effective. The next step in this process
is to take out the eraser and recover some of the
edges where your forms have gotten lost, with light
markings.

So far, we've just been drawing with dark, but
as your drawing has been brushed out with tone,
drawing with light becomes a great option too. Many
things we draw don't require dark outlines; rather,
they need light "outlines," such as the white roll
above the upper lip, the highlight on the nose and
lip, the wings of the nose, and some of the edges of
the lips. These areas need light in order to describe
our subject in better detail.

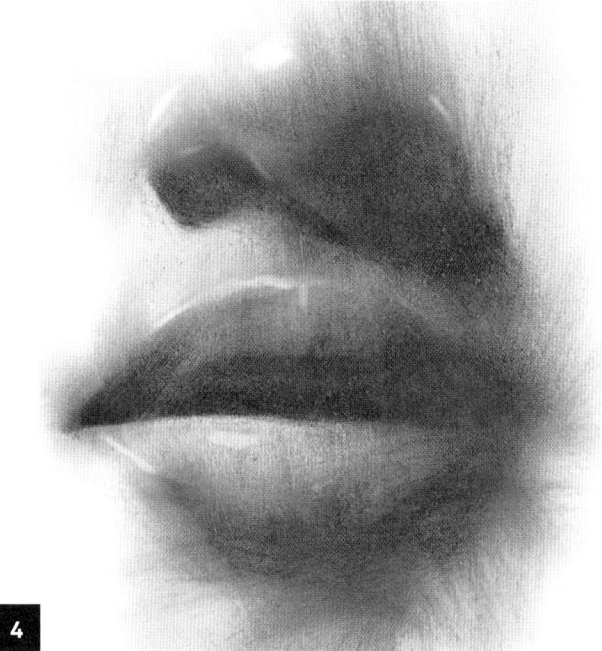

5. Occlusion Shadow—Lines within Shape. The same
concept is applied again yet in reverse, by drawing
in the dark lines that are considered accents in the
soft dark fog of the willow charcoal. I typically use
General's Charcoal Pencils to push these darks, but
sometimes I still stick with the willow charcoal to
create that soft blended feel of the tones that willow
charcoal does so well.

What you may notice is that after softening our
charcoal with a brush and lifting out the lights, when
we go back in there again to put dark marks down,
they actually stick out as more pronounced because
the dark flat tone we originally put in has gotten
lighter through softening. This is a phenomenon that
you must become aware of as a painter—that often we
put in a dark accent, or a highlight, and after we've
softened, the strength of this tone has been compromised slightly. This rhythm of putting in a mark and
softening, putting in a mark and softening, putting
in a mark and softening, is one of the acts of the
creation of subtlety.

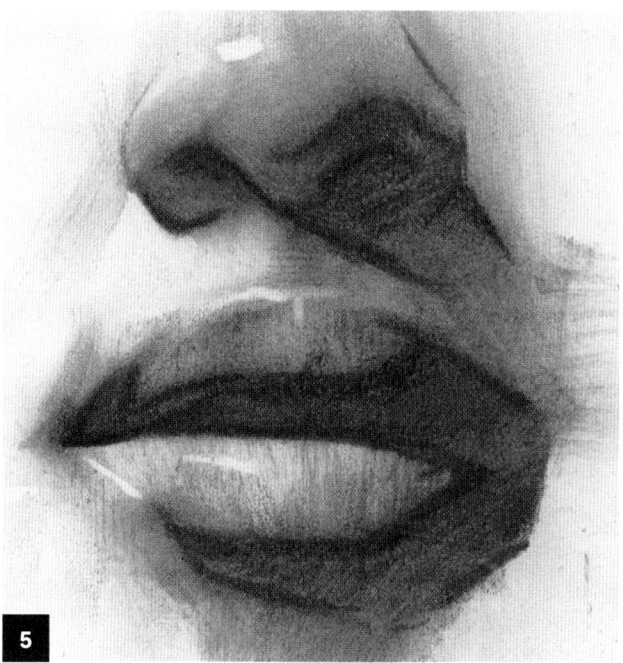

6. Create Soft Dark Transitions That Emanate from These Lines. Often, the finishing part of the drawing is low and mired in a thousand little tiny decisions. It's so fun to watch the beginning of a demo, but then the end of the demo almost looks like nothing is happening. What *is* happening in order to polish up our drawing is creating soft transitions that make our lines disappear. Whatever dark accents or light highlights that we put in the area immediately surrounding these lines needs to become a lot softer in order to look truly three-dimensional.

A line is a two-dimensional concept just as a shape is, and when a shape or a line is softened, it ceases to be a line or a shape and becomes a gradation or a transition. There are lots of little tiny transitions and softenings that need to happen in order for the portrait to become more believable and realistic. We won't be addressing those subtle nuances here, since these drawings are the foundation of our portrait and will be painted over.

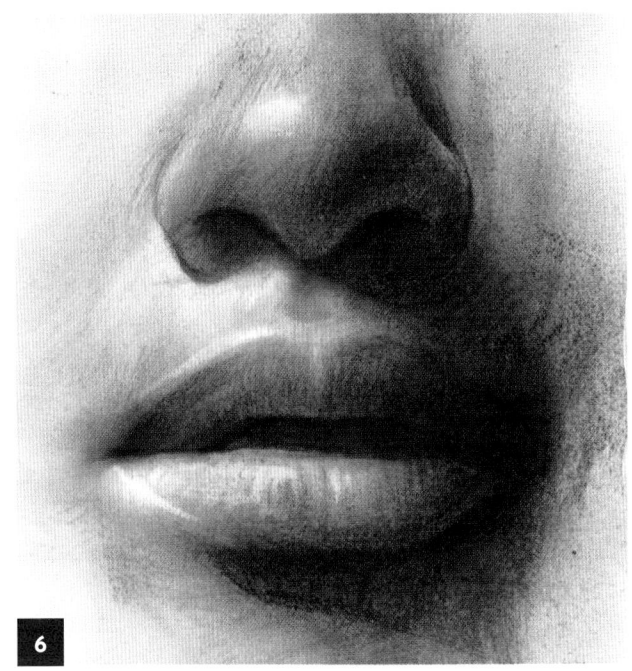

6

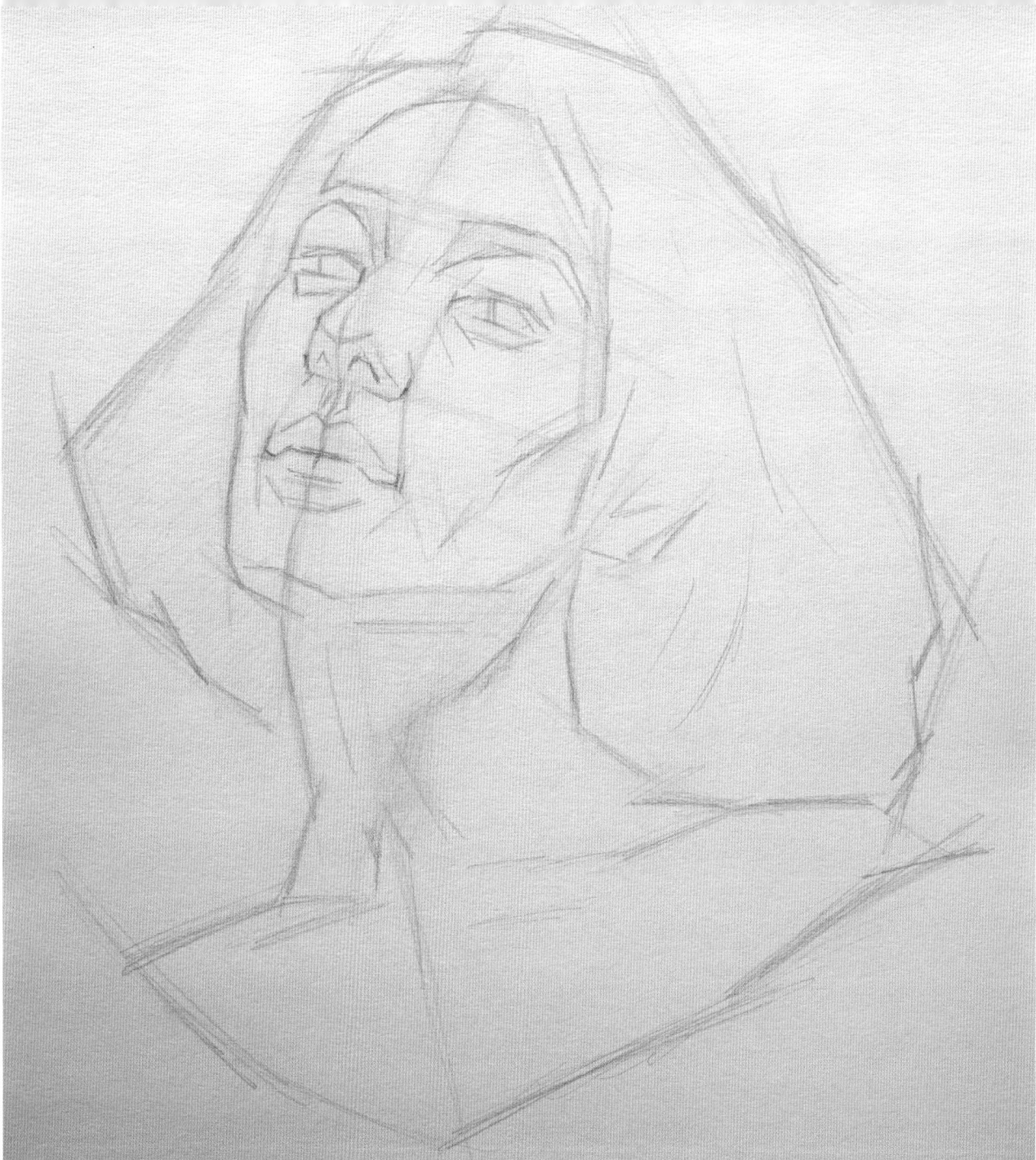

EARLY STAGES OF DRAWING

LINEAR STRUCTURE

In the early stages of a drawing, I oscillate between drawing the linear structure of the head and building up the visual impression of the head. In my opinion, getting the structure right is most important, but it's a harder habit to develop. Artists must learn to interpret everything they see with line. Also, I believe it's more important to draw the linear armature of the face in the same way that an architect might plan out a building—starting with a head without the features, the personality, or the likeness. This means that the centerline that runs down the middle of the face must be put in the correct place, and the features that go perpendicular to that centerline need to be laid out symmetrically, giving you something to build off of. There are innumerable books that go over the nitty-gritty of this process, and since that's not the goal of this book, I'll leave it at that.

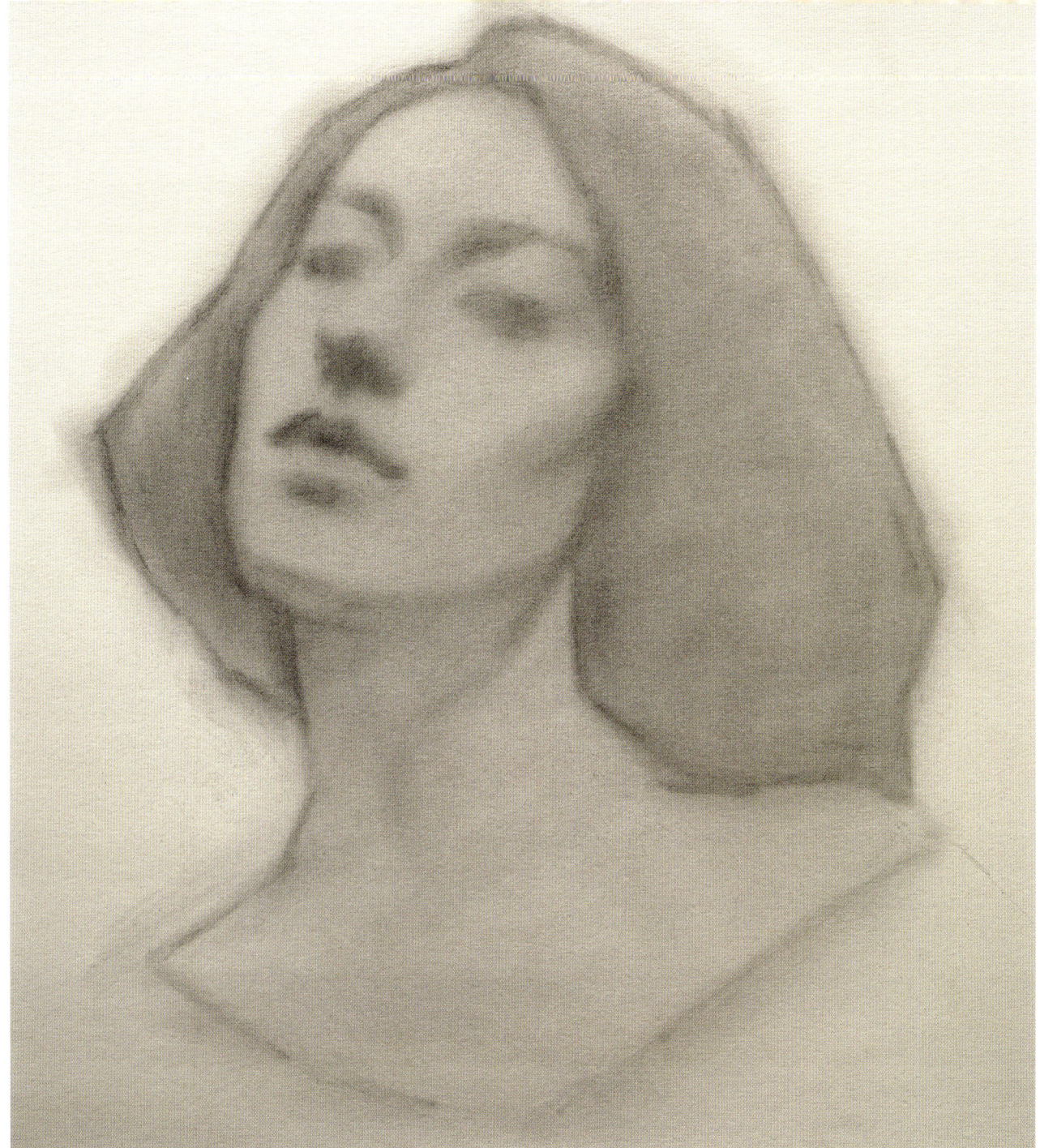

VISUAL IMPRESSION

Linear structure is of profound importance, but if the process is only based on structure, the soft impression that really makes everything come together as a whole will be sacrificed. Building up a portrait by going back-and-forth between these two extremes can be greatly beneficial as you chase the likeness. Very often in the beginning of our portrait journey, we commit too soon and the likeness is not there. Our lines are so hard and so resolute that we don't want to change them, and if we *do* change them, it would brutalize our drawing so badly that it may not even be worth fixing.

My solution is to never get so committed in the beginning that I can't make a change. If we honor the visual impression as well as the linear structure of the head from the start, we can slowly modify and improve the portrait as we see more and more. The following pages describe in practical detail how ghosting and redrawing can keep both of these ideas simultaneously present as you work.

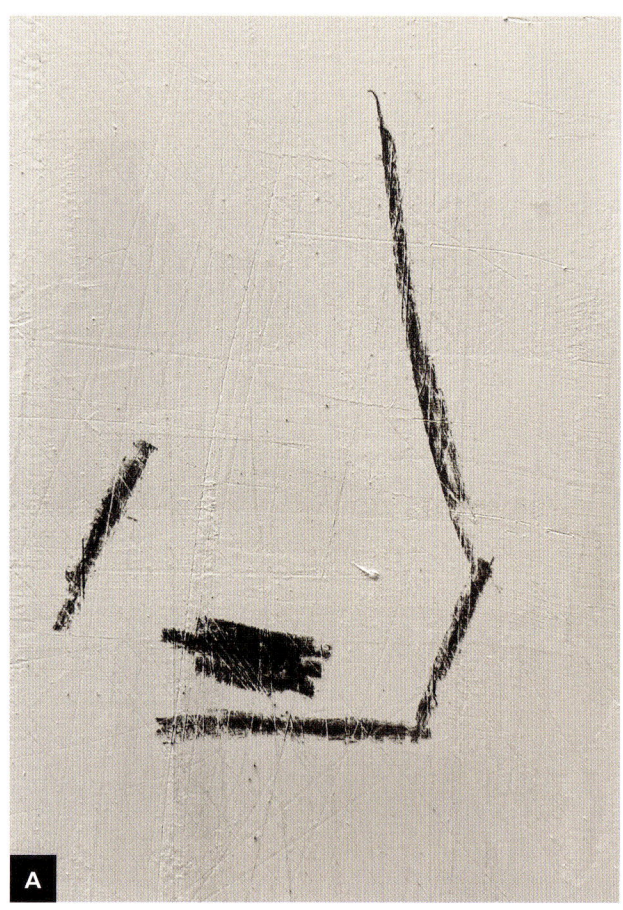

A

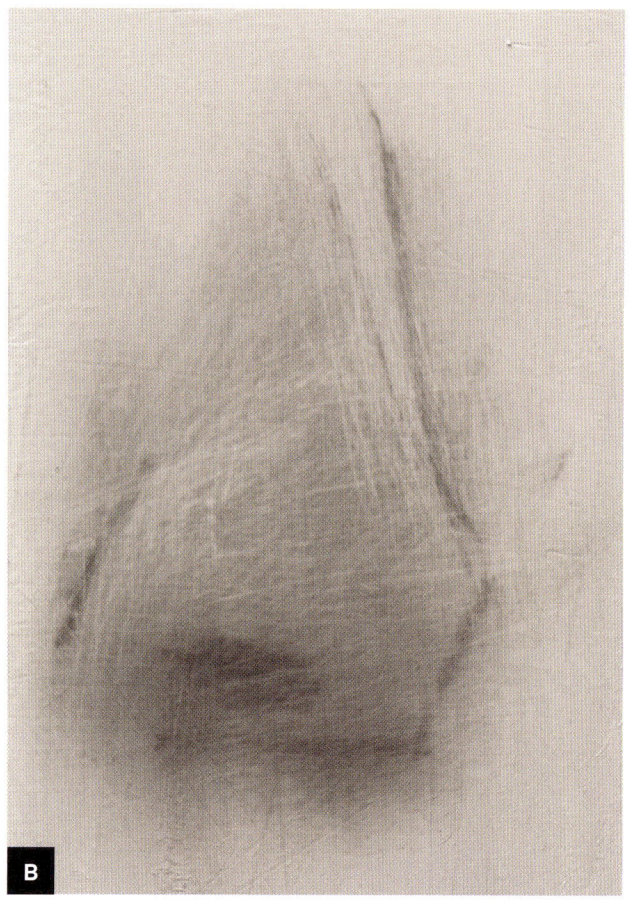

B

GHOSTING

A SOLUTION FOR FIXING DRAWING PROBLEMS GRACEFULLY

No matter who you are and how much experience you have, there will always be accidents, and if we don't have ways to gracefully fix them, progressing with a drawing seems hopeless. One of my solutions for fixing drawing problems is to ghost out the drawing. What this means is to reduce the contrast of the area that I'm working on by either rubbing, sanding, brushing, or scumbling, to reduce the impression created by that mistake. This allows me to continue to see where the mistake is, but also opens up possibilities to fix it.

In Figure **(A)**, I purposely drew a nose in the style of a beginner drawing. In teaching portraiture for many years, I've seen many noses drawn like the one above. Before we even learn how to draw a nose, we need to learn how to fix our mistakes when they inevitably come. In my teaching, I'm a big believer of learning the "how" and the "what to draw" in a drawing. Ghosting becomes an element of "how" to fix a drawing; it isn't the "what" to fix to make the nose correct.

After ghosting is done, the best thing to do is to find the edges of your forms using harder lines so that we start making some clear decisions that cut through the fog of ghosting **(B)**. I'll start with one tone, such as the highlights, and only work on where the light needs to be placed **(C)**. Then, I'll also start putting in the darks again to find the edges of their forms **(D)**.

Ghosting is a concept that can transcend many different media, from drawing to oil painting, acrylic painting, watercolor, and so on. This is the technique I typically use in my underdrawing beneath my oil painting. Ghosting isn't only a method for fixing big problems, but also a general way that I slowly build up my drawing. By working up the structure and then ghosting it down, I oscillate between the linear structure and the visual impression.

You must experiment with your materials in order to truly understand how your unique medium can make use of ghosting. When drawing on paper, it's most easily achieved with a flat pad made from a paper towel, using a fresh part of the paper towel as needed. Sometimes when ghosting, the tone can

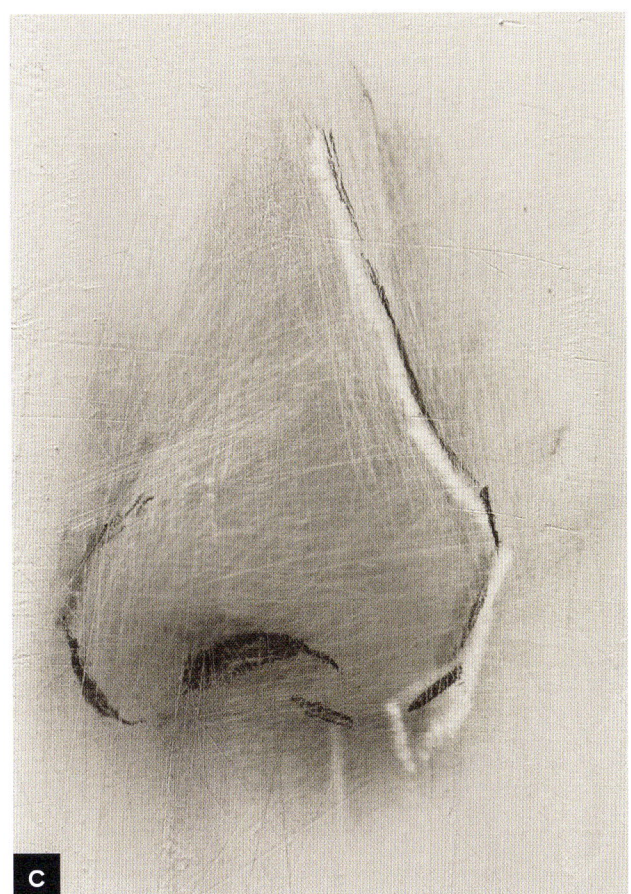

C

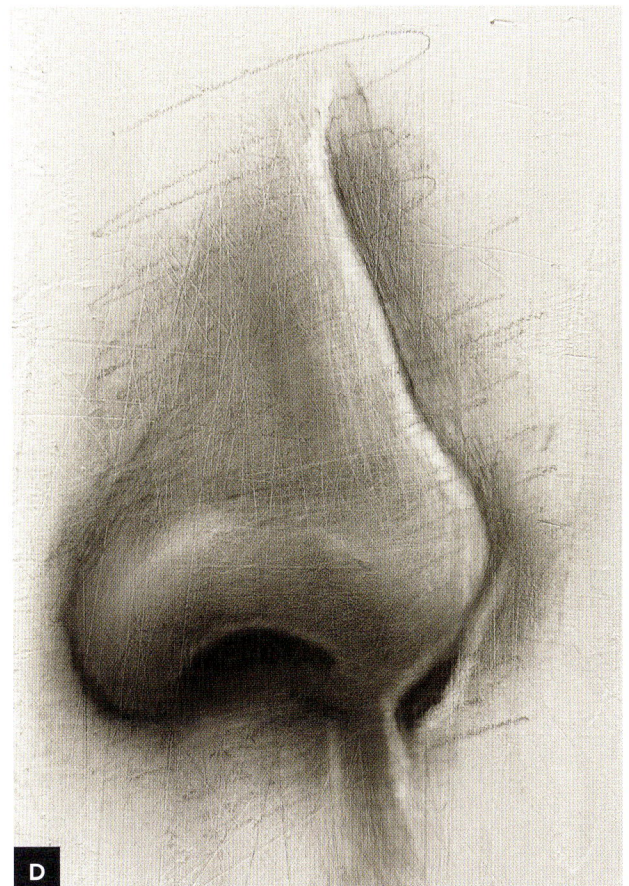

D

get too dark, and using a fresh piece of paper towel will gently lift off a little bit of the graphite, lightening the drawing as well as evening out the contrast between the light and the dark.

When working in charcoal, a brush may be more appropriate for ghosting, depending upon the surface. Often, I'm making my underdrawings on a wooden panel in preparation for painting, and then ghosting is best done with 400 or 600 grit sandpaper and a paper towel. The images at the right show the different ways that some of these materials can ghost out an image.

Sometimes, even my fingers can be tools for ghosting.

Ghosting in oil paint is all too easy and should be done with extreme care on a wet painting or you may push it too far. Using a soft brush and being as delicate and gentle as possible is key.

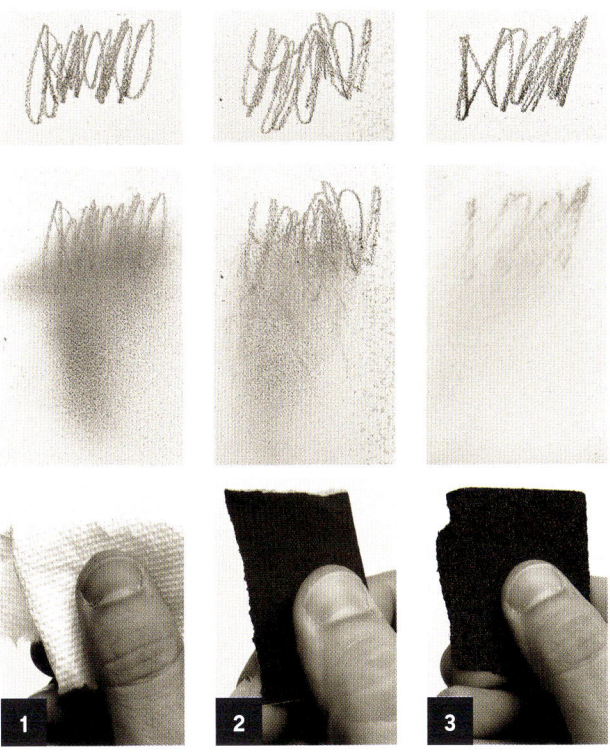

1. Paper towel: evens out the tone, but also slightly darkens. 2. 400-grit sandpaper: takes off a little graphite but evens out. 3. 80-grit sandpaper: most aggressive; erases graphite and roughs up surface.

DEMONSTRATION: DRAWING FOR A PAINTING—
GRAPHITE AND CHARCOAL

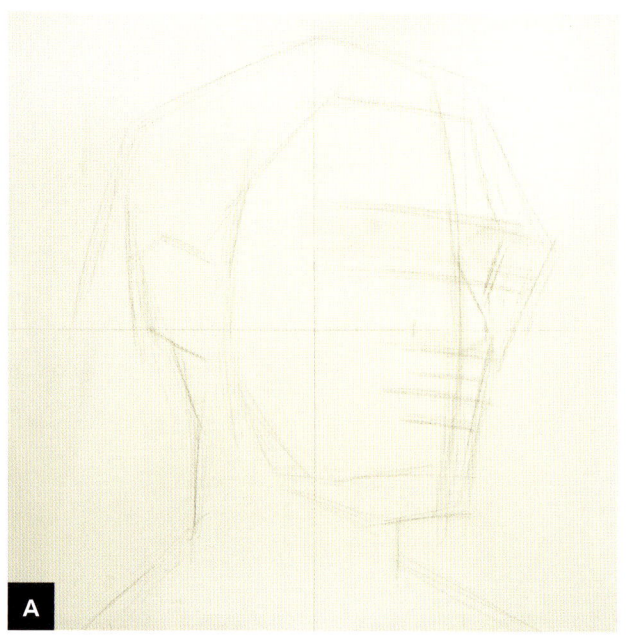

A

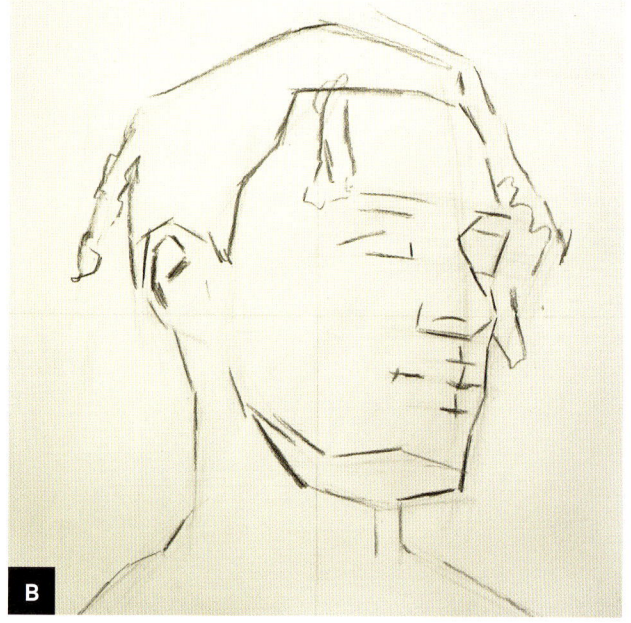

B

WIRE ARMATURE (A)

PENCIL

Keep the drawing very light by using a light touch
with the pencil. You must not make lines that can't
be erased or subdued easily. I usually use a dull 2H
pencil. Within this light way of drawing there are
four main objectives.

**1. The placement of the head in an aesthetically
pleasing way.** This is subjective, but avoid having it
go off the canvas or having a key feature (such as the
nose) too close to the edge.

2. The four main proportions of the head: Height
to Width; Top to Brow to Chin; Back to Side to Front;
and Brow to Nose to Chin.

3. The facial armature, which starts with the centerline of the face and continues with the facial grid with
parallel lines that start to define where the features
are going to land.

4. The envelope shape of the portrait's silhouette.
This includes the angles that create the shape of the
head and its orientation.

MAJOR FORM OUTLINE (B)

WILLOW CHARCOAL

The process of refining the four major objectives
continues with the addition of starting to draw them
in with a sharp piece of willow charcoal, as we begin
to feel a little more confident about our placement
of things. Another aspect of this stage is to begin
outlining the major shapes of shadow and darker
areas of the portrait. This is done to prepare us for
aggressively laying in dark, solid passages of willow
charcoal to begin the process of building form.

When possible, continue to use sharp, straight
lines; when lines are too round, they often lose
structure and character. Also, you're developing
landmarks that help you judge whether your
drawing is developing with the right character
of the major angles.

Scan to view a
video tutorial

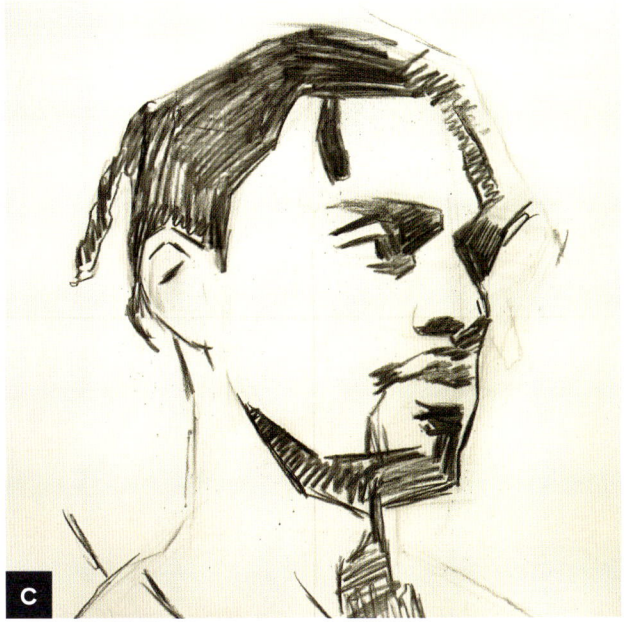

C

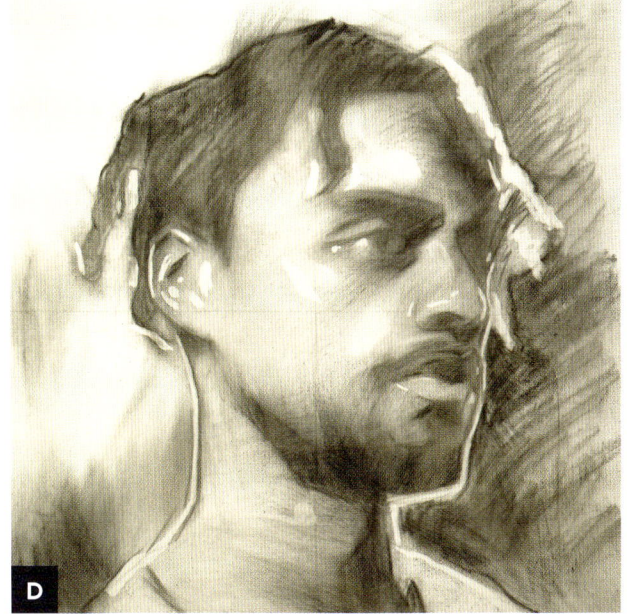

D

BLACK SHADOW SHAPE FILL (C)

WILLOW CHARCOAL

It's easy to think that it's too early to start laying in dark, solid passages of charcoal at this stage because we've barely begun to define the drawing. If you use willow charcoal to do this, however, it can aid tremendously in setting the stage for building the impression of the portrait.

I've found that many students want to get to the "shading part" very quickly, as it helps them to see what they're drawing, but this stage helps to take the drawing out of the abstract realm of outlines into a more solid, mass-driven approach, where you start to see the impact of your decisions. I highly recommend not creating a halftone or gray tones at this point, but instead keeping it strictly between light and dark, concentrating on crafting the shapes and trying to get the most character out of them as well as good placement.

GHOSTING AND PULLING FORM (D)

BRISTLE BRUSH

Once we build up all of that structure and tone, it's time to ghost out the drawing and pull the charcoal to help get a sense of three-dimensionality. Up to this point it's been line and shape only, and now, when the edges begin to be softened, the drawing becomes a little bit less definite, but also much more dimensional. This is a great rough draft that we'll continue to refine in the next several stages.

Here's a quick word on how to soften: It's a great idea to start pulling, or softening, the edges of your shapes by dragging them towards the light source. If this doesn't make sense, look at where your shape's edges need to be softened slightly and start to drag the charcoal with your bristle brush in that direction. Again, it's best to do this slowly and deliberately, possibly even suggesting movement in the drawing. Once this is done, there's an overall tone over the drawing, and you can begin lifting out the highlights to establish landmarks of light that will be useful in the next stages.

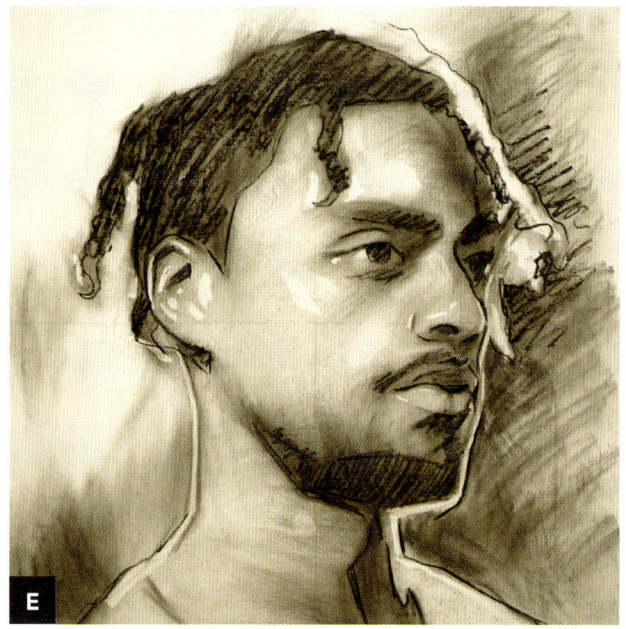

E

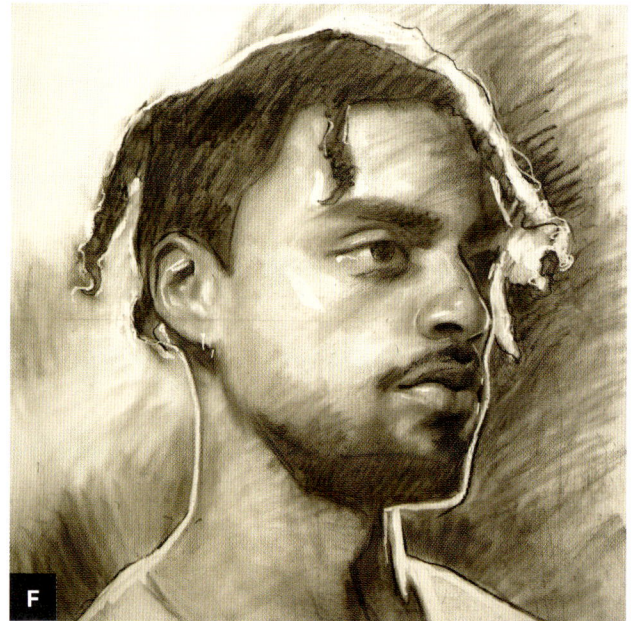

F

DEVELOPING FEATURES (E)

COMPRESSED CHARCOAL

The previous steps can be repeated several times until you begin to feel comfortable with the overall proportion and look of the drawing. Using the willow charcoal in this manner allows for mistakes—and for them to be easily changed—because it doesn't stick well to the surface. It's an easily manipulated media.

Once I have a good rough draft or impression, I'll begin switching over to using compressed charcoal. I use 6B Extra Soft General's Charcoal Pencils, and I find that they're able to get rich, soft darks that will also soften in a similar manner to willow charcoal; however, compressed charcoal sticks to the surface and doesn't just blow away in the wind like willow charcoal.

Of course, this makes compressed charcoal more of a commitment, which is really what you want when you start to develop the structure and the individuality of the features based upon the model.

PULLING AND GHOSTING (F)

THE CYCLE

All along, we've been going through this cycle, whether we're aware of it or not. And that cycle is drawing out lines and structure, then filling in the shapes, and then pulling and softening to create a sense of three-dimensionality. I often call this *line*, *fill*, *pull*, or in painting, *draw*, *paint*, *soften*.

- **Line.** Drawing in lines helps to create new boundaries and forces you to make those difficult structural decisions that can really drive the drawing forward.
- **Fill.** Filling in the shapes that are created by these linear boundaries gives contrast and material to work with.
- **Pull.** Pulling, or softening, allows you to create a sense of three-dimensionality and also lets you ghost out your image slightly so that it can remain flexible for the cycle to repeat all over again.

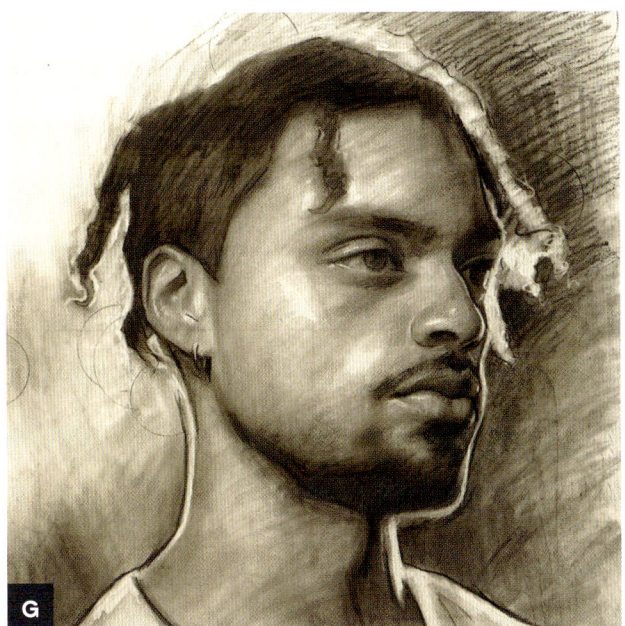

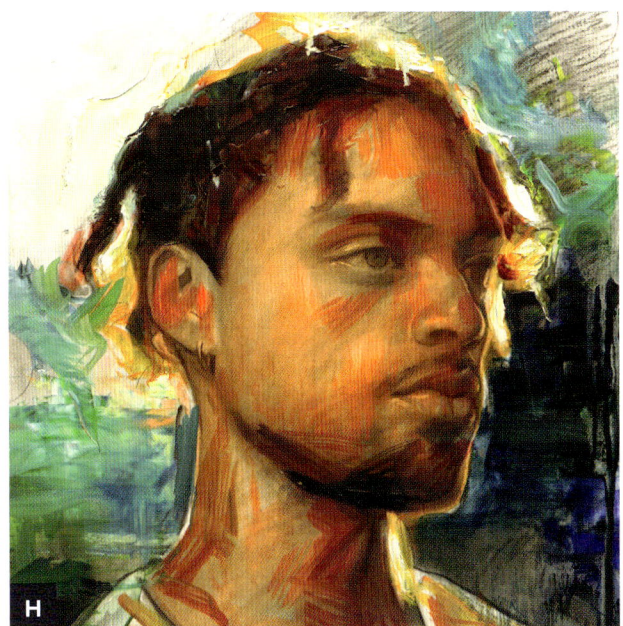

FINE-TUNING (G)

OUTLINING

It's amazing that after all of this structuring and ghosting, it finally starts to really come together and look like a true impression of our model. I'm a big believer in this back-and-forth process. It not only allows for mistakes, but it allows you to let the likeness of the model slowly develop through a refinement process, rather than attempting at a perfect outline and then filling in. There's a little dither in this drawing at this point because it's been lost and found several times already.

In the last go-round of this drawing, I really try to outline the major forms so they'll stick out and have extra contrast in anticipation of the future step of rubbing paint over the entire face. If the contrast is heightened in these areas, the drawing will survive and stick out a little bit, so that when we put a glaze of paint over it, we can still see the edges of our features and the most salient points in the drawing, so we don't easily lose them in the fury of paint about to come.

To make these crisp lines, I use sharp compressed charcoal and also a sharp eraser, such as a Tombow MONO Zero round-tip eraser.

ÉBAUCHE (H)

SEALING THE DRAWING WITH OIL PAINT

It may seem crazy that after all of that work drawing, we'd splash on color in the manner shown above, but it's nice to have the luxury of a well-refined drawing so we can focus on color and light without the added stress of getting a likeness.

The drawing is sealed with some kind of fixative that doesn't dissolve with mineral spirits, such as SpectraFix Degas Spray Fixative or clear spray shellac. This is important because if you wash the paint on with mineral spirits, it could potentially dissolve your fixative and thus dissolve your drawing. You may want to test this on a scrap drawing before you do it on a finished portrait.

The next step in an ébauche is applying color transparently over a sealed drawing. Typically, we want to cover our drawing with transparent, intense colors.

The one rule here is *do not destroy the drawing*. How do we avoid doing that? Keep the colors transparent. Every color shown above is used transparently. We need to use paint transparently to allow the drawing to shine through. If it becomes too opaque, wiping away can also be a solution.

THE CRUX OF THE ÉBAUCHE METHOD

This section may be the most important of this book. You can see in great detail what has been lost and what has been gained by putting on a wet and wild *ébauche* (French for first pass, or quick sketch). There are three things to notice as we compare back-and-forth between these two images: One, significant areas of the drawing are outlined, and there's a high degree of contrast, so that when the ébauche is put on, the main forms don't become lost. Two, the drawing is sealed so well that the head has not moved or significantly changed with the addition of such wet paint. Three, this securely sealed drawing allows for a lot of experimentation and improvisational color and brushstrokes that may not happen otherwise if I'm instead concerned with drawing out the portrait and getting some degree of a likeness as I apply paint.

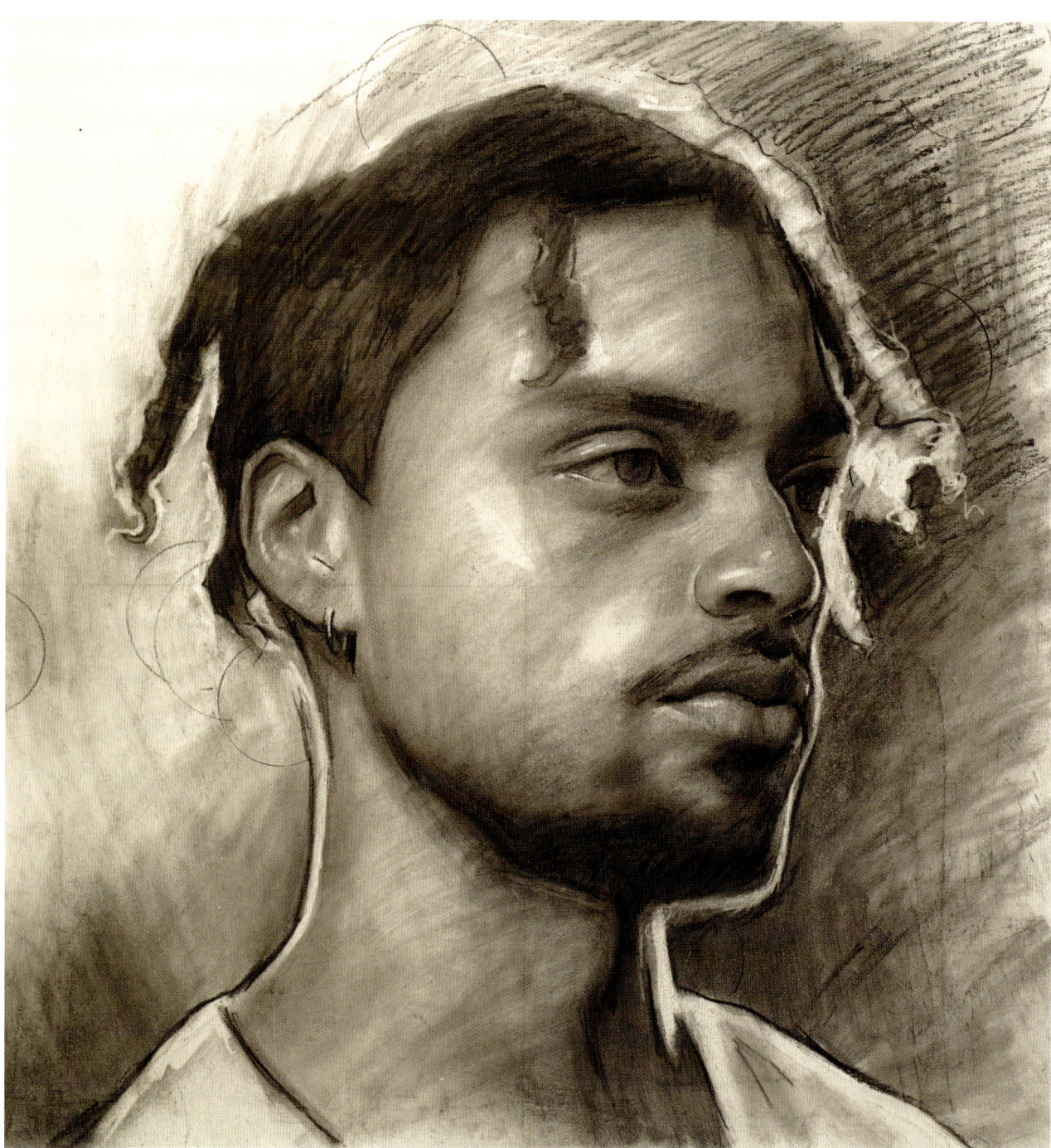

This improvisational approach to the ébauche layer is a revelation. In teaching this method over a few years, I've noticed that once somebody has a decent drawing, they become conservative in their painting, as they understandably don't want to lose what they have. For me, one of the purposes of drawing out the portrait first is so that I can actually let go and be loose and experimental with the paint application, not having to worry about the likeness at all in this stage. It's almost like I'm using two very separate parts of the brain to create dynamic tension in the portrait. I definitely encourage using the paint transparently for the ébauche. There are also areas such as the hair and some parts in the background where I'm already using a palette knife, boldly building up visual interest in areas that I know are safe to play around in.

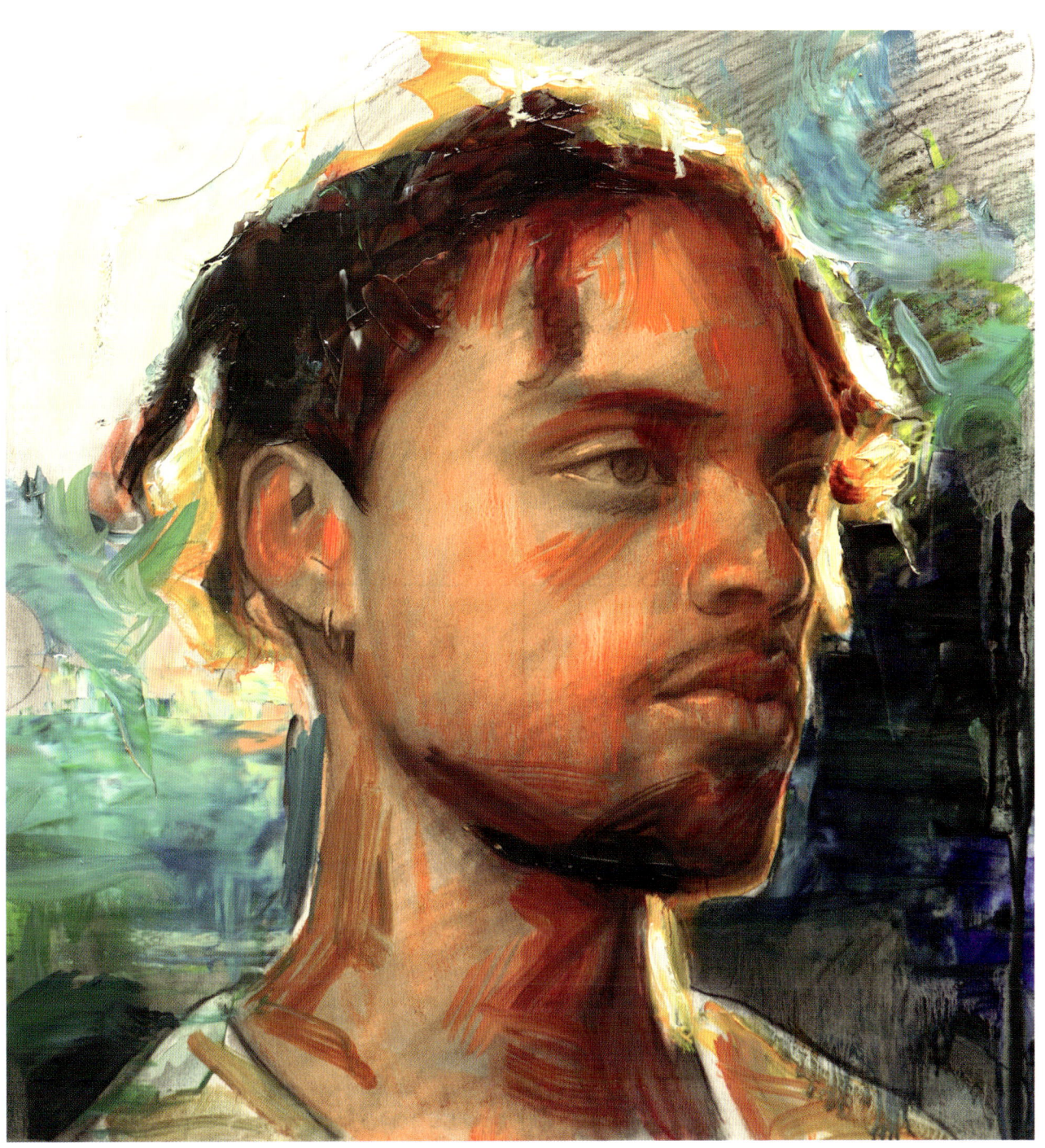

These pages show the development of the rest: the painting and the slow erosion of any trace of the drawing. I try to enjoy every phase of the painting and make it look interesting. This doesn't always happen. Sometimes, it becomes ugly, but it's still a virtue. In the plate below, notice that the main points of the features have been gone over with a small fine brush and held onto from the drawing phase. Even after the crazy, wet and wild ébauche layer, the drawing is enhanced so that it doesn't disappear, and I'm fully taking advantage of the drawing that was there. This also includes the highlights of the portrait. You can notice the structural qualities of the light that are lines in the ear and also in areas of the nose and eye.

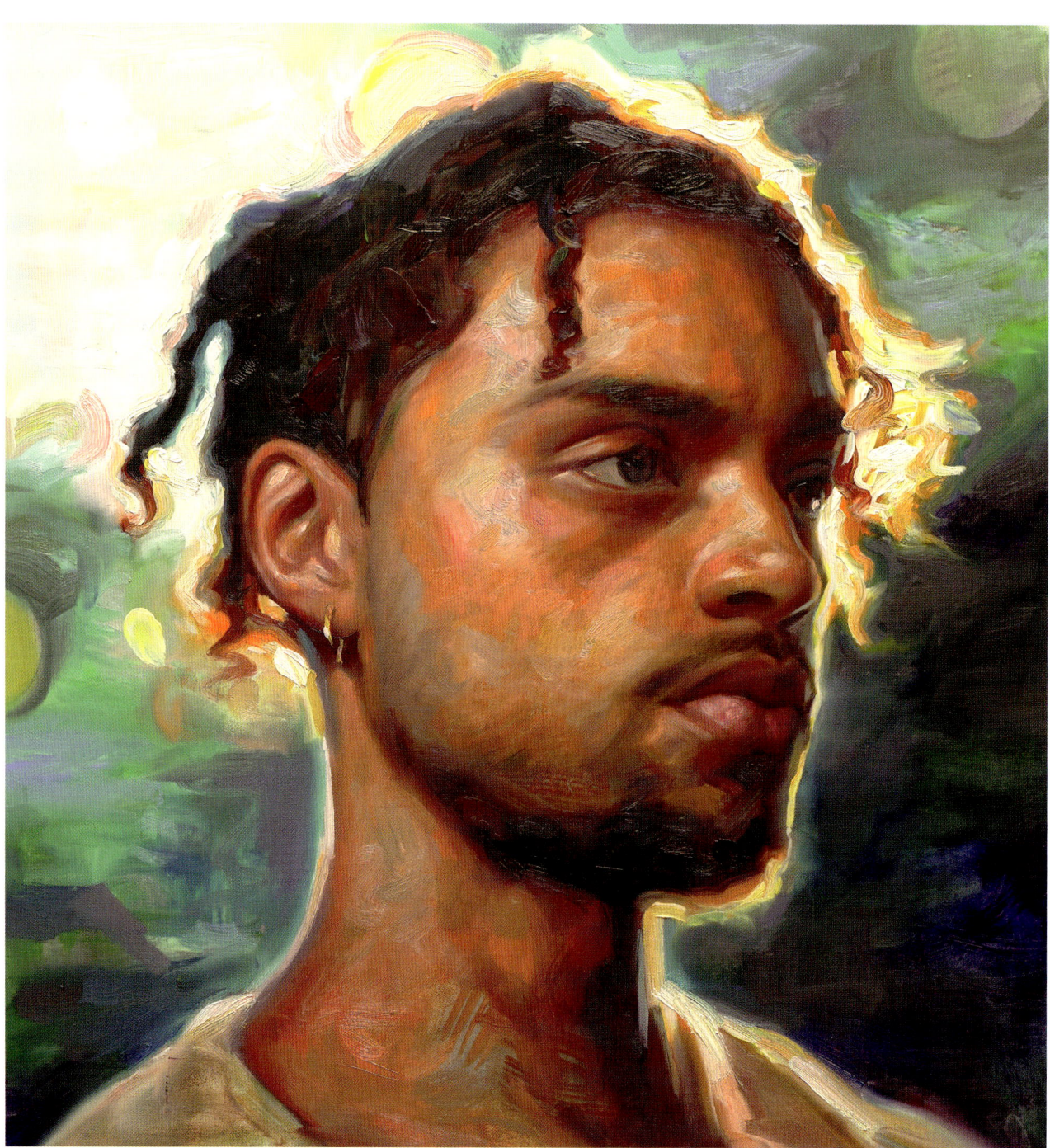

This image brings the painting to a conclusion, and we no longer see the pencil or charcoal drawing at all through these layers of paint. Often, when someone asks me about this painting technique, they wonder if the pencil or charcoal may bleed through the painting and somehow compromise it. This happened in the old days, when artists transferred drawings with carbon paper, and they had special inks that bled through easily. If your drawing is a well-sealed pencil and/or charcoal drawing, and you paint thickly enough, the drawing doesn't come through unless you want it to. Sometimes, a little bit of that gray or traces of the drawing shining through can be a nice touch.

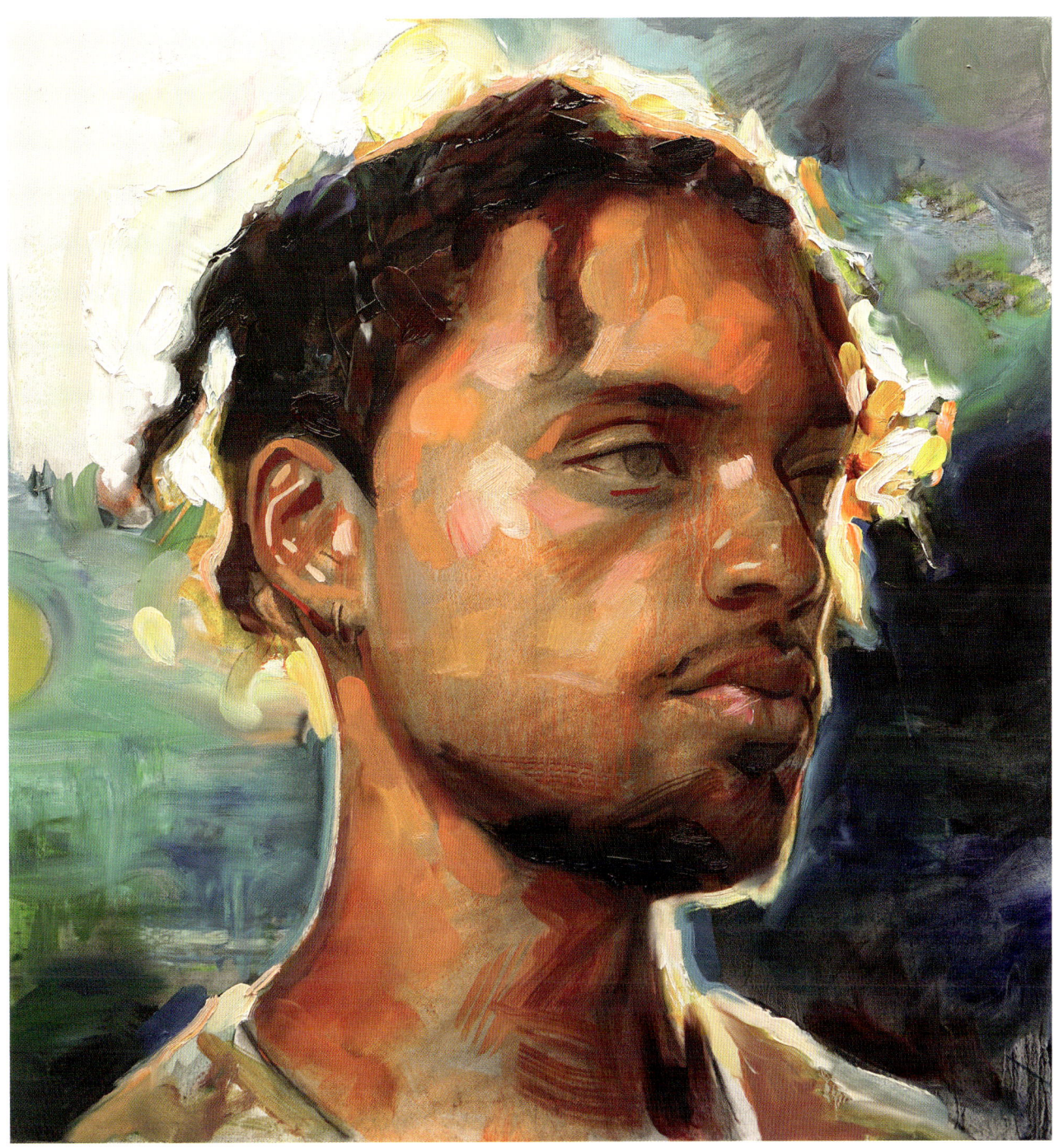

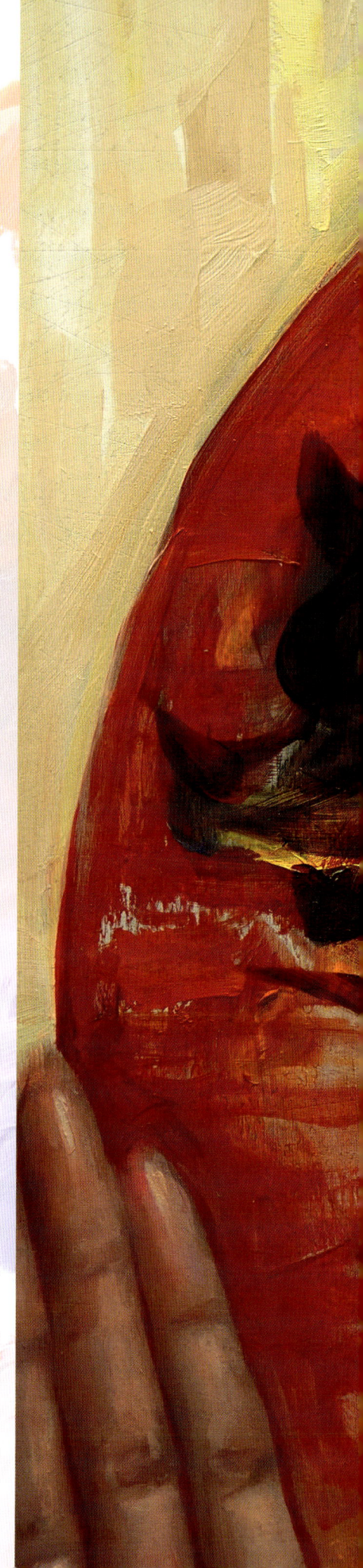

PART II

—

DYNAMIC FLESH COLOR

‣ Steve Forster, *Detail of Avie (Present Tense)*, oil and charcoal on aluminum, 46" × 40" | 116.8 cm × 101.6 cm

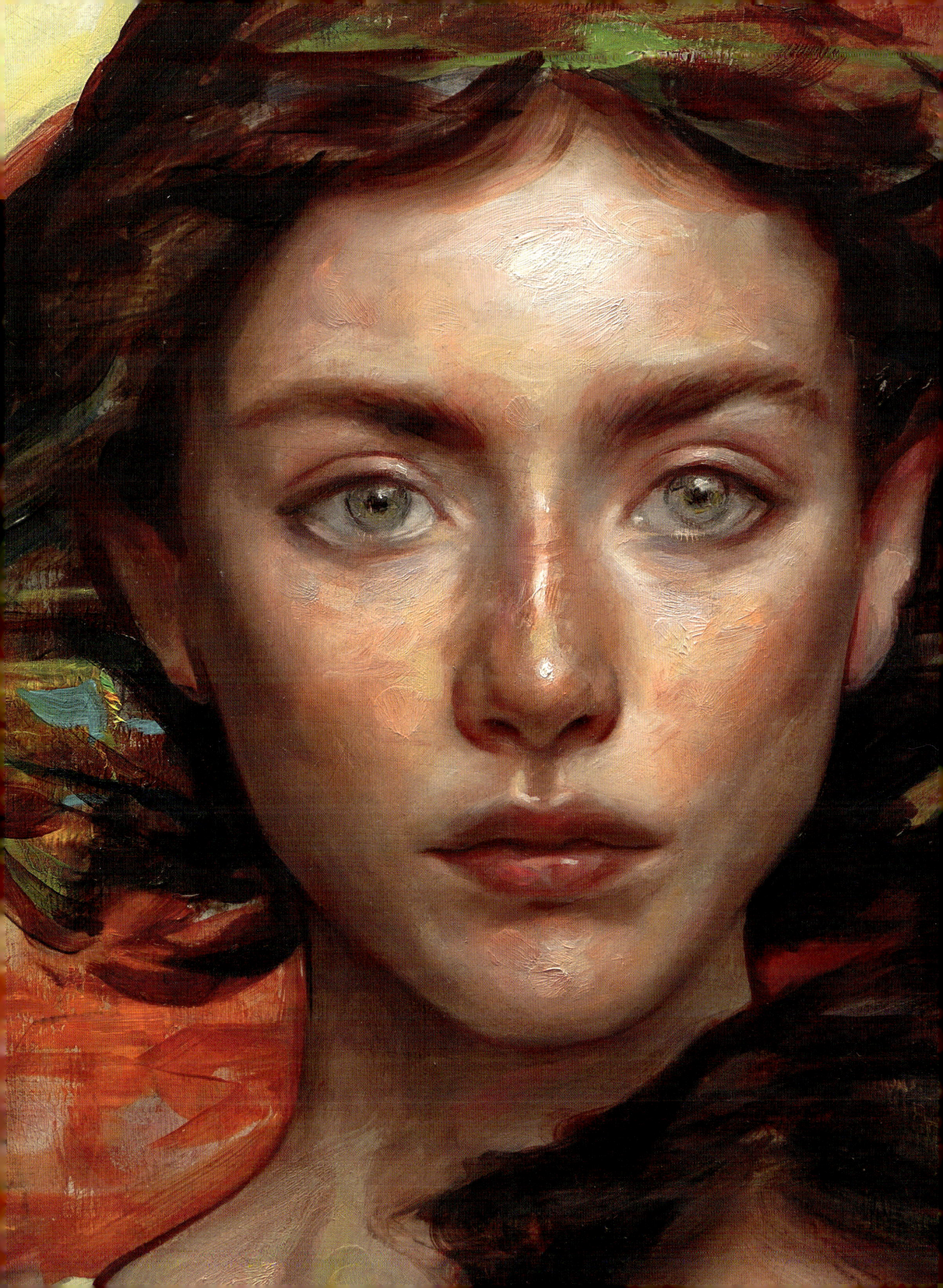

PAINTING MATERIALS

TYPES OF BRUSHES

I like to have a great variety of different kinds of brushes. I believe it's good to experiment with as many distinct types of brushes as you can get your hands on, as they'll increase your knowledge of what's possible to do with a paintbrush.

The standard portrait painting set for beginners should include a variety of sizes of bristle filbert brushes, a few cheap small round brushes for drawing, and at least one soft sable-like brush or a long dry bristle brush for blending.

That will get you started, but build up your brush inventory so that you have a lot of different brushes at your disposal. You want to be able to experiment and interpret the possibilities with them, never feeling bored with your choices.

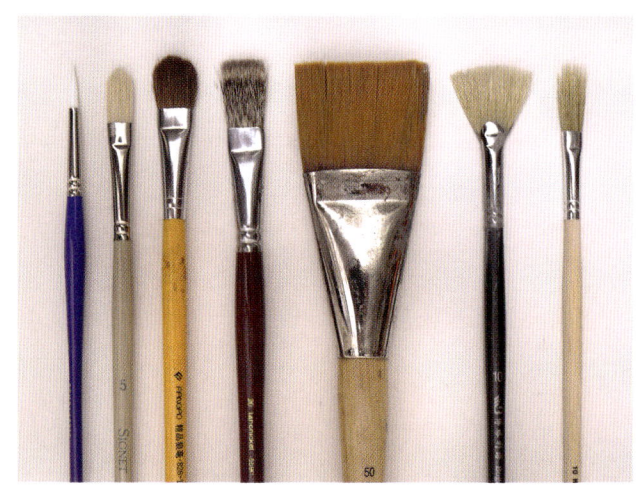

SHAPES OF BRUSHES

It's worth mentioning a few things about the shapes and length of brushes that can often be overlooked. In the second image at right, there's a flat, then a filbert, and then a round. Flat brushes make square marks and are great for blocking in and painting architecture, such as a window. The shape of the brush should match the type of form being rendered; therefore, a filbert is often the choice of many portrait painters because there's a broad, rounded edge that relates to the human form. A round brush is great for drawing and putting in smaller details. There are many variations of these basic shapes, such as a bright (a shorter version of a flat), a cat's tongue (a pointier version of a filbert), and some rounds that are more blunt or more pointy. Every artist has individual preferences, and experimentation will lead you to yours.

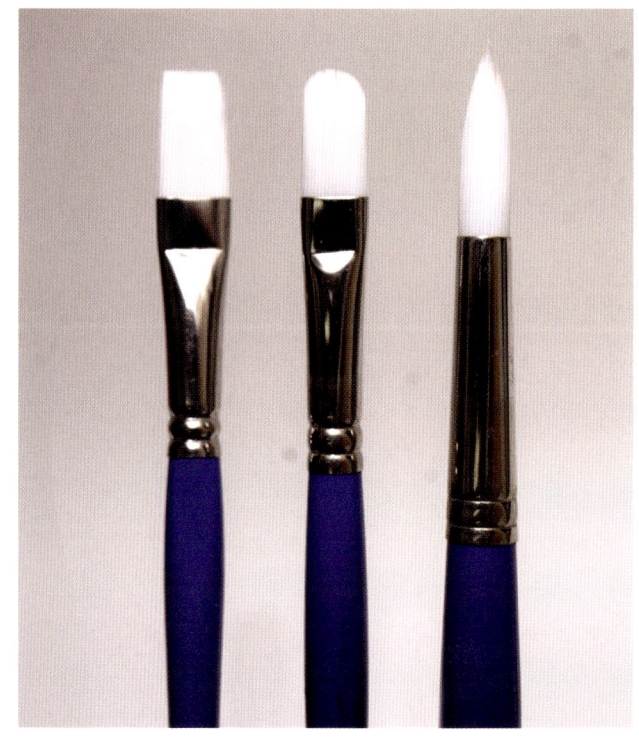

LENGTH OF BRUSHES

The length of the brush matters but is often overlooked. As we use our brushes, they get stubbier and lose their ability to lay down paint. It feels wasteful to throw them away, so artists love to save their bad, used-up brushes and not give up on them, hoping that they'll find a use for them. But keep in mind that a longer brush is a healthier brush that will lay down more paint and probably give you more expressiveness in the brushstroke. This is why I usually prefer flats over brights because a flat is a longer version of a bright and will eventually wear down to a shorter length anyway. Dispose of your stubby, dried-up brushes that are not helping you to make beautiful paintings.

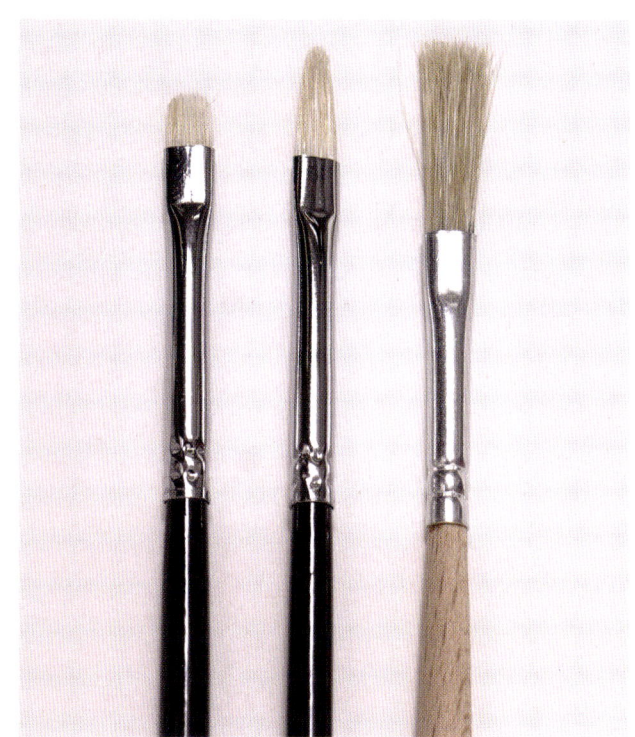

PAINTS

It's not necessary to spend a lot of money on paint, but it *is* definitely necessary to not get the cheapest oil paint available. Student-grade paint made by Winsor & Newton is a decent place to start and is a good standard brand of paint. As you slowly acquire more colors, you may want to switch over to the professional-grade versions. If you'd like to get the nicest paint available, Michael Harding, Old Holland, and several other makers are making exceptionally fine paint.

What I *do* discourage are cheap starter sets from craft stores that don't have a name brand. They'll make the painting process more difficult than it needs to be, and ultimately, you need to know if it's you that's the problem or your materials. It's hard for anyone to paint with cheap paint.

I also believe it's a good idea to have a nice mixture between earth pigments (ochres, umbers, siennas) and prismatic colors (cadmiums, phthalos) in order to achieve a full chromatic rainbow of tones.

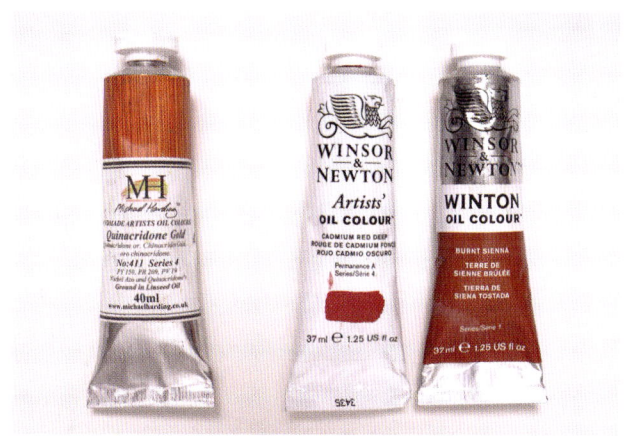

OIL, SOLVENT, MEDIUM

You'll need oil, some kind of solvent, and probably a medium as well. All three thin out the paint in different ways that are distinct.

Oil is already ground into paint, so it naturally extends the paint; however, using oil alone to stretch the paint often results in a sticky, tacky surface that takes an exceedingly long time to dry.

Solvent breaks down the oil and is what we use to clean out a brush that's loaded with paint. It's also mixed with oil to create what's called a *medium*, which is blended in a precise ratio to thin the paint in a desirable way. The

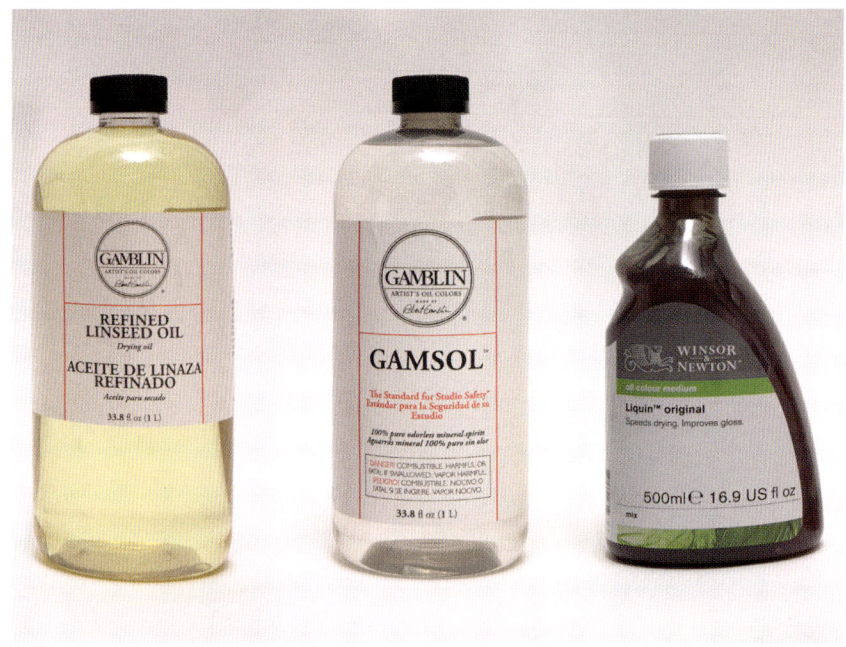

mixture of oil and solvent creates the best of both worlds; the solvent cuts down the oil just enough so that it dries more consistently and quickly and makes it less sticky. Using more solvent can also keep the paint surface from beading up. When blocking in a painting, sometimes I use only solvent alone and introduce a medium progressively as the painting goes on towards the finish.

Some people like to keep a solvent-free studio, and if there's any health concern about oil painting, it would be because of the solvent. However, with good ventilation and a product such as Gamsol, which evaporates slowly thus minimizing vapors, it can be used in moderation.

After a long search for the perfect medium, which can be concocted from numerous exotic oils and ratios, I've found that the best medium for me is a mixture of 50 percent Liquin, 25 percent linseed oil, and 25 percent Gamsol. Sometimes, the proportions of this change slightly, such as when hot weather dries out the paint faster. For me, the perfect medium stays wet all day long but is dry the next day—this medium accomplishes that.

  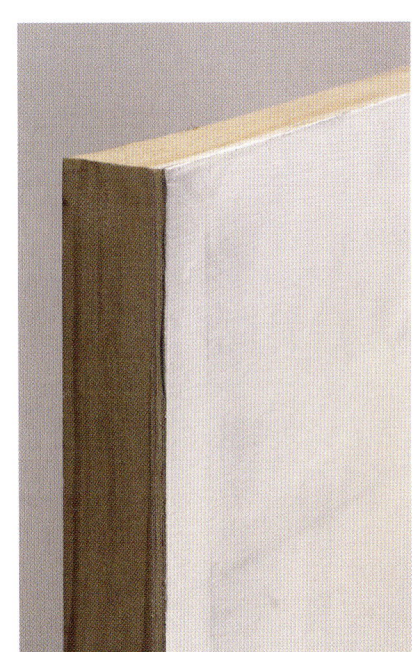

PANELS

Panels are my preferred surface to paint on. They're rigid and rugged and receive a drawing well. I typically paint on an aluminum panel called DIBOND, which can be bought at a signmaker shop or even at some art stores. The next best thing is a wooden panel, and I've used those for years, preferring a Baltic birch panel with a higher-grade wood quality. There are also cradled wood panels readily available at most art stores. Some of them come in a variety of surfaces textures, from extra smooth to having some tooth to them. Most people prefer the panels that have a little bit of tooth; you can always sand it to your preferred texture if you'd like it to be smoother. Paint doesn't always stick well to extra-smooth panels, so I recommend a panel with a slight amount of texture.

CANVAS & LINEN

Most people paint on canvas. It's easily available and quite inexpensive, but a better product is linen. The downside is that linen can be difficult to stretch. Canvas and linen can sag over time. To mitigate this, you can buy canvas or linen pre-attached to a panel and get the best of both worlds, but this does come with a higher price tag.

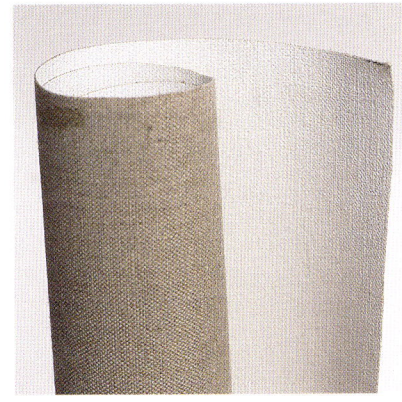 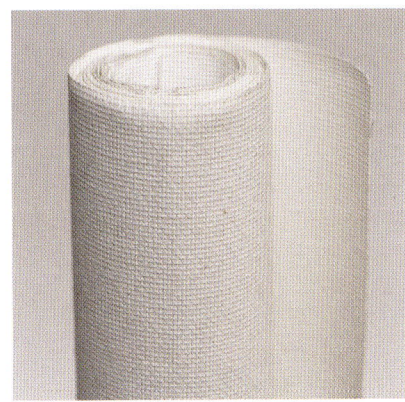 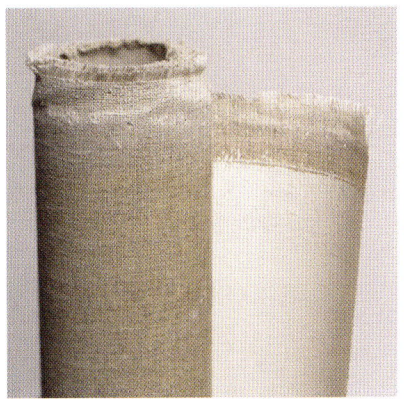

PALETTE

I use a white paper palette for convenience. I've used a glass palette and a wood palette in the past. If you have the time and the patience, it's nice to have a beautifully crafted, aesthetically pleasing palette that makes you feel good when you paint on it. If you prefer efficiency and convenience, a paper palette gets cleaned off with a simple fold of the paper and a toss in the trash. A paper palette also promotes the mixing of fresh colors (which I encourage!). A permanent palette requires maintenance, using oil and solvent to clean it with diligence, every day.

What's more important to me is the tone of the palette, whether you're using a wood, paper, or glass. Tone your palette to the typical tone of the canvas that you paint on. If you usually paint on a white canvas, you should have a white palette. If you typically paint on a gray-toned panel, you should have a gray-toned palette. This allows you to judge the colors and the values with greater precision. If your palette and painting surface are always different tones, you have to become a translator. If you're painting on a gray canvas but your palette is the tone of an orange, you'll have great difficulty judging the colors accurately. You'll be seeing the colors in one context, but then trying to form other subtle relationships from them in another context. Few things are more difficult than having to make this translation in your head; it's an unforced error that's easy to avoid.

Most paper palettes come in gray or white to aid in this decision. If you use a glass palette, you can put a piece of colored cardboard or paper under the glass to "tone" it. If you use a wood palette, slowly patina the palette—a couple of thin layers of oil paint, then shellac or varnish over this color.

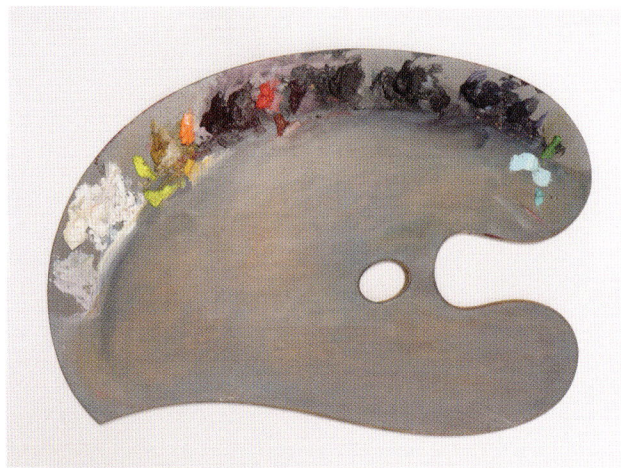

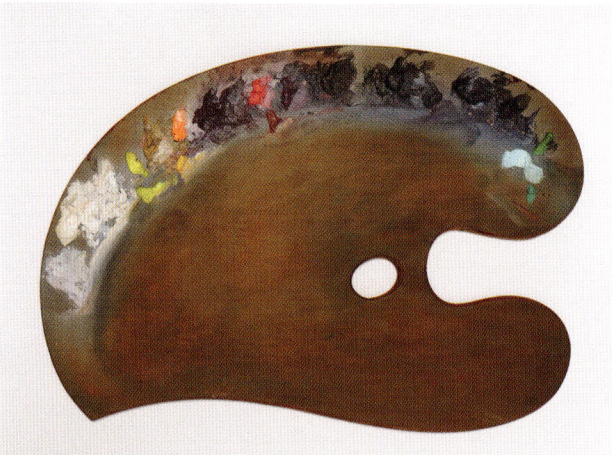

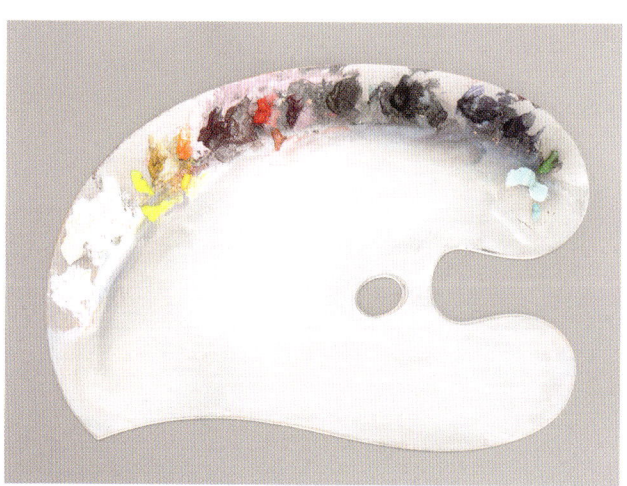

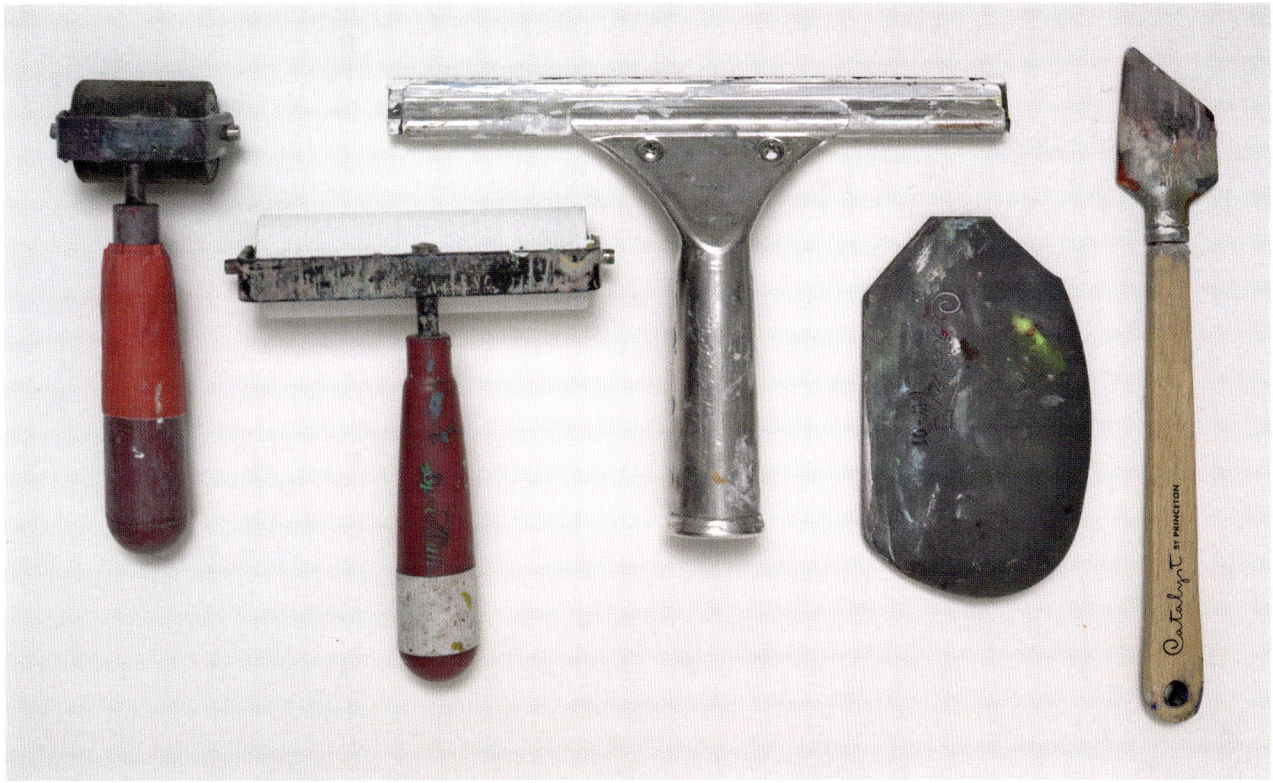

SQUEEGEE

Over the years, I've become a squeegee connoisseur. I use a variety of different kinds of paint appliers, including a brayer.

Squeegees can perform a variety of functions, including being a fantastic way to lay down a fresh, clean coat of gesso on a canvas or panel. As opposed to using a brush that makes streaks, a squeegee puts down a thin, even coat of paint that gets pushed into the cracks of the surface. It can also be used to create straight lines in landscape painting or to make an architectural element. I mostly use squeegees to create unexpected variety in the paint surface. I often use this in conjunction with a palette knife. The squeegee, since it lays down a thinner layer of paint, blends paint a little bit more readily than a palette knife, which often lays on a thick coat. Brayers also can provide that little bit of disturbance or variety that the exclusive use of brushes can't create. It's just another creative way to introduce a different texture and invite a little bit of serendipity into the paint surface.

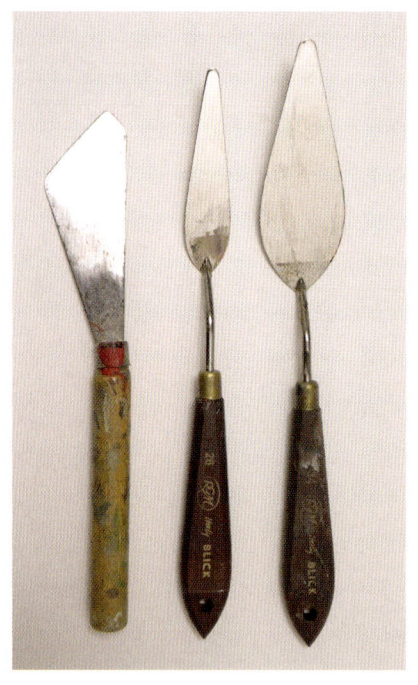
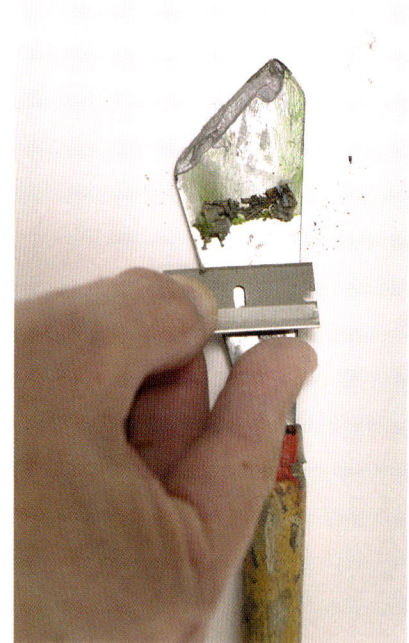
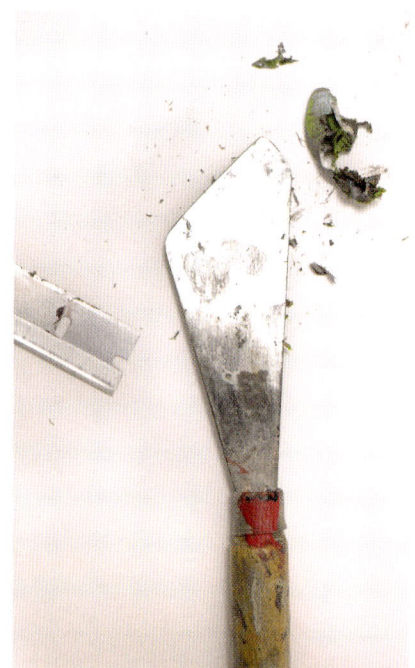

PALETTE KNIVES

Palette knives are one of your most important tools. Most artists use them to mix the paint, and they allow you to mix up big swaths of color without dirtying up your brushes. They're also used to paint with, to create hard edges and textures.

Dried-up, crusty paint diminishes the effectiveness of your palette knives so keep them clean! When you do have paint dry on your palette knives, use a sharp razor blade to scrape it off.

FIXATIVE

For the main techniques that I use in this book, the drawing must be sealed in order to paint over it. This is to prevent smudging and accidentally graying down the color that's being painted over it by the charcoal mixing into the paint. I like to use fixatives that don't dissolve with mineral spirits, in case I'd like to put a mineral spirit wash of color over my drawing, so this eliminates most retouch, varnishes and other kinds of fixatives. The most readily available fixative is clear shellac, but it should be sprayed as thin as possible to be effective. If it's sprayed on too thick, it can cause problems with paint adhesion. The better solution is SpectraFix Degas Spray Fixative, an all-natural fixative made from casein, which is a milk protein. I usually need to put on three or four coats of this in order to seal the drawing. If you spray SpectraFix too closely to the drawing, it can make the drawing look speckled. To apply it properly, make sure that you have about a two-foot (61 centimeter) distance from the drawing and apply it in several thin, misty coats.

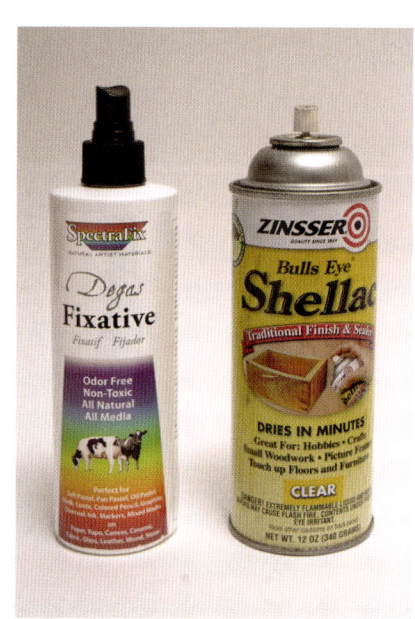

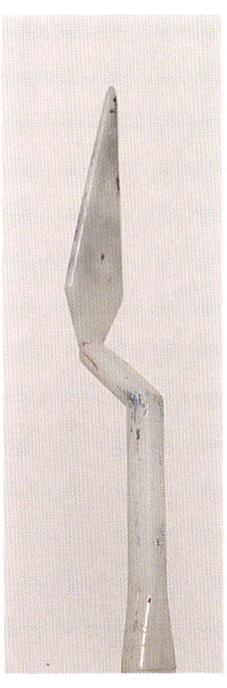 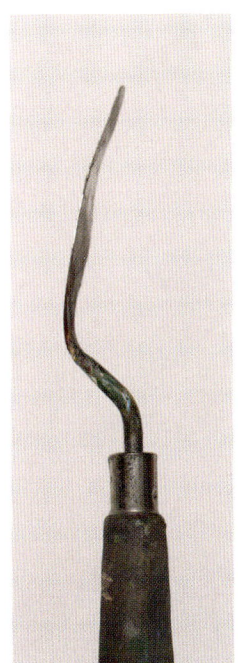 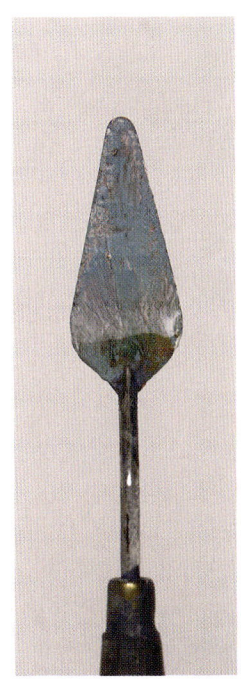 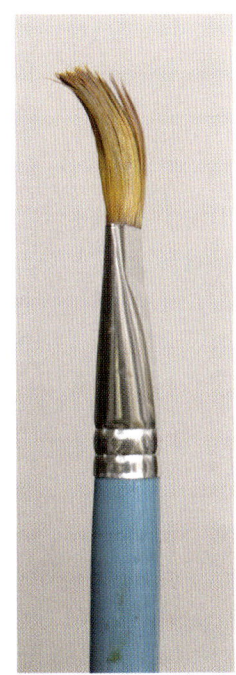 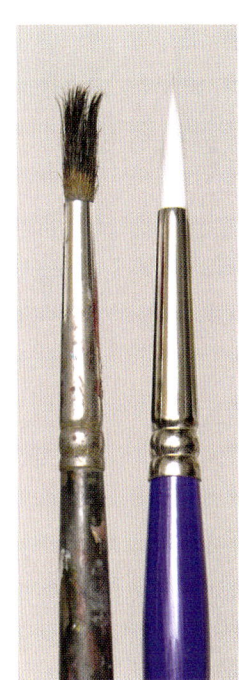

BAD MATERIALS

Let's spend a little moment on how using bad materials can negatively affect the painting process. Plastic palette knives, bent palette knives, and crusty palette knives are all a poor representation of what the tool is meant to be. The same can be said for brushes, which is usually a symptom of not having a good brush-cleaning process. Bent brushes and splayed brushes don't help us unless we're trying to create texture. Having clean, proper materials aids us in the process, as well as having decent quality paint and surfaces to paint on. They don't have to be the most expensive materials, but certainly don't buy the cheapest. I'd prefer to have lots of fresh, decent materials ready to go than expensive materials that have been ruined by a lack of care. The last picture above represents a contrast between a bad brush and a new brush. You can imagine how different the painting experience would be between the two. If we're trying to paint a delicate detail, a bad brush will do the opposite thing to what we're trying to do.

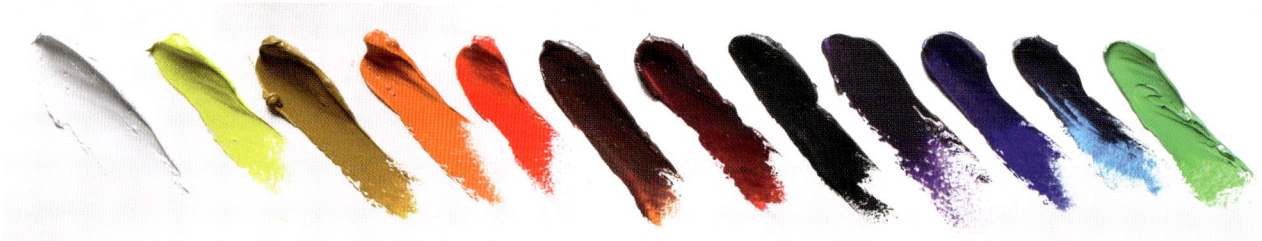

MY COLOR CHOICES

After many years of trying out many different palette and color combinations, these are the pigments in the arrangement I have arrived at, and quite honestly, I don't think it's going to change much in the future. It's a mixture of earth colors and prismatic colors, and occasionally towards the end of my painting, I may use some neon colors to give an added spark to my image through some glazing. I find that this creates quite a dynamic range, allowing the earth colors to mellow out the prismatic colors, but also having the prismatic colors gives me the boost that I need when I feel it's too gray. I also like the arrangement of yellow to orange to red to purple to blue to green similar to the way a rainbow flows, while still incorporating light to dark.

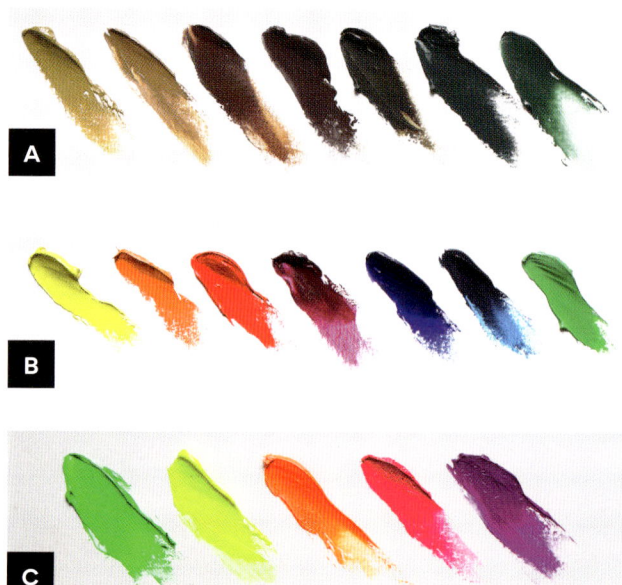

Earth Colors. (A) Earth colors, broadly speaking, are pigments made from naturally occurring minerals. They're typically grayer and more mellow versions of the different hues of color. They tend to favor a warmer spectrum and lean towards the orange, yellow, and brown family. There are also cooler tones such as blue ochre or terre verte, which can be useful to temper flesh tone. In many cases in art history, terre verte was used as an underpainting color so the greens shine through the flesh tone. All of these colors can be created by mixing prismatic colors with gray; however, it's nice to have a few of these on the palette as a shortcut to desaturate your colors quickly and gracefully.

Prismatic Colors. (B) Prismatic colors are generally represented by strong, chromatic pigments such as cadmiums, phthalos, and many dye-based colors with exotic names such as quinacridone magenta, and alizarin crimson. They're strong colors and are not able to be mixed from any other combination of colors. In some ways, they're considered primary and pure, and without them, the world is a much grayer place. Even if you prefer more gray tones and subtlety, you still need a few molecules of these prismatic colors to pull those grays in small directions this way and that. They provide greater variety and control over your grays.

Neon Colors. (C) Neon colors are a recent addition to my palette, and they're rather thin colors that lack body, mainly used for glazing a color to get it stronger. As technology becomes more pervasive, and we get used to vibrant colors from media, there's a sense of a need for painters to be able to hit these chromatic notes that are more and more a part of our lives. When we look at an image on a screen, the color is very vivid and strong. Neon colors help you reach chromatic notes that are impossible any other way, but they're perhaps too obnoxious to be used as the major colors in a painting. These are strong, beautiful colors, but they come with a word of caution as to not be overused, and their intensity can diminish with time.

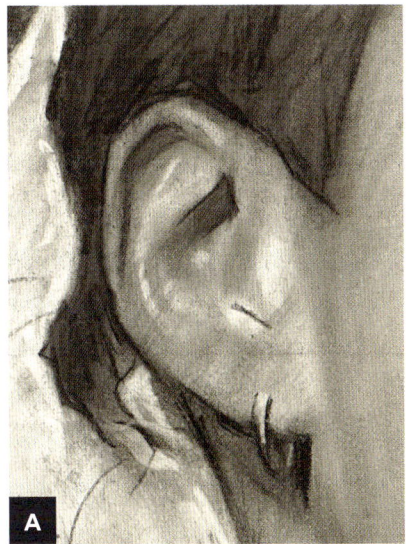
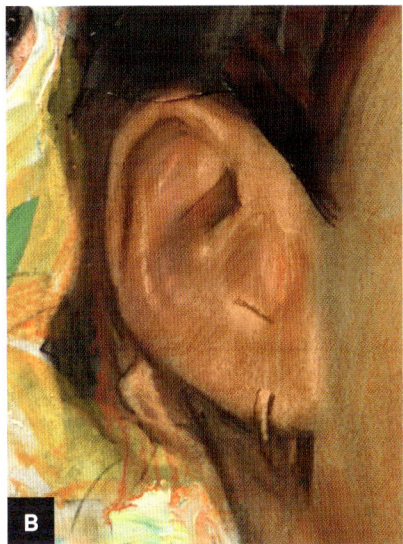
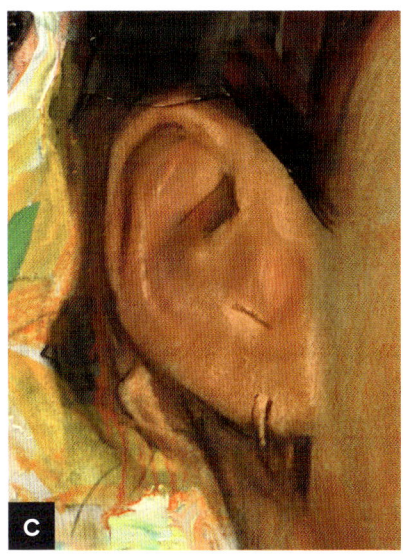

USING COLOR TRANSPARENTLY VS. OPAQUELY

The first step in painting over the underdrawing is using a transparent palette. When we're using colors transparently over a gray drawing, the colors need to be strong to hit the right color while still being able to see the drawing shine through. This is an extremely difficult thing to understand and even explain, but if the desired target color we want for the ear is a slightly grayed down orange **(A)**, then we need to use a strong glaze of orange transparently over our gray drawing to achieve the right effect. If we used the target color as a glaze, then it will become too gray and weak as it spreads out thinly over our gray drawing. To get the right color, you have to use something stronger because it's being compromised by the gray drawing underneath.

The middle image **(B)** shows how strong that glaze color is. The third image **(C)** shows how the glaze color is spread out more thinly and becomes the right general target color for the ear as it interacts with the underdrawing.

When trying to thinly paint the right colors over a gray drawing, often it requires a lot of experimentation and improvisational mixing through washes of color, seeing how they react with the gray underdrawing. I prefer to not have an elaborately mixed up subtle palette when doing this. I prefer to have a wet, transparent, washy palette and then clean it off and mix up a really nice subtle palette for the second pass.

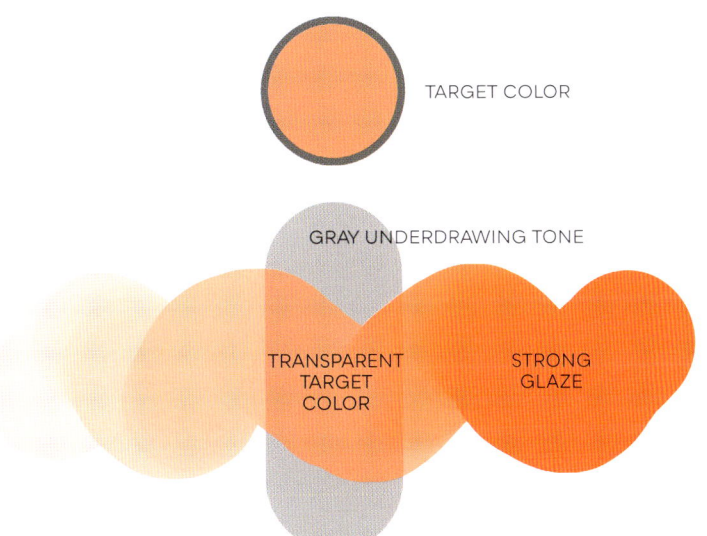

TARGET COLOR

GRAY UNDERDRAWING TONE

TRANSPARENT TARGET COLOR

STRONG GLAZE

Scan to view a video tutorial

ÉBAUCHE: TRANSITIONING FROM DRAWING TO PAINTING

Most techniques in art are rarely codified to the point in which everything is repeated exactly the way that it was meant to be. Meaning that when I say ébauche technique, not everyone will agree about my definition of it. But in my world, an ébauche technique is typically a very thin, transparent color layer rubbed over a sealed drawing in which the color is going towards the final effect indirectly. Often, using this transparent paint makes it challenging to achieve the perfect color because we're simultaneously trying to hold onto the essential quality of the drawing while moving the color towards a state of finish. So, there's a dynamic problem we're faced with. We must not lose the drawing, but we also want to get as close to the right color as possible.

The solution is to use oil paint almost like we're using watercolor. In watercolor, you don't use white, so you must use the paint transparently to achieve the desired effect. And nothing is really painted opaquely and solidly, perhaps until the end. On the contrary, oil paint is typically used rather solidly and is easy to blend; it's almost too easy to blend. In order to force oil paint to behave in the way that watercolor does, you must make it transparent. This may sound easy, but it can go wrong in a variety of ways. I typically recommend two ways of creating this transparency over the drawing: one is to use odorless mineral spirits and stronger colors so that you can create a wash that then sets up quickly, and two is that sometimes I prefer to use my finger and a latex glove to rub the color over the drawing without any mineral spirits.

When using mineral spirits to put on the ébauche, I call it the *wet and wild technique*. It usually creates a spontaneous crackly and drippy effect to the paint. This can add a lot of visual interest and really make the painting feel bold and spontaneous. It's difficult to control the mineral spirits, however, and it can drip all over the canvas to a point to work to where it's extremely hard to keep the color separate and clean. With practice, it can be a fresh and invigorating experience for creating a more painterly portrait. This is the method I used for the picture at right. For the longest time, I avoided mineral spirits for this way of painting because I didn't let the paint set up after the mineral spirit color wash. If you immediately start painting into a wash of mineral spirits, the paint doesn't stick, and you fight the surface with it, lifting off with every brushstroke. After you put on a color wash with mineral spirits and modify the colors while it's wet, you should really give it ten to fifteen minutes to set up so that it's not too watery and fluid when you begin a second more opaque pass. I typically mix up my palette or draw in some of the outlines of the most important parts of the portrait while this mineral spirits ébauche is setting up.

Of course, especially with this technique, the drawing must be sealed rather well. It's a fine line between not sealing the drawing enough and putting on too much sealer. If the drawing isn't sealed enough when you put on a watery ébauche, it's going to rub the graphite and charcoal around and compromise your drawing. Then, you'll doubt the whole technique and how it could even work. If you spray on too much sealer and create a thick, glassy layer, the paint doesn't adhere quite as well and could possibly flake off later on. No matter what surface you're painting on, if it's too glassy, the paint won't adhere well, and if it's too dry, it doesn't blend quite as well either. But this is explained more thoroughly later on.

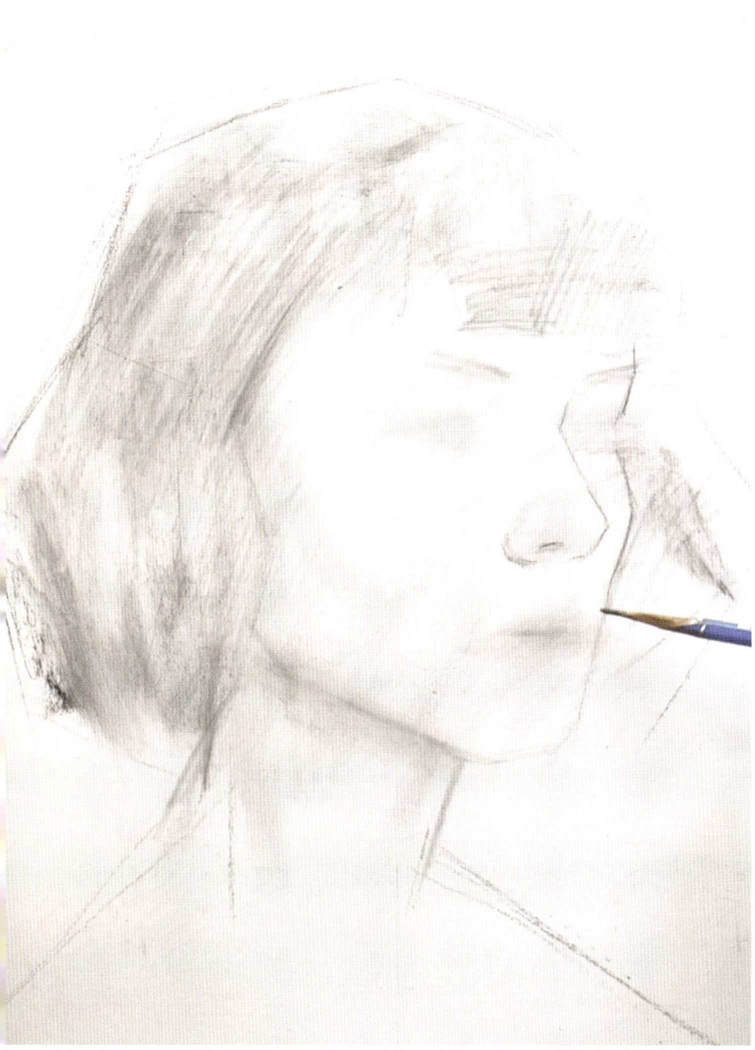

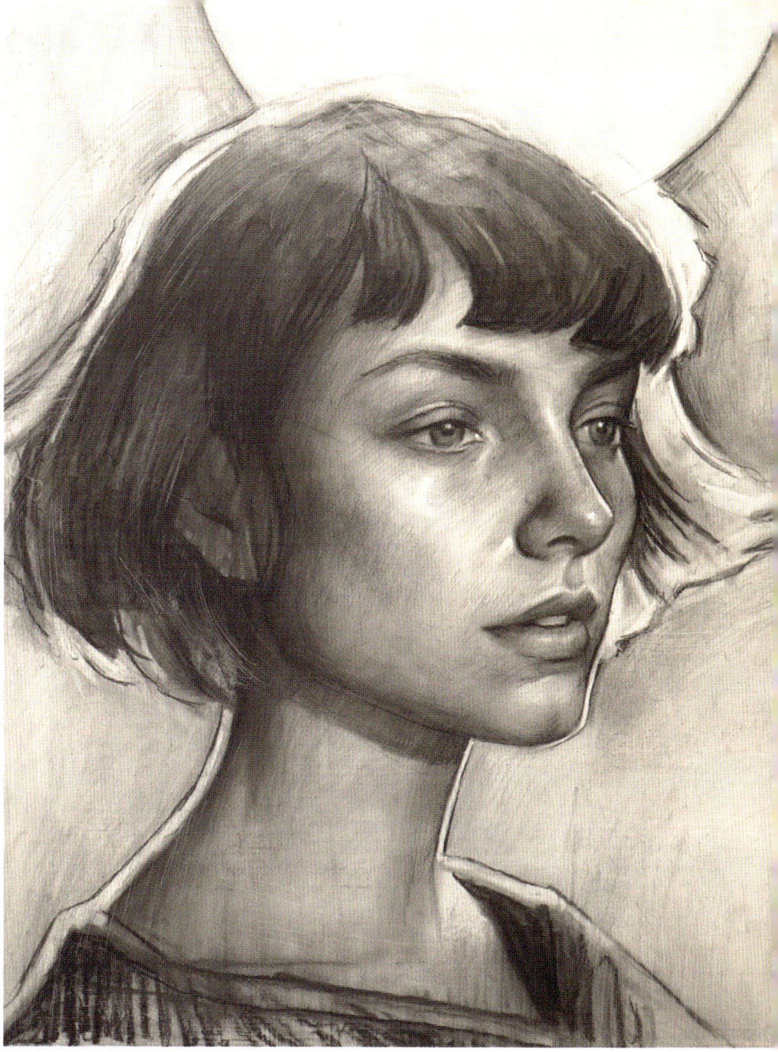

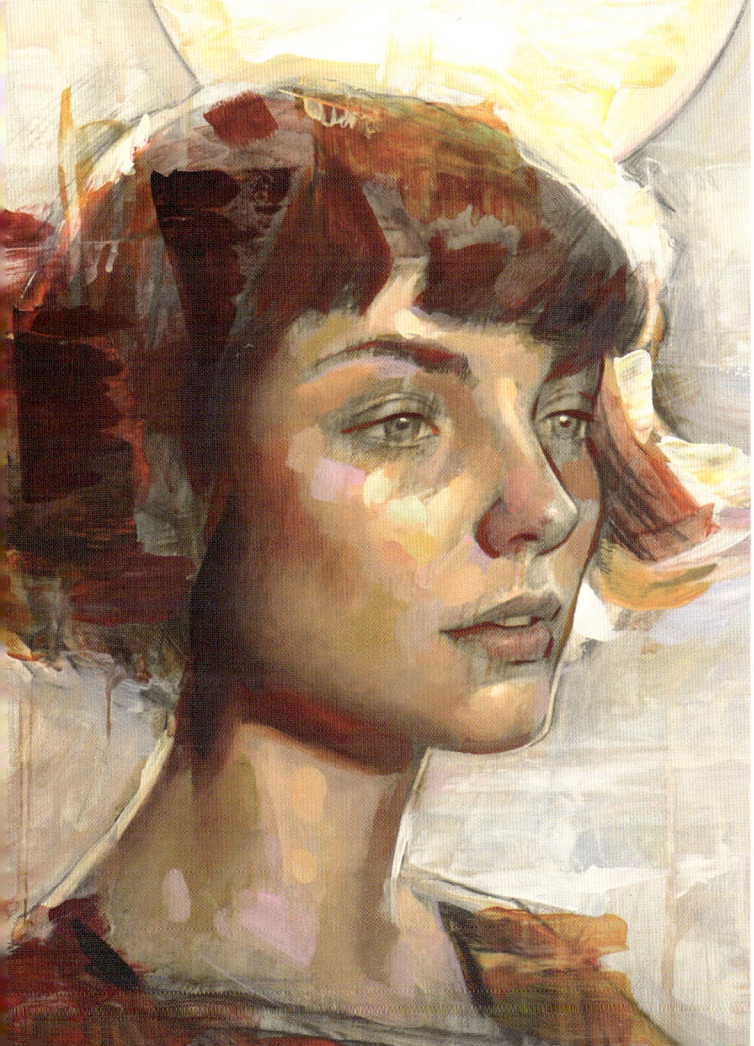
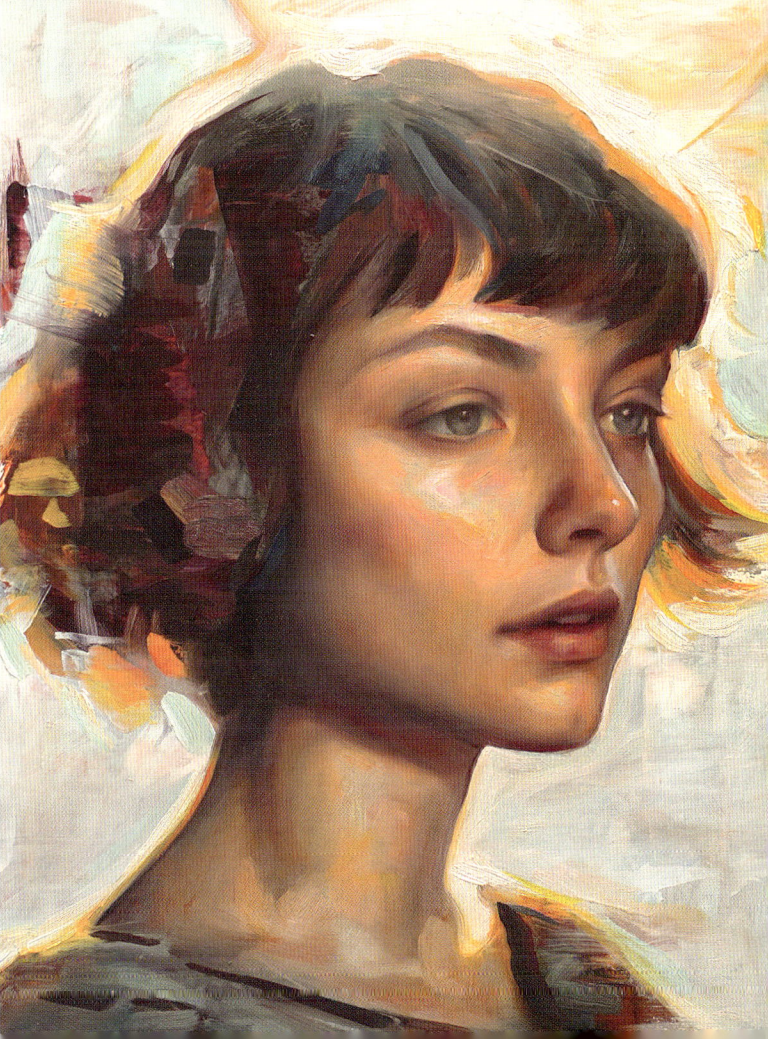

5 | VISUALIZING COLOR CONCEPTS

MUNSELL COLOR SYSTEM

Just like the order of musical notes on a piano, or longitude and latitude degrees on a map, we need boundaries to define where something begins and ends. This helps us to understand where we are and where we are going. Standard notation in music helps us to express musical ideas, communicating them in a written language, without ever having to hear the music directly, and also helps, by its confines of having specific notes, to measure if we're in tune or not.

If you carry this idea of a notation system into the world of color, ask yourself, "When does yellow cease being yellow and become orange?" Or "What does a really dark yellow look like?" Everyone will have a different concept of this if not formalized, so we need to be able to make color more concrete with color systems such as the one we'll use in this book—the Munsell color system.

Around the time of the industrial revolution, many scientists, inventors, and artists were trying to figure out how to talk about and analyze color in a systematic way. Originally invented as a way to classify different colors and types of soil, the Munsell color system is now considered to be one of the most successful of these models from the nineteenth century. Since then, it's become a widely used model for colorists to visualize and understand the dynamics of color space in a three-dimensional model.

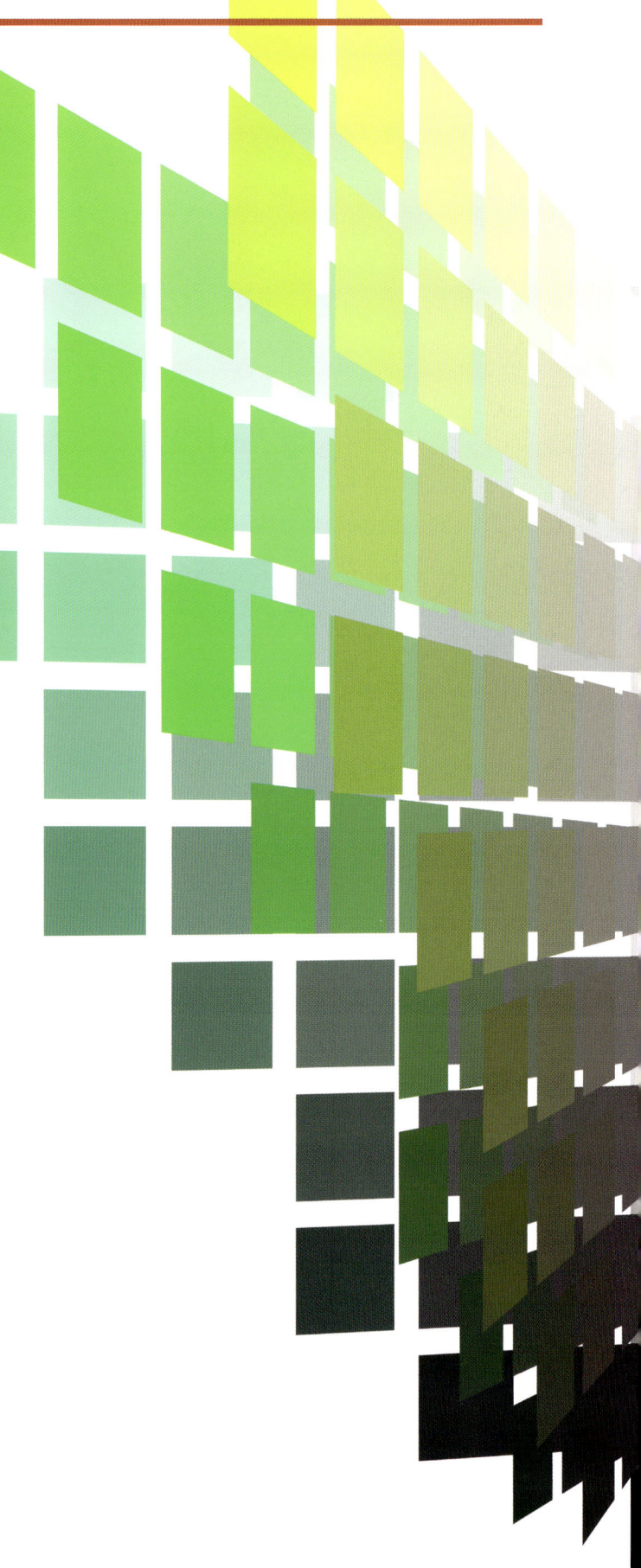

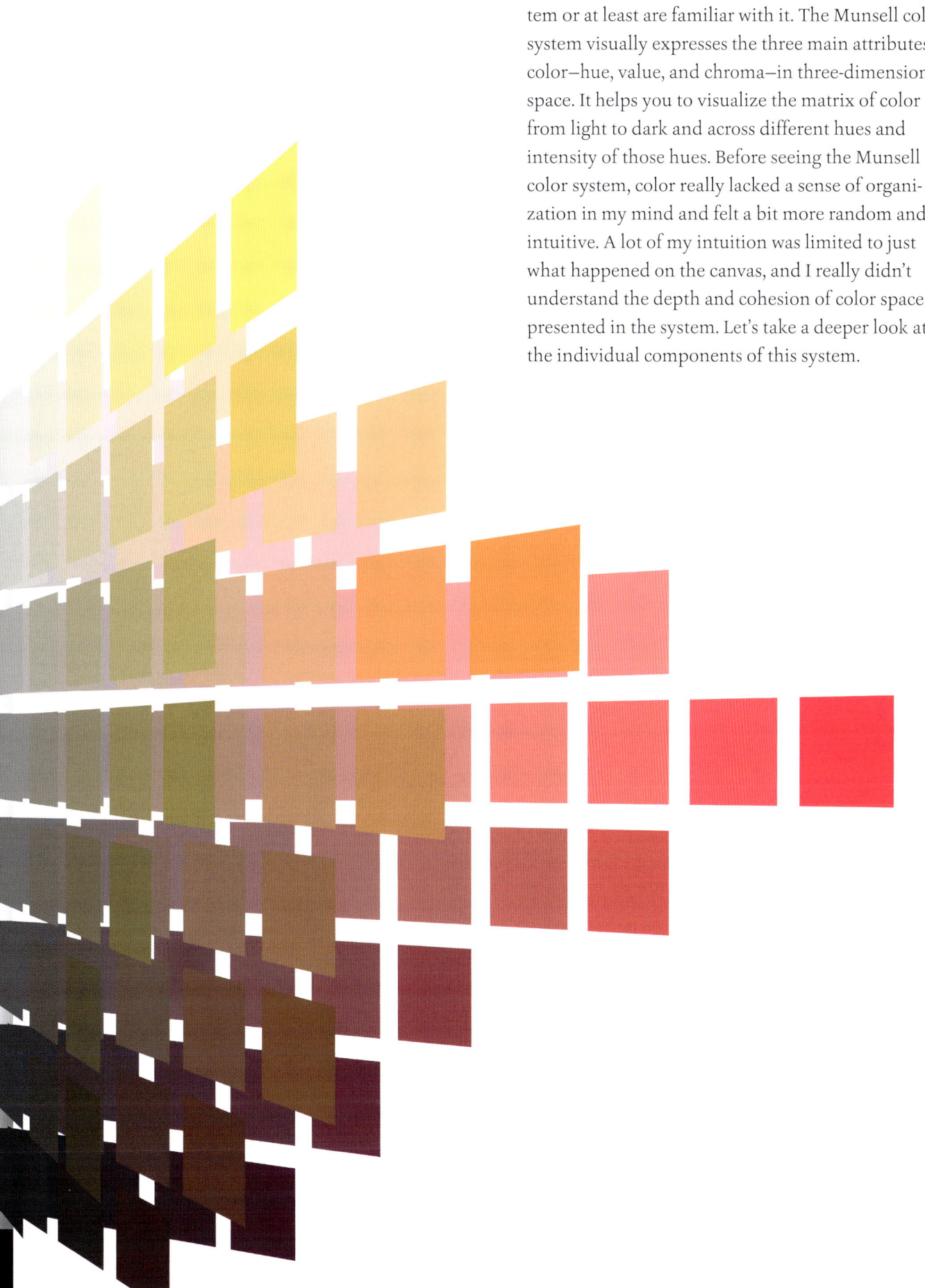

Many of the best realistic painters utilize this system or at least are familiar with it. The Munsell color system visually expresses the three main attributes of color—hue, value, and chroma—in three-dimensional space. It helps you to visualize the matrix of color from light to dark and across different hues and intensity of those hues. Before seeing the Munsell color system, color really lacked a sense of organization in my mind and felt a bit more random and intuitive. A lot of my intuition was limited to just what happened on the canvas, and I really didn't understand the depth and cohesion of color space as presented in the system. Let's take a deeper look at the individual components of this system.

HUE, VALUE, AND CHROMA

HUE

The attribute *hue* refers to the actual color. The six major hues are red, orange, yellow, green, blue, and violet. Hue is purely a color decision. Hue can describe more than these six primary hues, which are man-made ideas. It can also describe red orange or blue green, which helps to fill in the space between these large differences. This is helpful when describing pigments because most won't easily fit into the neat category of a true hue. Pigments mostly live in the space between these major categories. Some of the colors, such as white, black, and gray, don't have a hue but are considered neutral. Sometimes, on a pink tube, there will be a pigment called, for example, cadmium red hue, which isn't related to our previous depth definition. In this case, cadmium red hue means that they have mixed other pigments to approximate cadmium red, but no cadmium red exists in the paint; therefore, it's called cadmium red hue.

VALUE

The attribute of value is purely a light and dark concept. This includes white, black, and all the shades of gray in between. But the shades of gray are not purely just a mixture of black and white because that creates a *cool* gray. Nor are they brown and white mixtures because that creates a *warm* gray. They are perfectly *neutral* grays that are neither warm nor cool. One of the problems with value is that it's rarely presented purely in this black-and-white scale, but also applies to colors themselves. A red has a value or a blue has a value that's typically darker than red and so to break down color space, this separately can sometimes feel esoteric because we're really defining our attributes in a vacuum and not in a context.

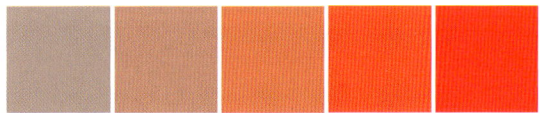

CHROMA

To understand chroma, the attribute that defines intensity of color, look at the image above not as a changing hue or value, but a color losing its colorfulness (a red losing its redness toward neutral). The hardest attribute to understand and difficult to control in application on the palette, students are tripped up because they see a chroma change as a value change. In the end, it's easy to either have too colorful a picture or something that's mired in gray. The tension between colorfulness and gray-colored grays can be such a beautiful tension in a painting and requires a lot of control. That means you must be able to make the color stronger with powerful pigments, but then also be able to neutralize them at a moment's notice and find all of the tones in between. I can't stress this enough—it's the hardest thing in color mixing, the notorious colored grays.

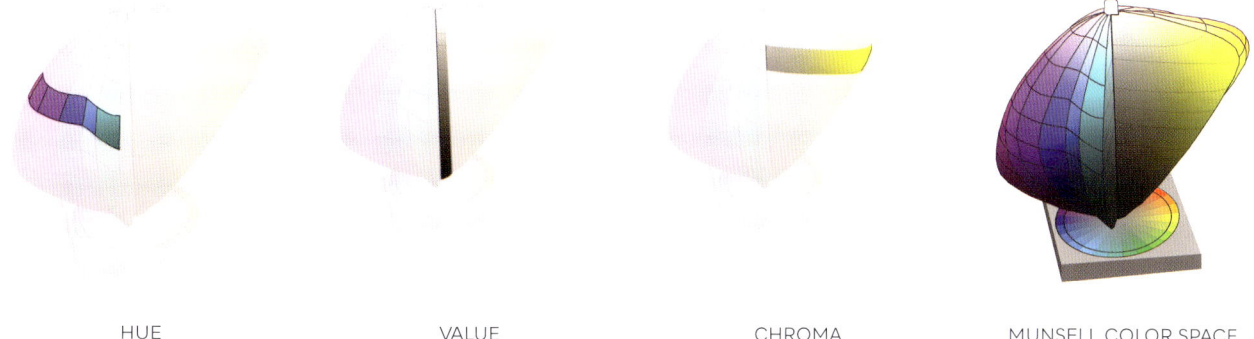

HUE   VALUE   CHROMA   MUNSELL COLOR SPACE

COLOR HAS A SHAPE

The attributes of hue, value, and chroma add up to a model that produces an *X*, *Y*, and *Z*, meaning it has a shape. As a color system, it's helpful to see it as a shape, called the Munsell color space, so that you can view the totality of the color of the world within a form. In the images above, you get to see the isolated attributes of the system with these overlays blocking out the other options, thus helping to explain how all three are at work.

There's a gigantic spectrum going from neutral at its core, a vertical axis that is darkest (black) at the bottom and lightest (white) at the top to the most colorful, those colors with the highest chroma, spreading radially to the edges. You'll also notice that the yellow extends further out in the lighter values and the blue and the violets stick out in the darker values. This clearly shows that certain colors peak at certain value ranges.

USING MUNSELL

Using the Munsell color system in the traditional way can sometimes be cumbersome, so I'm presenting a simplified version below where each hue has a letter combination, each value a corresponding number from 1 to 10, and the chroma has a range from 1 to 5. A zero on the chroma scale would be perfect neutral.

The color square at left is my rendition of a certain kind of pigment, and it has a hue, a value, and a level of chroma. What is its hue? Value? Level of chroma? Each color that we look at has an answer for these three questions, and sometimes, getting this perfectly dialed in with each color that you mix is nearly impossible, so it's beneficial to mix a few options and allow your eyes to determine which is the right color rather than trying to mix one perfect tone. However, it's also a great exercise for trying *to mix* that one perfect tone successfully. I'd call this color a yellow orange with a value of four and a chroma of three. The best way to understand is to put the color in action and try to repeatedly do this for many of the colors that you see. Whenever you need to lower the chroma of a given color, try to use a neutral gray that's the same value of that color.

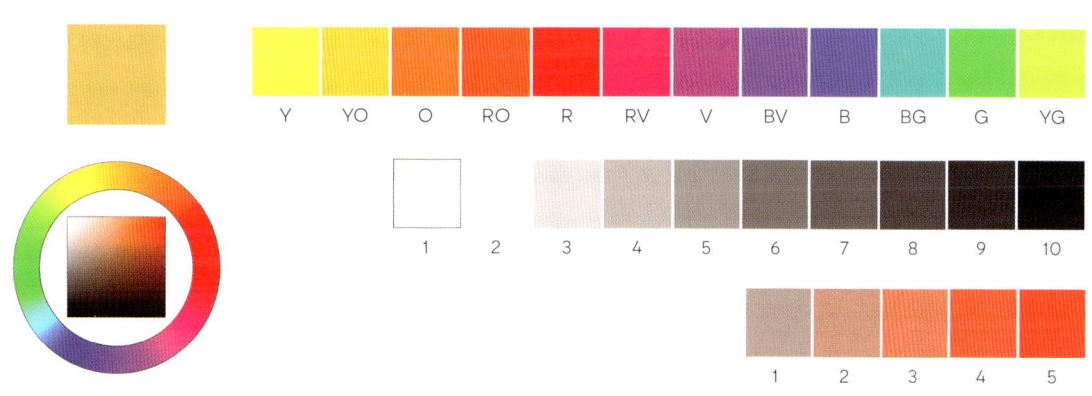

Y   YO   O   RO   R   RV   V   BV   B   BG   G   YG

1   2   3   4   5   6   7   8   9   10

1   2   3   4   5

HUE AS IT RELATES TO PIGMENTS AND WARM/COOL

Figuring out which pigments to buy and how they relate to the Munsell color system takes a bit of effort and experience from the painter. A paint tube called cadmium yellow might actually have quite a bit of orange in it, or a green, such as viridian, might be so cold and strong that it's unable to produce the type of warm green that you need to paint a tree in a sunset. Thinking about how each individual paint pigment that you purchase has a spot on the hue spectrum and that there's actually a spectrum of reds or spectrum of greens that have subtle hue variations within them is really illuminating, which leads to an understanding of how to use your pigments the most effectively.

One of the ways to simplify language when talking about paint is to talk about it as if it's warm or cool. Often, this warm and cool distinction becomes more difficult to understand, but basically speaking, warm colors tend towards orange and cool colors tend towards blue. Take the hue red for instance. There are lots of different reds, but one way to think about cadmium red light is that it's a red orange or a warm red; whereas alizarin crimson is considered a red violet or a cold red. So more often than not, a given pigment paint won't perfectly be a true red or a true blue. It will have some tiny shift towards another adjacent hue.

Knowing this has many different applications too numerous to mention in this book, but one example is trying to mix a violet by using red and blue. If the red you are using is a red orange and the blue is a blue green, the violet produced would be a brown violet because the two colors being used are not pure forms of red and blue. They're somewhat compromised and thus create a limitation to how much chroma your violet can have. There's actually a little bit of the opposite color of violet, which is the yellow in the red, and that neutralizes the violet being made.

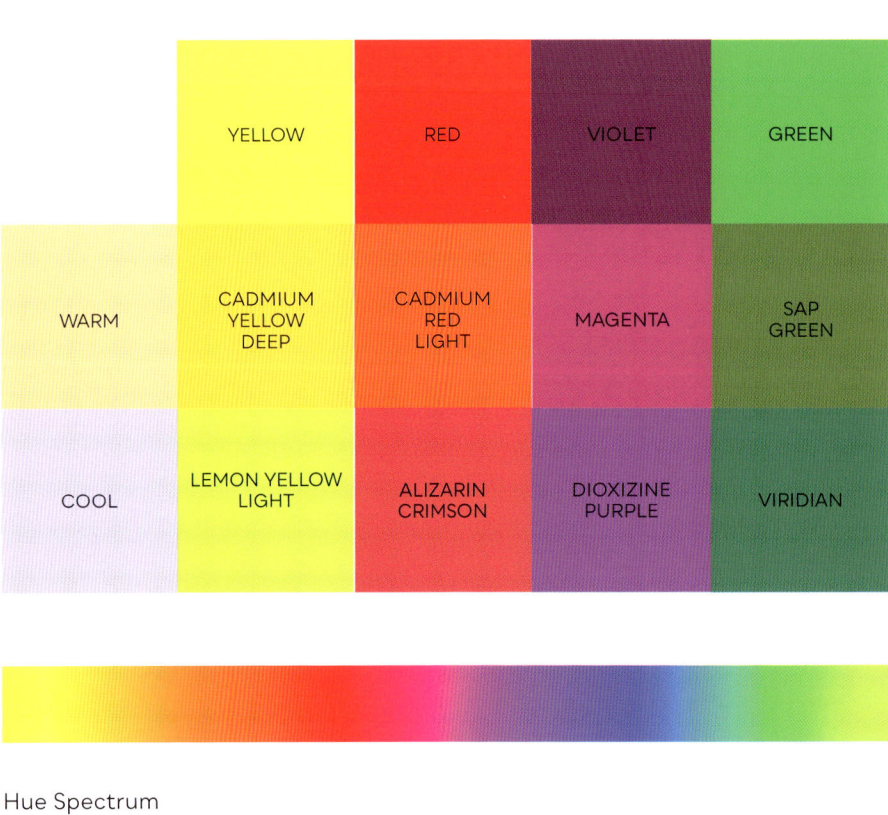

Hue Spectrum

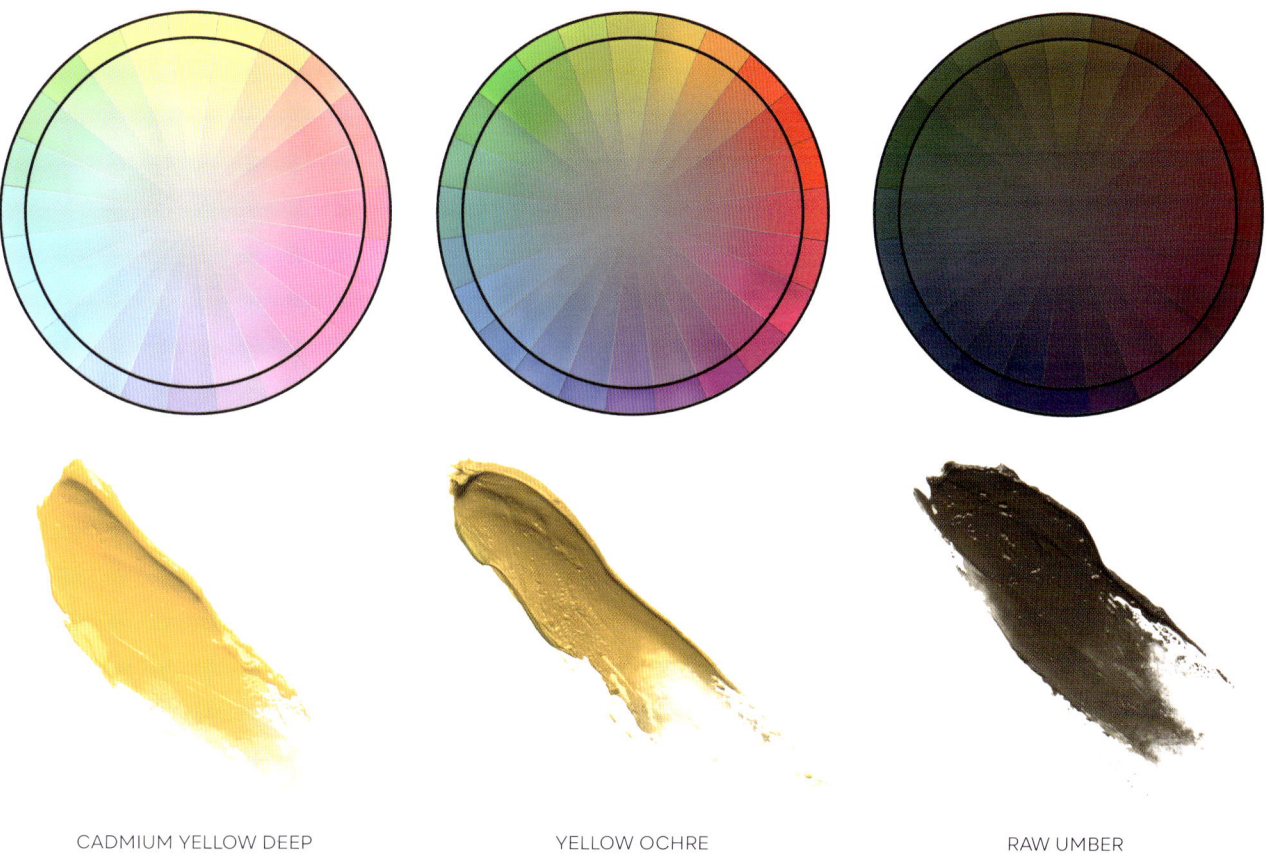

CADMIUM YELLOW DEEP   YELLOW OCHRE   RAW UMBER

PIGMENTS AND WHERE THEY PEAK

One of the more interesting things that the Munsell color system illuminates is that different hues peak in different value ranges in terms of their chroma. Therefore, a yellow orange is the most chromatic when it's the lightest in value, cadmium yellow deep.

The spectrum of neutral to chromatic becomes much more limited in the dark ranges. And that's why it's really difficult to identify a very dark yellow because there's almost nothing to work with. Seen in this light, you can understand that a color like raw umber could be used as a dark yellow rather than just seeing it as another brown, and you could also look at yellow ochre as being one of the more chromatic versions of a yellow in the middle range of values.

One of the unique challenges of many pigments is that you can't see what they are until you add a touch of white, such as with alizarin crimson or ultramarine blue. That's due to the fact that as colors generally darken, this chromatic range disappears, and so you need to bump up the value of your color in order to see its full chromatic possibilities.

This also explains why we need to have stronger colors in the darks on our palettes, so that we don't start to make mud in this dark region and have more color clarity options, rather than always leaning on umbers and blacks to solve our shadow problems.

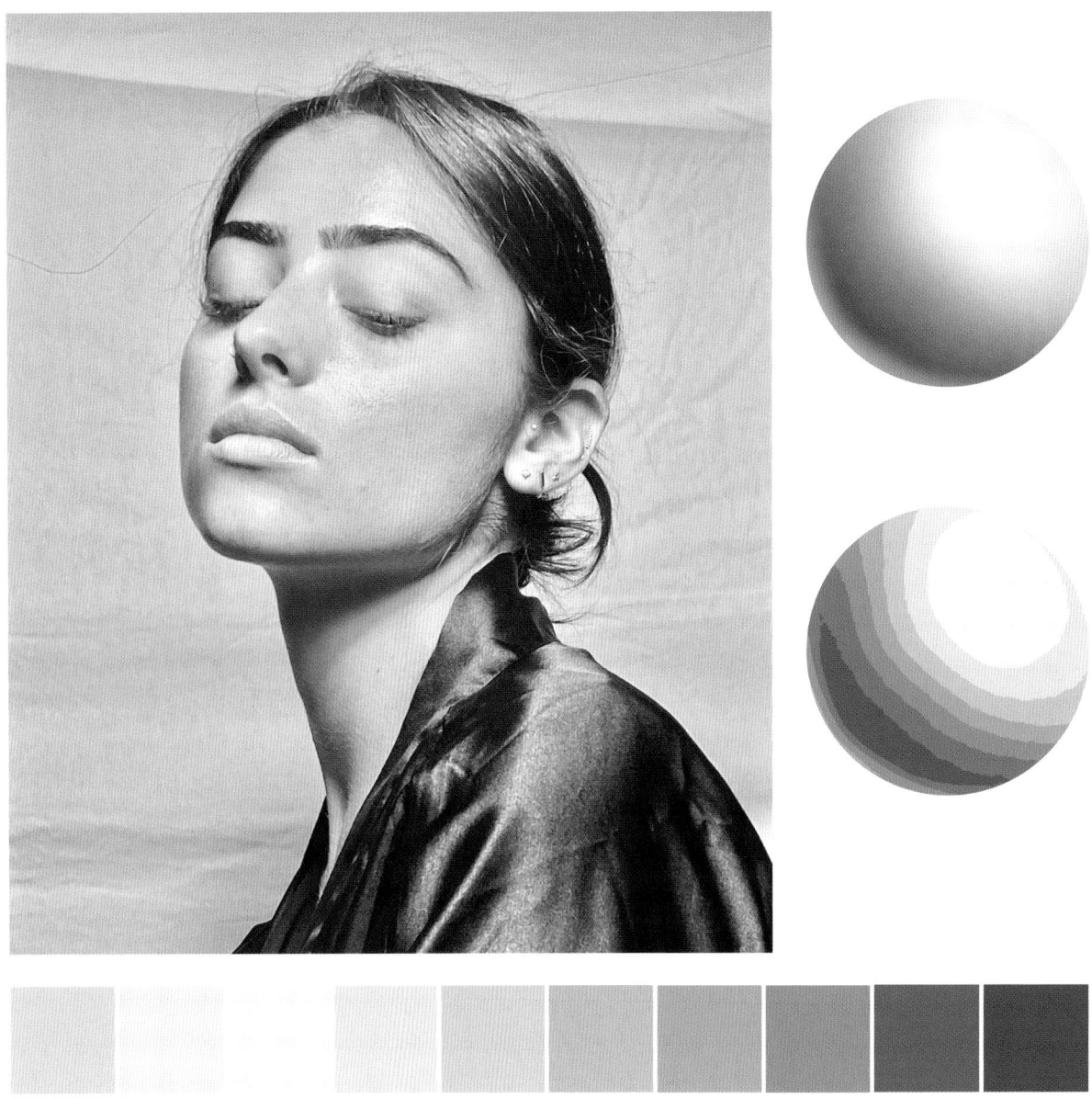

VALUE AS IT RELATES TO FORM

When I was in art school, one of the biggest insults was to hear that your painting was flat. In some ways, I found this to be quite amusing as a very academic way of insulting somebody, and in other ways, I found it to be a difficult concept to even understand what was being said or how to fix it. Because often, I might be painting from a photograph, and the photograph had little exposure. Or even if I was painting a model from life and there was flat lighting there, through my lack of skills, I may have made it even flatter.

Something can be true in the way the camera represents the light in the image above, but still lack dimension. This could be from a variety of factors. Our camera is a lens that interprets what we're seeing and isn't actually a perfect rendition of our subject; sometimes, the darks are too dark, the light gets washed out, or details translate stronger than they are. Sometimes the lighting is just flat and lacking a certain sense of drama to showcase the three-dimensional qualities of our model. But for many artists, we shouldn't just stop there and accept the way that the photograph is rendered. We can adjust the lighting when taking the photograph to create more of a sense of dimension.

I believe one of the secrets to making something appear round is to push the darks as dark as they're going to go, in order to get darker halftones that pop the light. In the photograph opposite, you'll notice that the shadows have become darker than the previous photo, and that this has allowed me room to retouch this

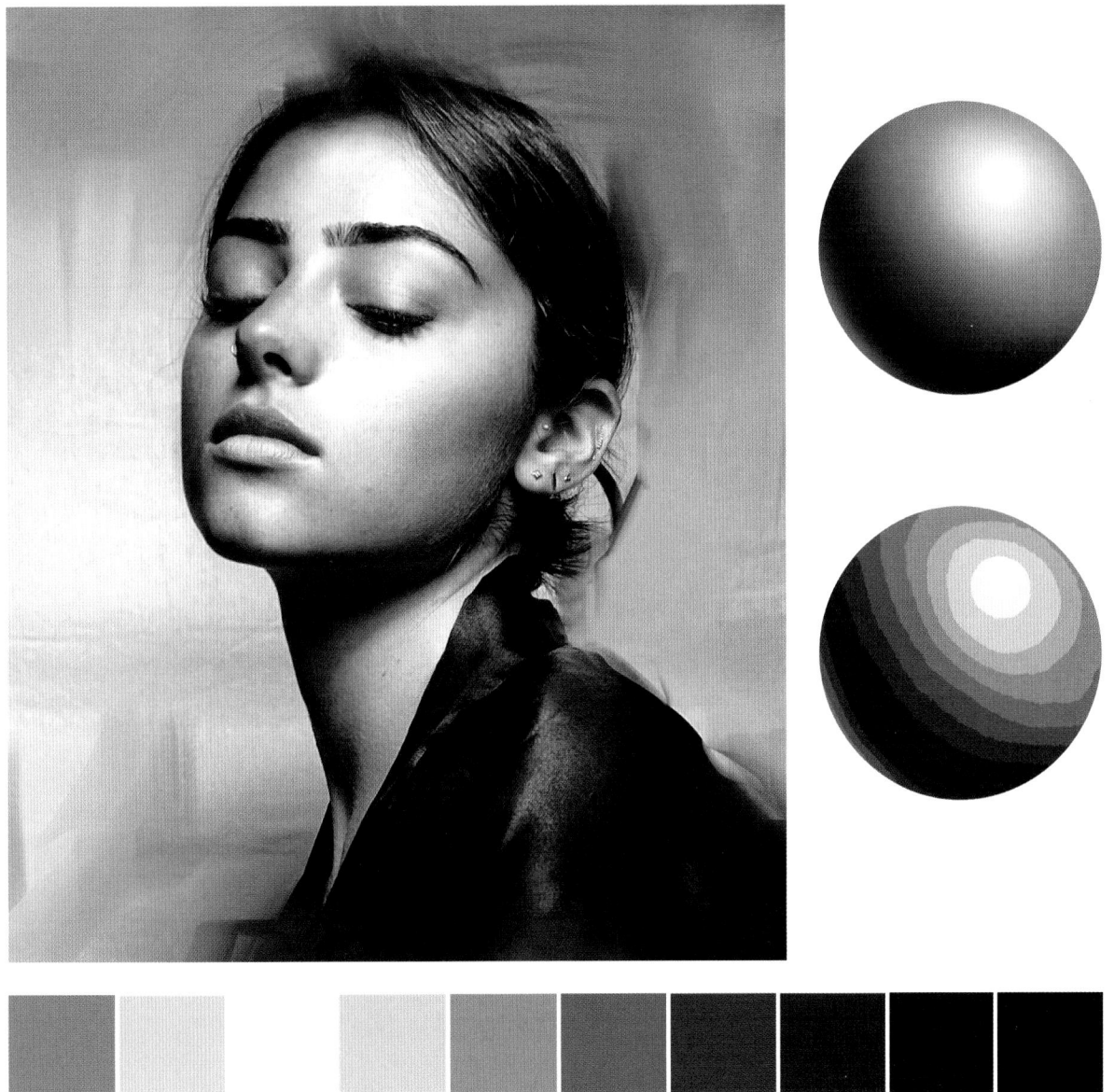

photo and push the halftones darker in order to create more form. The halftones are basically all of the shades in between the highlights and the main shadow.

This increase in form is especially noticeable in the eyelids where you get a sense of a focused highlight that pops more. This effect is also more noticeable in the highlight on the nose and on the cheek versus the side plain of the face and the range of values between the highlight on her left cheek and the side plain. The left side plain of her face by the ear has quite a bit of depth when compared to the previous photograph.

When you push the darks dark, it opens up the range from the dark to the light to expand and gives you more of a spectrum of tones to describe the three-dimensional qualities of the face. So if the dark isn't very dark, you don't have as many options between these two areas. Often as a teacher, I have to tell somebody you need to push the dark darker and more colorful to achieve the greatest amount of depth on the face. Don't be afraid of the dark because without it, the light doesn't shine.

Form, dimension, roundness, and 3-D are all synonyms for what's being talked about here. One last note about this subject is that frequently when dealing with drawing issues, color issues, and painting technique issues, this concept is often neglected. It's represented here in black and white so as to not muddy the waters by adding color.

CHROMA AS IT RELATES TO FLESH TONE

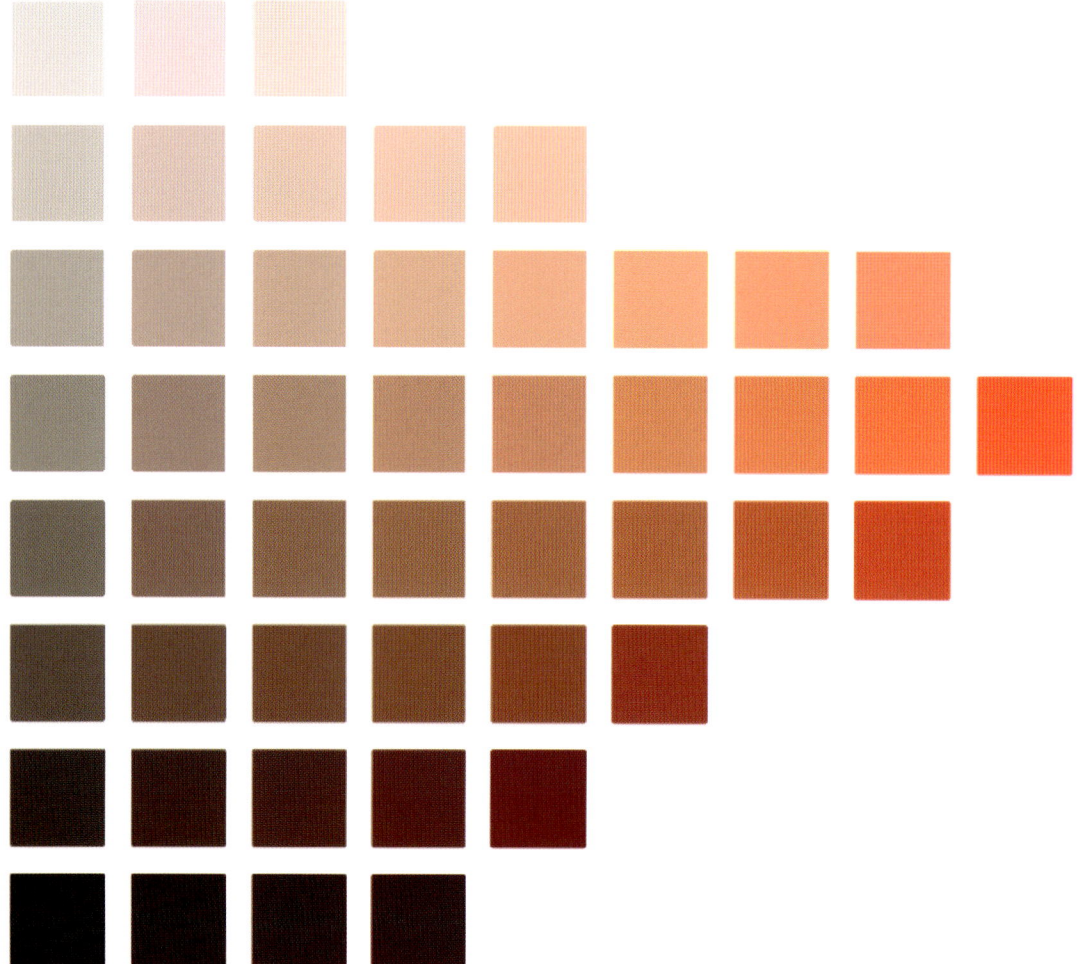

CHROMATIC AND NEUTRAL (WARM AND COOL)

One of the most basic ways to understand painting flesh tone is to see skin as either being more chromatic or less chromatic (more neutral).

When seeing flesh tone through this lens, one can see it as a spectrum of color intensity (chroma) rather than monochromatic or even random colors. First, it's good to paint areas of the face that have more intense color to them; they're easier to perceive. Typically, lips, ears, eye sockets, noses, and cheeks have a little more color chroma to them, as well as some shadows that receive reflected light. Then, it's good to look, and begin to define, the least chromatic areas of the skin, which are cooler. Often these are located in bony areas, in the whites of the eyes, the teeth, in the skin around the lips, and in the darkest halftones or the turnings. There are always a variety of factors at play when we're looking at somebody, but those are some good places to start exploring.

Once you have the most chromatic tones (warmest) and the most neutral tones (coolest), you can also find that middle ground, which would probably be the average flesh tone in between those two extremes.

When viewing flesh tone through the lens of chromatic and neutral, the main objective is to realize that flesh is a spectrum of chroma rather than a singular type of chroma. This approach to flesh tone is very helpful, particularly when painting from a photograph or in some other situation where there may be an overall homogenizing effect to the color in a reference image that obscures this reality, which you *would* see when painting from life.

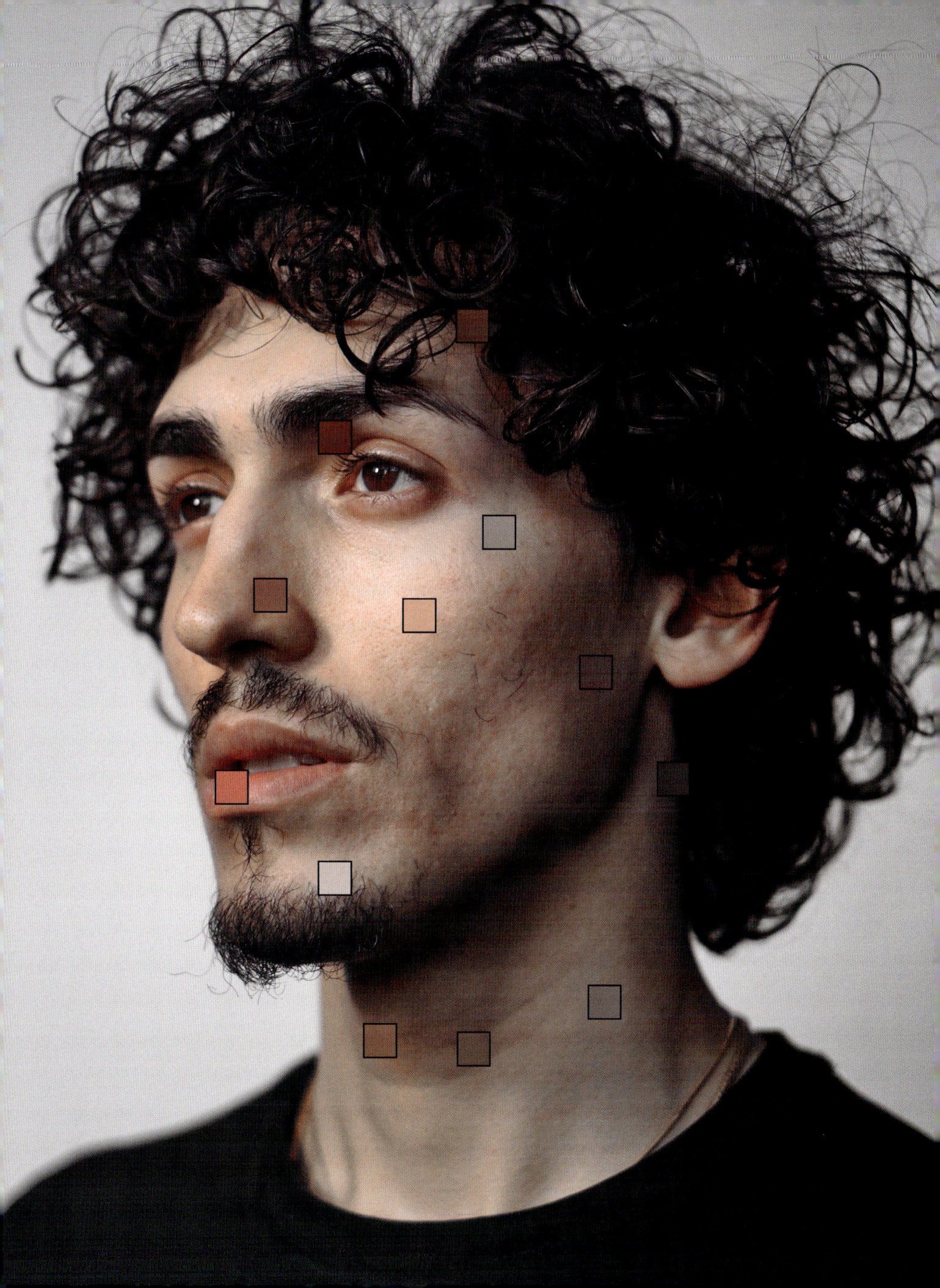

HUE AS IT RELATES TO FLESH COLOR DIVERSITY

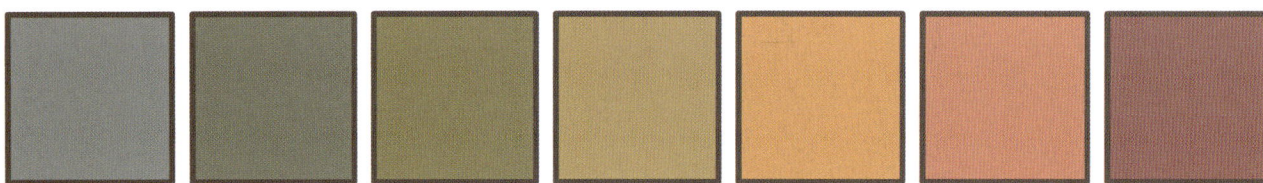

Probably my favorite way to think about flesh tone is using the concept of creating color (hue) diversity that centers around a primary hue. So, if we take this model's general average flesh tone, which is called the *mother color*, represented in the big square in the middle of Figure **(A)**, and we create variations on that tone with all of the different colors of the rainbow, signified by all the colors surrounding this square, this denotes flesh color diversity.

To create this on the palette, develop a pile of a flesh tone color that you just can't live without, meaning the one color that ties everything together. This mother color may not be the most interesting one, but if you didn't have it, everything would just feel random. From here, find a redder version and a grayer version. Sometimes, this gray tone can appear green or blue or even yellow gray and is typically the more difficult color to mix. If you get too zealous when mixing this color, mix a little bit of this mother color into the offending tone to bring it back into harmony. These unexpected tones, however much frustration they create for the artist, are worth the effort and can take your painting to the next level.

Mixing up flesh color diversity creates a unity and variety that's a full-bodied expression of what flesh tone can be. Because secretly, I don't want to just mix the right flesh color. I want all of the flesh colors that are possible because it portrays a liveliness and a fresh quality to flesh that is, perhaps, the reason oil paint was even invented.

And if you start looking for hue diversity in skin tones, you may just find it. Most people are just looking for the one type of flesh tone that they think will get them to the finish line. But typically, you need to have variation in your flesh tone or it lacks that liveliness in the color. So if you're looking for all of the colors in your flesh tone, you might start to see the natural deviations that typically occur on a face and start to control that more in your work.

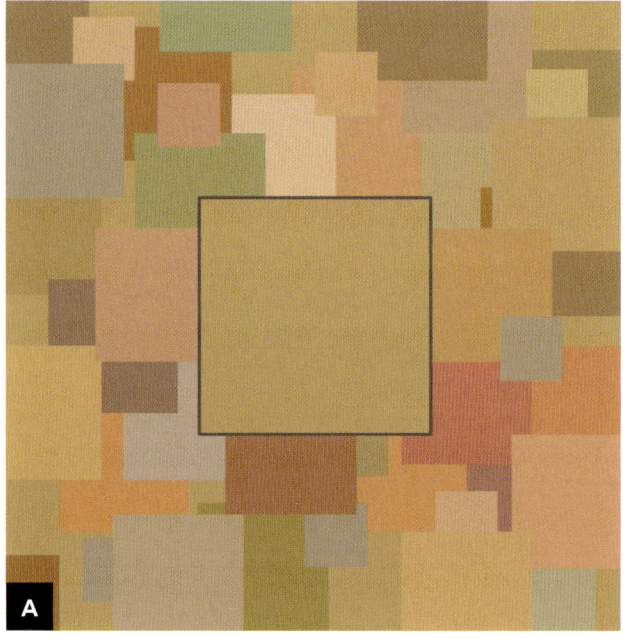

A

Often, there's a little bit more yellow in the neck, or the darker halftones around the jaw can be a cooler gray, green, or blue. Purple is frequently found around the eyes. And sometimes, the color of the light or the color of the atmosphere can also play a role as to bending these colors into a slightly different version of themselves, creating color diversity. But we'll explore that later on.

I think in order to genuinely appreciate this quality of flesh color diversity, we need to look at renowned artists that achieve this in their work. Artist like Bouguereau, Aleah Chapin, Lucian Freud, Stephen Assael, Odd Nerdrum, as well as many of the paintings in this book, have this effect. It may not always be well represented in a photograph on the Internet, but when you see paintings like these in person, they awaken your sensibilities of color and what's possible in painting.

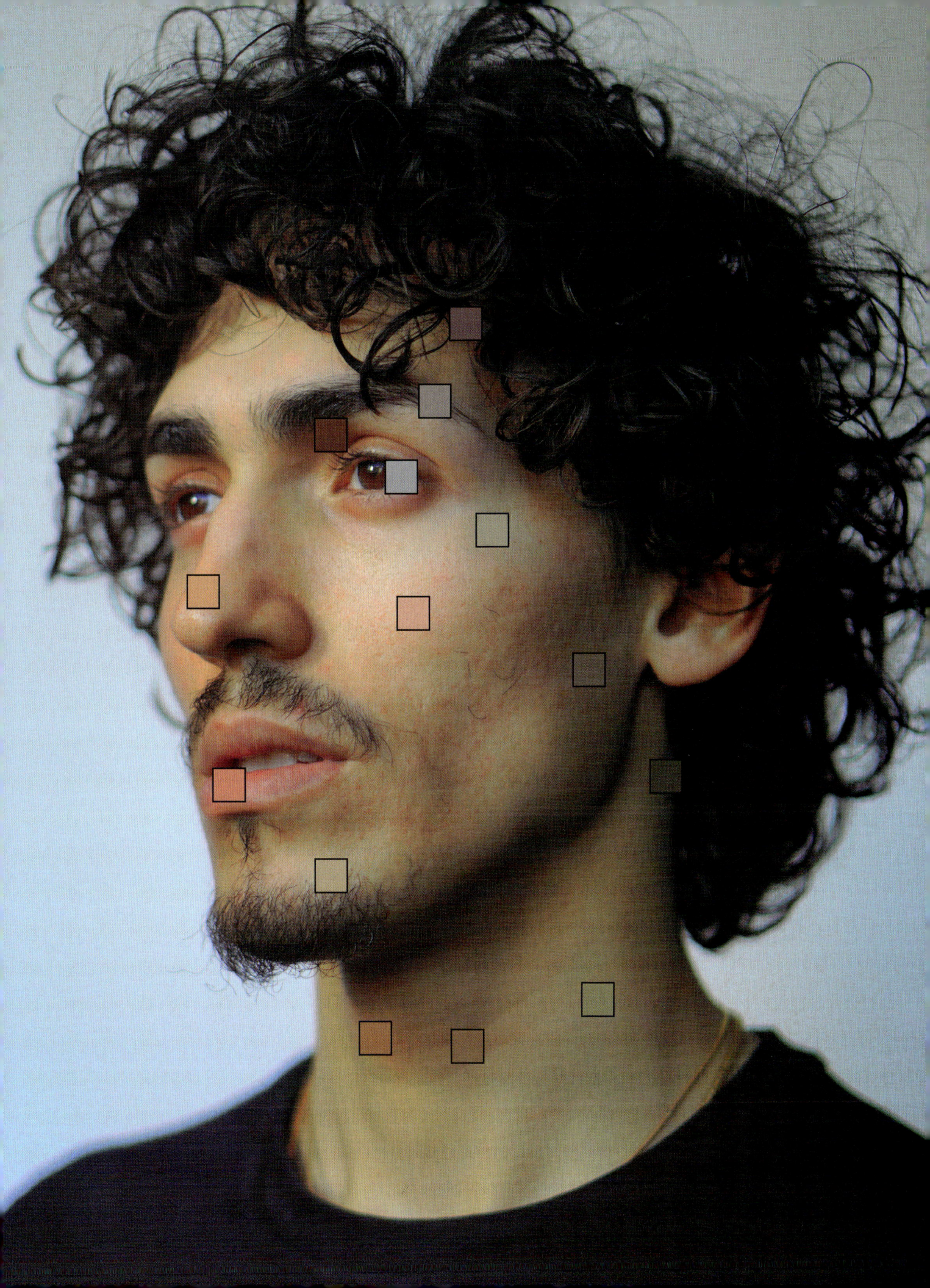

AMPLIFYING COLOR INFORMATION FOR DIVERSITY

Using this many examples may seem redundant, but with a topic so difficult as painting flesh tone, it's well worth it to explain and talk about some of the problems.

Often, the question that I get asked the most is "How do you see all of those colors in the flesh tone?" This singular topic is probably the most sought-after skill among my portrait painting students that I have, this amplifying color diversity concept. And many of these concepts are more easily spoken about than done, and this is especially true if your reference material has limited color information. Often, I find myself as a teacher having to really amplify the color information on the photo, for students to be able to make a little progress towards a colorful flesh tone.

As we previously discussed on page 98, the easiest way to think about flesh tone is, "Is it chromatic or is it more neutral?" This means, "Is the flesh tone redder or grayer?" Creating variety in chroma with this method is a great building block in painting flesh, and many artists stay within this concept for many years with enormous success.

Trying to create flesh color diversity is quite difficult, even when you'd like something to be quite subtle such as **(A)**. I've found that students need to see something like **(B)** in order to paint something like **(C)**. Some artists have a great practice doing this, and they can just pick out a color on somebody's face and amplify it to a great degree to push these concepts. Others need training wheels, such as taking the photo into a digital photo editing software and bumping up the Vibrant several times and/or

playing with different exposure settings to get the most amount of color information possible. The better the photo, the more likely it is to have color information that can be amplified, but the main thing to look at when doing this in an editing program is to make sure that everything doesn't turn orange. So sometimes, when you bump up the vibrations or the saturation or the exposure, the flesh tone goes to orange, and you may have to play with the color balance settings as well to emphasize the opposite tones of orange. That may mean increasing the blues and the greens a bit in order to create this amplified sense of diversity.

I've found this to be one of the most elusive concepts to gain confidence in as a painter for so many reasons. But one that truly comes to mind is just the fact that when we're painting, so often we blend the colors and values that we put down in a way makes things look smooth and finished. Blending isn't a bad thing necessarily, but in order to push the color into our work, sometimes painting with slightly stronger colors or having a reference that has slightly stronger colors depicted will help us to bust out of the gray-brown haze that so many portrait paintings are a victim of. I've painted way too many brown, sad, dark paintings in the past, and now I really love to emphasize luminosity and color diversity in the painting of my flesh tones.

So hopefully, I've convinced you to amplify whatever color information that you have in your reference to a much more extreme place so that you can see the temperature and hue variations that exist in the photo. Even if you fail or make a way to chromatic painting, you'll have learned something that can be made more subtle in the future with more control.

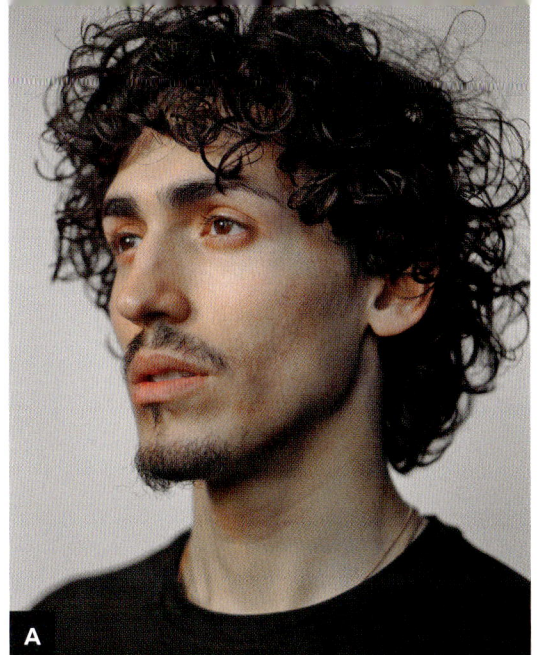

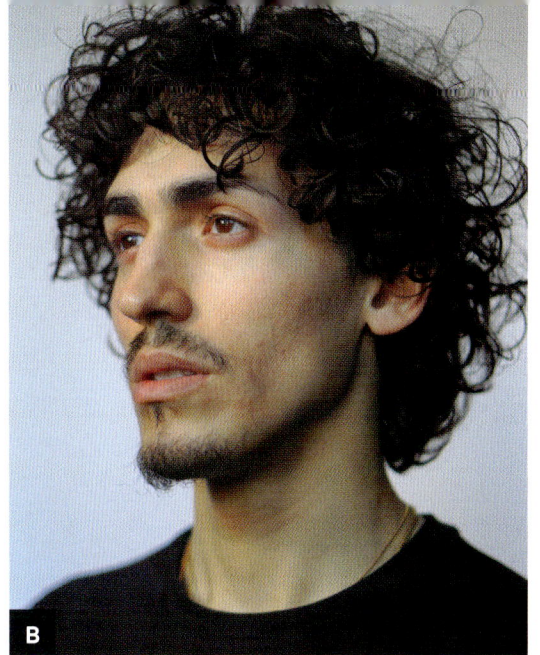

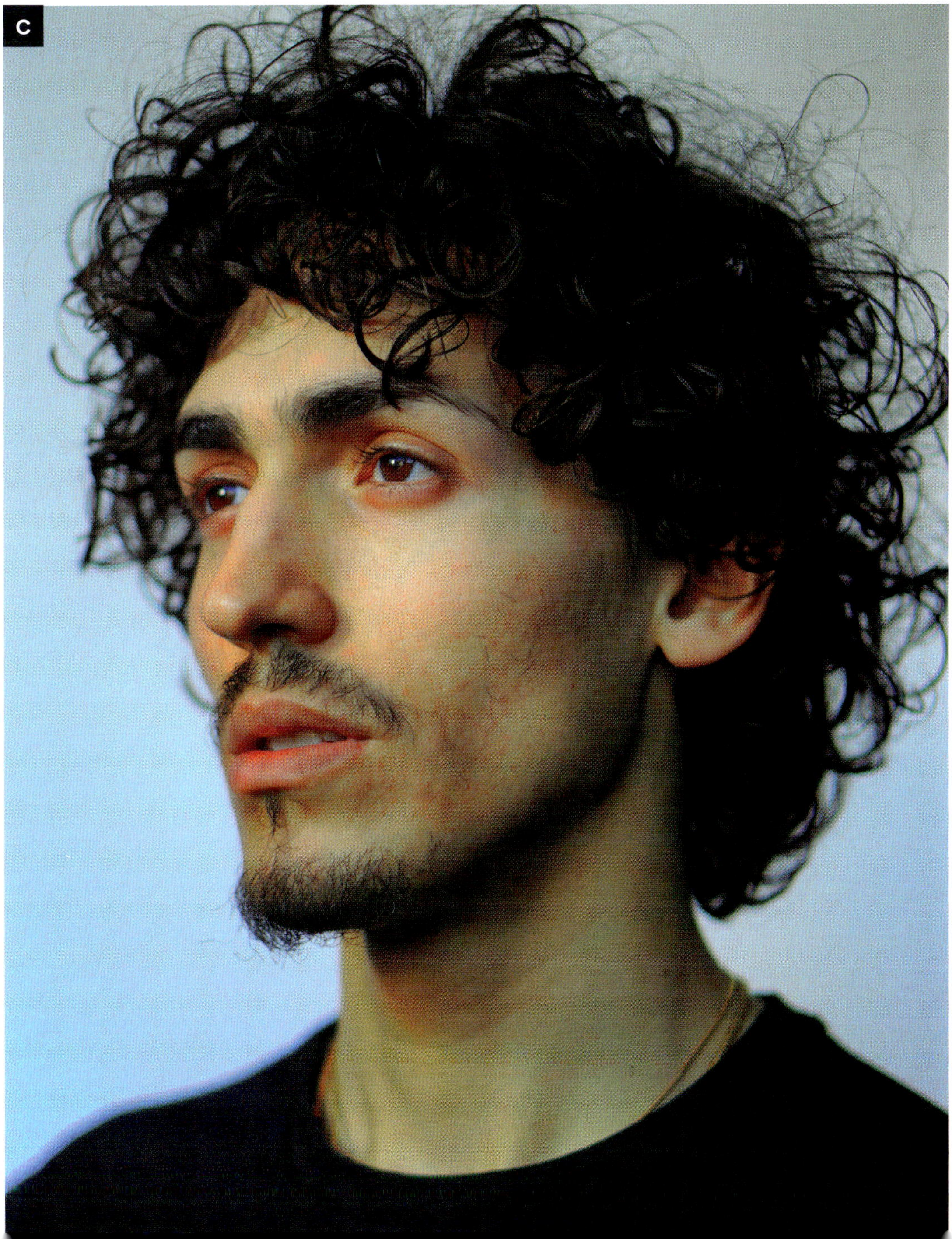

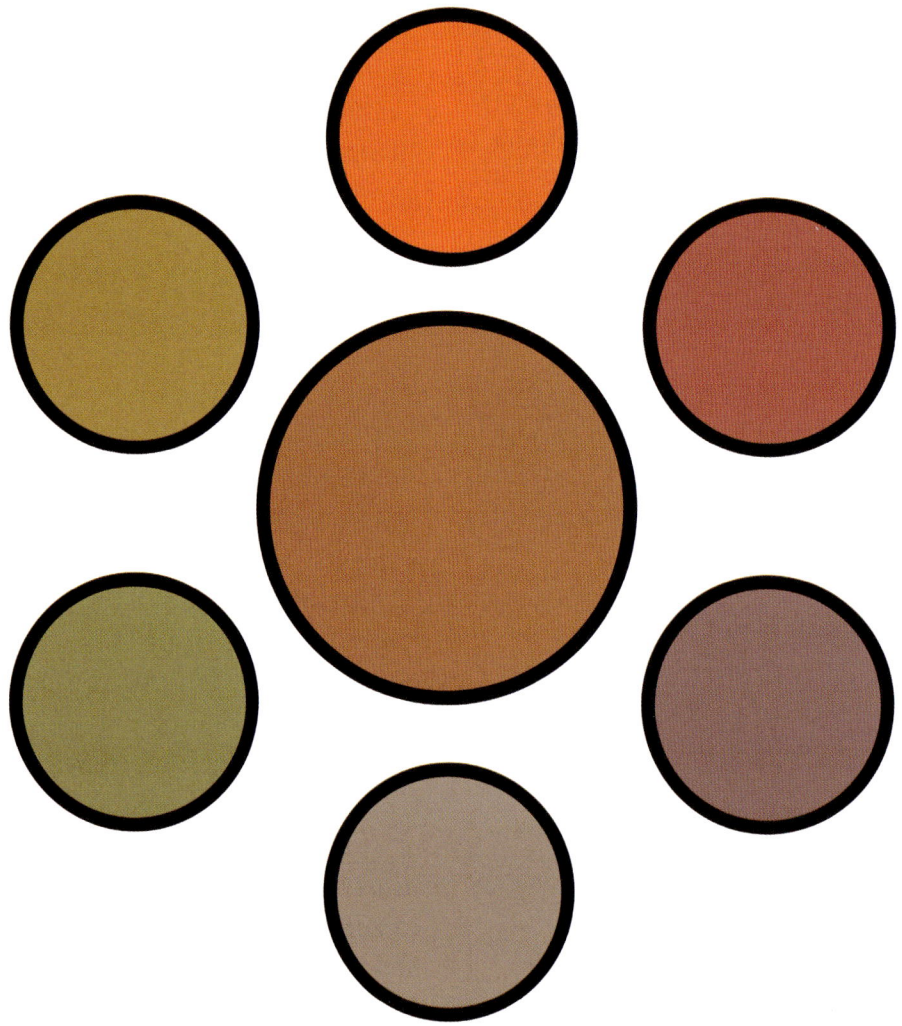

A WAY OF THINKING ABOUT HOW TO CREATE COLOR DIVERSITY ON THE PALETTE

We've spent some time talking about color diversity and different concepts of it as it relates to our perception of our model, so now it's time to get more practical and clearer with what's happening when you create color diversity within color space and on the palette. The color wheel and chroma square in the three diagrams on page 105, really help you visualize and make the connection between Munsell and flesh tone diversity. Many people who are digital painters, or are familiar with the Photoshop Color Picker, will be able to quickly relate to that color wheel and chroma square. It's a practical way to mix color digitally and intuitively.

This is my number one go-to palette concept for creating diversity off of a local color or a mother color. It's so great to have this concept ingrained in my brain for the times in which either my reference material isn't very colorful or I'm having a difficult time locating the color of my subject.

Scan to view a
video tutorial

DIVERSITY THROUGH CHROMA SHIFT

To create color diversity based on a mother color, the easiest way to start is to shift the chroma of that major color. So for this mother color, being a gray orange, I'd add a more chromatic orange to get a more intense version of the mother color, and I could also add a neutral of the same value of the mother color to get a less intense and desaturated tone moving towards a blue.

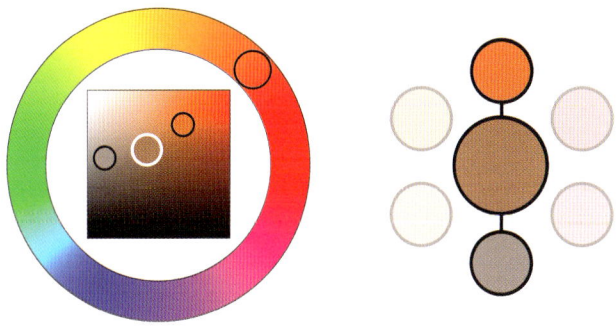

DIVERSITY THROUGH HUE SHIFT

Another way to build out more color diversity is to create a hue shift. Again, taking the mother color, shift it towards red, but don't increase the saturation too much. And then for a second color, take the mother color and shift it towards yellow.

Most flesh tone is generally orange—darker or a lighter version of orange. And sometimes, somebody is more red, orange, or yellow orange. So this same way of creating diversity exists; it just may have a different subtle variation.

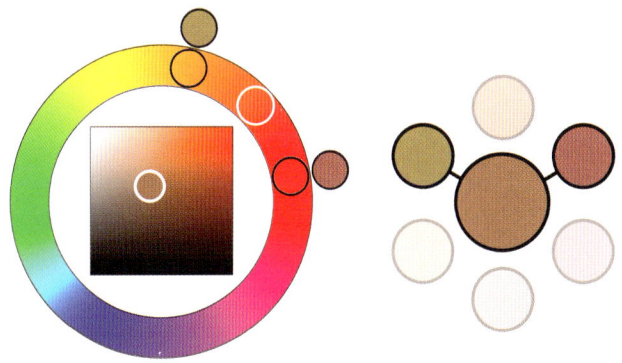

DIVERSITY THROUGH HUE AND CHROMA SHIFT

The last and most complex way of creating color diversity is to do a tone and chroma shift towards the often more subtle and hard to identify colors of flesh tone. If most people have warm flesh tone, say red or orange, then purple and green are often a subtle complement and therefore should not be too saturated. I love the idea of having all of the colors of the rainbow in my flesh tone somewhere. It's just that some of these colors need to be barely identifiable, scarcely noticeable as green or as purple. It's almost more of the context that defines them as those colors than them being perfectly identifiable as those hues. For example, the purple may look purple next to all the other colors, but in fact it might just be a very gray red.

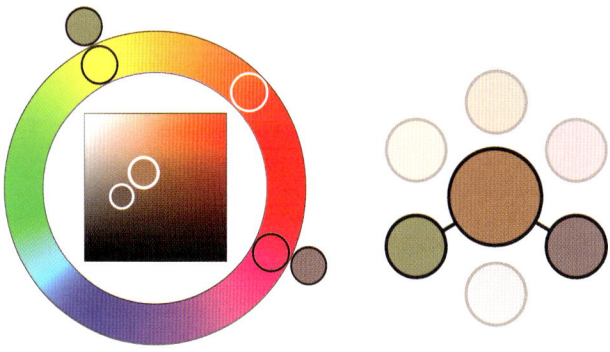

ACHIEVING DYNAMIC RANGE

Undoubtedly, talking about color diversity in isolation of one tone is probably the simplest way to introduce the concept, but there's the tricky issue of getting this concept to attach onto a larger value structure for our painting. As a teacher, I've noticed that color diversity is often first understood in the light and middle tones of the portrait, but then often the darks are neglected and not really considered in the larger range of values in the painting. I'd consider the full-bodied spectrum of light in a painting as having a dynamic range of values. What this means is dark darks, light lights, and colorful middle tones. It's not to say that there aren't extra colors in the lights or in the darks, but that there's a dynamic sense of contrast with the values as a whole and that you don't cheat yourself with the dark range, making sure that those tones are colorful and vibrant.

In order to achieve dark darks that have a sense of chroma, more medium in the darker tones must be used. Darker tones often dry a lighter gray if you use them straight from the tube. If they're really dry looking straight from the tube, they often show up as more dull even as you're painting them wet. So adding a bit of medium to your darks certainly helps, but also having a range of prismatic colors to use in your darks also helps that dynamic range.

Achieving dynamic range also includes making sure your whites are thick enough and clean enough to project a sense of luminosity. Often, that means that they need to be painted thickly (impasto) and have more pure prismatic colors in them, so keep the gray out of the light. If there's no dynamic range in a painting, often the painting can look chalky, which is a result of not having enough darkness and chroma in the darks. Or it results in the painting looking muddy, where the light tones aren't light enough and the dark tones aren't dark enough and because there's no contrast, the tones blend together and the colors get homogenized.

MAKING IT DANCE

If this dynamic of range is achieved, and it is the first priority, then adding color diversity into all of these value ranges to make it dance is the next step. This feeds into the notion that even though we love color and the diversity of it, the larger value structure, once it's established, makes color diversity more easily achieved and is more of a way to finish the painting.

The values lay the foundation, and the color diversity creates the beauty that only color can describe. It's the thing that adds the spark of life to the picture. But if color diversity is achieved before the larger value structure is established, often it becomes undone by placing the correct values on. It's much easier to change the color of a certain value than to change the value of a certain color. That may sound like semantics, but it's true because if you change the value of a certain color, often graying occurs.

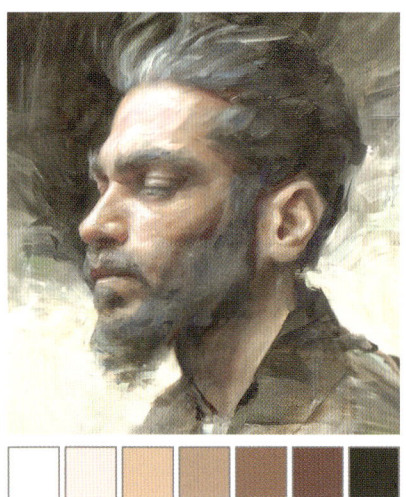

Chalky

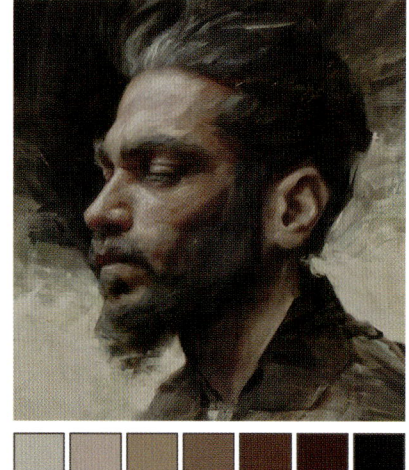

Muddy

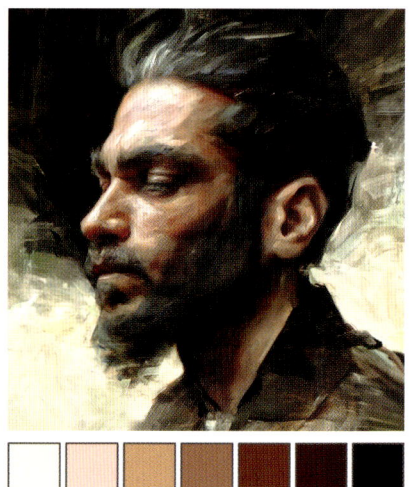

Dynamic Range

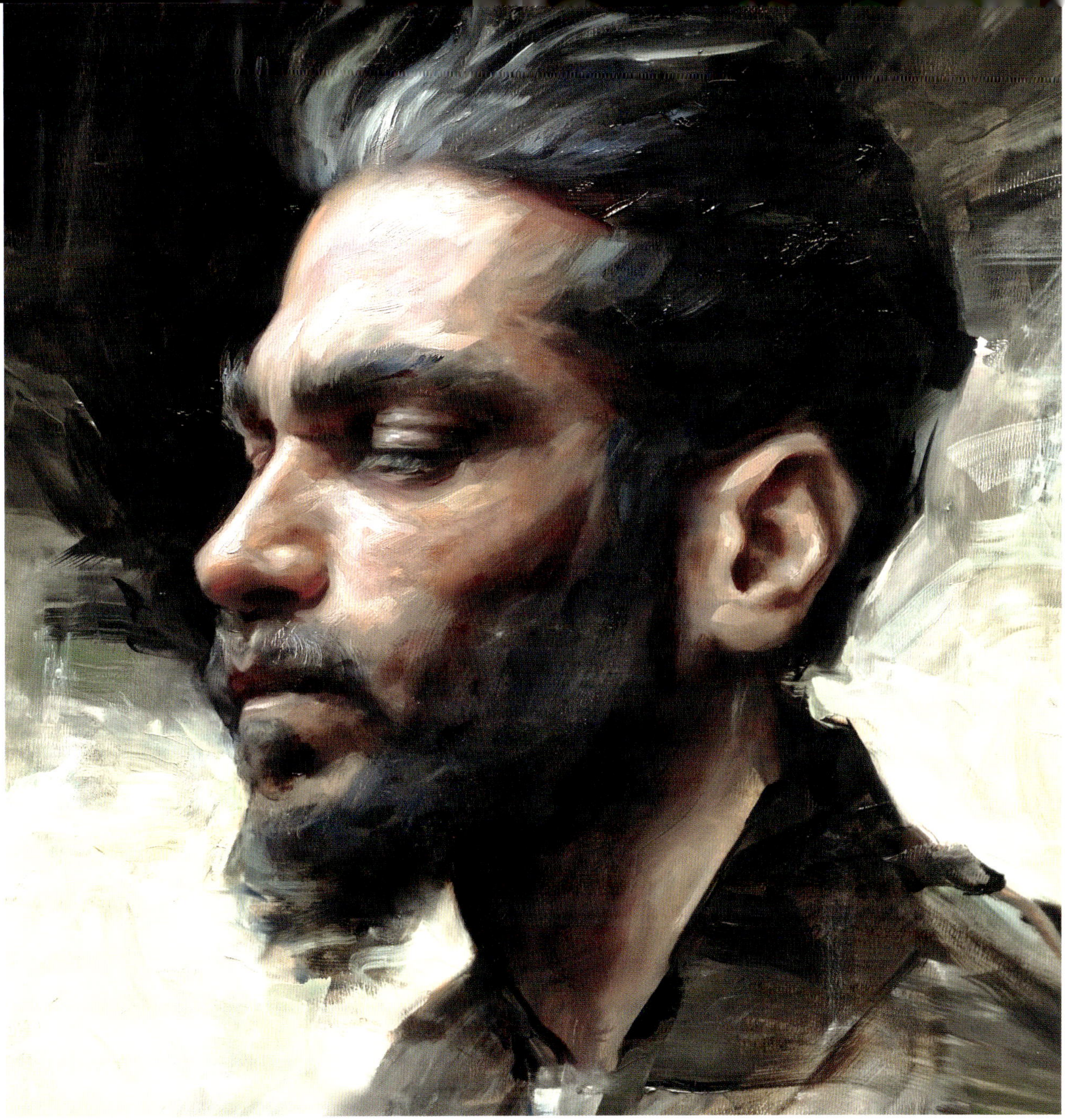

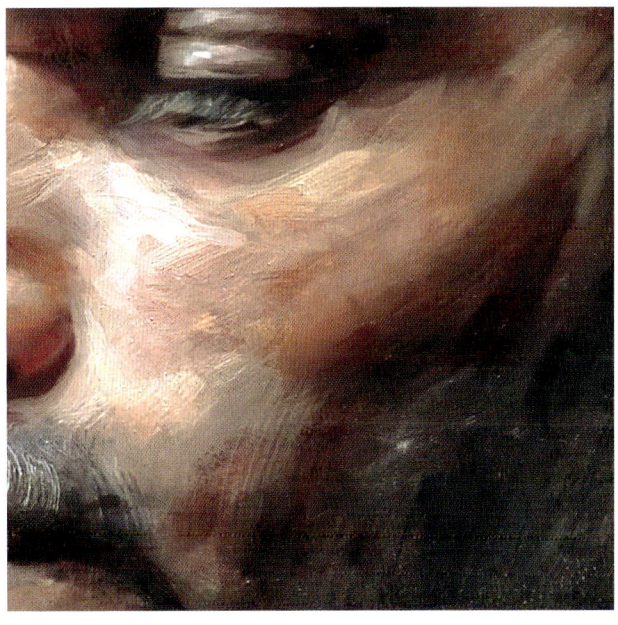

So, establishing a dynamic range and larger value structure allows for freedom and experimentation with a dance of color that fits into a larger scheme holding it together.

Steve Forster, *Ivan*, oil on aluminum,
14" × 18" | 35.6 cm × 45.7 cm

BROKEN COLOR THROUGH A BRISTLE BRUSH

With older skin or skin that has a little bit more texture and variety in it, try painting it directly with a bold bristle brush and have the color variation blend into each other in a rougher manner, as in the painting opposite. The directness and the freshness of this approach is invigorating and exciting to execute. A word of caution though—it does require a lot of continual palette maintenance to keep the colors fresh and subtle enough to be used on the face. Palette maintenance means that you're continually adding to and modifying your mixed colors so that they don't become homogenized and gray as you use them. If you consider your palette as a bank, if you keep making withdrawals, then there won't be any color diversity and variety left. Palette maintenance is continuing to mix and make new deposits of fresh color onto your palette.

Note in the example opposite that that all of these tiny strokes have not been blended. They partially blend into one another, just by virtue of the fact that all of the color notes are being painted into one another. This idea should not be underrated. Those who like a more lively paint surface may need to break the addiction of over-blending, and a great way to break yourself of this habit is to *never* blend! Rather, always paint one color tile into another color tile, and with the use of a bristle brush, this "blends" those tones as you lay them down next to each other. They don't need your help. In fact, often the reason why we blend tones in the first place is because they're the wrong color, so to compensate, we smush them together. If you shift your focus to putting down the right value and the right color to begin with and keep layering and layering, then the blending often just takes care of itself. It's no longer the major focus of the work at hand.

BROKEN COLOR THROUGH GLAZING

On a smoother face such as the one featured in the painting on page 110, putting in flesh color diversity and/or broken color is made much more achievable through glazing. A smoother face requires blending and lots of transitions that stretch out the color. If you paint directly wet to wet, these subtle variations often get blended away and evaporate through the blending process. This can be disheartening because as hard as you work on putting down all these individual colors, if you blend them to create the smoother face, all of your beautiful colors will become homogenized.

One of the ways around this is to almost not even really focus on color initially, but focus on drawing values and painting a beautiful face. Then, when that's dry, now you go about creating color diversity with tiny little spot glazes that then are blended into the face seamlessly on separate days.

You can go about tweaking and modifying the face color with small glazes for many sessions, and in fact, this is a terrific way to continue to work on a painting after the majority of it's been painted well.

There can be more than just tweaks to the midtones; brighten your lights by using a more transparent white (such as lead white) and enhance your darks with deeper color to create more form.

▸ Steve Forster, *Nick*, oil and charcoal on aluminum, 14" × 18" | 35.6 cm × 45.7 cm

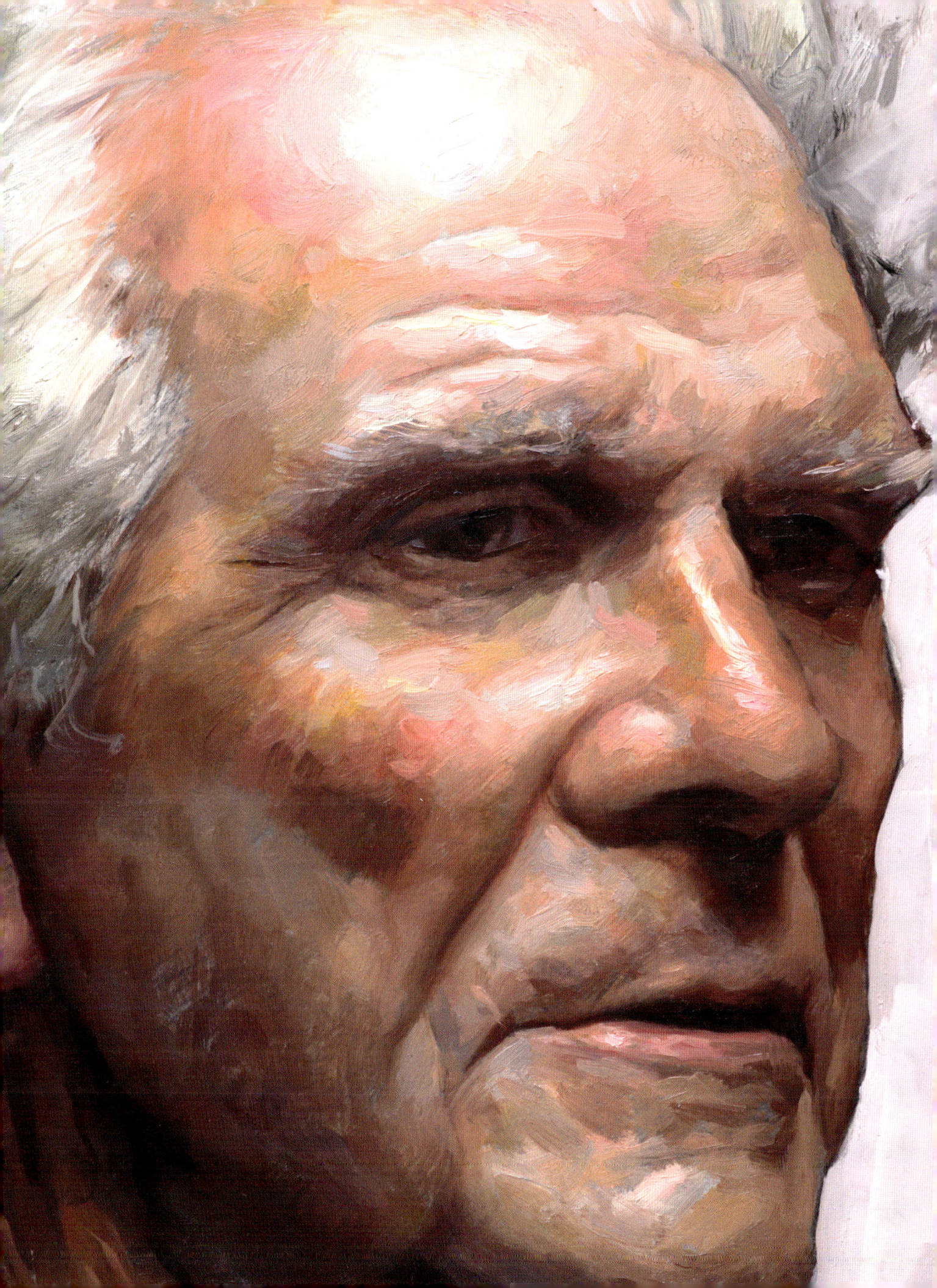

CREATING A FLESH PALETTE MATRIX

The central flesh color mixing idea of this book is to get familiar with the process of building a color matrix for your flesh tone—building a flesh palette that gets progressively more complicated and nuanced as it goes on. You'll get acquainted with how to start off with the basic major scale of colors, that then influences and helps control the variety and diversity that flows from the central core of tones. I know of no other way that's more effective for getting a full range of values and a beautiful set of diverse colors all based on a central core complexion tone, or mother color.

THE MAJOR SCALE

The first and most crucial step to building your color matrix is starting with a simple light to dark string that acknowledges the color of the light, the mother color, and the darkest dark. The mother color is the average flesh tone that isn't the lightest, nor the darkest, and it's the central complexion tone on which you must focus. Getting a large pile of mother color and really spending your time getting this right will influence the rest of your decisions. The color of the light isn't necessarily the mother color plus white, but try to see if there's another hue that it can bend towards to make things more interesting. The darkest dark isn't necessarily black. Try to find a color within that darkest dark, such as cadmium red plus black or alizarin crimson and ultramarine blue.

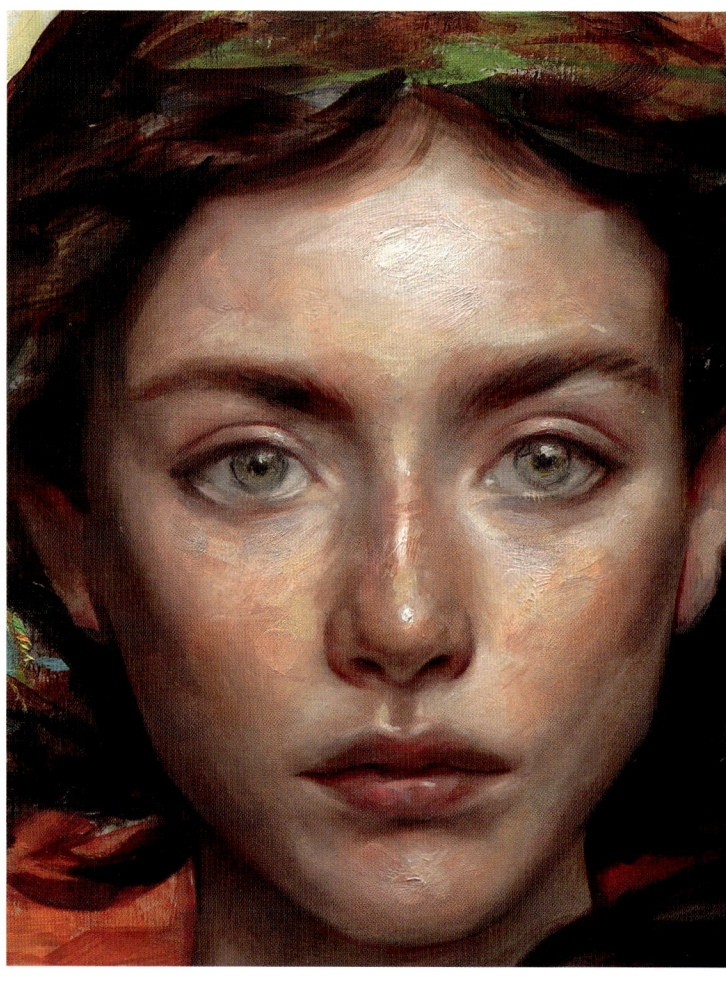

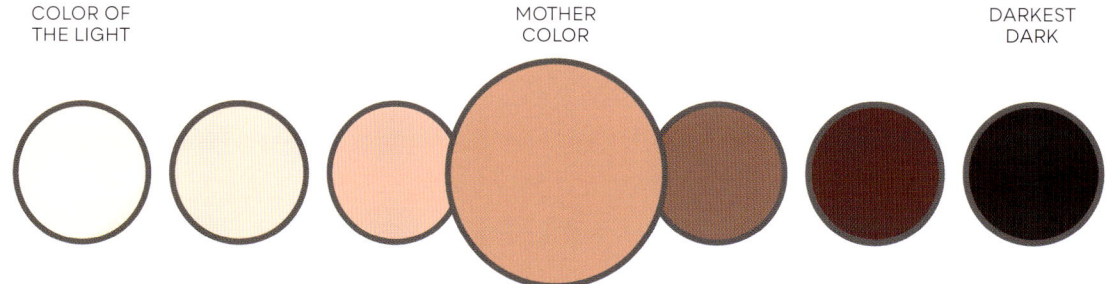

COLOR OF
THE LIGHT

MOTHER
COLOR

DARKEST
DARK

THE WINGS

Once the major scale has been established, build out variations on the wings of that string. Typically, it's safe to say that most people are in the orange family, whether they're a lighter or darker version of orange. Therefore, one of the preliminary wings should probably be in the reddish family, and the other wing should probably be in the yellowish-gray family. I say reddish because sometimes this red can be red orange, red, or red violet. I say yellowish because it can mean yellow orange, yellow, or even yellow green.

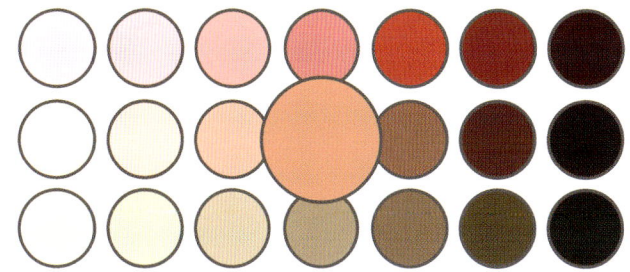

BUILDING IT OUT FURTHER

Usually, if the main string and the preliminary wings are built out, that's often enough variation, but in some cases, it's nice to add even more and build out your flesh tone to have extra variations. This could be a background color that starts influencing the skin tone or some other special circumstance in which the flesh tone is very colorful or even has a bit of all of the colors of the rainbow. Setting up your palette this way can inspire you to see colors that you might not have seen before. This structure, however complicated looking, gives you an excellent framework to sensitively perceive color.

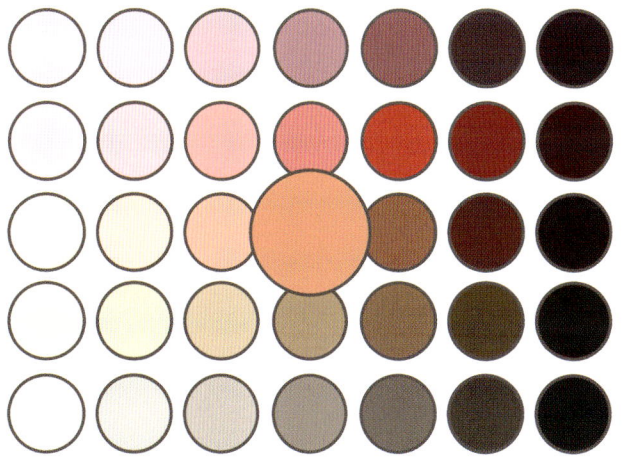

PALETTES ARE MESSY

With all of this planning and explaining about the many variations of flesh tone based on the main string of color, let's be real and acknowledge that the palette is often organized chaos and will probably end up looking like the one at right. This is what a palette often looks like when I'm actually in the process of painting—not a sterile, pristine example. The goal in the previous illustrations of the color matrix isn't to expect you to create perfectly arranged tones of color, but to show a target to hit, even if it gets messy in the process.

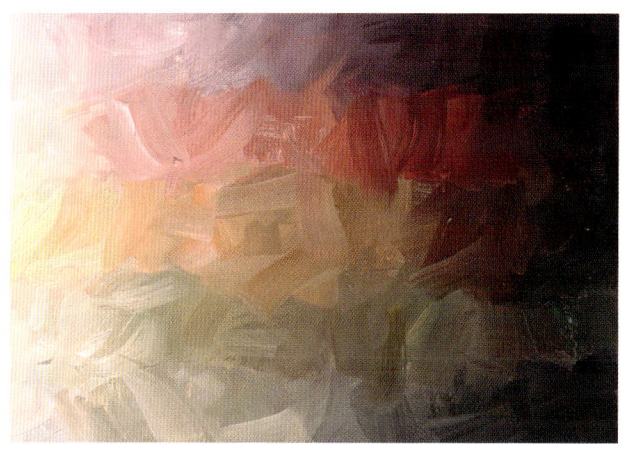

SITUATIONAL VARIATIONS ON FLESH PALETTE MATRIX

The flesh palette matrix has many situational variations, including those of all the different skin complexions that you can paint. Let's pause here and demonstrate how this general idea of a palette matrix can have many different situations that it attaches to, including various lighting situations that involve filters such as assorted

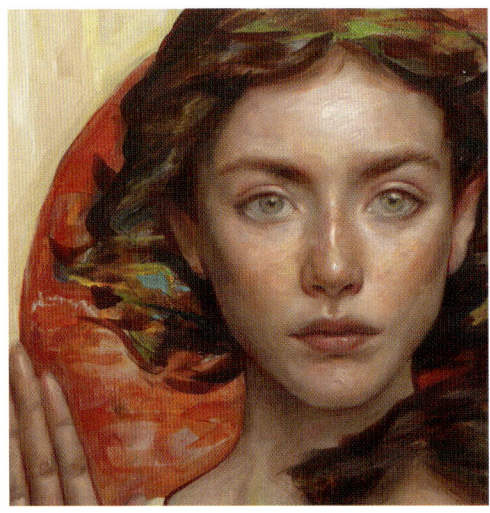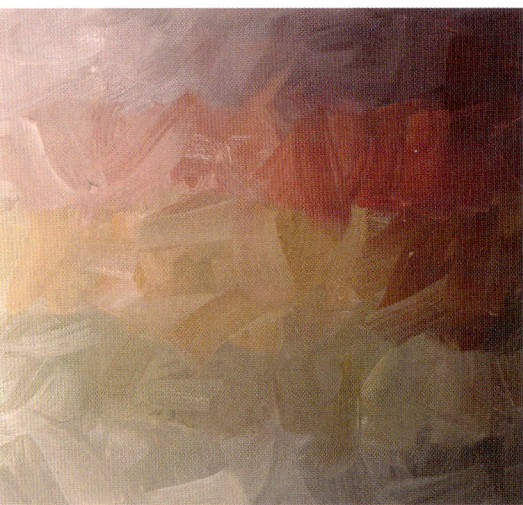

PALE

In this variation, notice that the overall tones are slightly grayer, and there's a limitation to how light the highlights get and how dark the darks get. Even so, there are still variations in skin tone. The reds, purples, greens, and yellows can still be seen through this slightly dustier lens.

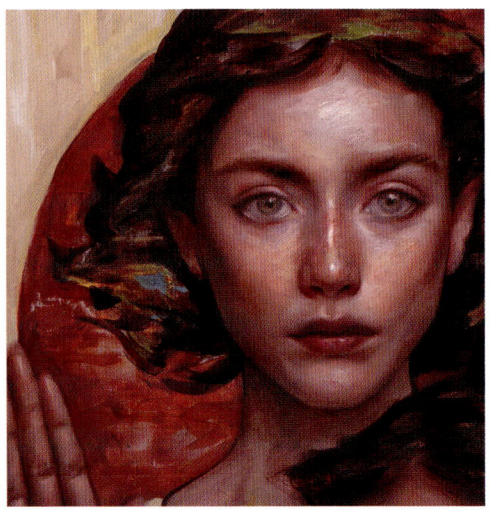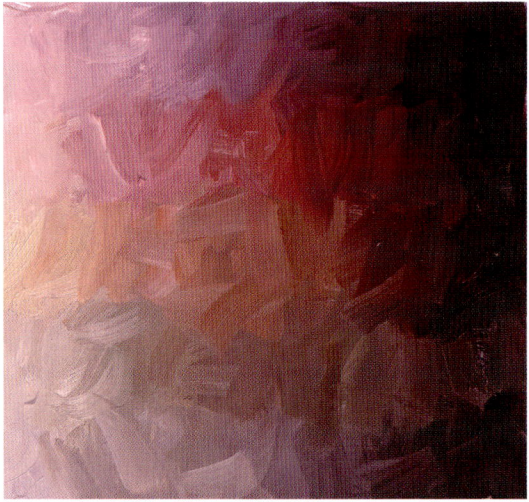

DARK

This darker and more purple version of the image still manages to hold onto the green, the red, the yellow, and the purple. If your image has a lighting situation like this, you may find that painting a global glaze over the whole painting can set this darker tone, and then you can paint nuance and diversity into it.

colors of light, as well as more saturated versions of normal colors. Your reference may have different characteristics and mood shifts depending upon the environment. Often, these situations can throw you for a loop because they inflict their will upon the flesh tone and turn it into something that isn't expected. The lesson here is that there's diversity even within these strong environments.

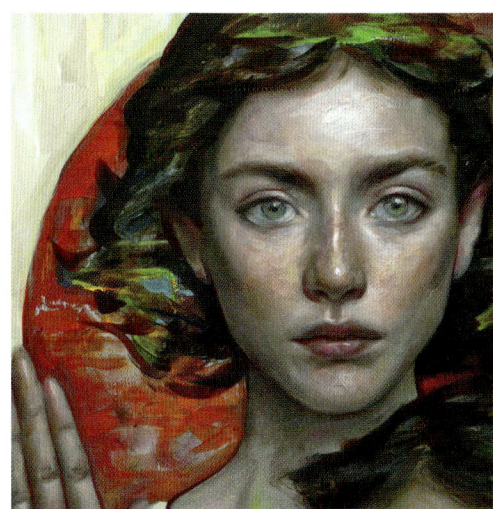 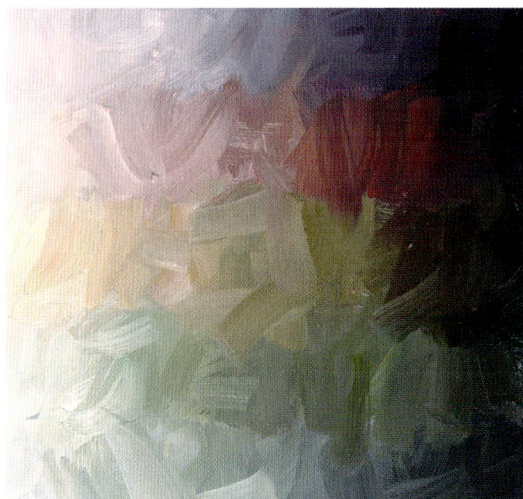

COLD

The mother color in this image might not be anything we'd think should be a normal flesh tone. It's a somber gray-green-yellow. What prevents images like this from lacking life is the variety of the other flesh tones, even within this cold lighting situation.

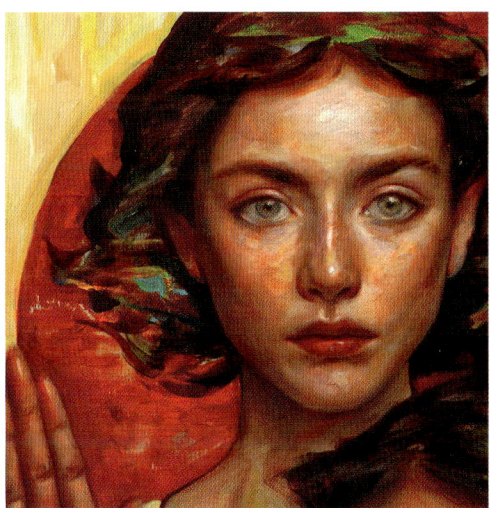 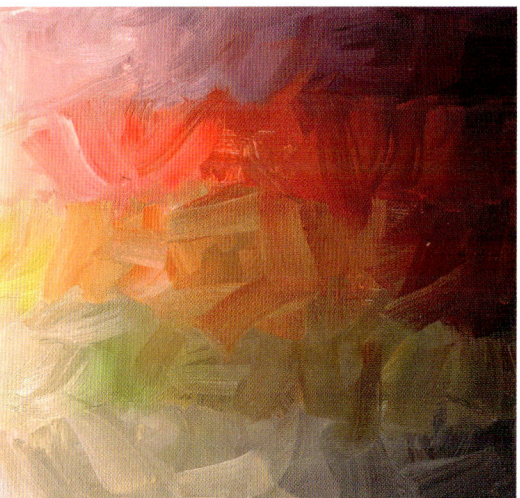

SATURATED

Even as the tones open up and become much more distinct and vibrant, there's still a diversity that makes the flesh tones dance and have variety. Without those subtle greens, purples, and grays, this easily would turn into an orange face, and the portrait wouldn't succeed.

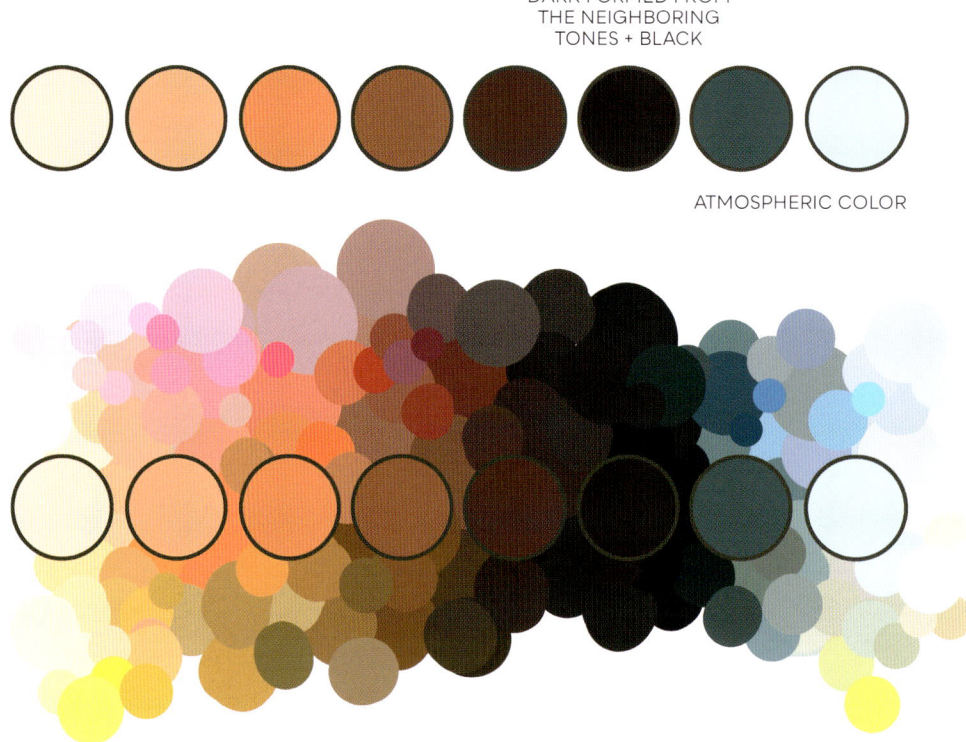

DARK FORMED FROM
THE NEIGHBORING
TONES + BLACK

ATMOSPHERIC COLOR

ADDING BACKGROUND TONES

Even while explaining that a flesh palette matrix is a messy thing and showing the variety of tones within it, I have to admit that it can get even messier and have several other variations that can expand it. For instance, I like to include a bit of the background (atmospheric) tone. This is a way to balance out the major scale of flesh tone. First, I'll mix the major scale flesh tone colors. Then, I'll include two more steps beyond the dark flesh tone that show the background tone and then make a slightly darker version of that atmospheric color that I can integrate and flow into the flesh tone. This gives a sense of balance to the colors and an overall acknowledgment of the environment. I can make a new darkest dark by mixing that darker environmental tone with the darkest shadow tone of the flesh. In this way, my darkest dark can be formed by elements of the environment and the flesh, rather than just mixing an arbitrary black color, thereby bringing consequential color into the darkest darks that connects to the rest of the painting in a unifying way.

CREATING A FLESH COLOR FIESTA

A "flesh color fiesta" just means anything goes color-or-wise, but there's a method to the madness. These colors are organized around the major scale of tone that incorporates the atmospheric color, opposite. Setting up the palette around that major scale of tone provides some amount of organization to the wild color that could occur in a painting. I like to display all of these dots and variations to show you how messy and varied the palette can become when you're actually mixing colors. Sometimes, the values are too dark or too colorful or too gray, and that's okay! It adds to the fun of finding more colors than perhaps are actually in your reference. If you have enough time to mix these colors, it's a wonderful way to inspire you to paint. How fun would it be if, at the beginning of the day before you paint, you can quickly and efficiently mix something approximating this flesh color fiesta—how inspirational it would be for you in your paintings, allowing for so much color creativity while still maintaining organization, purpose, and order!

Scan to view a
video tutorial

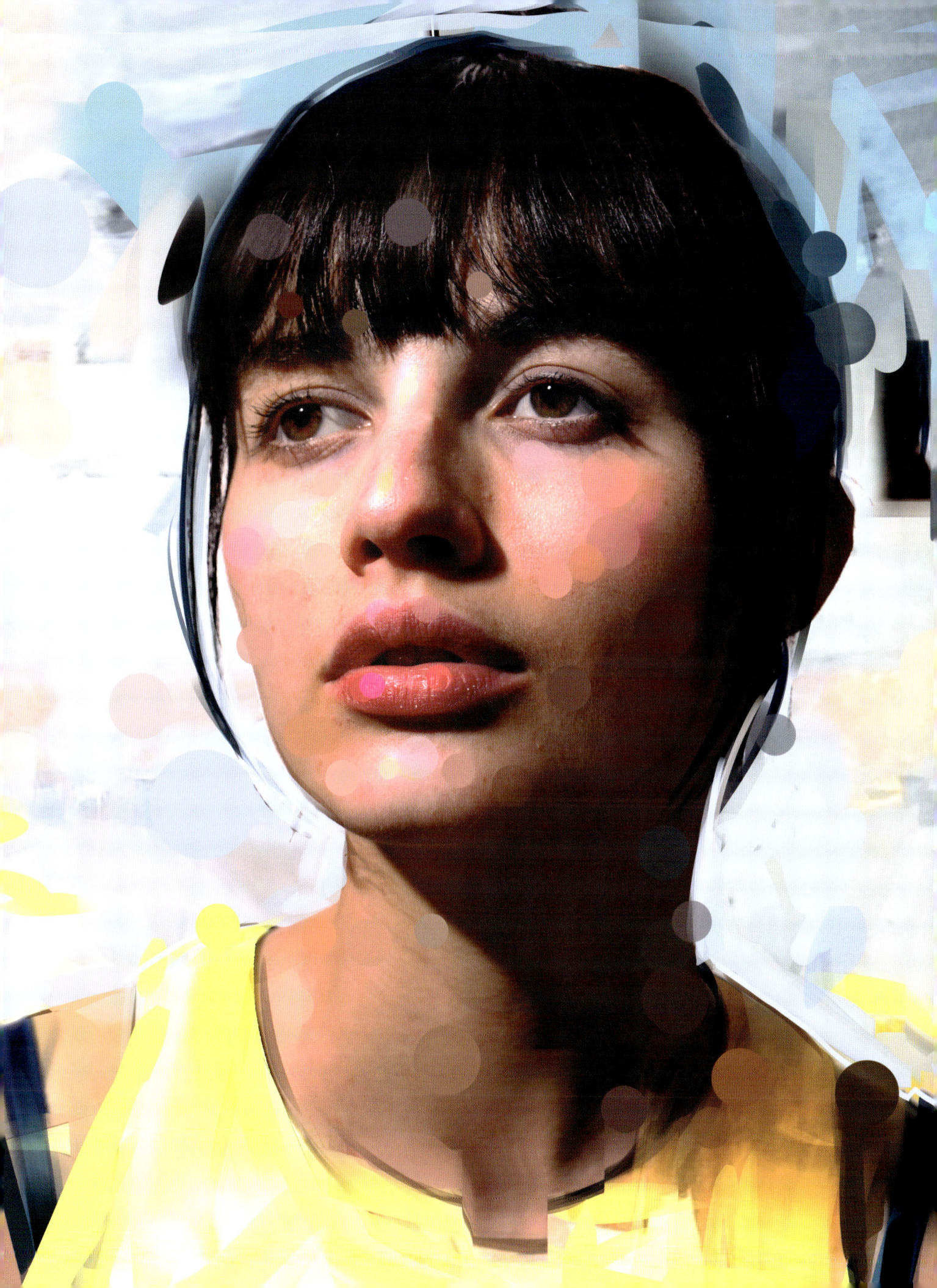

COLOR FLOWERS

As we've now seen color diversity on a simple scale with one color and also color diversity with the flesh palette matrix, we'll now think about a painting in terms of zones that have their own mother color with color diversity, which I call *color flowers*. The painting opposite can be broken apart into four major zones: the hair and shadow, the flesh tone, the greenery, and the lighter teal tone that makes up the sky and the shirt.

Before we even get into the diversity of those zones, consider that designing a painting with three, four, or five consistent shapes (zones) is a good design principle that helps organize a painting with graphic clarity—even though there's a lot of overlap and blending in a painting so that the zones may not be immediately obvious. Nevertheless, keep zones in mind so that your painting doesn't become muddy from lack of value organization. A great way to practice this is to do Notan or marker sketches to jot down your design ideas and understand where the major shapes and zones of value are in your painting.

If your painting has been designed to have these zones, then getting a mother color assigned to each zone allows you to then explore color diversity within that given value of the mother color. For example, if we only had one tone to block in the hair, it would probably be a very dark gray. But then there would be all of these accents and deviations within that dark gray, including black, maroon, dark blue, and even green. So, creating a zone from this dark hair allows me to borrow other colors from other areas in the painting and tie it all together; if there's a green somewhere else in the painting, I can also represent that green within the dark zone of the hair, as long as it doesn't get too light. Or if there's a blue somewhere else in the painting, I can take that blue and have it represented within the dark zone of the hair as well. I can be creative with the hair color as long as it doesn't overall lighten it to the point in which it ceases being dark. The same can be said for the flesh. Overall, there's a warmth to it, but you'll also find cooler tones, yellow tones, and even some green snuck in here and there.

On the palette, instead of having such a clean organizational matrix like the flesh color matrix, we use these color flowers to fit into these major zones and create variations of the zone's main tone. This palette strategy gives you the ability to not only just paint the flesh, but also gives you ways to conceive of the other main shapes in the painting.

Rather than getting hung up on flesh tone alone, color flowers bring diversity into all areas of the painting in an organized way. I find this a useful way to always be thinking value in relationship to color. As you may notice in all of the color flowers, the value I've chosen doesn't go too much darker or too much lighter off of that main tone. That is some of the secret code to creating iridescent color that is fresh and vibrant—don't try to create too much light and dark texture in your color flowers, but rather only show what only color can show above.

▶ Steve Forster, *Detail of Chyna (Pass Through Light)*, oil and charcoal on aluminum, 24" × 24" | 61 cm × 61 cm

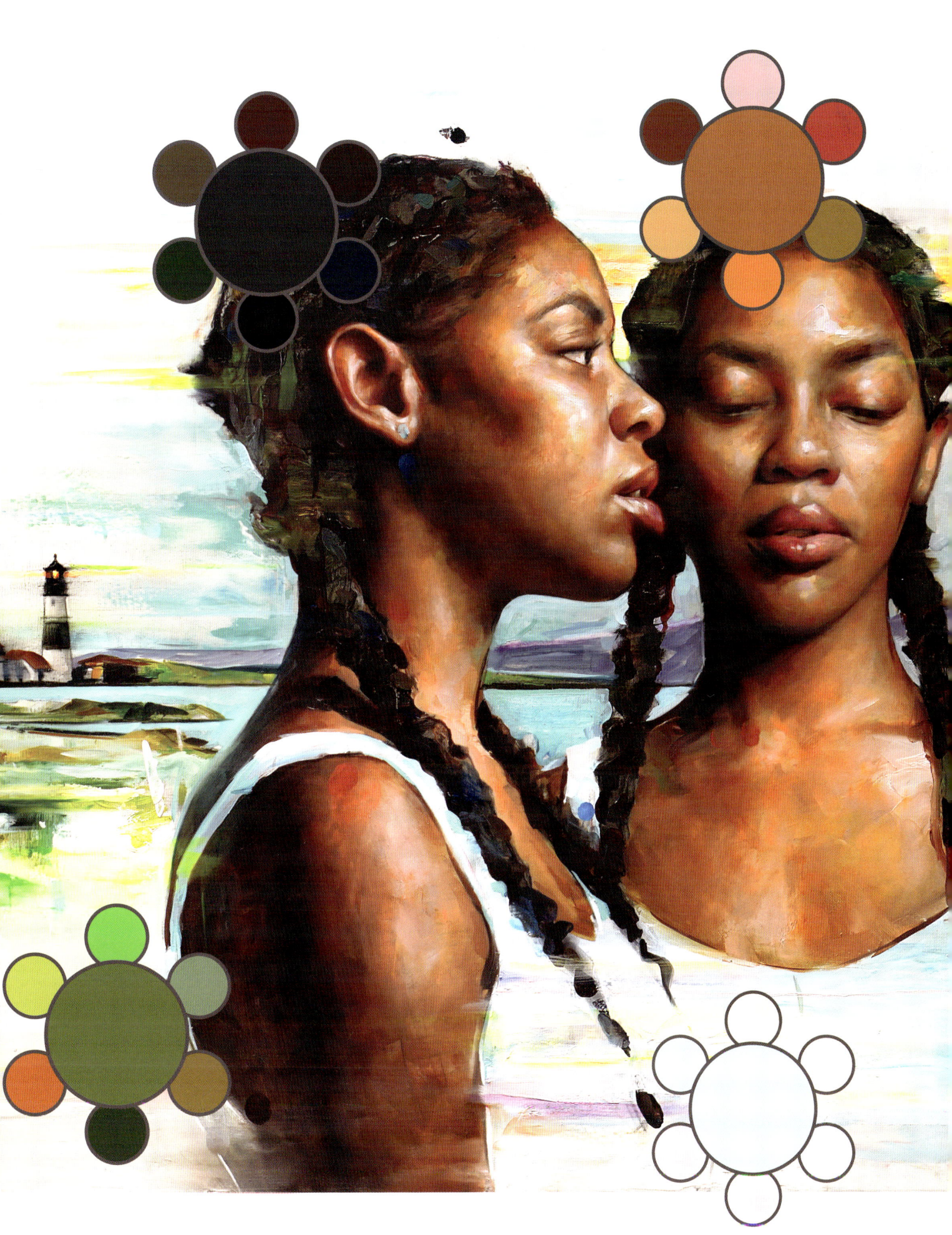

7 | ALTERNATIVE TECHNIQUES IN PAINTING

UNDERPAINTING TECHNIQUE

As has been previously said, the main technique put forth in this book is to create a solid drawing, seal it, put on an ébauche, and paint up the painting. However, there are a lot of different roads to Rome, and with there being so many different ways to paint, we need to at least represent a few of them here because each one of them teaches you something unique and powerful about painting.

Since the majority of this book is dedicated to color and luminosity, we won't spend much time with the underpainting technique opposite, which is really just a variation of the underdrawing technique I previously demonstrated.

The first step is rubbing a tone over the canvas or panel, preferably with a small amount of medium or mineral spirits, but I caution against using too much **(A)**. It's a fine line between applying enough paint and using too much medium. Typically, I have a small piece of a T-shirt or a rag, I dip it into the medium slightly, then dip it into the paint, and rub the mixture over the entire surface. You should use a general middle tone that you find interesting and helpful for the overall appearance of the painting. This is commonly represented as brown or gray, as in a grisaille technique, but there are many different colors that could be used, including green. Here, I've chosen this purple-gray tone.

The next step is to roughly paint out the main angles of the head with a small brush **(B)**. Try to do this with straight lines, going point to point from the major angles of the portrait. I try to think first with line, and then tone starts to fill in the boundaries I created with line, and then I go back-and-forth between these to draw the rest of the face. In Figure **(C)**, see the new lines in the various important points of the features (more line), and then we rub out the light tones with a rag instead of using paint (more tone). This technique is also known as a rub-out painting.

The last stage is just repeating these steps again and again with increasing clarity, so there continues to be new lines for the dreadlocks and new areas of light for the highlights, followed by more extreme darks and lights—but still no white paint **(D)**. To get a light accent without using white paint, I sometimes use a cotton swab dipped in mineral spirits. The reason why I don't want to use white paint right now is that if you'd like to transition to color on the first day, then the wet white starts to mix into your colors. If instead you use mineral spirits to pull off the color tone of the canvas, it starts to set up and dry so that you can still get into the painting on the first day. If you plan on separating these two layers and just making an underpainting for now, then it really doesn't matter.

When you do not use white in a rub-out painting, it's known as an open grisaille, and if you start using white, it's called a closed grisaille. The benefit of an open grisaille is that you can easily transition to color on the same day. The benefit of a closed grisaille is that you get a little bit more control within this monochromatic expression of the face because it can be difficult to control the light on the face when all you can do is wipe away.

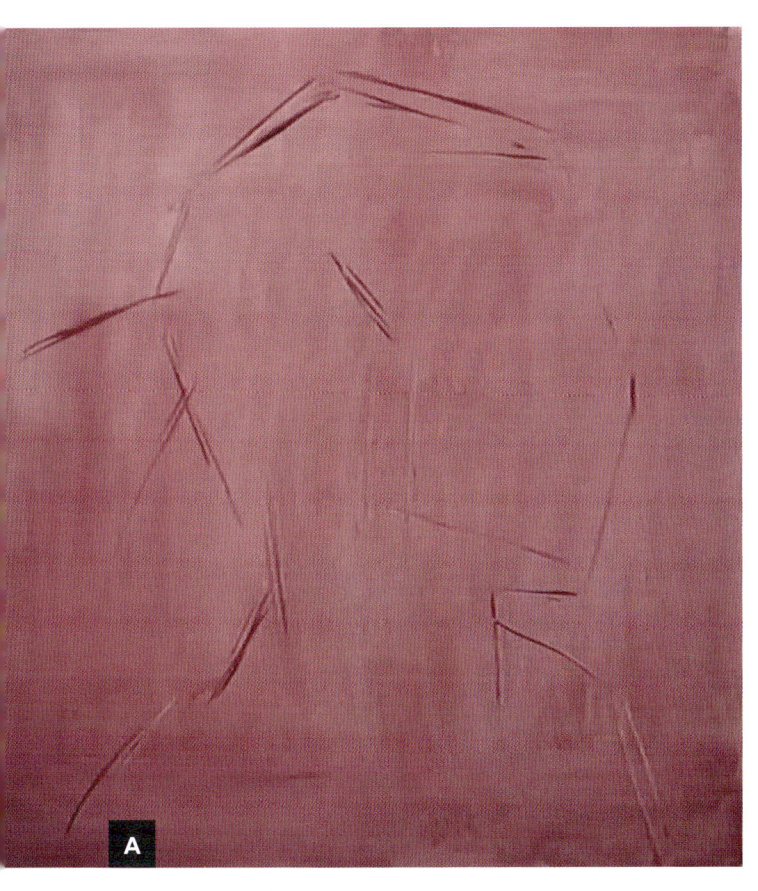

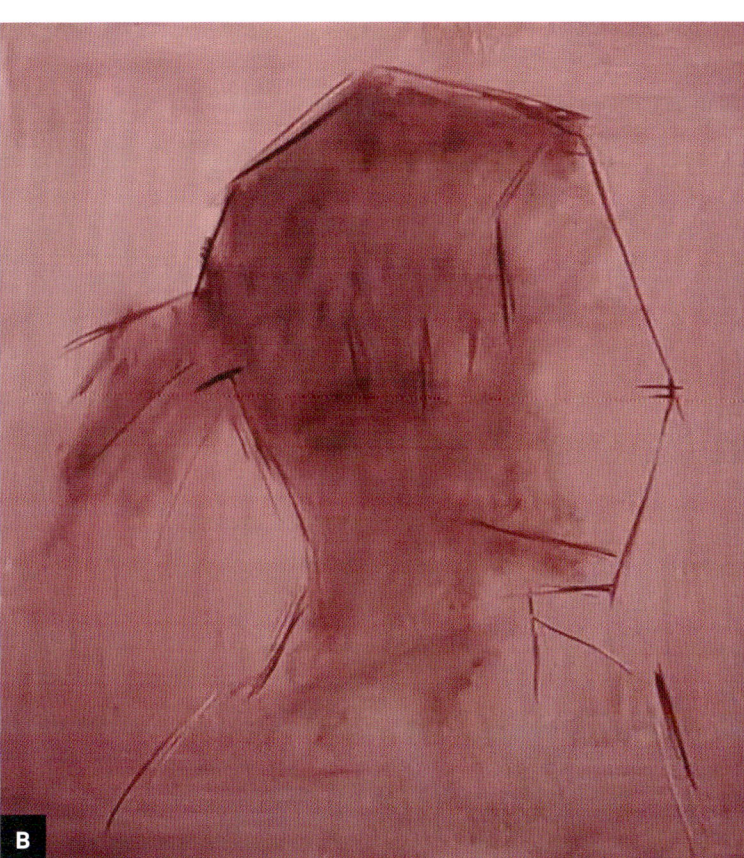

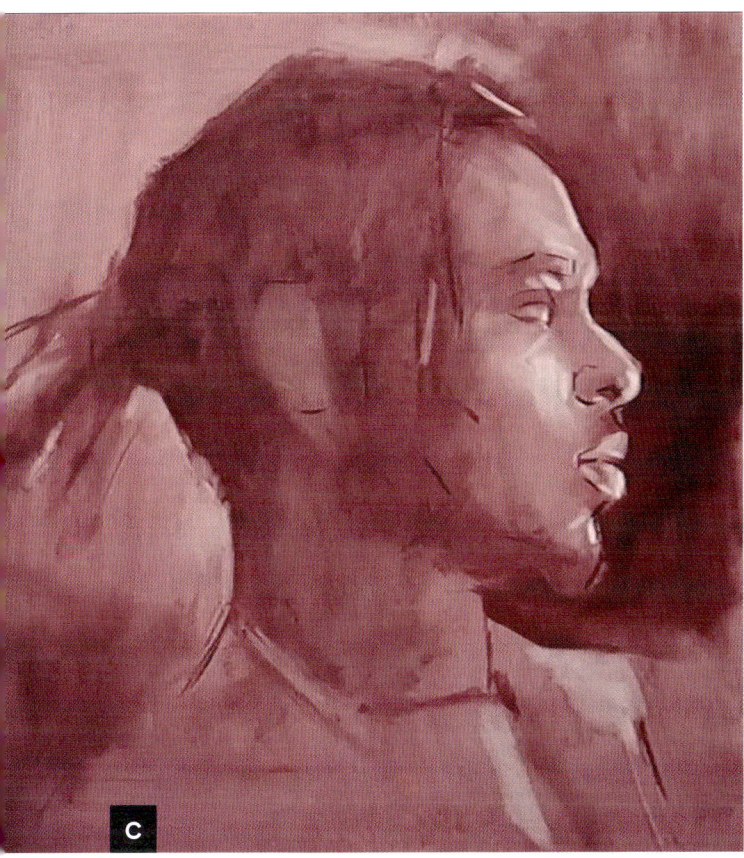

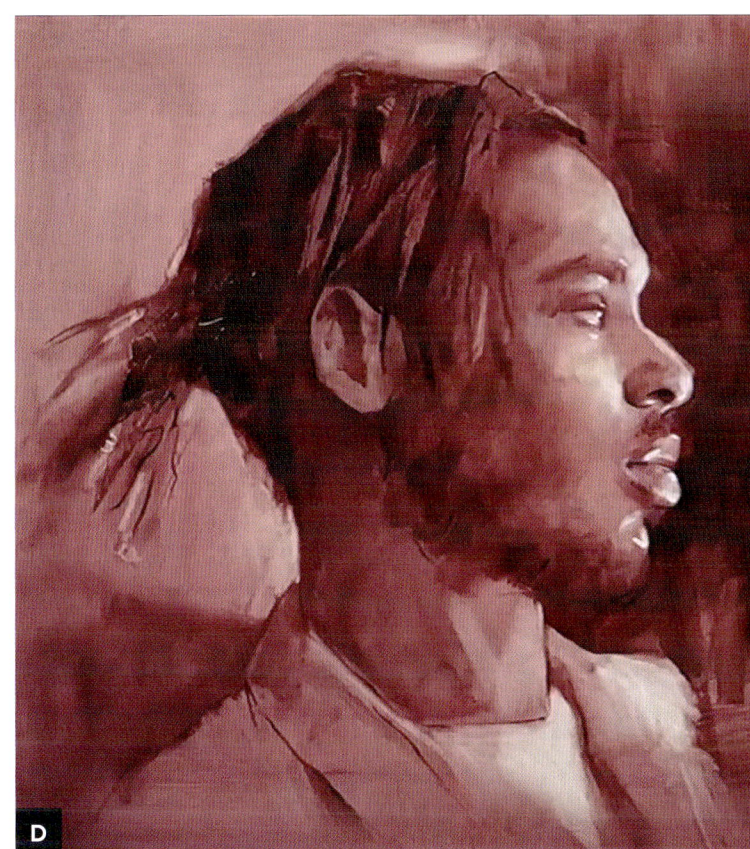

DEMONSTRATION:
COLOR SPOT PAINTING

In fifteen years of teaching painting, I've often been asked "How do I get better at mixing color?" This is probably the best exercise I've created for teaching color and value mixing in painting. There's almost no blending at all in this project. Blending or softening often truly hinders our progress of hitting the right color notes; therefore, attempting to make a painting without blending at all will help us not run away from the problem of actually trying to mix the right color in the right relationship to the colors around it.

MAJOR SCALE

Beginning with the major scale, we start with a mother color, but then shifting towards the color of the light, we have many hue variations. This is because the model is by a window, and there's a yellow light hitting the under-planes of the face and a blue violet light coming from the sky that hits the forehead. From there, we descend into a darker redder tone for the shadow on his face, and then through the dark hair, into the bluish shirt, and finally atmosphere. Noticing the many subtle hue shifts will definitely make for a more uniquely colorful painting.

VARIATIONS OFF THE MAJOR SCALE

Once the major scale has been established, creating minor variations leads to other colors, helping you to start seeing options and diversities based on your preconceived ideas. If you missed the right colors in the major scale, you're starting to dance around them and get ones that might be more appropriate. The more options that you develop, the more likely you'll see them in your subject.

IT GETS MESSY

While it's nice to start off with the major scale structure, undoubtedly, it'll get messy! You're working with these colors and also searching, constantly coming up with new mixtures. Don't feel as if your palette is a place for perfection—but for organized chaos.

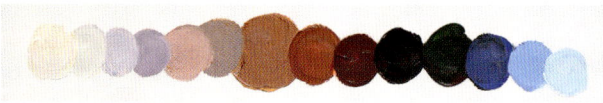

Major scale

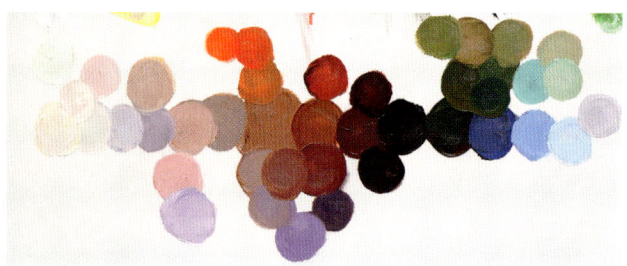

Variations off the major scale

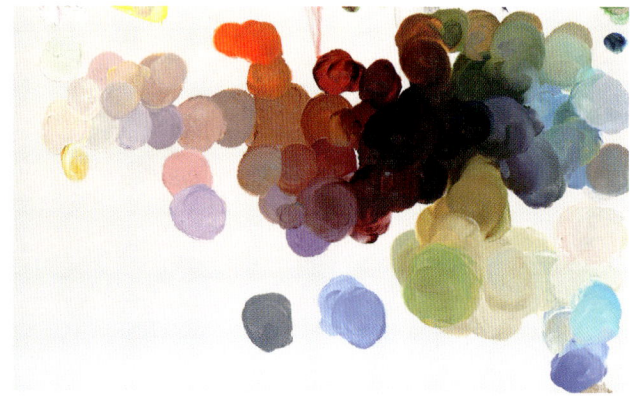

It gets messy

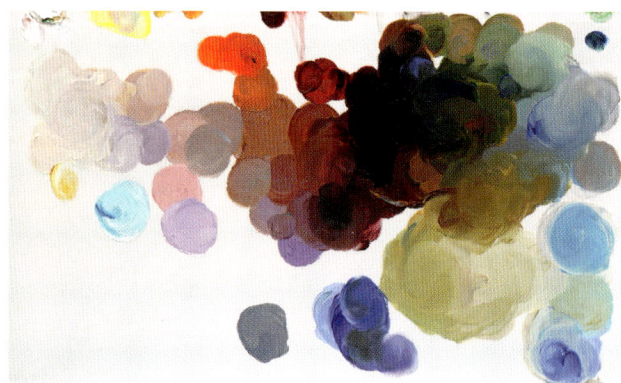

Keeping it going

▶ Steve Forster, *Fradin*, oil on aluminum, 16" × 16" | 15.2 cm × 15.2 cm

Scan to view a video tutorial

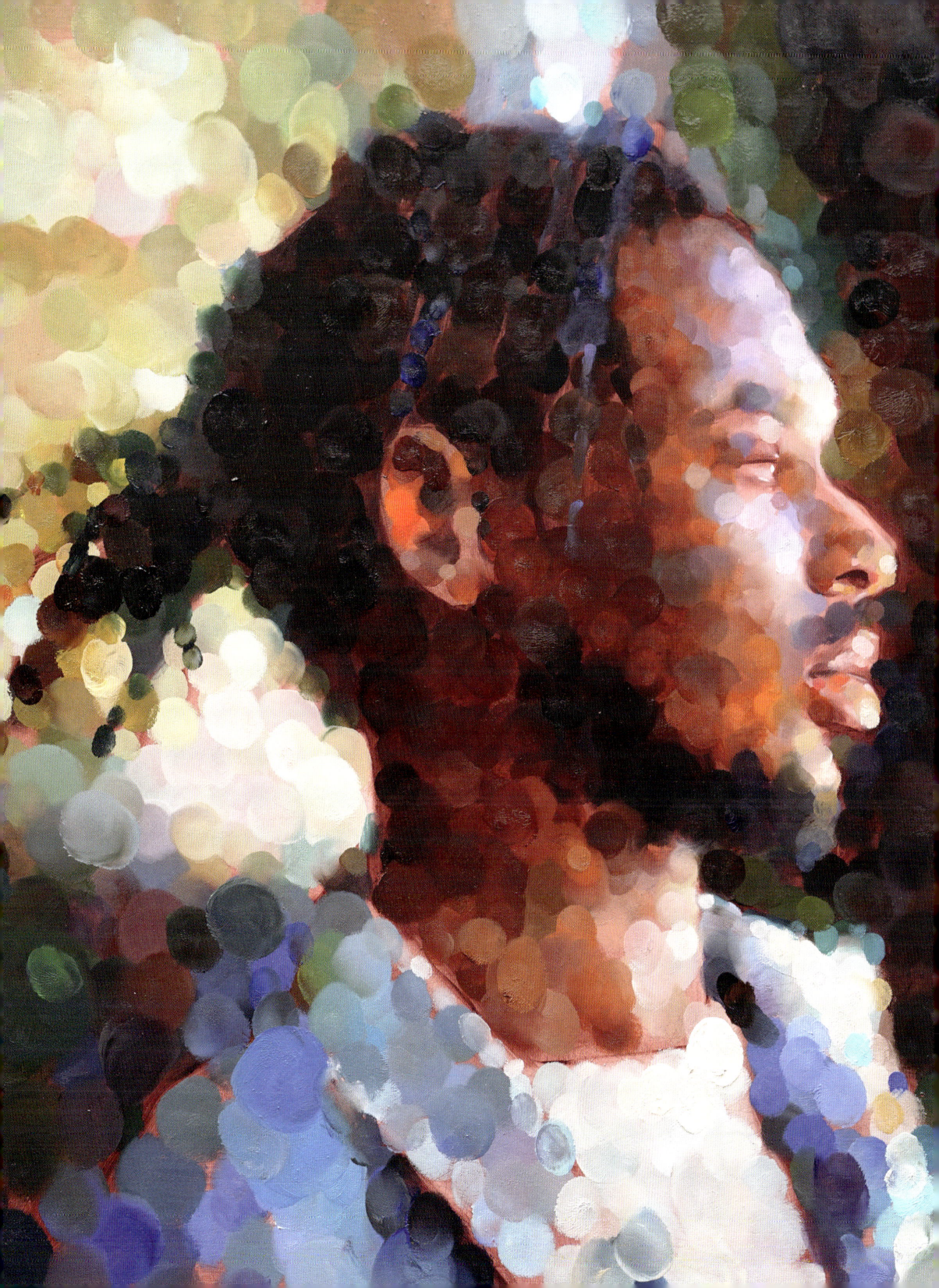

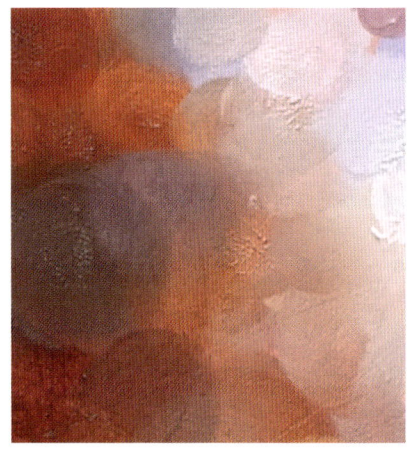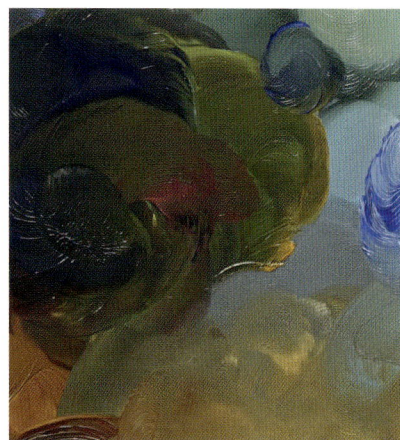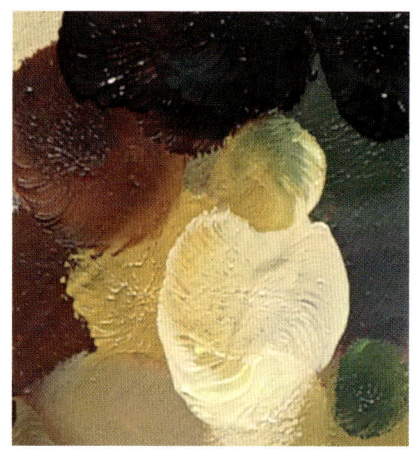

MARBLEIZING COLOR

This dot painting exercise can be taken to a higher level where you begin to marbleize the paint. That's the term for what happens when you have layer upon layer of wet paint, and there begins to be a swirling liveliness of unblended color. If you look at the series of images below, you'll notice how not only does each new stroke of the color "blend" with the previous one, but it also leaves its own trail of unblended color (most obvious on the far right). This effect is known as *marbleizing* because in that single stroke there are many colors. This is a curious thing in painting, especially in illusionistic painting, where we're trying to capture a sense of reality. Usually, when we're trying to create illusion, there's a lot of blending and strokes like this marbleized one never happen. I want to take a moment to pause here and talk about the virtues of continuing to not blend. If you try this color dot exercise, there will come a point in which you're tempted to blend everything away. Just continue layering new dots upon the previous dots to build a sense visual interest and even a color texture. In several of these spots on the face, you begin to see this layered marbleizing happen in the images above.

This technique can be used in many wide applications, even that of illusion. Artists like Nicolai Fechin and digital painters like Mike Hernandez are masters of this technique. Marbleization an extremely useful piece of vocabulary for the painter, especially the oil painter who suffers from over-blending and lacks words for how to describe a fresh, unblended mark. There are many ways of actually marbleizing color, but the main quality behind it is restraining yourself from blending. It requires that you continue to lay your new fresh decisions and paint into the soupy mess of your oil painting unhindered by your previous decisions.

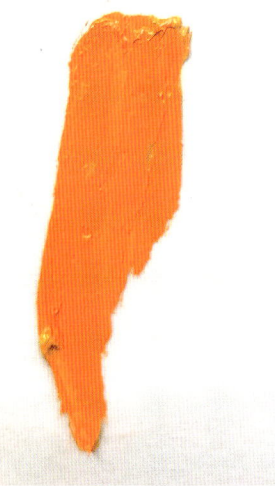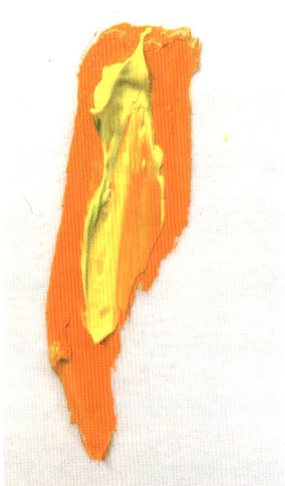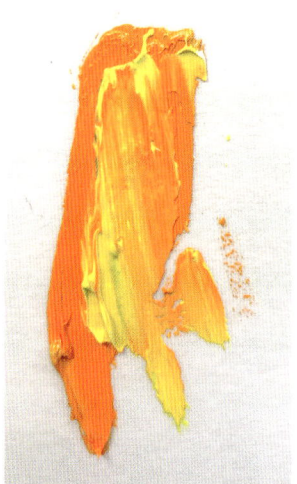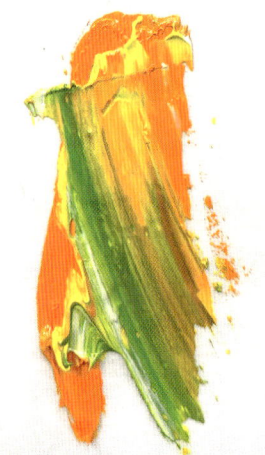

MARBLEIZING VS. BLENDING

As much as I greatly believe in this principal of color dots and not blending them, and I think it might be one of the most healthy practices for painters to learn about, undoubtedly the day will come when there will be blending. That soft quality may be the aesthetic that a painter admires the most, so I don't want to discourage people from blending altogether. There's this tension between softening—making something feel natural and beautiful and smooth—versus the painting becoming over-blended and dead. Even if you'd like to ultimately end up with something soft and as beautifully smoky as the *Mona Lisa* is, if you love color, it's still not a bad idea to go through this color dot exercise in order to understand the individual tones of the face.

One way to think about blending and how it intersects with color dots is that you can add dots everywhere, then blend a little bit, and then dot it up again, and then blend it again. Working in this cycle allows for sensitivity, but it also encourages making new decisions, which is one of the biggest problems of blending; once it's smooth, it feels finished and we don't want to mess with it again. It's hard to have the courage to interrupt our polished areas to find a new color or correct a mistake. But if you get into the rhythm of dotting and blending, you anticipate this cycle, and it allows you to build up something that has slightly more character and is more of a process that works.

The image on page 107 and at right is a digital representation of the workflow of dotting, softening, dotting, and softening.

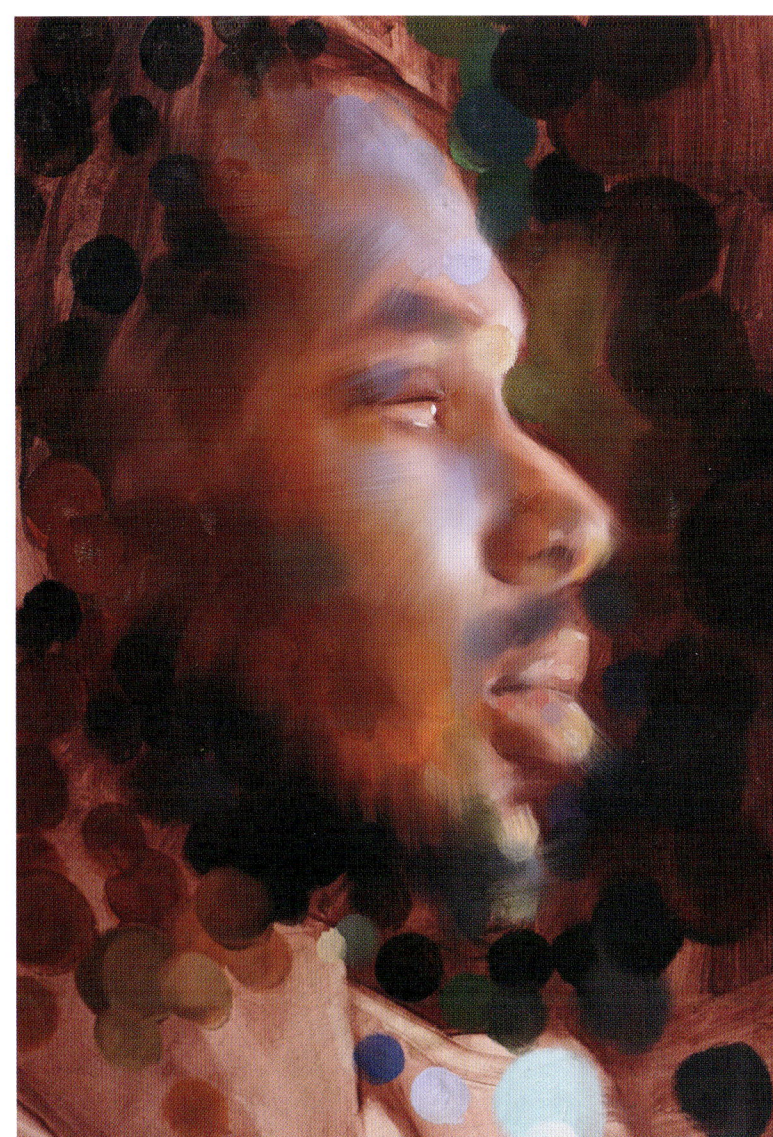

BLENDING: THE AGONY AND THE ECSTASY

To further break down this idea of dotting, softening, dotting, and softening, here's another example or variation on the theme. I made this for a video lecture on Art School Live with Eric Rhodes. The topic of the lecture was "Blending: The Agony and the Ecstasy," which is a tongue-and-cheek acknowledgment of the place that most painters have been in their experience at some point. The fact is that blending can take just about everything away from your painting, but it always seems to be this thing we're drawn to and have a compulsion to do.

I tried to show that you could have this really raw, ugly, finger-dotted start, with no drawing, but good colors and values in a rough approximate place of where the features would go. These tones may even be slightly exaggerated in order to keep the painting interesting and nonrepetitive. Then, with a long soft bristle brush, I delicately blended these tones. Blending is one of those words that could mean lots of things. It's a catchall word that means you smudge some things around and they became softer. But what I want you to notice about how I blended these tones in the images on page XX is that I actually draw while blending. I love to push this concept as a teacher: blending isn't merely softening or smudging or blurring. It can also be drawing! In Figure **(A)**, the nose and the mouth have not been shaped into anything. They're just abstract splotches of paint. Through blending, I have formed them into a soft, out-of-focus, slightly lower contrast version of the nose and mouth. This often continues throughout the whole painting process whenever I blend; sometimes I push the nose up or I push the mouth down using blending to do so. When we draw and we practically outlined the features, there's no possibility of them moving anywhere. But if you're constantly pushing and nudging things around by blending, you're more flexible and not afraid to question if something is in the right place. This flexibility allows you to chase the model's position and get a better likeness by not committing too early.

This phase, which John Singer Sargent called the *wigmaker's block*, which is an antiquated way of saying mannequin head, is a phase in the blocking process of the painting, where the features are painted into the face and the face into the background so that nothing is crisp and everything is slightly soft and painted into its surrounding areas. In this way, the features sort of emerge out of a soft impression and are really quite flexible and changeable because nothing is crisp and set in stone. This is a great way to block in a picture because you're hovering around commitment, still able to make changes while yet being able to have an impression of your subject rather than a blank canvas.

This wigmaker's block is also a wonderful foundation to paint into and really develop the detail in the color from. It's best done if you can develop the color and detail while this wigmaker's block is wet, and that's why, while it's not important for the wigmaker's block to be perfect, it has to be done quickly, so that you have time while it's wet to paint in the nuances, accents, and details that it doesn't have. So Figure **(B)** shows we've dotted, then we've softened, and then drawn in the major features with low contrast and less of a sharp appearance.

Then, in Figure **(C)**, we're dotting in the color diversity and value diversity that really starts to bring the nuances out of the foundation of the wigmaker's block. So in a funny way, I'm repeating step number one except smaller and finer with a smaller brush. If only I had a small enough pinky to dot in those tones, I'd use my finger instead because I like finger-painting. But I don't, so I need to use a small brush to dot in the nuances of these colors.

Then, in Figure **(D)**, let's change the word *blending* to *swiping* in the color to create *directional* blending. This gives our painting movement and instead of a generic soft blob, each brushstroke is carrying the light somewhere or pushing the dark somewhere else. So instead of dots of colors, they become swipes of colors. They create form texture and movement.

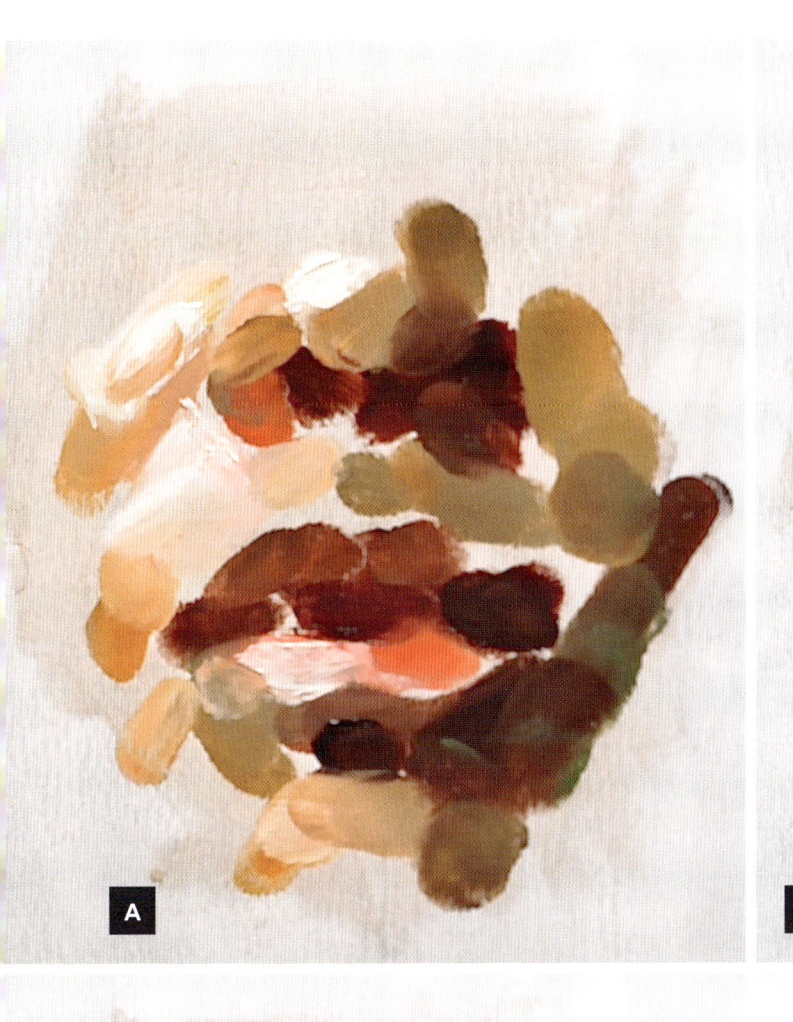

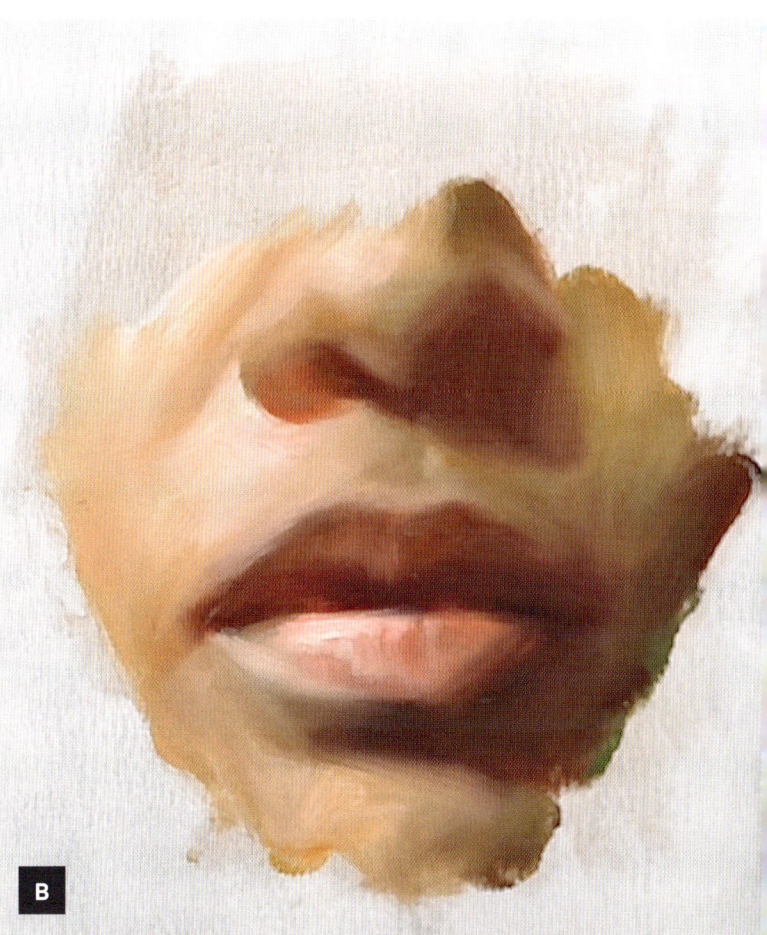

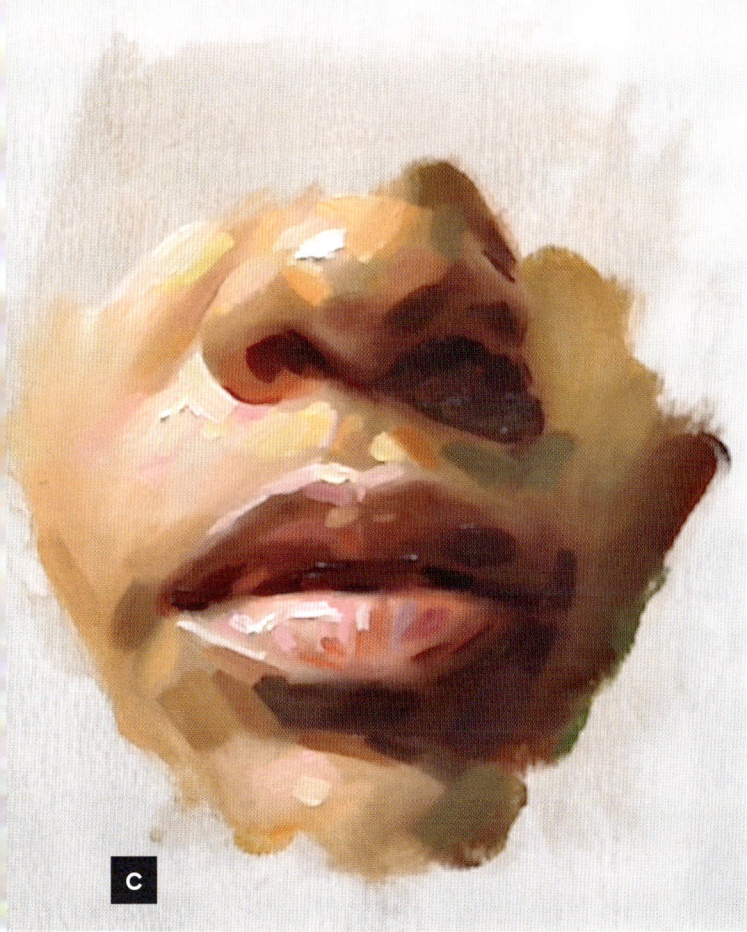

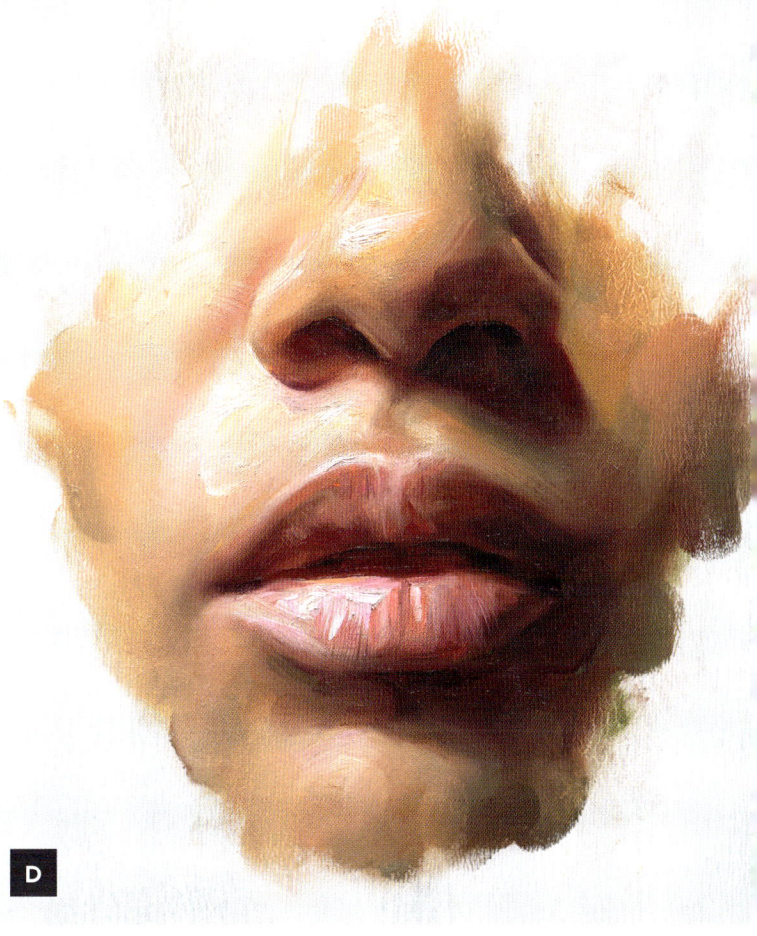

DEMONSTRATION:
ALLA PRIMA

SAVING THE BEST DRAWING FOR LAST

In a completely antithetical approach to the painting technique put forward in the beginning of this book that utilizes an underdrawing and generally a careful way of keeping that drawing all the way through the painting process, the demo in the following pages really is a more virtuosic approach that requires some experience and in general, saves the best drawing for last. That best drawing really develops organically through a more splashy painting approach that privileges color and value first. It's actually really not particularly different from the approach in the beginning part of the book except there's no drawing to start with. It skips all of that and jumps right to the ébauche process and the drawing develops out of that. This can be very freeing and help you to learn how to be looser and inventive, but it does require a lot of experience if you'd like to capture a likeness and have a finer degree of realism.

I generally wouldn't recommend this technique without quite a bit of drawing experience. The main painting technique put forward in this book really allows you to work on your drawing skills and then also transfer that to painting skills in a formal way. Developing that drawing practice is huge when it comes to confidence in painting. After those skills have been acquired, it's fun to challenge yourself by just going for it with this approach. It'll help you to loosen up and find your personal balance of tight drawing and loose painting.

I've found that all of my different painting experiences, whether it be making brown underpaintings, underdrawings, alla prima glazing, and so on, have increased my paint knowledge and helped me to become a more well-rounded painter. If you're looking for a fun challenge, this technique is for you.

Scan to view a
video tutorial

▸ Steve Forster, *Alina*, oil on aluminum,
14" × 18" | 35.6 cm × 45.7 cm

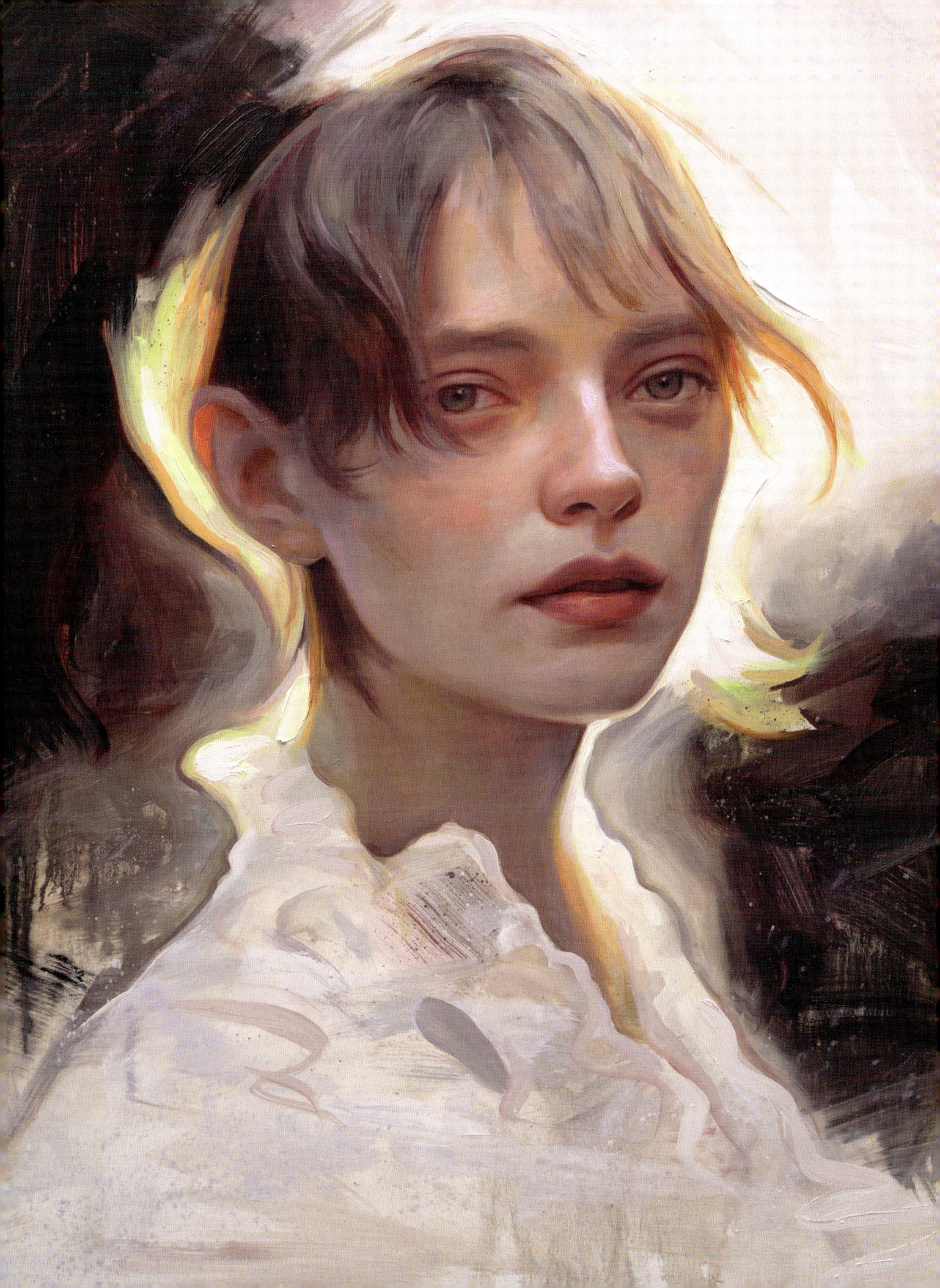

WASH TO KILL THE WHITE

It can be quite a challenge to work on a white canvas and develop a finished painting in one session, but one thing I've found that helps is to start with a Gamsol wash of the mother color in the main areas. So, for the face, there's a general wash of burnt sienna with a touch of red, the background has a general wash of red and a little violet, and there are some touches of yellow on the rim lighting of the hair. All of this is done thin with clean, fresh Gamsol. This Gamsol then evaporates and causes the paint to set up, almost giving you a semi-dry primer layer for a second coat of more solid paint to cover more thoroughly. If you don't let this Gamsol set up and dry sufficiently, you'll be painting into a wet mess that's slippery and the paint won't stick.

The very light areas of the painting are left alone, so that the lightness of the canvas can help create that luminosity and brightness that this image requires. Using this wash can subliminally awaken you to the different chemical reactions paint can have. And sometimes, my favorite moments are when a bit of that wash shines through in the finished painting, keeping that broken apart speckled look.

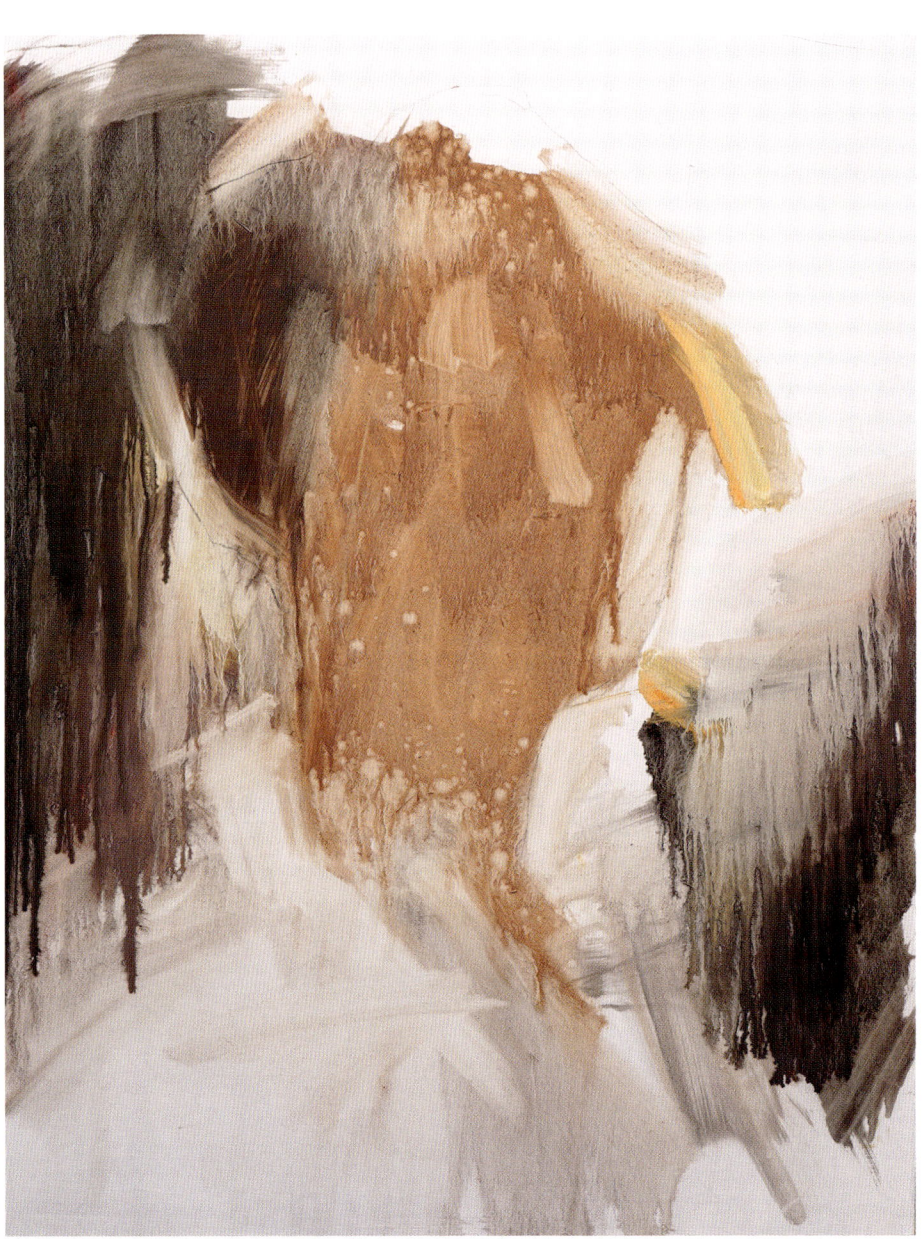

COLOR TILES

The next stage after leaving the washes of color to set up is to mix up your palette more thoroughly with solid paint and broadly lay in color tiles to establish a basic general idea of the head. In the previous stage, we used the paint wet and thin, and it may have even caused a mess on the palette. You should clean the palette after the wash phase, and while that wash is setting up, you'll have time to patiently mix up all the colors you need because there's no rush to get started. You need at least fifteen minutes for the Gamsol to set up. If you mix all of those colors then, putting color tiles on over this tacky wash is so much more fun because you'll have the variety and options to begin creating color diversity. Just don't be stingy with the amount of paint that you mix because one of the number one problems in finishing a painting on a white canvas in one day isn't using enough paint.

Also notice that the lips are blocked in with one tone, the nose is blocked in with one shadow tone, and the eyes, even though they're not dark eyes, have been simplified and made graphic in order to place them. Proportion and the facial grid are still being used; however, I consider it a rough draft in that a lot of it will shift as refining is done.

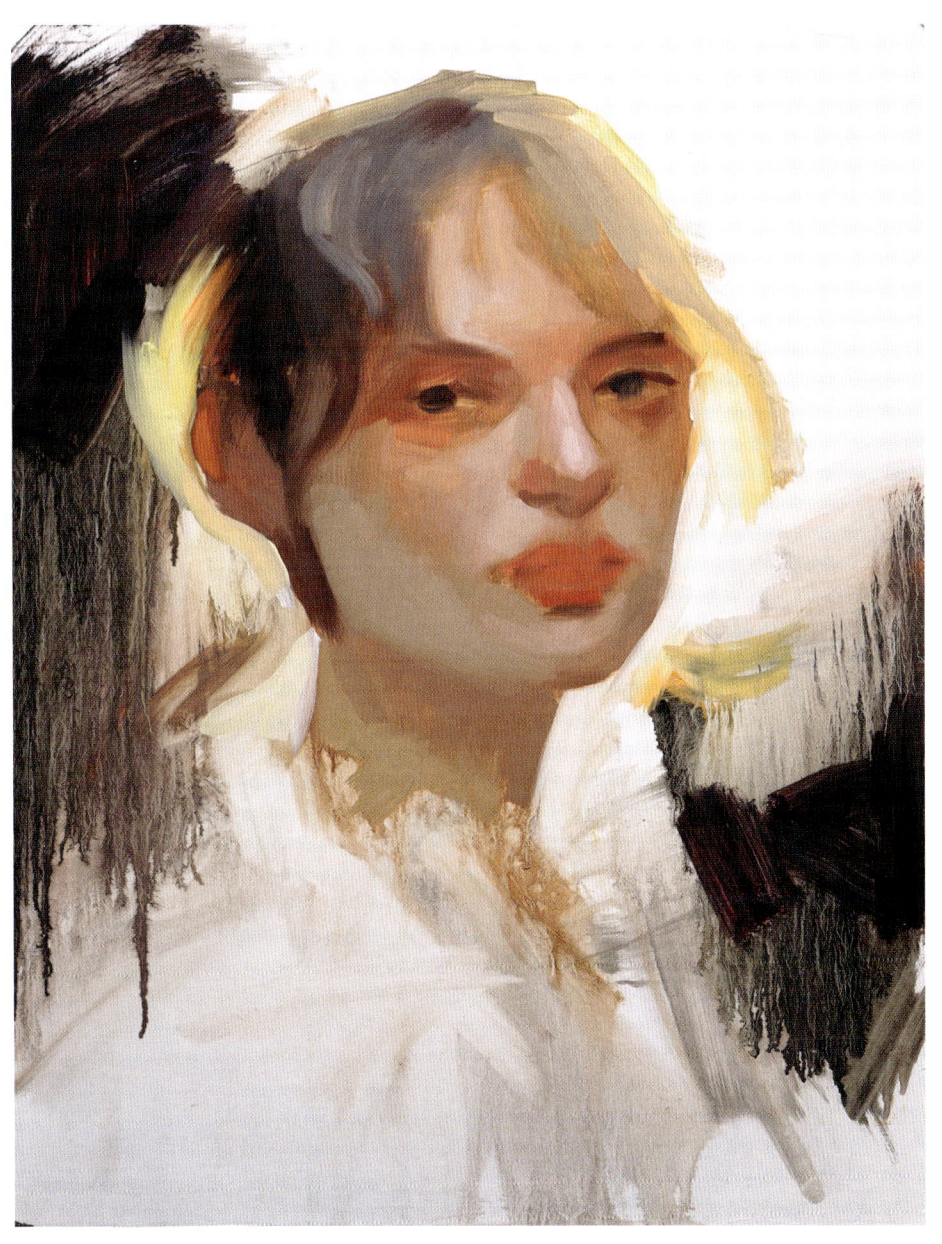

DEVELOPING THE DRAWING

Even though we were able to put a wash over the canvas as a primer and start developing the colors more thickly with the second coat, the painting can still get quite wet and difficult to manage. So often I pause painting, get out a little round brush, and start drawing in the features and working up the details and the edges with clarity.

I've found this to be important for a variety of reasons, one being that the painting just needs to be drawn more clearly to develop the features, and this usually looks the freshest when it's painted into surrounding wet paint so that it doesn't have a cut-out look. Also, when you take time to slow down and draw, you still give the rest of the paint a little bit of time to set up and dry and stick just a little more to the canvas. So if things are getting a bit mushy and hard to control, stop painting and start drawing. I've found that almost all of my paintings that don't get finished don't suffer from a lack of painting, but they suffer from a lack of drawing.

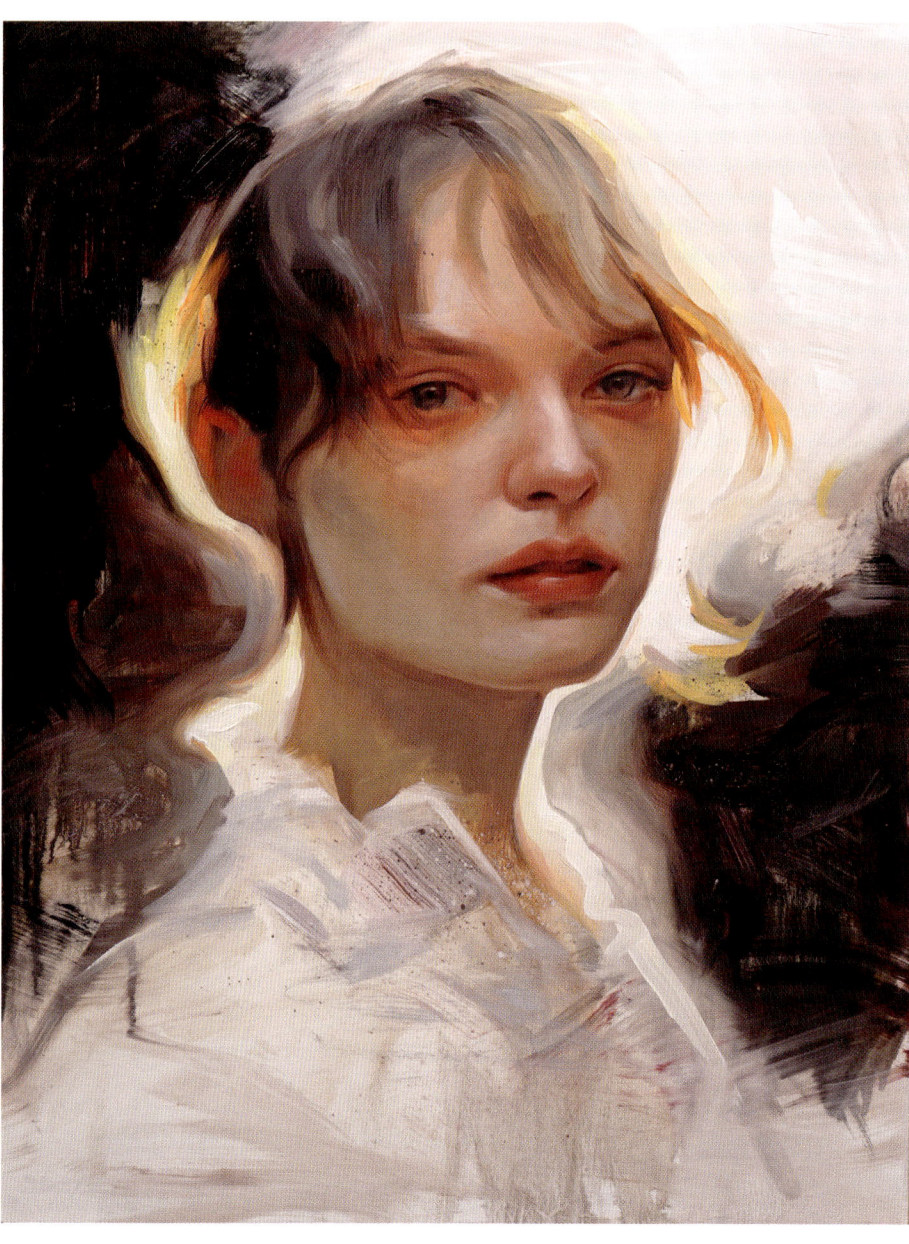

TIGHTENING THE SCREWS

In a lot of ways, finishing a painting is just spending longer on the details than you think you're supposed to. But one of the things you may notice in the evolution from stage three to stage four is that the color has changed. Often when I'm painting, I slowly get used to the colors that I'm using, and also their values. What I often have to do is step away from the painting for a little while and go get a coffee, and when I come back, suddenly my eyes are a little fresher and I might see that there's a missing color or a missing dark value that if integrated into the portrait would make all of the difference.

So I want you to notice how the last stage has more of a presence of violet in the skin tone and that has added to the diversity of the main tones established in the beginning. Also notice that some of the darker half-tones that really make the light pop on the face have been added so there has been more of a darkening and a shift in the color that creates a subtle amount of variety in the skin tone that really starts to pull it together. There's also a little bit more outlining and flair and attention to detail to finish up this alla prima study.

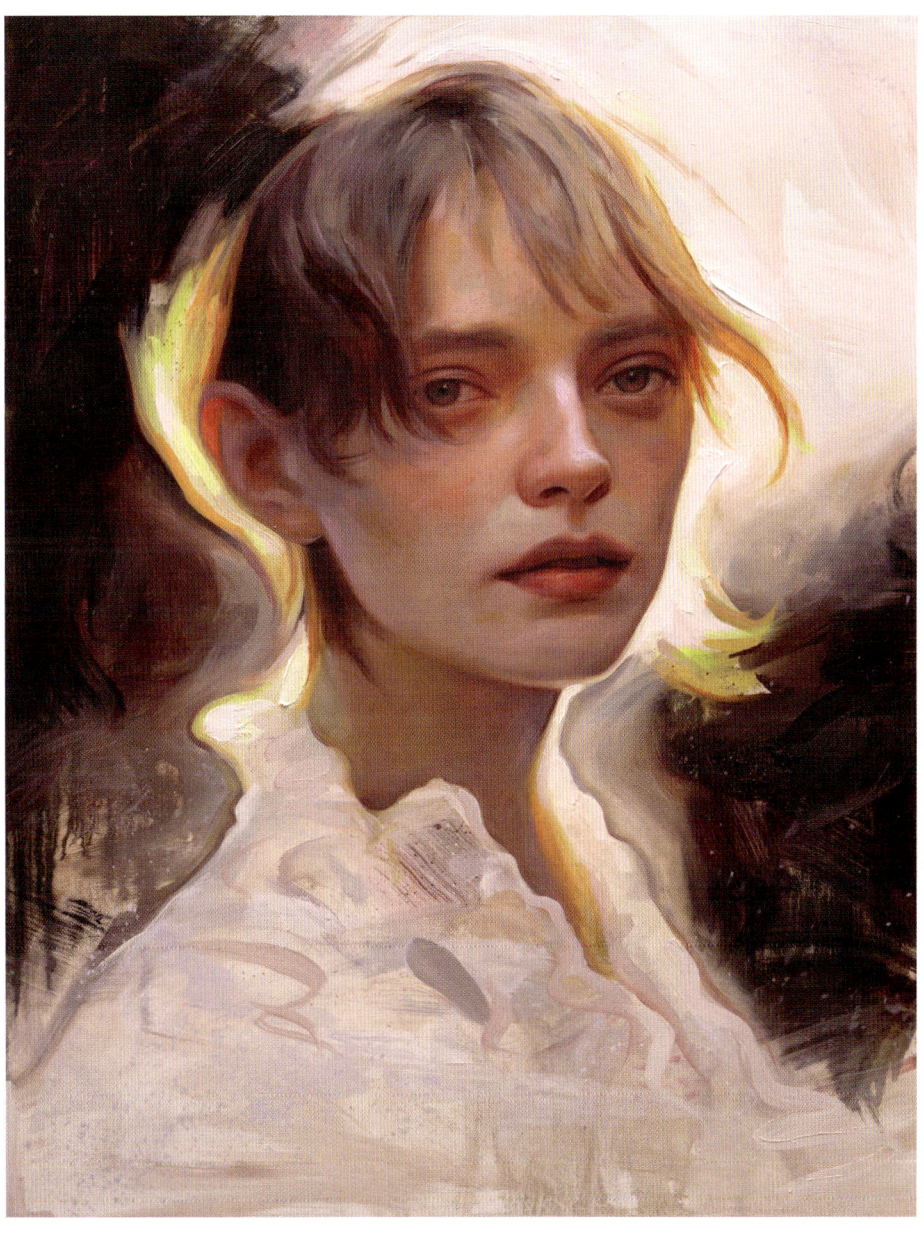

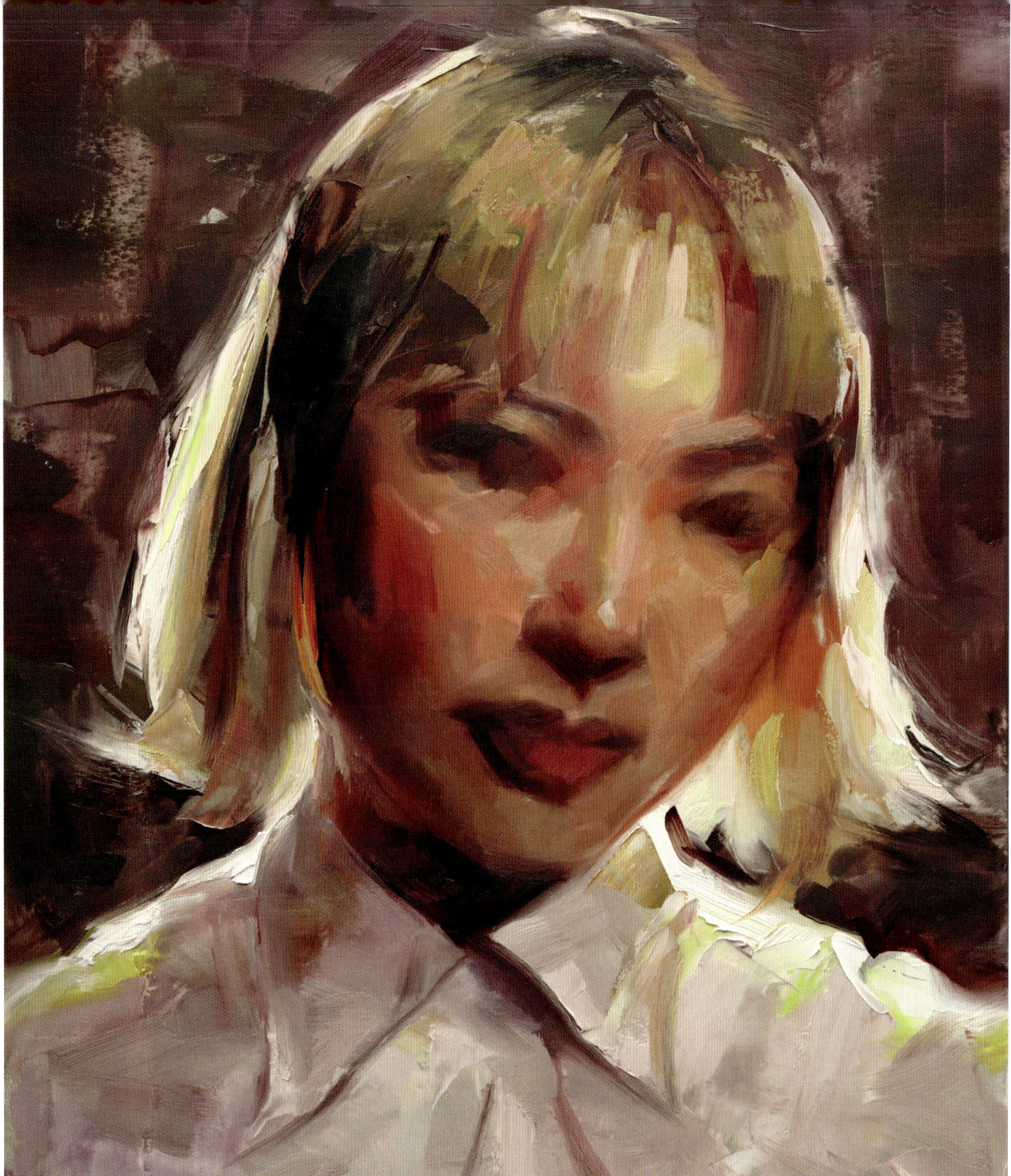

ABSTRACT START

A slight variation on the previous approach is one of trying to truly embrace the abstract painterly qualities of the face when blocking it in and still reserving the best drawing for last. Here, I'm trying to get the general block-in of the head with good proportions and good values, but really not fully committing to the drawing just yet. I find that if painters really want to embrace their artistic characteristics and have a love for alla prima painting, they should really consider the beautiful qualities that can be sought after and explored without the pressures of perfect drawing. Granted, it's taking me many years to be able to have a painterly approach, where the drawing somewhat resembles the model, but what I'm really talking about is leaving the features vague, simple, and movable, so that we don't obsess over them. This allows us to zoom out and think about

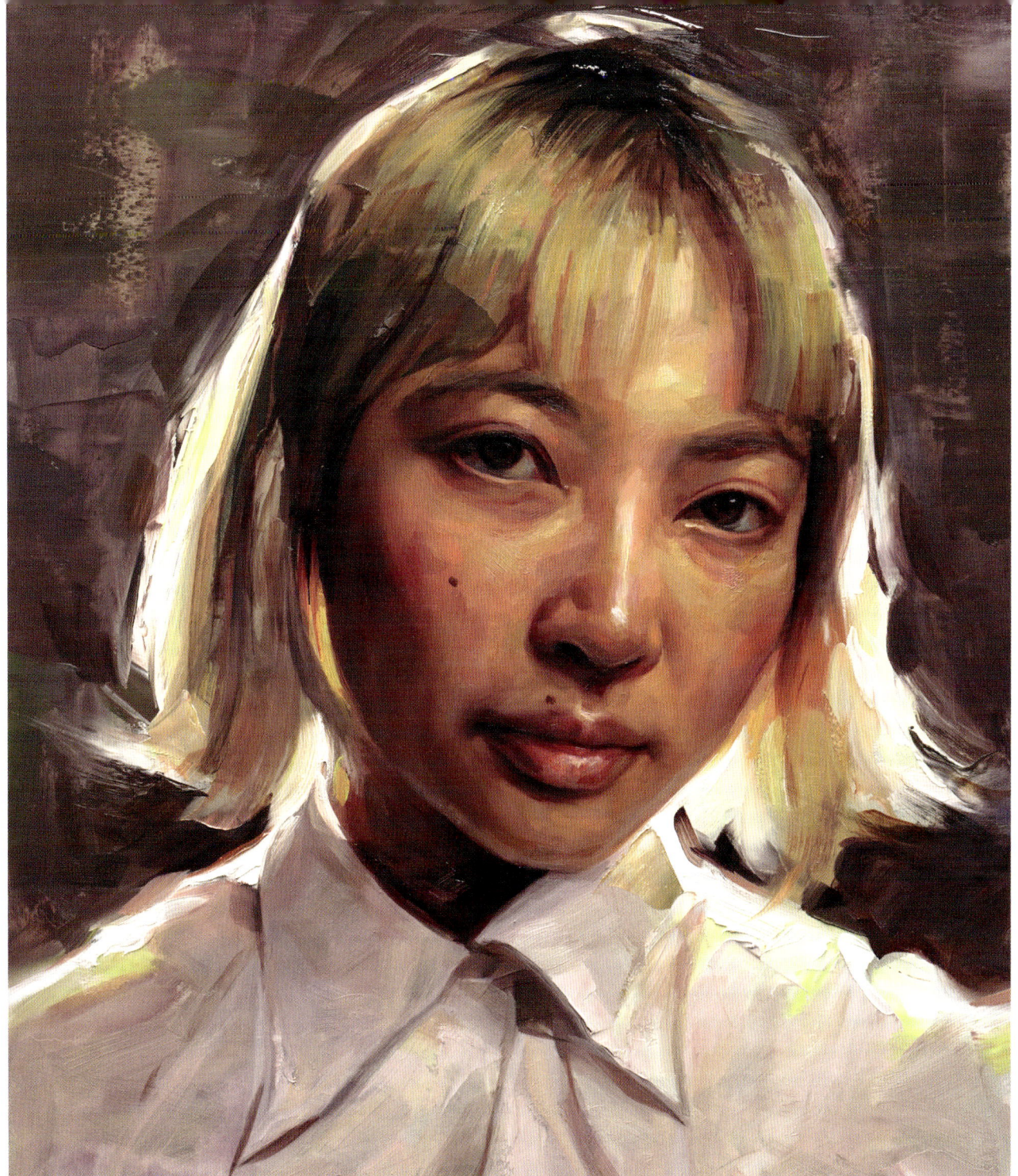

the larger, bigger abstract qualities of the head and fully explore them with a greater focus. For me, this means that even though I want abstract mark-making and brushstroke diversity, I still want good values and an intensity to my decision-making that builds visual interest rather than resolving the drawing too quickly.

This abstract start allows me to paint the entire head in general and have enough time to do a decent job of it without spreading myself so thin. This is especially helpful if you have a limited amount of time to paint the head and block it in, and you plan on coming back to it later on. This block-in was done in about an hour and a half for a Zoom class that I teach on Saturdays, and then there were two more hour-and-a-half sessions to finish up some details and glazc in some subtle changes.

Steve Forster, *Junyi*, oil on aluminum,
14" × 18" | 35.6 cm × 45.7 cm

HOLDING ON TO ABSTRACT MOMENTS

Perhaps I spent too long in a classical painting program, but part of me just loves and deeply appreciates the more abstract moments in my paintings these days. When painting from a photograph, constantly comparing your painting to that never-changing reference, there can be a stiffness and an obsession with creating the illusion of reality rather than the freedom in the expression of paint. I find that when painting from life, it's much easier to be more expressive and create variety because it's an ever-changing reality, and we're not constantly comparing ourselves to a lifeless photograph.

As many painters have found out, usually in the beginning, we are freewheeling and loose, creating bold, brushstrokes and interesting moments in paint and then slowly by softening and refining and painting over and over again, our paintings lose these moments of freshness.

Make it a priority to create certain areas in your paintings that just look interesting from a paint perspective rather than an illusionary perspective. With a portrait, I don't think that everything can be done in this way; otherwise, it wouldn't be recognizable as a specific person, which I think is the definition of a portrait, rather than a head painting. But it doesn't mean that we can't be loose and free with our paint quality, always seeking variety. One practical thought in trying to create this for yourself is to have at least have four different brushstrokes, each one unique, and alternate those brushstrokes so that homogeny is not created. This could be a small liner brush, mixed with a flat graphic brush, mixed with a palette knife, and then mixed with a soft brush. Having these distinct voices allows for brushstroke variety and for you to fully embrace the language of paint and how it can be expressive.

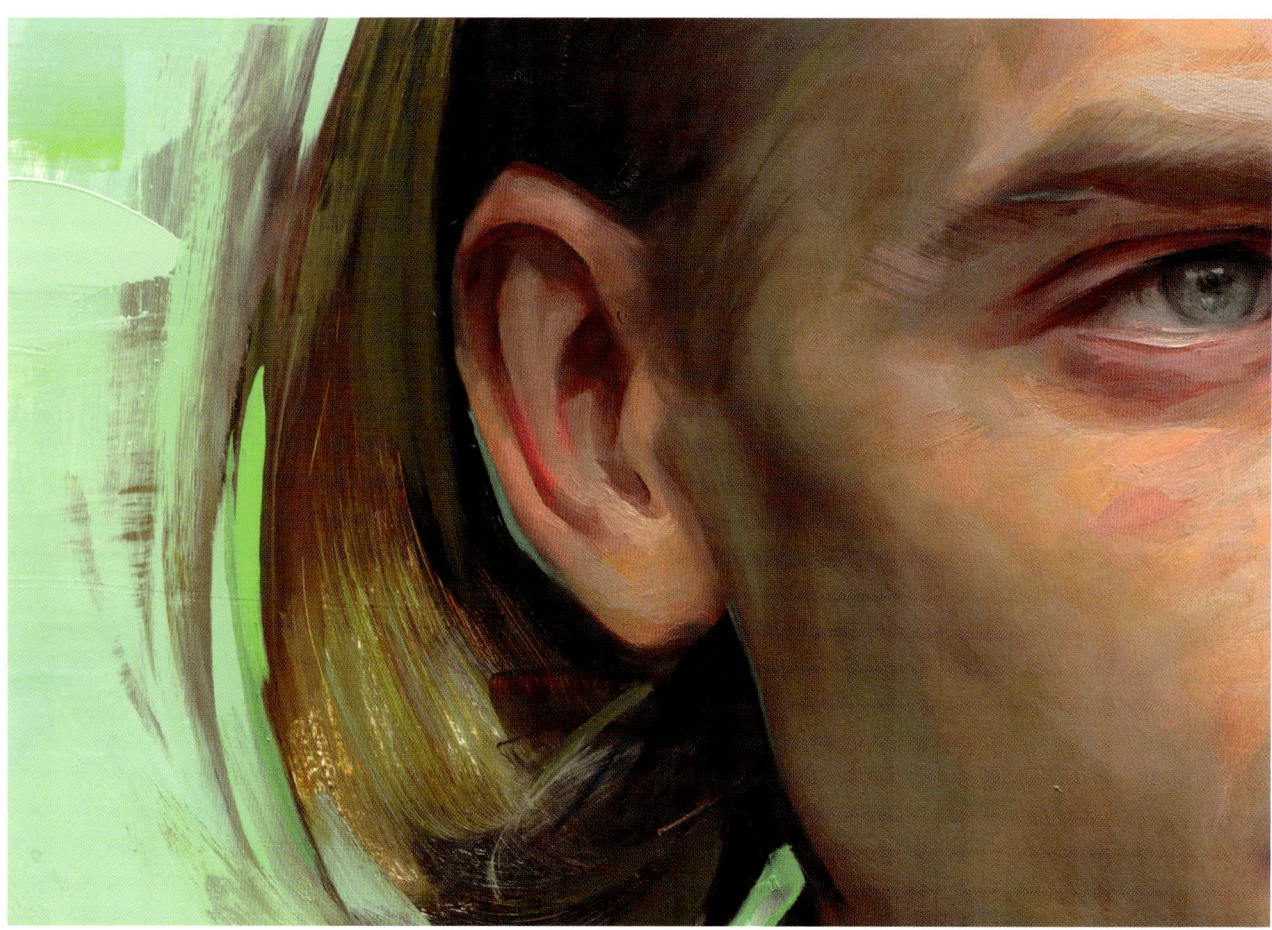

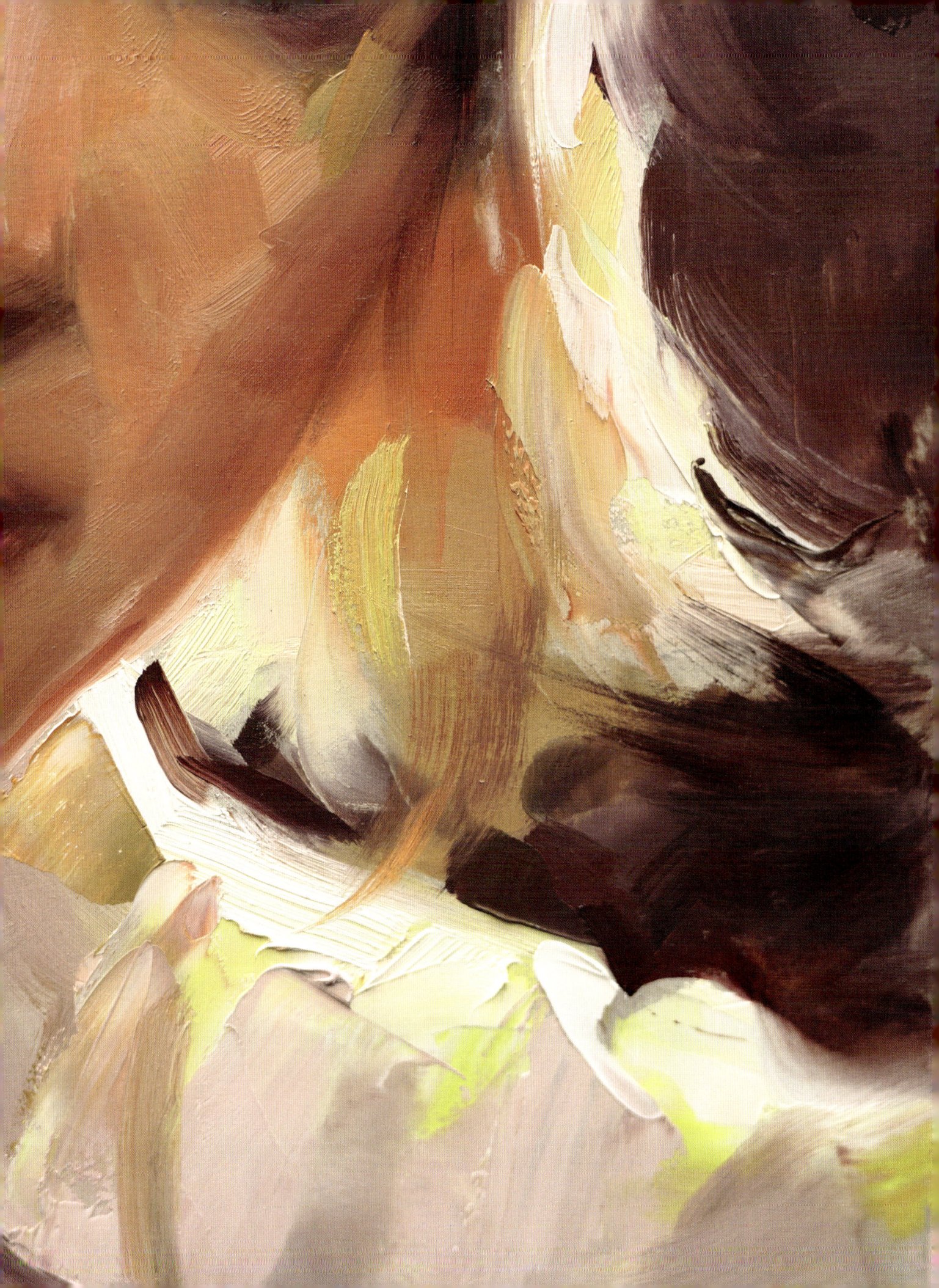

BRUSHSTROKE VARIETY

On opposite, this painting mixes the effect of realism with the brushstrokes of a more digital and modern quality. I find that many people are interested in this style, which could be associated with a sense of "disrupted realism." When delving into the unknown such as interpretation, it's probably the most helpful to create a set of rules that gives some sense of guidance to your own way of interpretation. I say this because sometimes people ask me how I make these marks or what is that kind of a brushstroke, and it's truly an evolution of a certain set of rules that I made for myself that created those marks.

Granted, in the beginning, it's all experimentation, and the more different strokes and vocabulary you can develop to create brushstroke variety, the better. Often, when somebody discovers a palette knife for the first time, they go crazy with it and try to figure out all the different things they can do on the painting with it, and it gets to be a thick, crusty mess. If we think of that as an experience that we can draw from and then integrate into other brushstrokes that we've already mastered, that's how research and development works with your brushstroke vocabulary. We may go over the edge with a new tool, but if we're smart, we learn how it can play with other marks and other vocabulary we already have.

I like to have all these marks mixed together, almost like a tapestry of different brushstroke choices. In the detail image below, you'll see lines that help shape some chaotic marks. You'll see soft areas that keep all of the marks from being crisp. You'll see squeegee marks that add a bit of chaotic disruption. And you'll see a highly polished area that presents a contrast to the abstractions.

▸ Steve Forster, *Junyi*, oil on aluminum,
16" × 16" | 15.2 cm × 15.2 cm

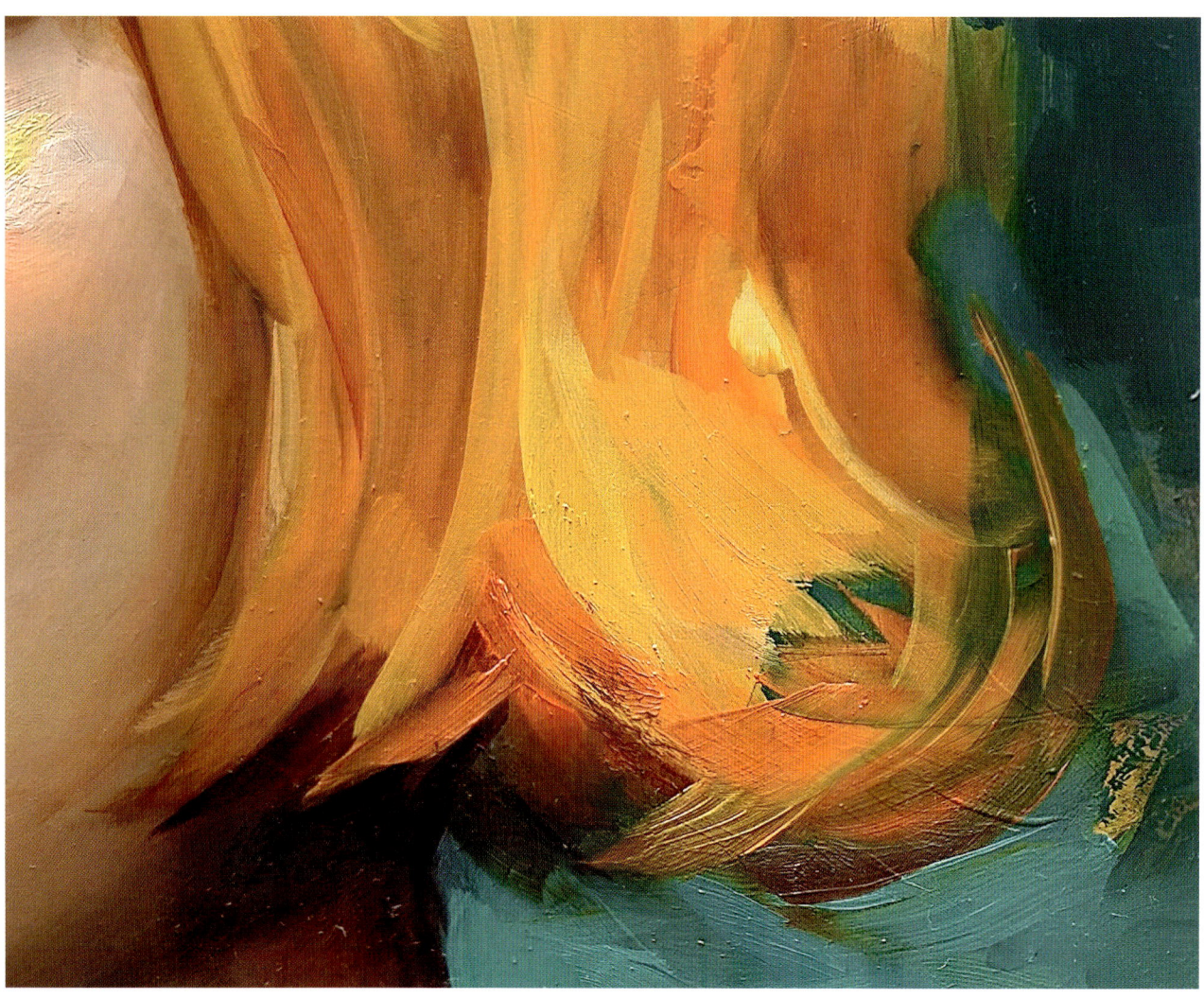

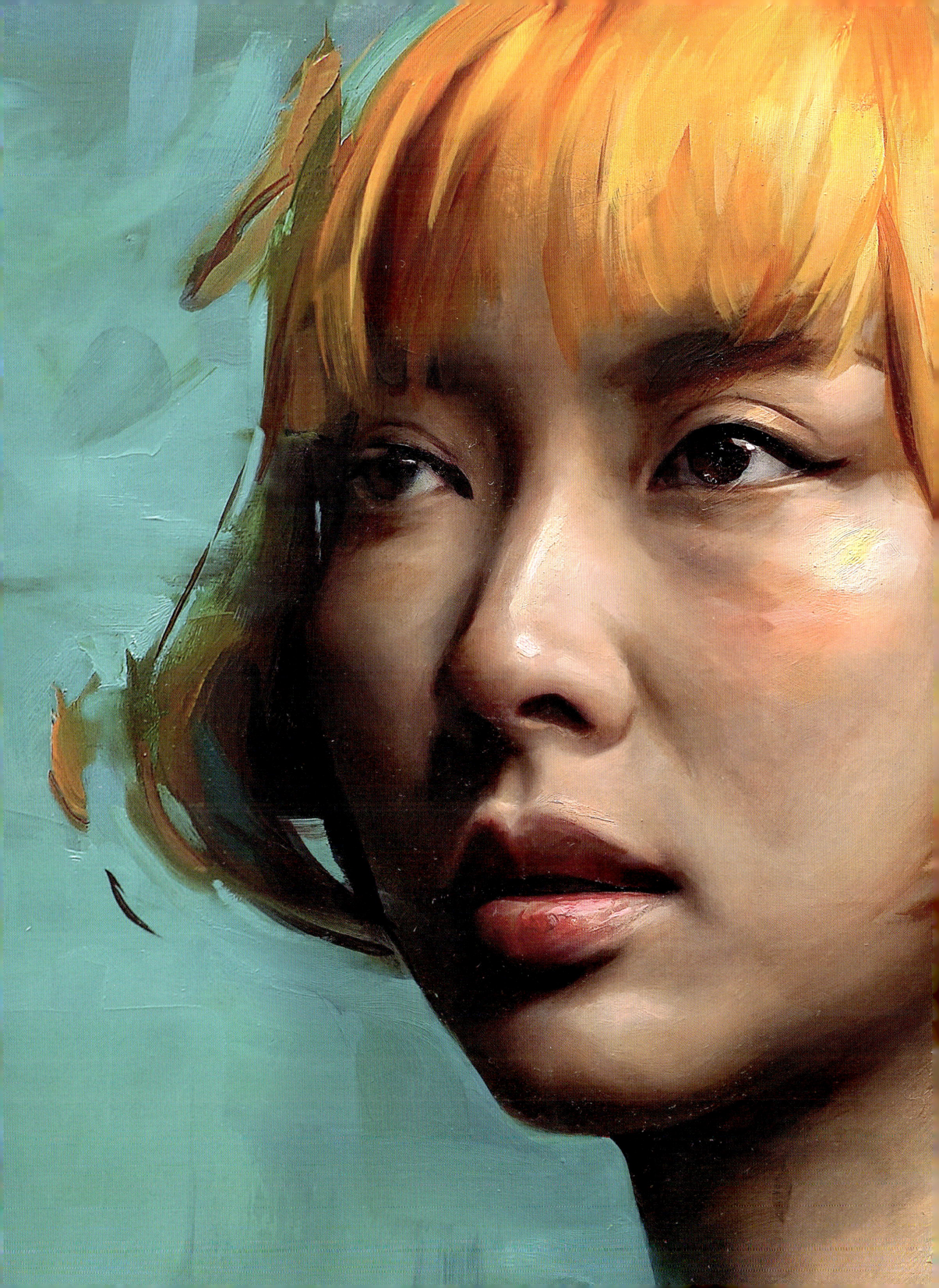

8 | ADVANCED COLOR CONCEPTS

CLASSICAL FLESH MODEL

"Flesh is the reason oil painting was invented."

—WILLEM DE KOONING

Flesh color is one of those seductive mysteries of painting that compels us to want to learn how to paint. In a way, it's like alchemy to the painter, turning the flat surface on which we paint into a human being using a little bit of dirt, paste, and hair attached to a wooden handle. If you manage to do it, you're hooked for life.

It can be one of the most frustrating things to try to paint because it's ever-changing—it's skin color along with form, issues of complexion/ethnicity, and the practical application of paint to canvas.

In classical painting of the seventeenth century, there begins to arise a notion of what beautiful flesh color is. Through a combination of observations and aesthetics, we arrive at what I refer to as the classical flesh model. Of course, every figure painting from this era doesn't necessarily line up with this theory, but a vast majority of traditional classical paintings do. The best examples are Jacques-Louis David, Rembrandt, Rubens, and so on.

How did the classical flesh model develop? One of the main contributors to this idea is Peter Paul Rubens, who wrote a book on color that's now lost to us. I can imagine that in that book, he described this process, and it was probably used as a manual by his many assistants, who did quite a bit of painting for him. It would illustrate how the anatomy of light could be transcribed to color from one of his drawings without having a live model or photo for reference. This color coding of the anatomy of light would have been explained in a way that was easily understood by those many assistants, an incredibly useful tool for keeping consistency across a huge canvas with multiple figures.

I've heard a variety of different versions of this methodology. Some have been helpful, and others have been more confusing than useful. But basically what I conclude is that the classical flesh model is a one-light mass with a cool neutral turning and a warm shadow.

This model works because people generally want to see warm flesh in a warm light—it looks healthy. Also, reflected light usually tends to be warm anyway. It tends to be what you see when flesh is lit beautifully in an environment that showcases it.

There can be many applications of the classical flesh model, but generally it follows this warm-cool-warm pattern. You *could* perhaps have a cool light, and then it would go cool-warm-cool. In some modern applications of color, this is especially valuable; however, it's rarely used in class painting.

All this may sound confusing, but the color of flesh is complicated; if you grab hold of the classical flesh model and try to really understand it, it gives you some sense of how to use color for flesh, even perhaps without seeing it in reference. Ideally with the guidance of these pages, when all combined and mastered practically, you'll be able to color a black-and-white photograph of a figure without ever seeing a color reference photo.

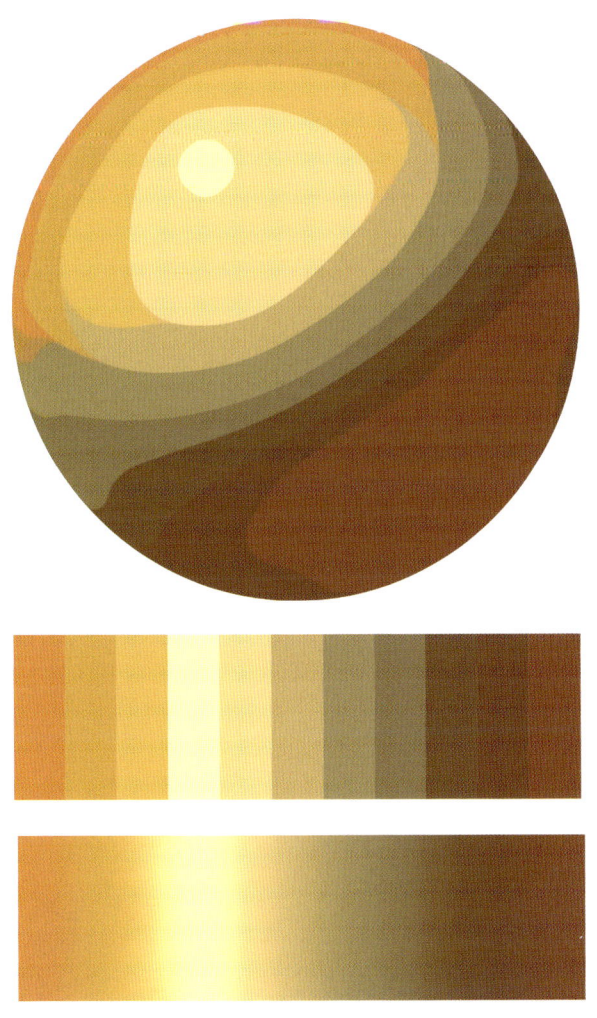

In the diagram below, we see the classical flesh model, which can be more exaggerated in color or more subtle in color than this diagram. All of its component parts correlate to the anatomy of light, which is the breakdown of the different identifications of light and shadow rolling over a form, such as a sphere. Generally speaking, we have a warm light mass that has warmer chromatic turning into the light, a cool turning into the shadow, a neutral dark shadow (terminator), and a warm reflected light.

The first one is the warm outside turning, which I call *turning into the light*. This has a warm cast to it. Then, comes the warm center light. Remember that in the classical flesh model, it's almost always a warm light. Then comes the neutral or cool turning, then a neutral dark core shadow, and finally a warm reflected light in the shadow.

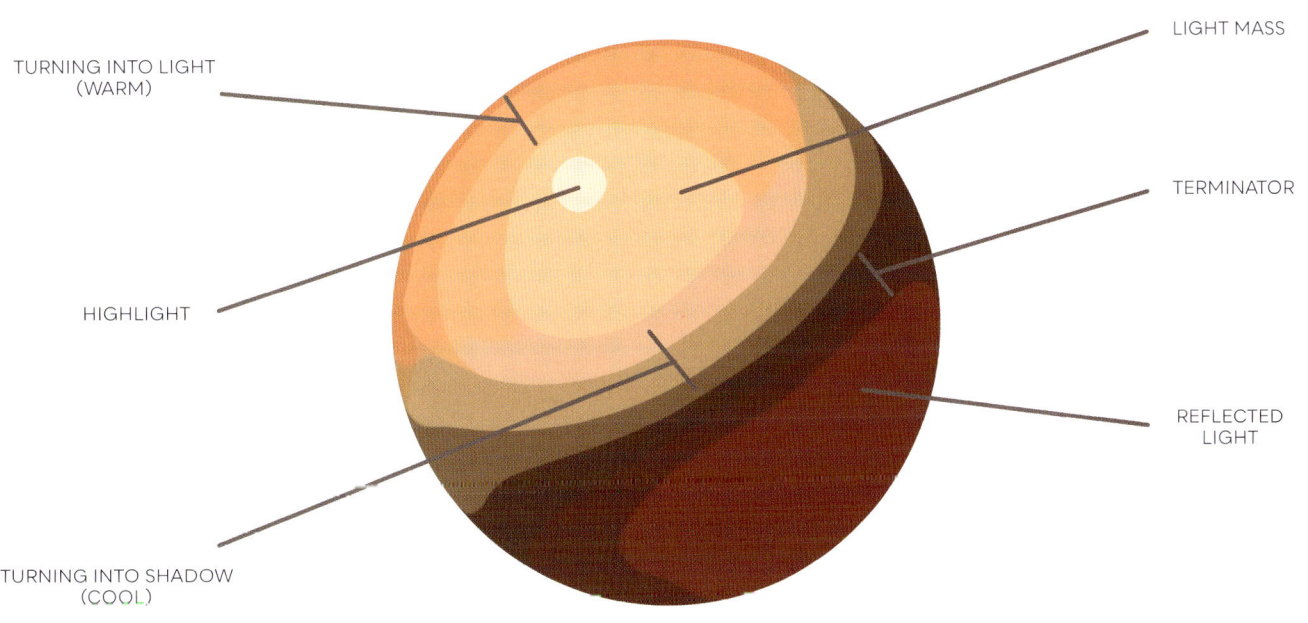

TURNING INTO LIGHT
(WARM)

LIGHT MASS

TERMINATOR

HIGHLIGHT

REFLECTED
LIGHT

TURNING INTO SHADOW
(COOL)

ETHNICITY AND THE CLASSICAL FLESH MODEL

I thought it would be worthwhile to try to examine skin tone varieties and come up with a starting point for the beginner to understand the differences in the types of ethnic color palettes and complexions. The classical flesh model still applies across all skin colors. It just tends to favor slightly different colors depending upon the complexion of the model. Darker skin can often be orange and violet with sometimes a bit of a cooler blue as well. Middle tone skin can have a more orange and olive tone to it that balance each other out. Very pale skin often has a pinkish quality with under tones of a green gray, as well as yellow to keep it warm.

Obviously, in the canon of European western art, many paintings tend to favor the complexion of Caucasians; however, there have been great examples of a variety of different flesh types by Rubens and Rembrandt and many others. Even within Caucasian skin, there can be quite a variety of colors used, depending on whether the person works outside in the sun and has more of a ruddy complexion or if they're more of an indoor person with a cooler pallor. Given that there's a range of differences within any given ethnicity, I put together an average that I consistently see when painting from life.

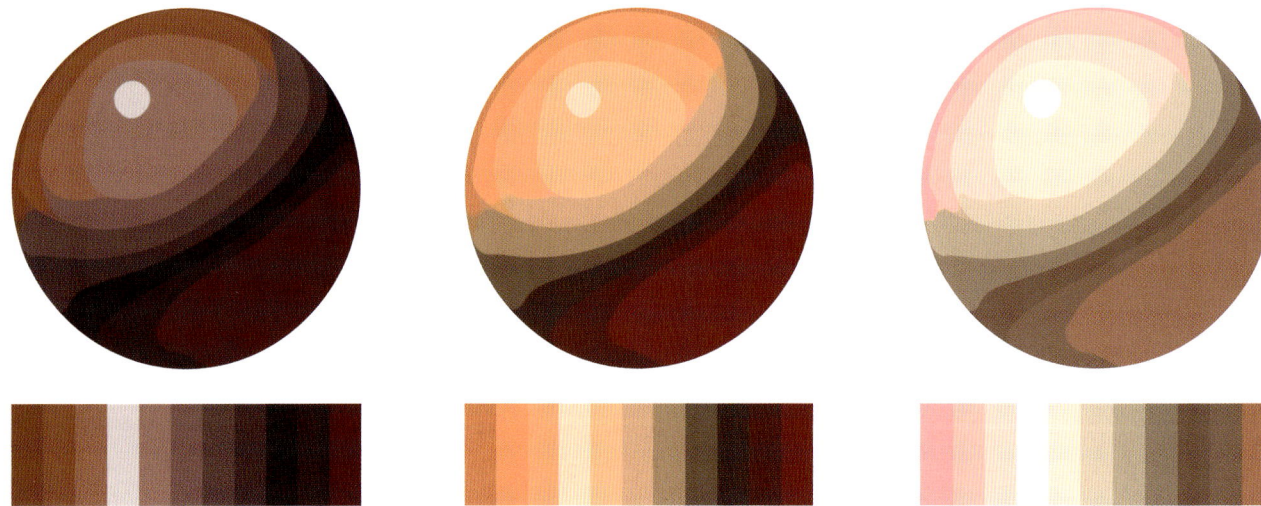

ETHNICITY AND COMPLEXION

Often, I am asked, "What's the difference between painting somebody with darker skin and painting somebody with lighter skin?" Yes, there can be many differences, as we've already noticed in the classical flesh model; however, there are usually more tones that overlap than are different. As we see in the diagram below, these two different skin tones could still be painted with the same palette. There are differences with how dark the shadows go and maybe how dark the halftones go, but in general, the colors are the same. It's the value structure that's different.

I've noticed in painting models of different ethnicities that you can have the right colors, but sometimes it's about a subtle variation in values rather than colors themselves that create the effect of ethnicity, especially if you're trying to make colorful flesh in the appearance of a healthier, warmer tone. It's easy to find yourself in the same exact color palette with two very different models, and the visual cues that would change their ethnicity go beyond color alone. This just goes to show how important values and drawing are and how perhaps obsessing over the different hue and complexion variation isn't always going to be the right answer.

On a side note, I enjoy how much we can all overlap and be a little bit closer to one another rather than so far apart. Of course, somebody can have a more pale complexion that favors pink while someone else has more of an olive tone, but keep an eye out for how often flesh tones are more often similar than different.

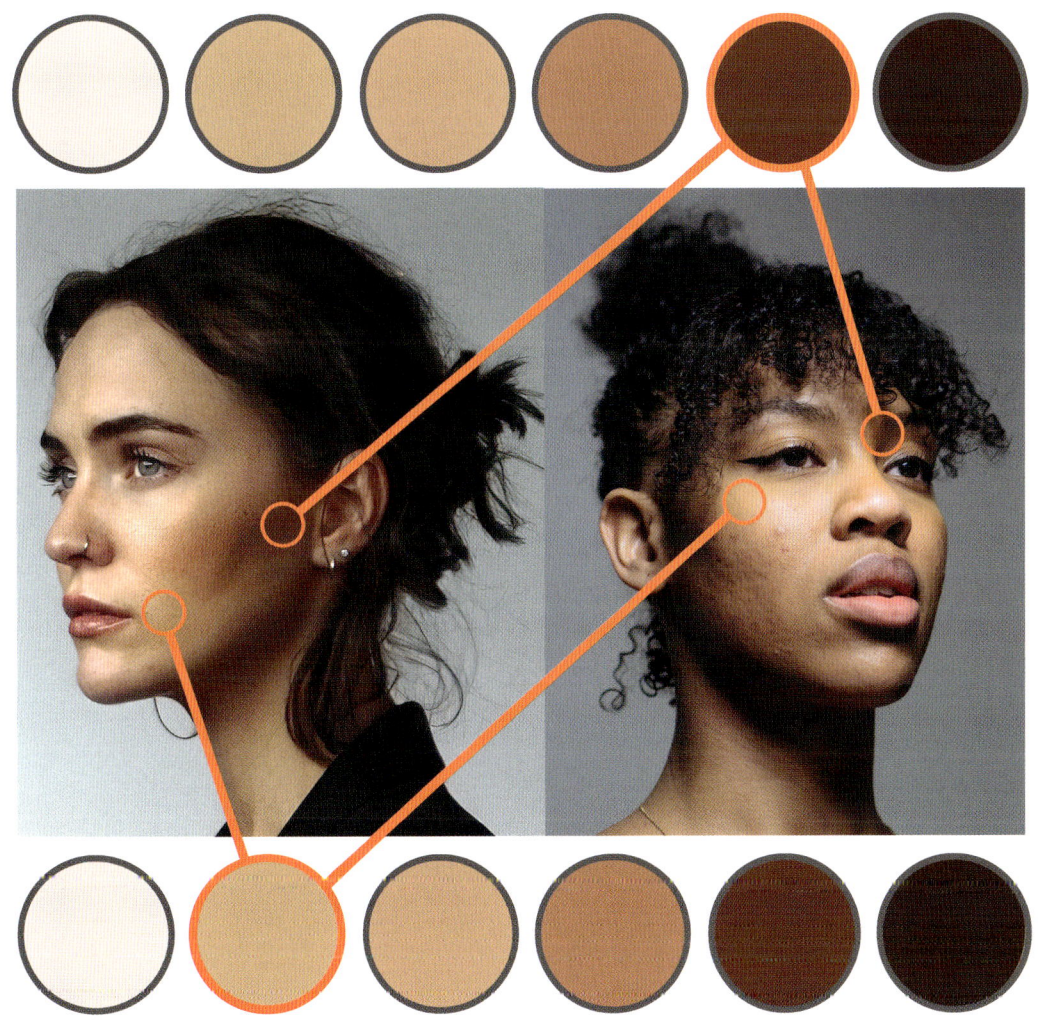

COMPLEXION AVERAGE

One of the main concepts put forward in this book is about creating a flesh palette matrix from a mother color, or said differently, a complexion average. Identifying this mother color with whatever lighting or atmospheric situation you may find yourself in is the first step in building the palette. It's a constant struggle to tune your palette to this note, so it becomes focused on.

In the images to the right, we see three vastly different complexion average tones: one that favors an olive tone **(A)**, one that favors an orange saturated tone **(B)**, and one that favors more of a pinkish, pale tone **(C)**. All of these relate to ethnicity and complexion in some way. Given different lighting situations, this is subject to change, and even the settings on your camera can vastly affect the color balance and how we perceive the skin tone of our model. When I photograph a model, I'm looking to balance out the color in order to be able see a full-bodied spectrum of color, so it doesn't look like there was an orange filter over everything or a blue filter, and so on. How do you know if your image has this full spectrum of color rather than looking filtered? In the images, notice that not only does the man in Figure **(C)** have pinkish skin tone, but he also has yellowish hair, the background has a tinge of green, and his shirt is blue. This tells me that I can trust that the skin tone is actually pinkish and doesn't just have a red or pinkish hue applied over the entire image; otherwise, those other color zones wouldn't present as they do. The same is true for all the other models depicted.

Perceiving this complexion average tone may seem easy in these images, but sometimes the relativity of many factors can make it a challenging thing to actually get on the canvas, and it may take several efforts. This is why it's important to mix up your paint fresh every day so that you can approach the canvas in a new way and not always try to just match what you previously painted. Whenever I'm painting

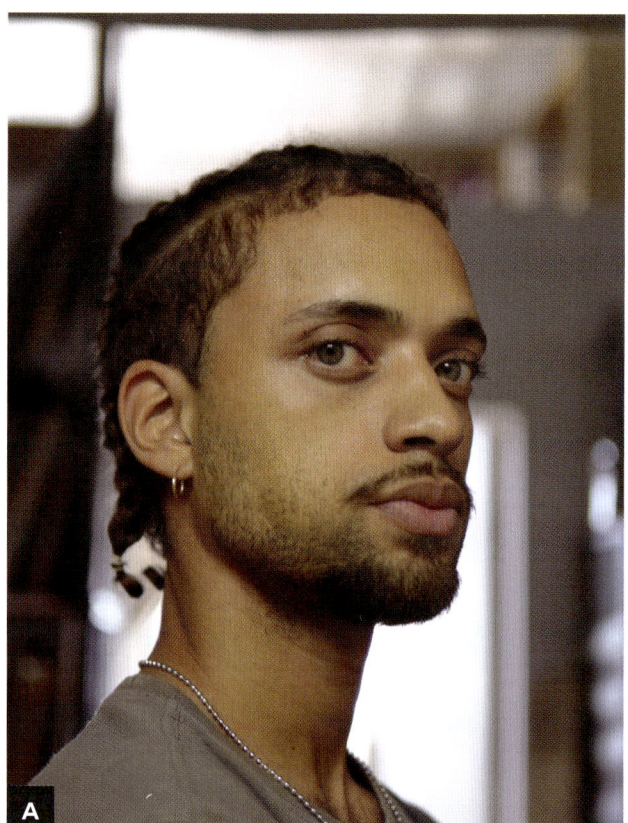

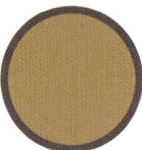

on the same thing over multiple days, I'll continually start mixing the palette from this complexion average tone, and I'm constantly trying to center my palette on achieving it. It isn't a loss or waste of time though; sometimes my previous mistakes add a little variety and excitement to the picture. For example, if I started painting the man in Figure **(A)** a little too orange in the beginning, and then I suddenly realize he has a little bit more of an olive tone, I may leave a little bit of that "mistake" orange to shine through. You may see that orange actually on his face, at the back of the neck, and also at the temple and other areas. Just remember to oil out your painting so that you can rub away or blend today's efforts with the

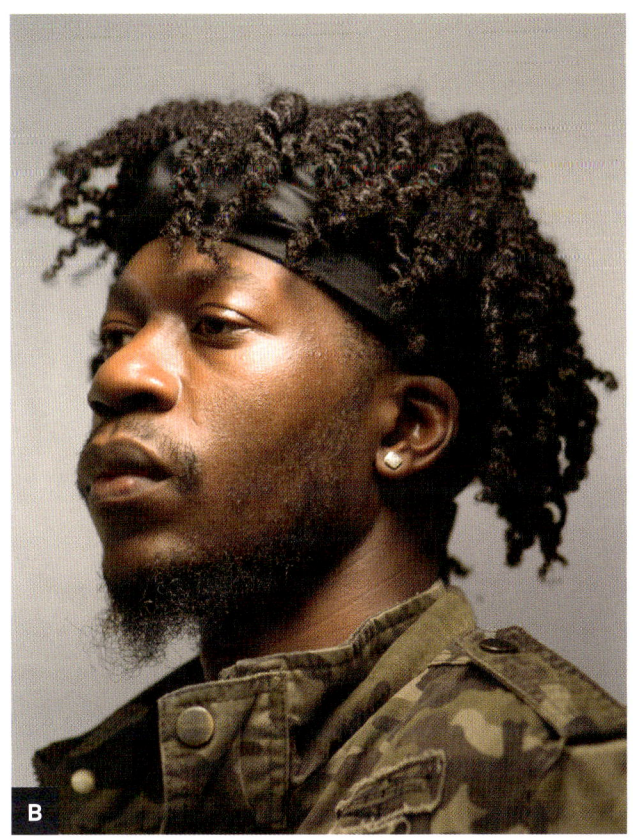

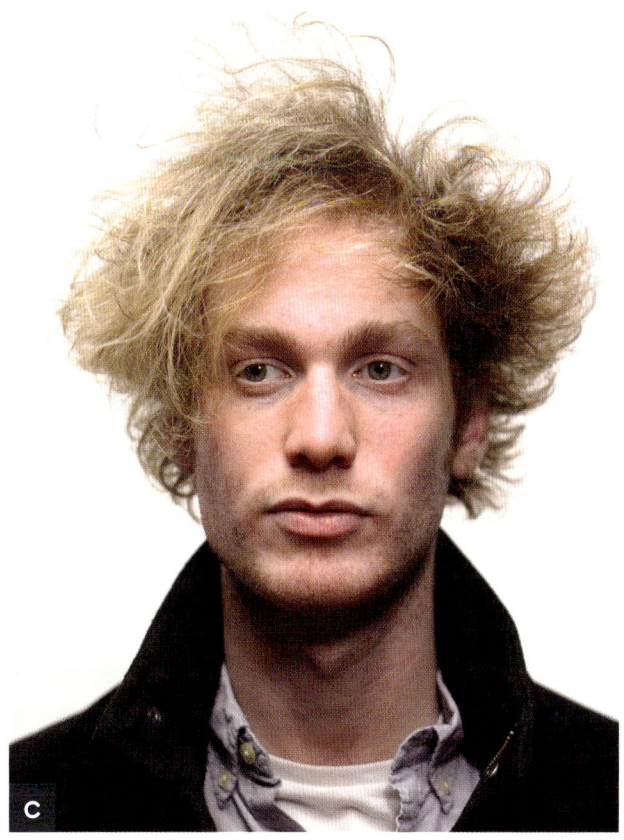

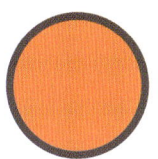

previous day's efforts more easily. As discussed in "Oiling Out and Glazing In" (see page 162), it's much easier to paint wet on wet (or oiled out) than wet on dry, which usually results in having to repaint the whole image.

One slight variation on this is that if you suddenly notice that you have made your subject too gray, you can glaze in this complexion average tone transparently over the whole surface of the painting to warm it up and pull it closer to this complexion average tone.

Getting the complexion average tone or mother color is a top priority, but the subtle variation that starts to deviate from this tone will be the very thing that actually adds excitement to the picture. Remember, the mother color is a centering point that helps you organize your palette and assess your colors, but it isn't the final goal. So as helpful as it is to identify the "right color" for the complexion, if this is all we get on our palette, there will be a monotone, boring quality to our painting that actually misses the point of flesh tones.

CLASSICAL FLESH MODEL WITH COLOR DIVERSITY AND THE ANATOMY OF LIGHT

BOUGUEREAU

William-Adolphe Bouguereau is perhaps the most influential colorist for me when it comes to flesh tone. Of course, his content and style aren't everybody's cup of tea, but he is perhaps the first and the best at tying together the classical flesh model with color diversity. Some artists use color diversity in a wild and crazy way, which at its worst can look like a skin disease or make someone's face look like a bruised piece of fruit. Bouguereau was able to achieve all of these colors while making the flesh smooth and fitting it within that classical sensibility of painters like Jacques-Louis David or Peter Paul Rubens, who pioneered the classical flesh model.

As we see in his painting *Portrait de Gabrielle Cot*, opposite, there are so many different iridescent and pearlescent tones to the skin that it's hard to take it all in. Somehow, all of these tones are organized into a larger context, the Anatomy of Light, where the light is yellowish, the light mass has a pinkish quality, the turning is slightly grayer, and the shadow has a warming red effect, which also has a yellow reflected light. To pull something like this off, you have to have extraordinary color control and a rich concept of what color is when it comes to how color shifts through different light zones (the Anatomy of Light) as well as different zones of the facial skin itself. Something like this doesn't happen by accident or by getting lucky with a specific colorful model. It's a concept-driven method of painting and seeing flesh color and its most beautiful possibilities.

Take a look at the classical flesh model sphere **(A)**, in which we get a sense of how the color of the light and the color of the atmosphere are interacting with the mother color of the skin. Through every light zone, it's changing color slightly, and it becomes a much more rich experience than just having an orange sphere that goes from light to dark with white and black. Having subtle color shifts in the zones of light will always make flesh color more interesting. Though this isn't necessary, it's a high view of the classical world of skin tone, and it demonstrates how a classical understanding doesn't have to be dry and boring but instead can be technically elevating and bring our sensibilities to a much higher place.

In Figure **(B)**, notice the variety in the diversity that gets placed into these different zones, while not straining too far from the overall tone they live in. These colors are all accents that depart slightly from the average tone based on different qualities of the skin. You may ask why there's a random purple on the sphere, but look under the eye, and you see how the skin itself changes to be slightly more violet. Or how in the lips and in the cheeks, you see a little extra pink, and how it departs slightly from the classical flesh model as an accented tone. Or you may see the bits where Bouguereau pushes the skin tone slightly cooler than it is naturally, just to create a color-shift contrast that makes the colors feel more vibrant. He does this too around the eyebrows, where we get a sense of the coolness of the skin, as well as at the jawline right before the shadow.

So to me, layering two complicated concepts like the classical flesh model and color diversity with unity, along with the various reasons the skin should change color based on the location on the face, is probably the highest understanding of flesh tone that you may come across. Layered concepts present sophistication rather than a one-size-fits-all approach that's too simplistic.

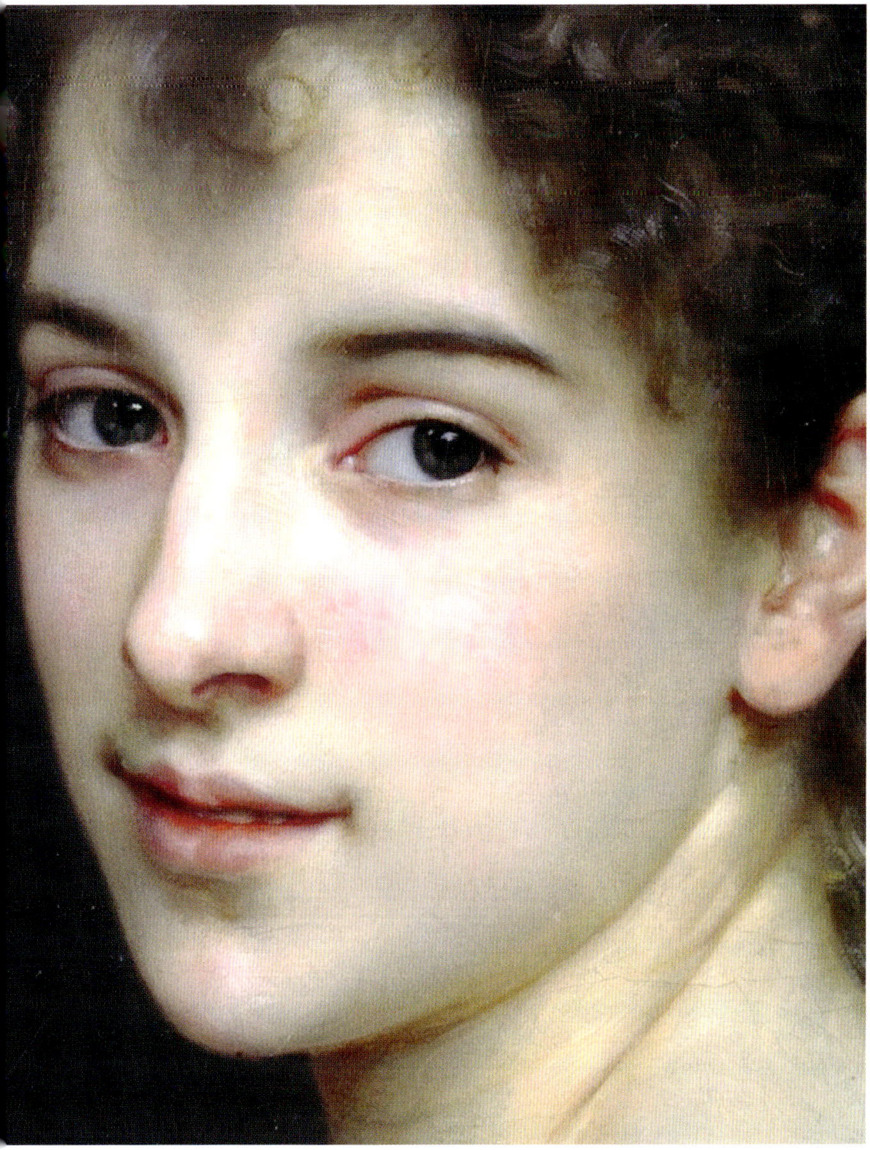

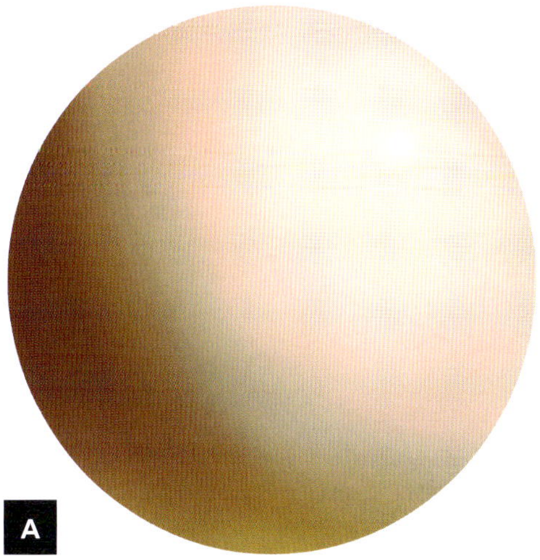

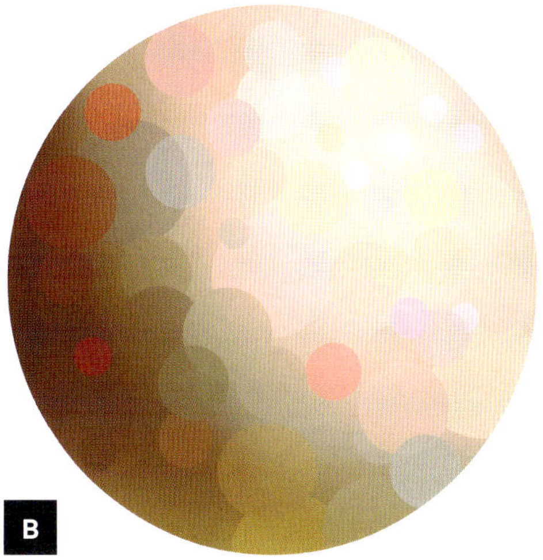

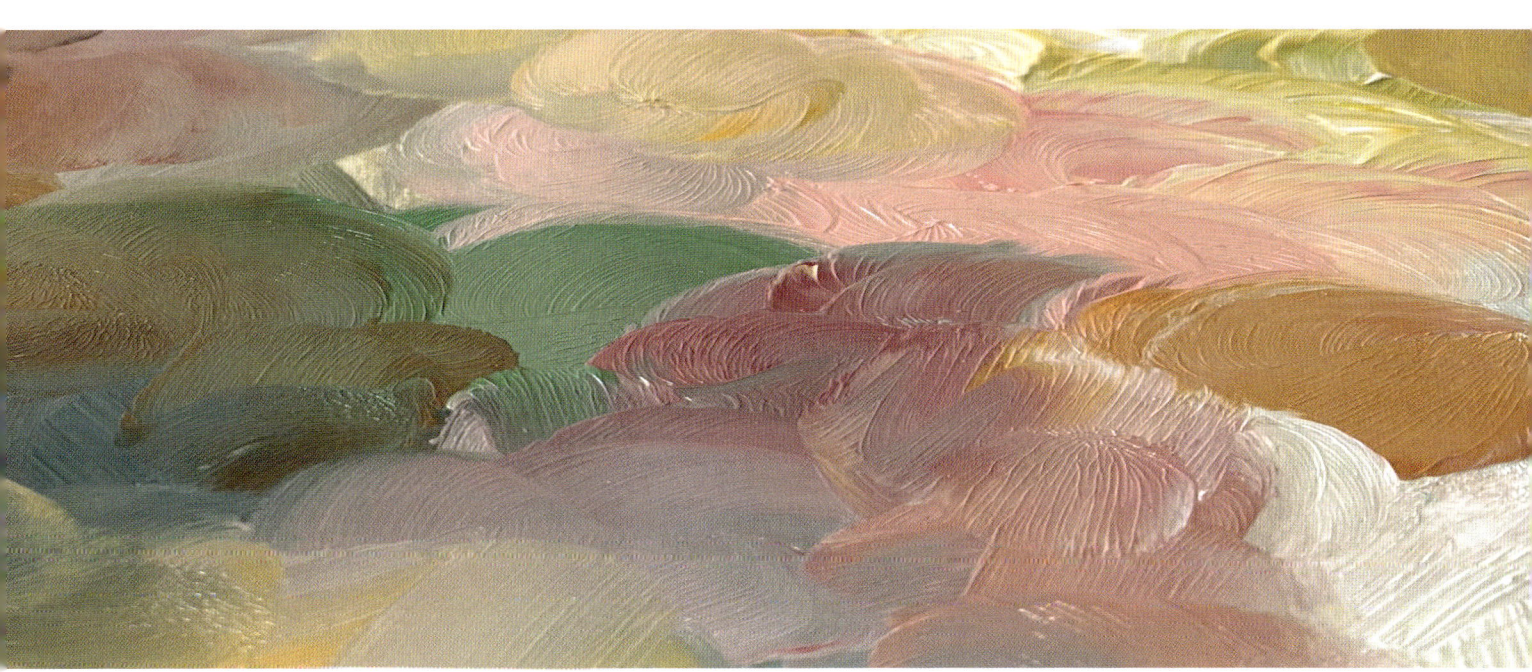

COLOR INTERPRETATION AND AESTHETICS

As I've become more in tune with the color concepts across history and different painters I love, as well as those found in nature, I've sought to put them into my own work and try to paint more from a sense of this internal aesthetic of color, rather than based purely upon what I see, especially when it comes to working from photography, which is so limited in scope of color diversity.

The camera tends to homogenize color tones, yet nature may not be exactly what resonates with you aesthetically. The artist's job is often to heighten or show our subject in a defamiliarized way so that we can truly appreciate it in a new light and not walk past it, as if it's a quotidian experience. This defamiliarization allows us space for interpretation.

To paint a subject in a different view, using assorted colors and diverse brushstrokes, to elicit the mood or the feeling that captures how you feel about your subject is part of the act of interpretation. This idea really shifted my whole concept of art-making as a somewhat "realist" painter. There's the school of nature where we're trying to learn from what we see and be anchored in reality, but there's the wild card of interpretation and feeling which we're also trying to visualize.

I think it's best to become thoroughly acquainted with and study the visual vocabulary of masters of art first, before trying to be an interpreter. One must first know a language before writing poetry. This language can be from historical artists, nature, or contemporary masters.

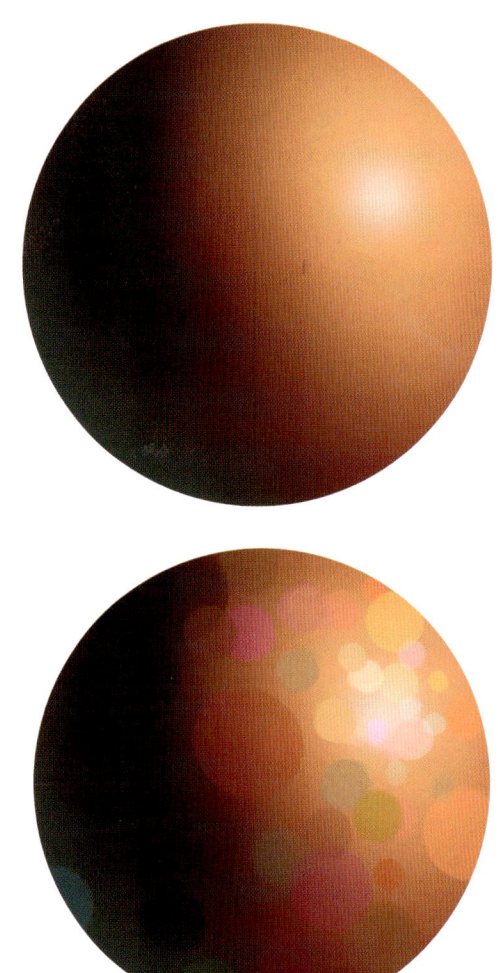

In these images, we see one of my interpretations of a subject using some borrowed ideas from classical art and also integrating some of my own ideas: the classical flesh model, flesh color diversity, color flowers, and even the concept of the compressed rainbow that we'll explore in the next section.

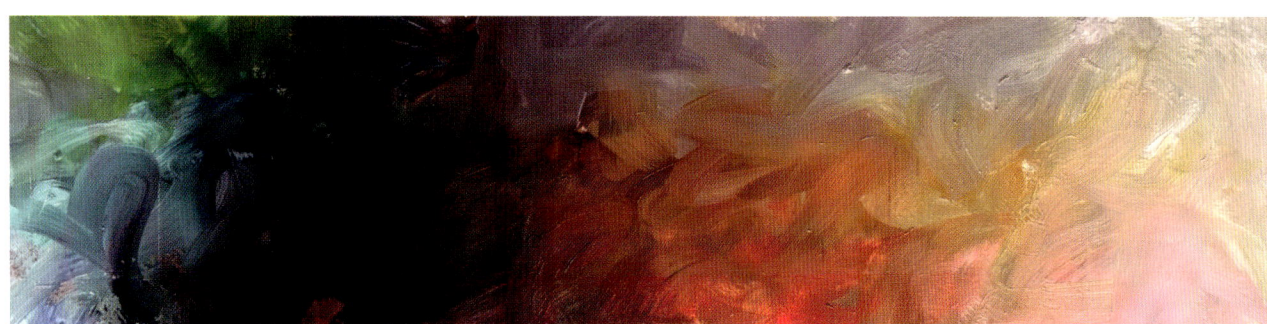

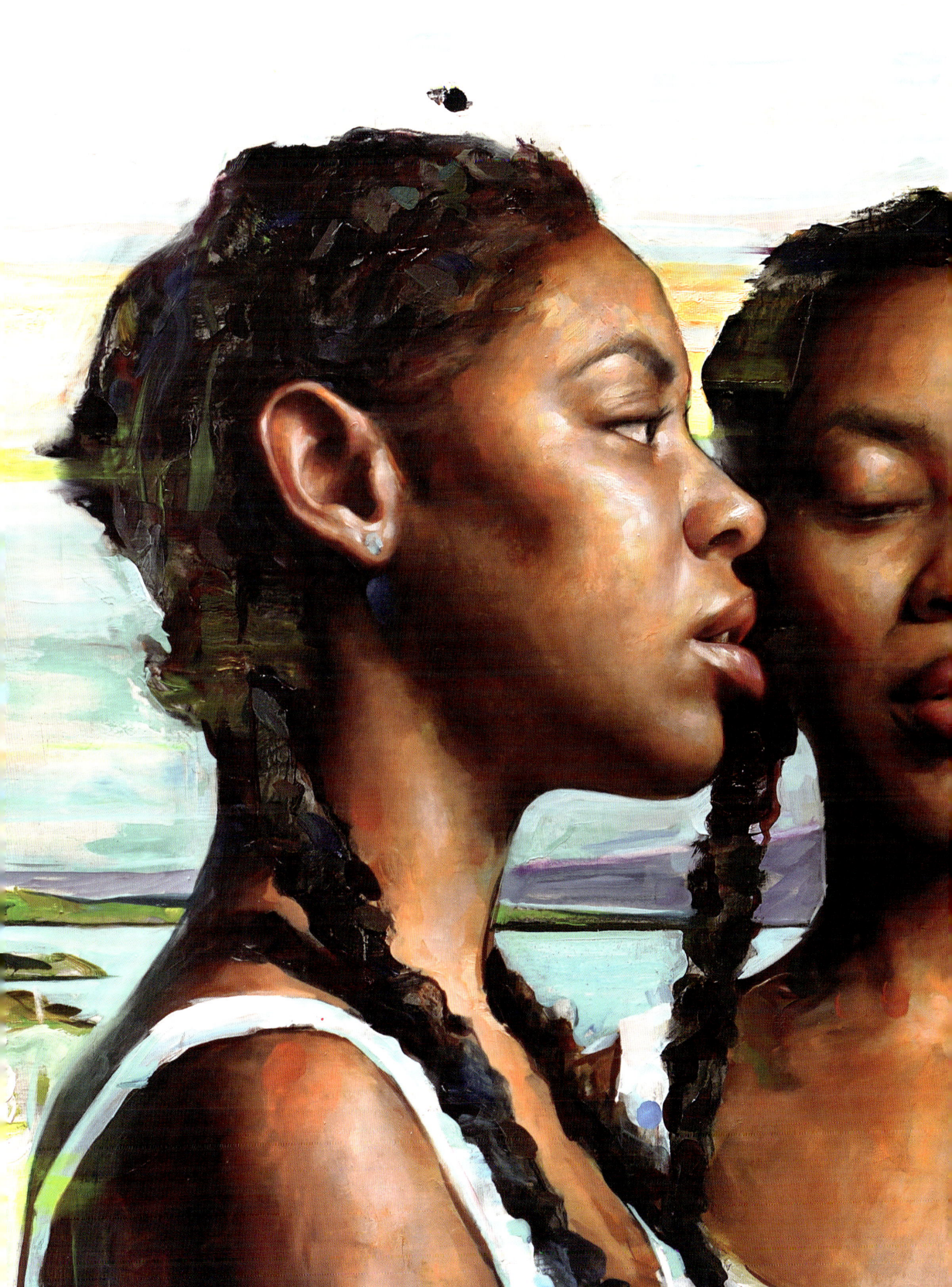

THE COMPRESSED RAINBOW

The compressed rainbow is a concept that I discovered as I continued to look at natural color harmonies found while landscape painting. The more you look for the compressed rainbow, the more that you'll find it in nature. You find it in the light of a candle. You find it in a sunset. You see it in the way a cool light from a window gently gleams across warm hardwood floors. Wherever you find it, it's a particularly effective tool to have in your painter's toolbox. It formalizes the notion that as things get darker, they change hue and temperature as well as value. More simply put, as a yellow light hits an object and slowly goes darker, it goes through orange, red, and violet to get to a darker gray or blue, as seen in the diagram opposite.

I call it the compressed rainbow because it's not a true rainbow in the sense that we aren't talking about a bag of Skittles where the colors are fully saturated to their maximum. This rainbow flow of tones is mitigated by graying down of these tones, to harmonize them in a gentle manner and keep them from being obnoxiously colored. Sometimes, this graying down happens more strongly at different areas of a progression. Typically, the darks are the most gray part of the compressed rainbow, where the colors may not be as chromatically blue as they look. The context of all the colors together can trick you into thinking that they're more saturated than they actually are.

I see the compressed rainbow often in flesh tones when there are multiple light sources, which generally make the confusing topic of painting flesh tones even more complicated. That's why there's a section in this book dealing with this concept, so that we can paint flesh tone in the way that Joaquín Sorolla did, not just with a singular light source in a room, but also acknowledging the atmospheric conditions that are all around us as well.

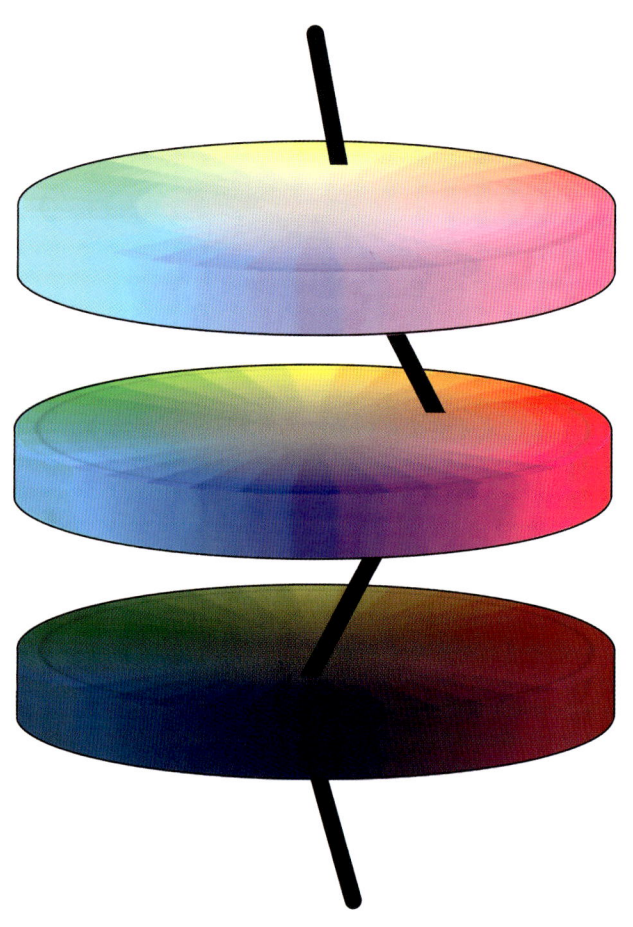

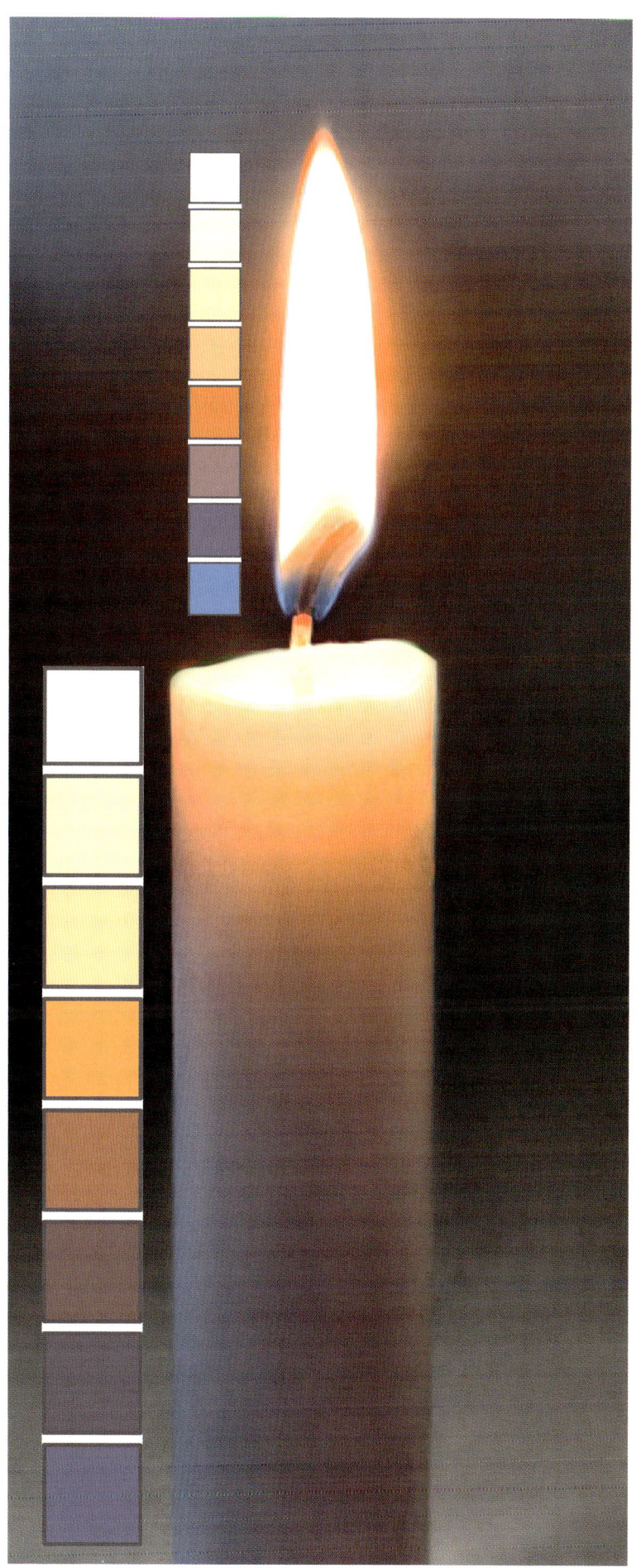

9 | UNDERSTANDING COLOR AND LIGHT

ATMOSPHERIC CONDITIONS

As I mentioned, I noticed this concept of the compressed rainbow while landscape painting, and where it comes from is the idea that you have a primary warm light ("the sun") and you have a secondary cold light ("the sky") that are both influencing the perception of your subject. It happens to be a beautiful thing, and this is why many landscape painters go out at sunrise or sunset to achieve the colors of these forces in full action. In the middle of the day, the sun rises and cancels out the blueness of the sky, and the blueness cancels out the warmth of the sun, making most things gray and hazy. If you've ever gone plein air landscape painting, you know that this is the worst time to go outside and paint for light effect. But these sunrise and sunset conditions are the optimal time to see the magic of color in nature.

In the diagram at right, there's a flesh sphere showing the forces of the sun in the sky acting upon it. If you think about it, the mother color or complexion tone of this flesh sphere is actually quite a gray orange, as seen in the center of the sphere. Things become more interesting when you notice what the sun does to this gray orange as it hits the sphere on the right. You get this beautifully chromatic yellow, fading to a somewhat chromatic red orange, and a little towards the top you get a touch of violet as these colors start to mix with the sky color. The sky also has its blue color reflected on the top of the flesh sphere. If we consider the sky to be very light and blue the further we go up, notice that light blue actually isn't found on the flesh sphere. That light blue bends the color of the flesh towards itself, but doesn't overtake it. The sky blue takes the flesh color on the sphere and pulls it towards violet and perhaps lightens it slightly, but not so much that you'd just take the sky color and paint on the flesh sphere with it. You have to mix the sky blue with the flesh tone first, and maybe you have to put a little extra violet in that mixture to create this rainbow effect that we see here on this sphere.

Let's look at the shadow at the bottom of the sphere, which I've left quite neutral dark. Imagine if this flesh sphere had green grass under it, causing green to reflect into the shadow. Then, you'd have color reflecting on this flesh sphere from all sides!

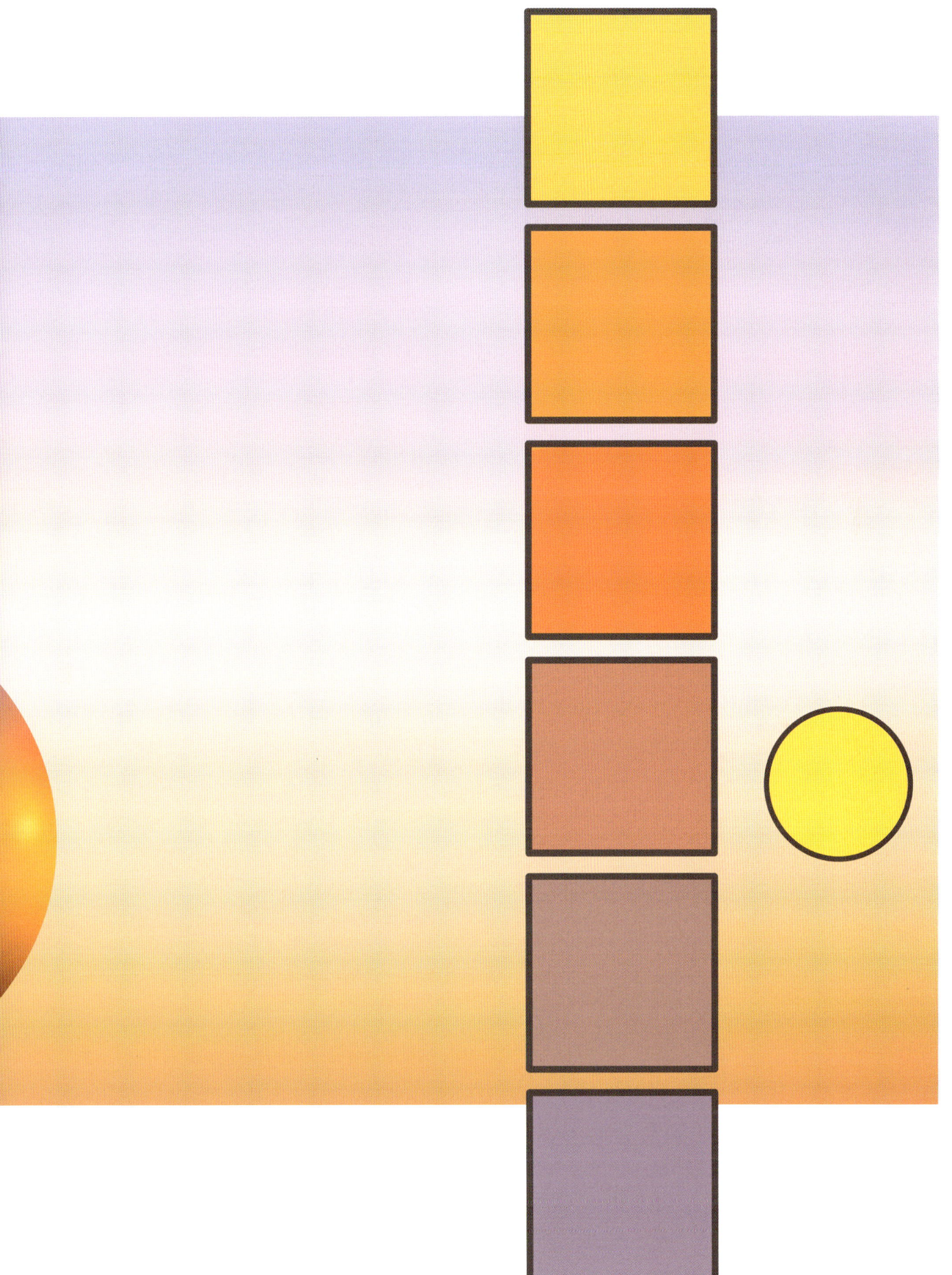

COMPRESSED RAINBOW WITH A MODEL

Now that we know what the compressed rainbow is and a little bit about what can form it in nature, let's turn to a model that has multiple light sources. This image, opposite, is definitely an extreme color version of the compressed rainbow, but I find that when trying to absorb these concepts, you have to start with extreme examples. Subtlety can be added to them as you find necessary. Aesthetically, you may not want the face to be this yellow or orange, but you can easily see the compressed rainbow at work because of this extreme version. If you'd prefer to make these tones slightly grayer in order to avoid such a saturated orange face, that's an individual aesthetic decision.

The compressed rainbow is at work across the forehead, but if you look at the nose and other areas on the face, you'll see the compressed rainbow in many more areas than just the forehead, and in fact, usually when this situation is happening, there are many different value ranges and slight variations of this same progression of tones. This means that sometimes the compressed rainbow is in a lighter range; sometimes it goes to a darker range; sometimes it's a little bit more saturated; sometimes it's more subtle; and so on.

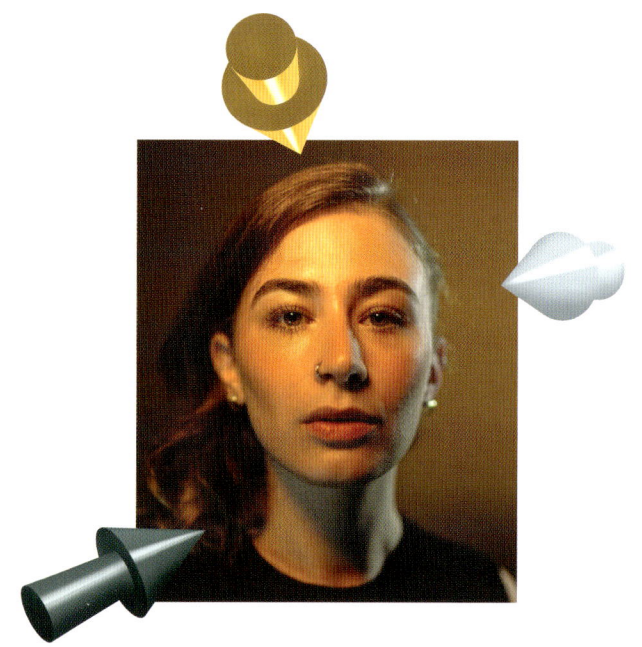

The smaller image above demonstrates the direction the light is coming from when it hits the face. I used three-dimensional arrows to emphasize the depths and the angles from which these lights are hitting the face. In professional portrait photography, this is known as a three-point lighting system: a rim light (light blue arrow), key light (yellow arrow), and fill light (dark green arrow). In this image, the yellow key light is considered the primary light for illuminating the face. The fill light is typically relating back to the rim light and perhaps represents the rim light bouncing off of something else to slightly illuminate the shadows, so that they're not black. This sense of lighting is dynamic and really shows off the three-dimensional qualities of the face.

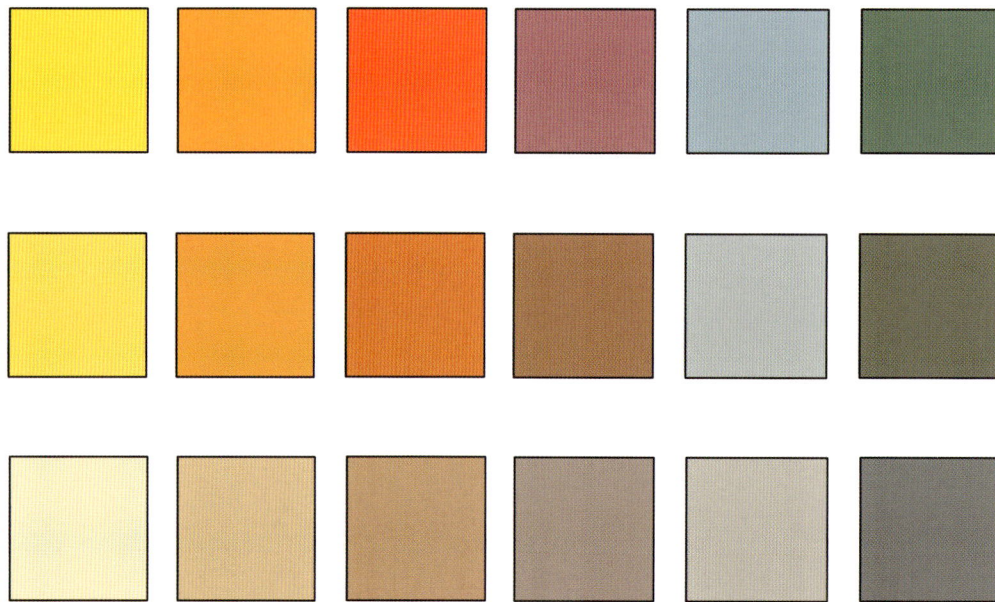

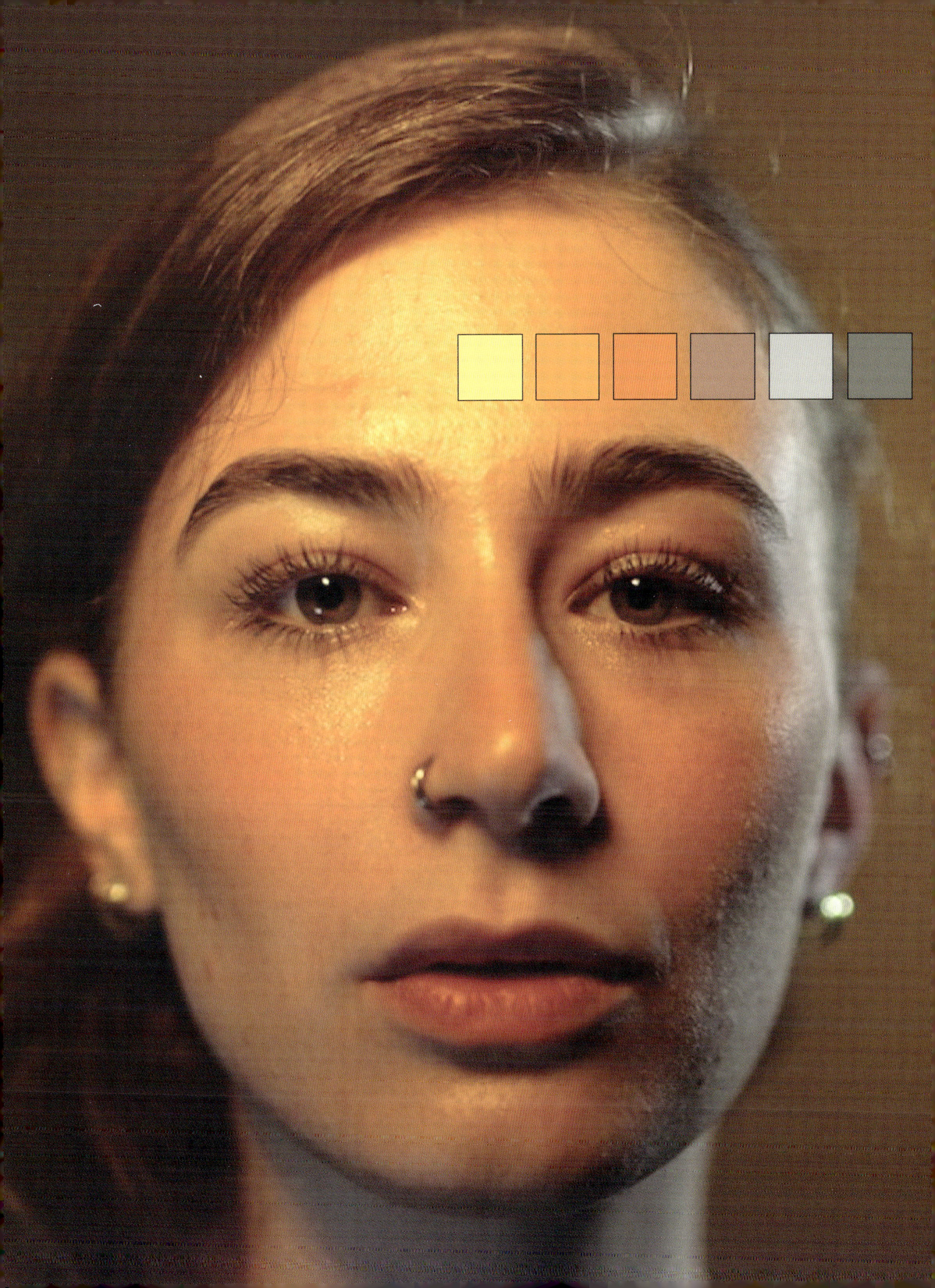

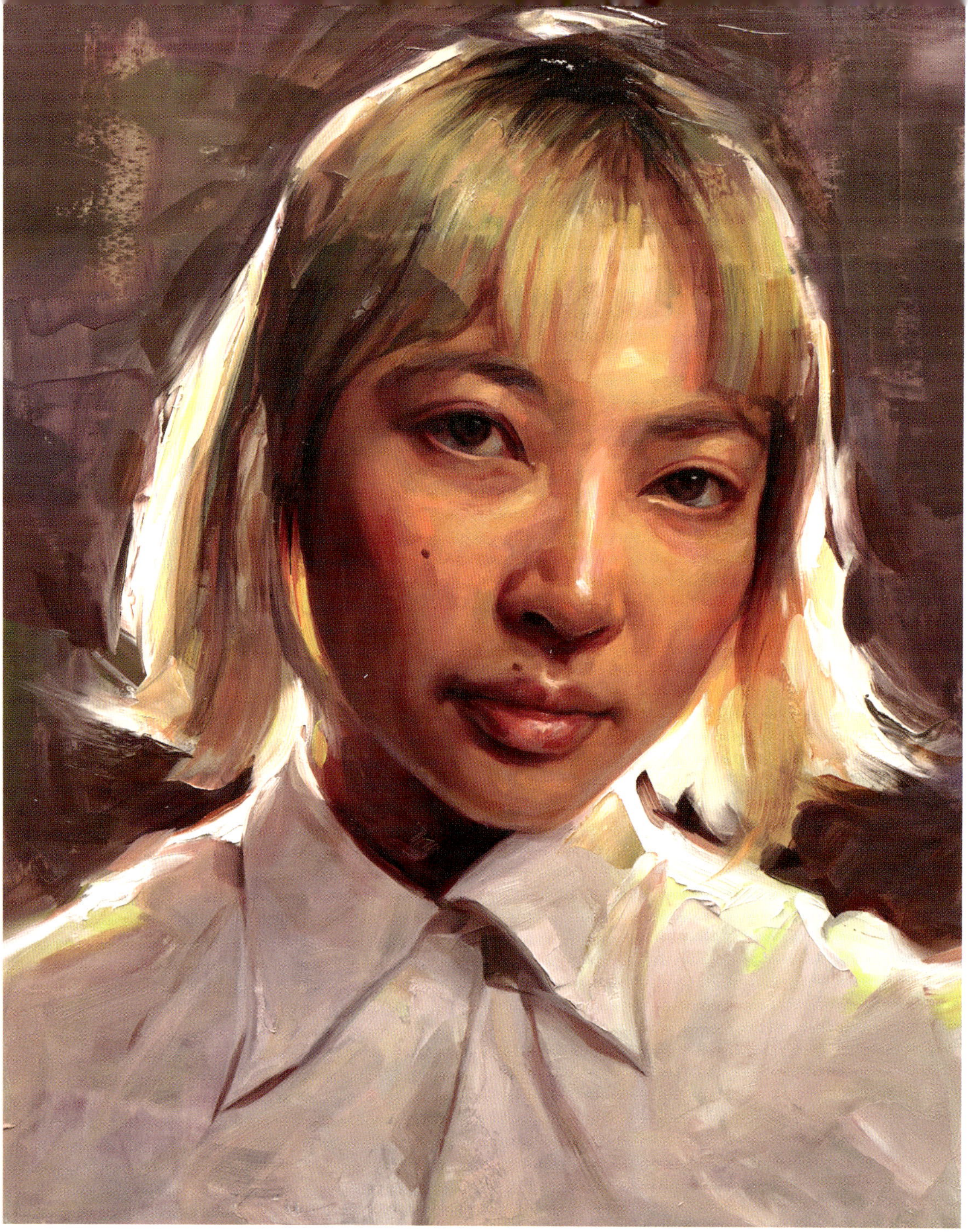

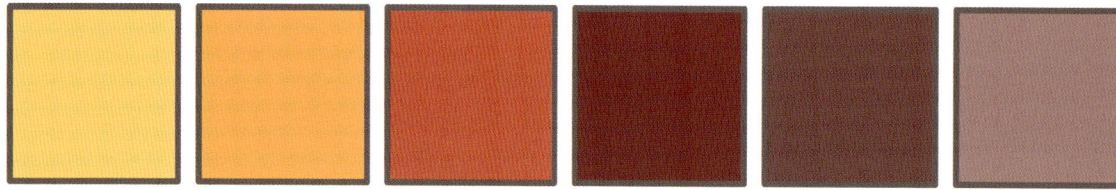

The image above represents the compressed rainbow in a painting with some of my artistic decisions also represented. Again, there's a complicated lighting situation here where we have backlight, but don't let that confuse you. The primary key light is warm. It's on the front of the face. Then, the shadow and atmospheric tones of the background are more violet, so you get this beautiful quality of yellow, fading to red, to a red violet, and then a gray violet. You could also imagine blues in this picture, and you might see little flashes of them on the white shirt, but the effect of the compressed rainbow is present here even in the absence of blue.

COOL TO WARM

In most traditional paintings and landscapes, the primary light is warm. Since the sun can't be cold, the effects of a compressed rainbow always go from warm to cold, but as we see in this image below, there's a reversal of this order. The primary light is actually the sky from a window. This picture was probably taken during the middle of the day in a dark room by a window. What do you think the secondary light source is? Is it another light in the room? Is it the sun? No, in actuality, it's also the sky! The sky is reflecting off of the yellow-orange coat, creating a reflected light that warms up the shadow and behaves as a secondary light. It's secondary because it's a less intense light source than the light coming in directly from the window. As you may notice, the light on the face is blown out and slightly cold on the forehead and cheek, but the shadow has a warmth to it from this reflected light and is a bit softer.

When trying to play with these patterns, perhaps in your own photography and/or painting, it's immensely helpful to privilege one light source as being primary and more intense than the secondary light source. Of course, you can make the primary and secondary equal, making two primaries, but usually this creates more of a busy-looking image that doesn't feel quite as natural or beautiful. This effect is mostly formed in nature by light reflecting off of something else, or there's a dimmer fill light. Two primaries usually aren't found in nature. I advise you to embrace these natural standards; when we try to produce light effects in the studio, it's easy to overdo it.

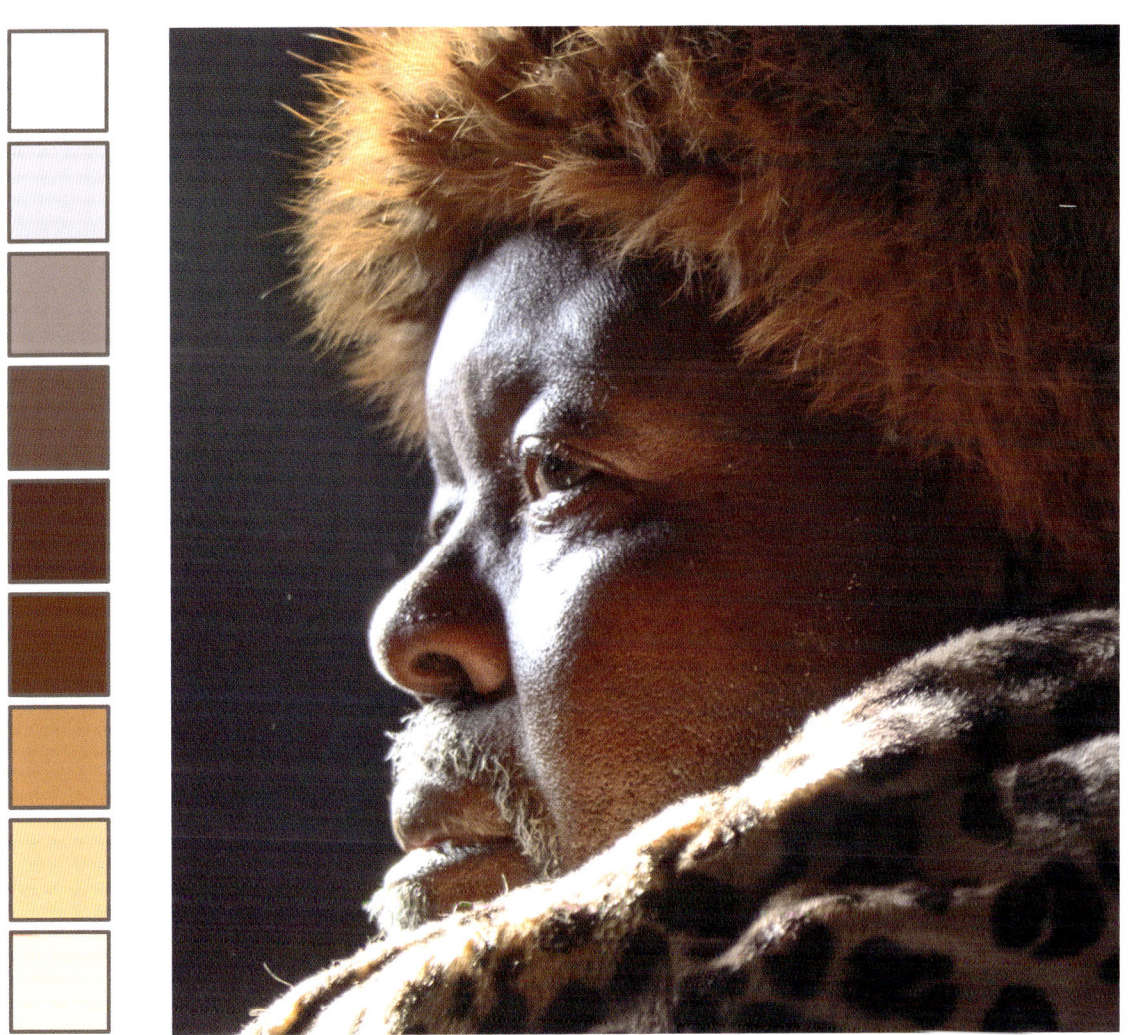

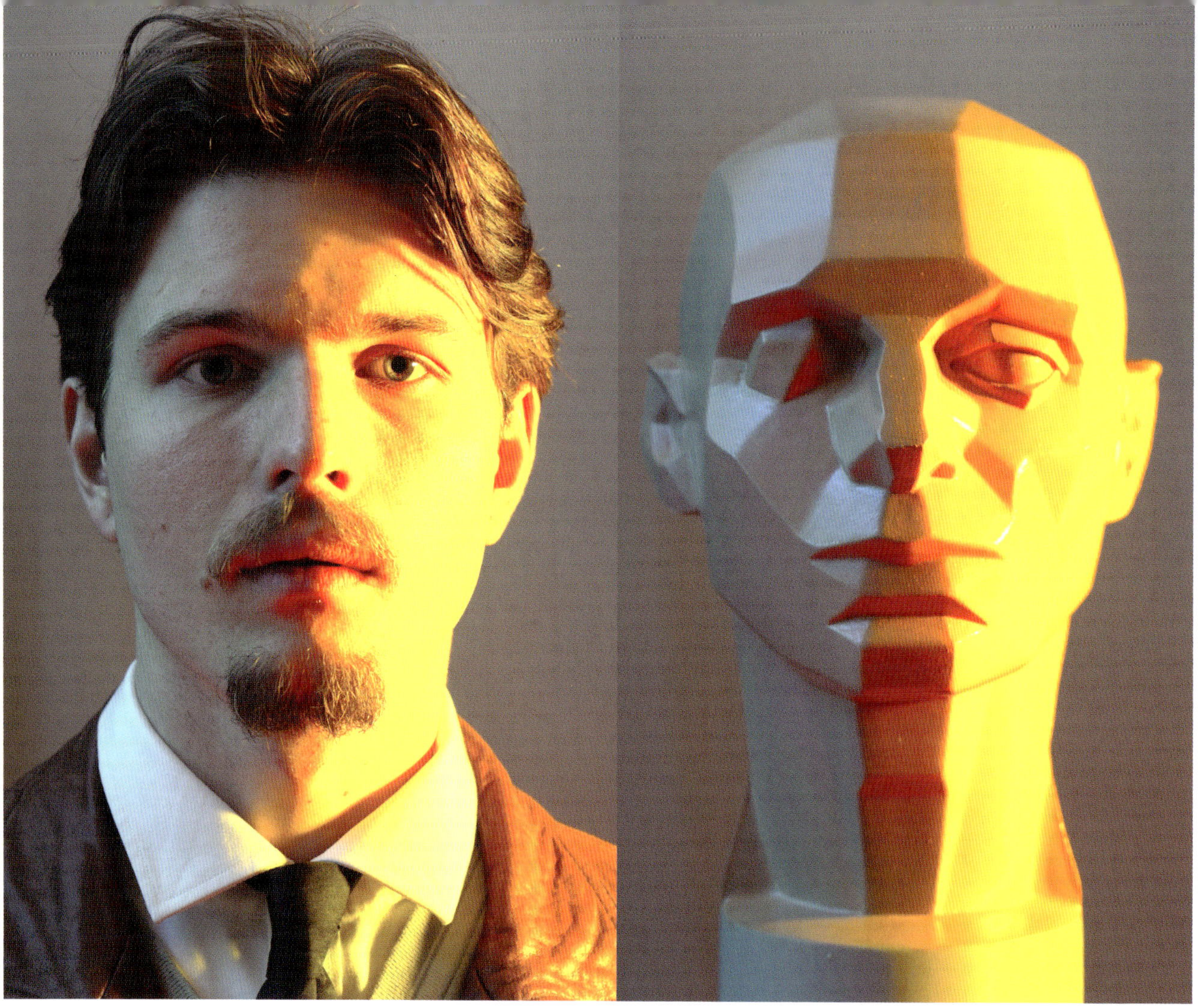

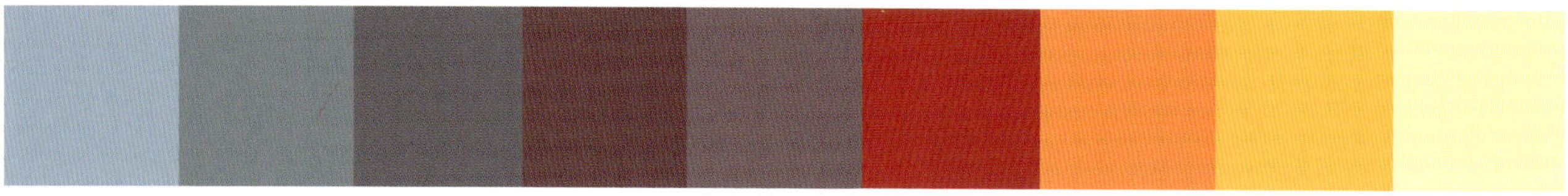

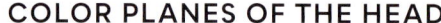

COLOR PLANES OF THE HEAD

As a student, I'd often hear about the planes of the head, and it was hard for me to understand its usefulness when painting a portrait. Why would I want to make my painting more of a robotic statement of the human I'm looking at, rather than just paint what I see, which would be much softer and more natural? I'm not alone; when I posted the image above to social media, I had many comments about how the bridge of the nose was wrong compared to the model, and why does my planar sculpture have two mouths?

The famous planes-of-the-head model that I'm using was made by John Asaro as a way to see how light hits a head from all sides and to study the dimensionality of the head in a generic way. He didn't make the sculpture to perfectly match my model. So of course, it's not a perfect one-to-one

comparison, but it does help us to see what is made slightly more subtle in the model. In fact, some of the color planes on the Asaro head are more interesting and tend to highlight some quiet lighting effects that are occurring on the model, such as the blue light and how it hits the skin above the mouth, the cheekbone, and the forehead.

This allows me to paint my subject in a way that's more dynamic and bold and to also see where that cold light is really bending the flesh tone towards itself. As a way of study, it gets me thinking about the face in a dimensional sense. It helps me perceive the dimension of the head by taking away the roundness or smoothness of the face. Also, it takes away the facial hair, the eyes, and even the eyebrows, which are a distraction from the way that light and color roll over the form of the face.

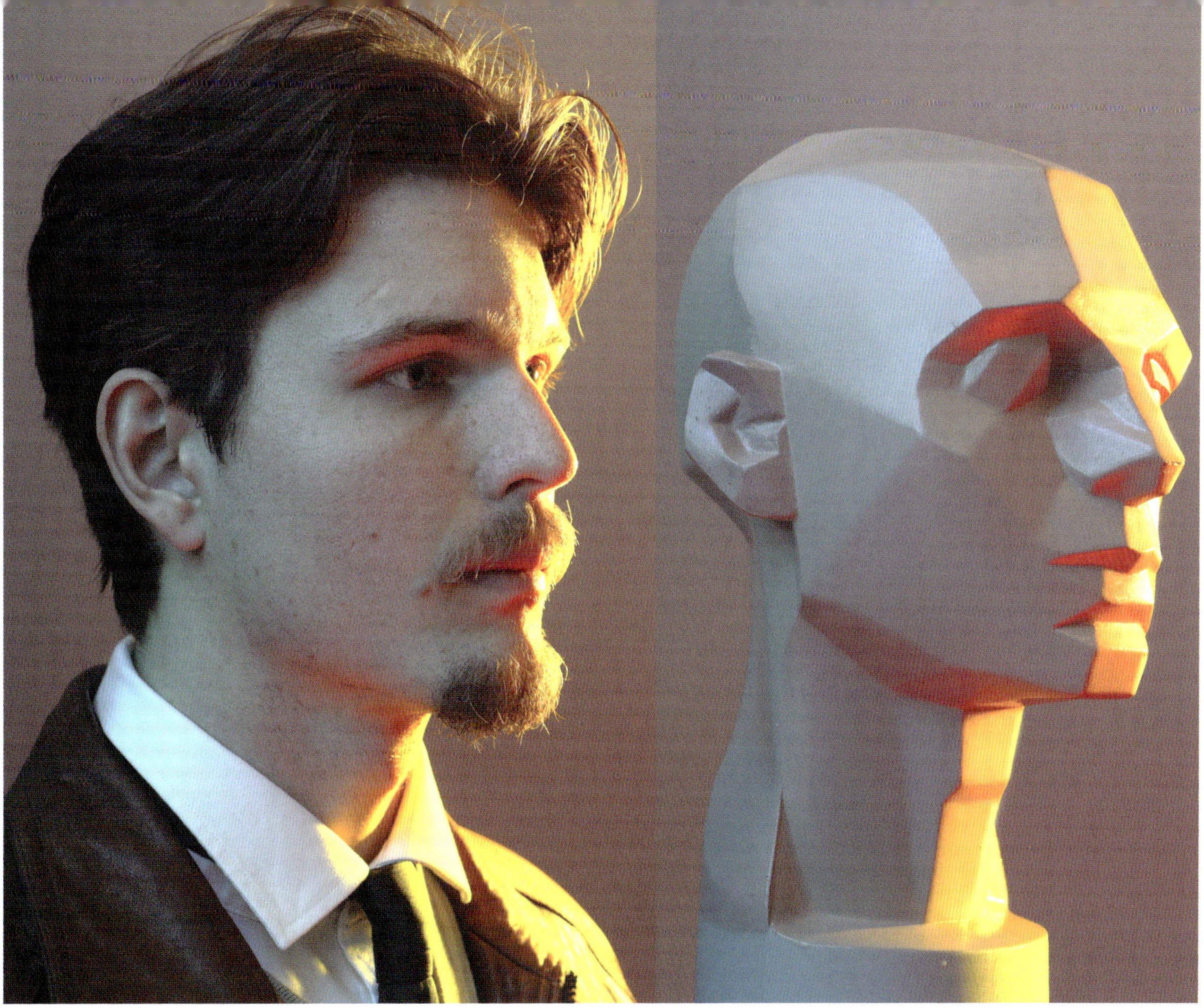

I've made one small modification to my Asaro head. I painted the head a generic warm flesh tone, so that when I photograph it and my model in the same light, they're fairly close. This could be done with many different flesh tone complexions, but I tried to match him as close as possible.

I used three different light sources on this. I was looking at some different movie stills that had beautiful color effects in their portraits, and I wanted to achieve those same color tones. In this lighting situation, there's a yellow-orange rim light, a cool ambient fill light, and a red reflected under-light. The underlight forces the color of this painting into a strange otherworldly quality often found in film.

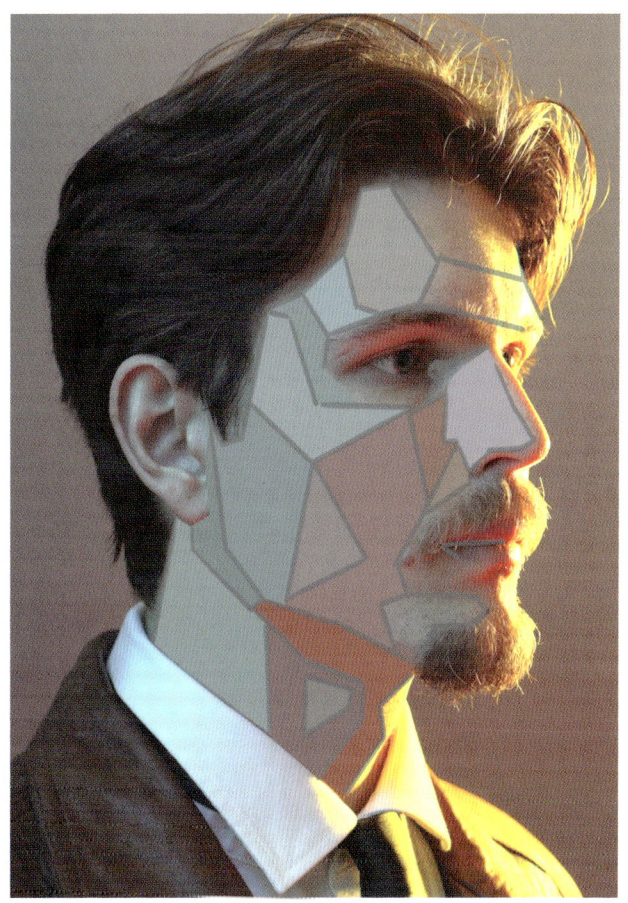

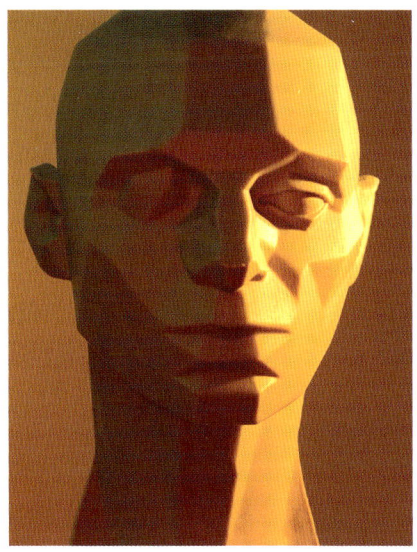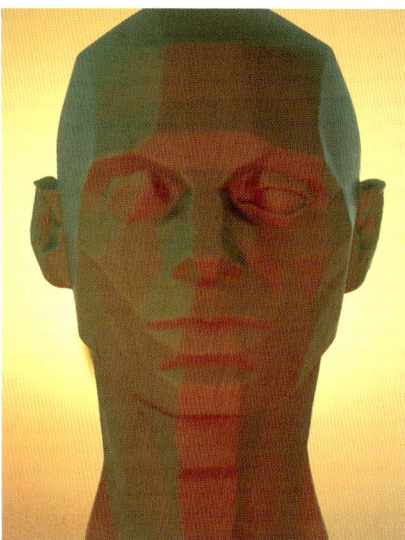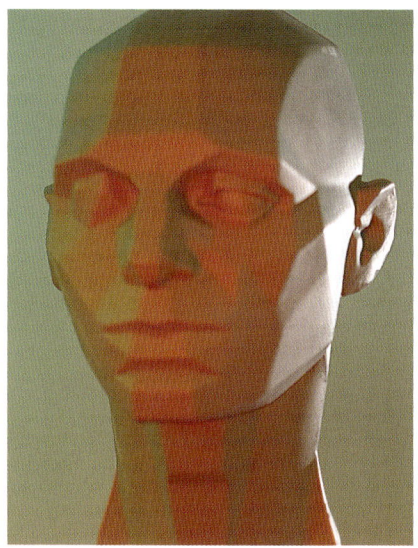

CINEMATIC LIGHTING FOR MOOD

Part of exploring the color planes of the head and how they create dimension with a portrait also has the ability to affect the mood. The mood of an image can be drastically affected by color choice and lighting. Since their time is precious and usually expensive, before you do a model shoot with your subject in your studio, you may want to consider how the light will strike their face prior to their arrival. Exploring color options and lighting options with an Asaro head is helpful in trying to articulate your vision before the live model shows up. I usually have this head on a tripod and can position it to the height of the model.

The three-point lighting system of primary light, rim light, and fill light (see page 152) can be quite a complicated equation to fit together in some intelligible way. You don't want them to conflict with each other, yet you need to maximize the dimension that you can create through illuminating the head. Three-point light is a little awkward at first and requires experimentation. I'd recommend starting out with just warm and cool lights, which can be very effective, and not to try to put in all of the colors of the rainbow. Try a warmer yellow-orange light with a cooler grayer light and just play around with the intensities of light and the angles of how you've positioned them.

I'll say it again: It's much more cost-effective and clarifying to play around in your studio with these angles and positions of lights before your model comes into the studio. Another tip is to get dimmable video lights that allow you to control which light is primary and which light is secondary. Often, these lights will also come with a way to change the temperature from warm to cool.

When it comes to experimenting with light, you need to get a pack or two of color gel filters in order to actually change the color. Gels can melt and burn up around hot bulbs, but if you use the LED video lights, since they don't heat up, you can freely experiment with the gels, attaching them to the lights with bulldog clips.

Obviously, if you're doing a commissioned portrait, you may not want to make a lighting environment that feels scary or anxiety-producing, so soft or more natural tones between warm and cool are often desired, but if you'd like to create more drama and experiment with color, this can be a fun use of your time. You might find this especially useful for a larger narrative painting—being able to position your model in an environment where it's truly engaging with the atmosphere, and the colors around the subject can be adjusted to how it fits your narrative.

Not only is this knowledge helpful for producing some creative results in the desired effect of your color and light scheme, it's mind-altering in a way that allows you to see the head more in a 3D space better than just about anything. Normally as painters, we think of the head in a flat, 2D way because we're painting it on a 2D surface. We're obsessed with the silhouette, the features, and the details. We have no concept of the dimension of the head. I've

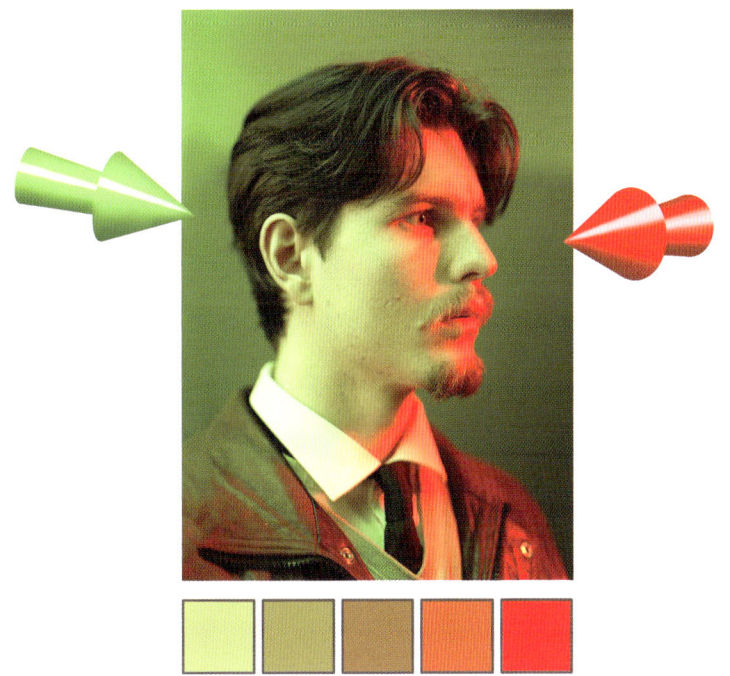

been around sculptors who really understand the planes and how the head occupies 3D space, whereas we painters are obsessed with shadow shapes and the visual appearance of the model in 2D. Cross-training and spending a little bit of effort trying to understand how to light a head in the cinematic way helps you to understand the dimension of the head in a manner that you may have possibly never considered.

IT ISN'T ALL RAINBOWS

Sometimes, when you're lighting the head in a cinematic way and especially if you're using opposite tones as in this image above, you won't produce the compressed rainbow. This disturbing lighting concept, which could easily be seen in an intense climactic moment in a movie, doesn't produce the rainbow (as shown in the color strip). That's maybe why it's disturbing! You'd never find this in nature. The sun is not red, and we tend not to like the way that we look in green light. This image goes against the natural color harmony found in nature that usually produces a compressed rainbow. When I see the light effect of a compressed rainbow, I've often wondered, what makes those colors so harmonious and easy to look at? Is it just my prejudice for what is naturally

occurring and easy to process? If I lived on Mars, and we normally had green lights indoors, would this then feel natural? And the way that we see things on earth, would that then feel strange? Regardless of what we feel is natural, there's a psychological element to the way the colors play out on the face, and you want to be aware of what this effect produces when lighting your subject.

This image is also slightly disturbing in my opinion because it has two primary light sources and not one dominating. This is a subtle thing that's easily overlooked in lighting design, as it's just exciting sometimes to play with lights and see what's happening with the face, but having a single primary, again, aligns with what we see in nature, and it therefore tends to be more pleasing.

All in all, these jarring qualities can have a dramatic effect, and of course, that's why it's used in cinema and sometimes in narrative paintings. Maybe this resonates with your aesthetics, in which case it may be the direction in which you choose to go. But if this doesn't describe you, just be cautious about the unanticipated psychological effects of your lighting.

10 | THE PHYSICAL REALITIES OF PAINT

THICK PAINT IS POWERFUL

Among the many different physical realities of paint that are dynamic and worth mentioning in a portrait book, the truth that thick paint is powerful is exciting and beautiful. For one thing, when we use the paint thinly, it doesn't truly become itself. If we use an orange color and we spread it out thinly, it's then compromised by whatever happens to be underneath it, which is usually something that will gray it down or darken it. When a color is placed on the canvas thickly, it's 100 percent itself in tone and color. Unless you just want to make a colored drawing, considering the attributes of thick paint is important as you're attempting to make a face out of paint.

Accompanying thick paint is the notion of *impasto*, as seen in the detail image, opposite. Impasto is an Italian word for thick, interpretive paint, and it's typically used to describe light, meaning that the thickest parts in a painting are usually represented as the lightest parts of the painting. This isn't a hard and fast rule; it's meant to be broken. I've seen many thicker dark areas in Rembrandt paintings, for example. But as a general rule, impasto is used to describe light and can especially be effective as a method for describing texture that's hit by light. For example, I'd see skin texture on this man's face in the light, but I probably wouldn't see his skin texture in the shadow because shadows are mysterious and vague and cause details to become smokier. That's why there's this natural phenomenon of detail and clarity in the light that's often interpreted with thicker impasto paint.

When paint is applied thickly, it becomes three-dimensional and picks up extra light in the room, allowing us to get a painting to actually look brighter than it is. Thin paint doesn't pick up light in the room as much. Thick paint can also be a way to show these tiny little wrinkles in skin texture by creating a fake sense of detail that it would take many hours to even attempt to describe with a tiny brush. Even if we could, it wouldn't have the same power and gusto of an artistic, bold stroke of thick paint. There is power in thick paint, and it should definitely be used as one of the tools in your toolbox of painterly tricks. Pair with a contrast of thinner paint so that it remains dynamic and not overused.

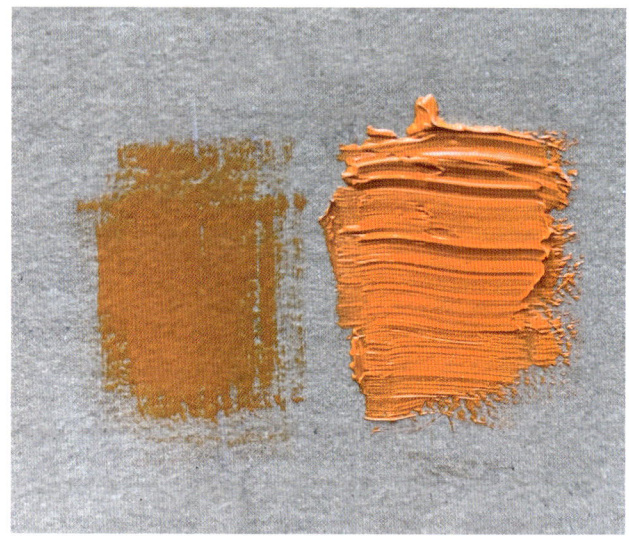

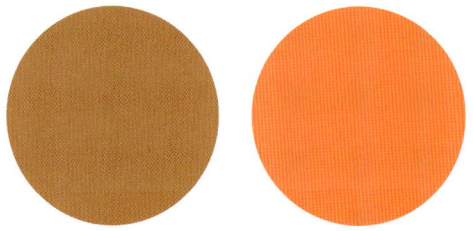

▶ Steve Forster, *Detail of Kevin*, oil on aluminum, 16" × 16" | 15.2 cm × 15.2 cm

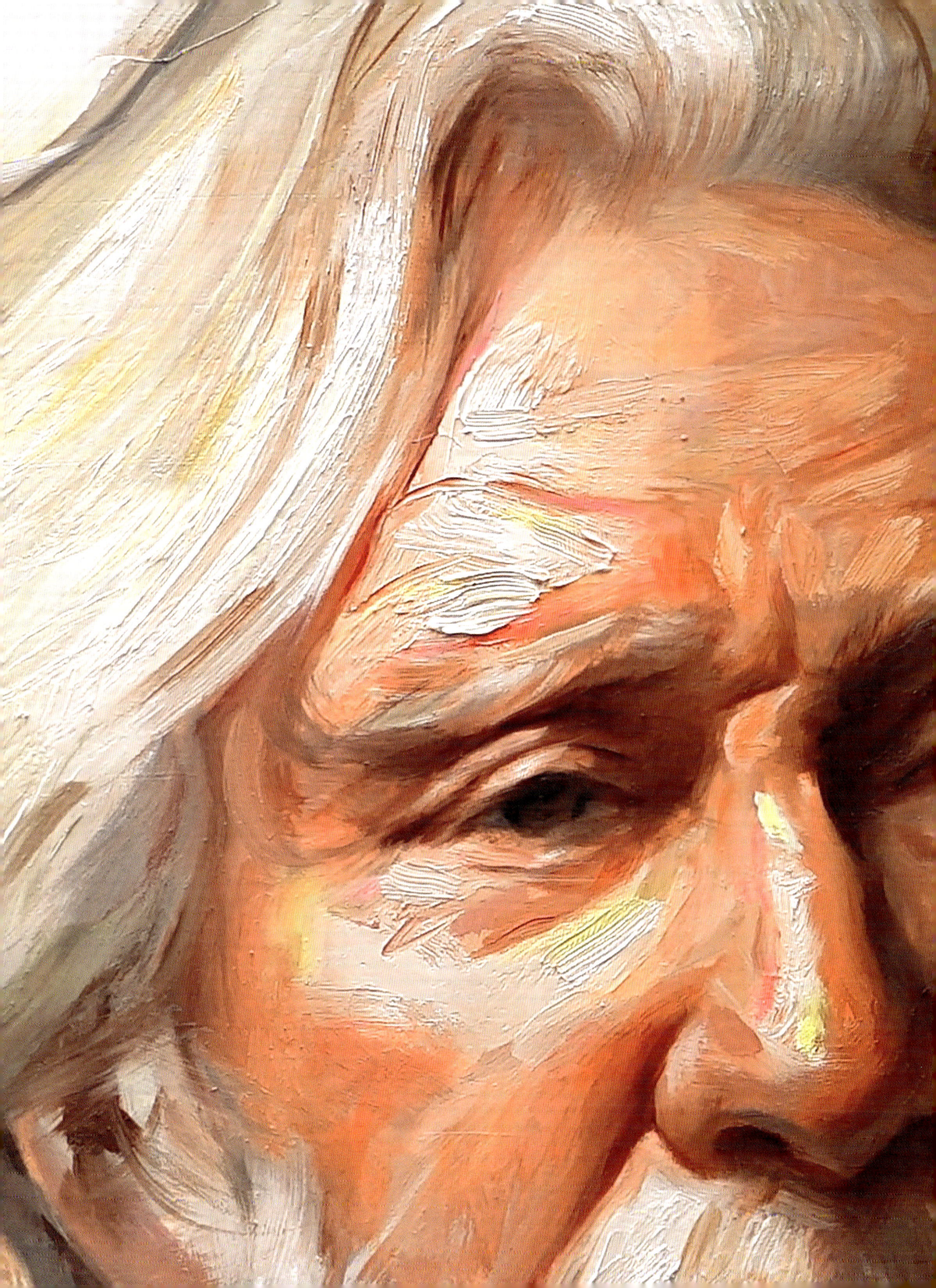

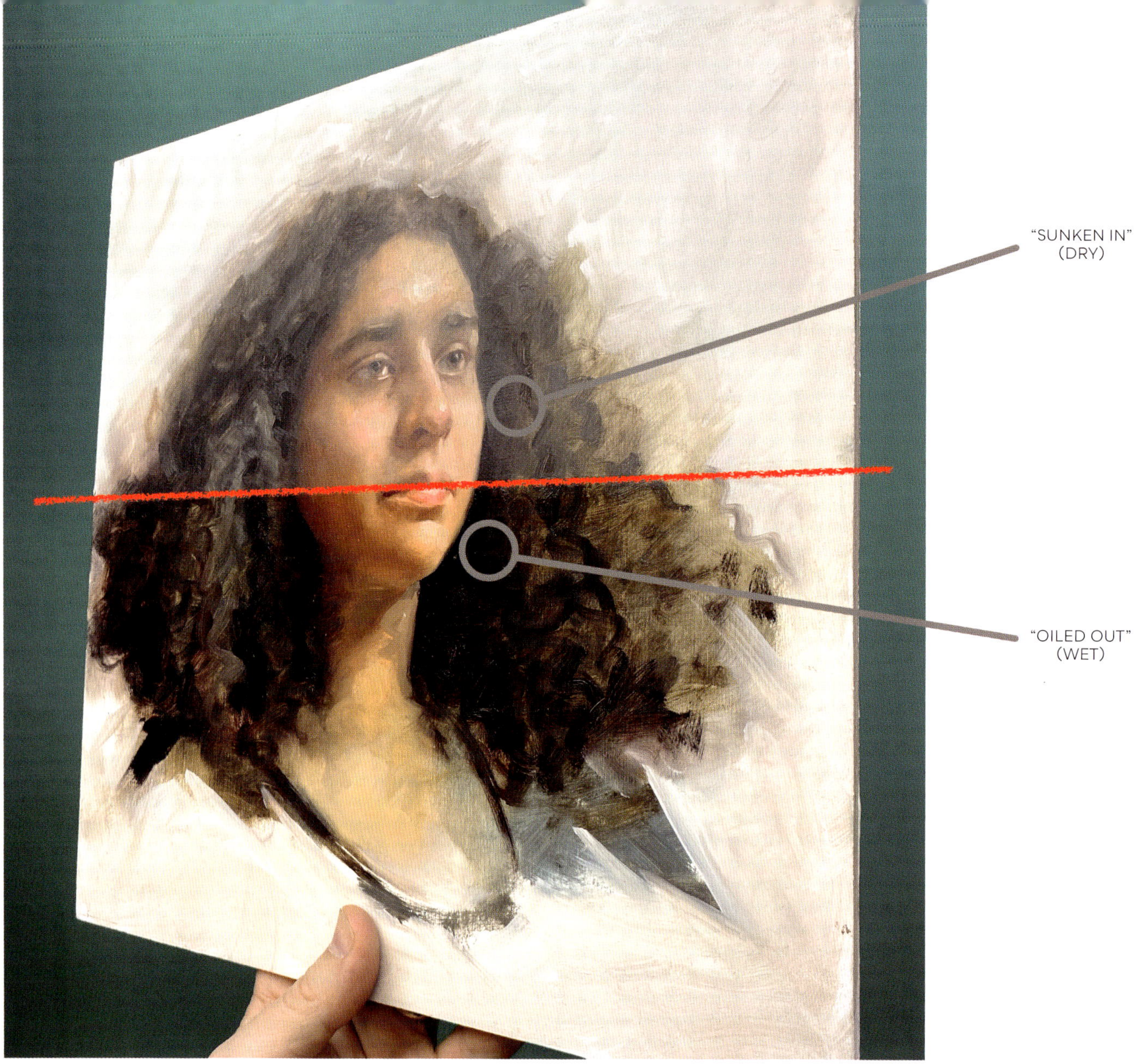

Image labels: "SUNKEN IN" (DRY) and "OILED OUT" (WET)

OILING OUT AND GLAZING IN

One of the sad realities of oil painting is that after a painting has dried, it usually dries duller than how it looked when it was wet. There's a slight disconnect between the decisions that we were making when the painting was wet and what happens when we come back into the studio the next day after it has dried.

When oil paint dries, the darks dry lighter, the colors dry grayer, and the lights typically dry darker. All of this lowers the contrast and diminishes our previous day's decisions. One way to counteract some of these problems is *oiling out* a dry painting. This requires a medium of some kind, preferably the one that I recommended in the Drawing Materials section (see page 22). The best way of doing this is to rub a thin coating of the medium over the painting with a lint-free rag. Don't do this if the painting isn't completely dry, as it will smear halfway dry paint all across the painting. Oiling out should restore the strength of the darks to the painting, making them darker. It should make the colors in the mid-tones more colorful and vibrant. This is a fantastic way to start a new painting session because it shows you what is truly there, rather than going into your painting session under the impression that the painting is actually lighter and grayer, an unfortunate mistake that would throw off all your new color decisions. This technique also gets the painting slightly wet again, which is a much more pleasant way of working on a painting. I almost always prefer to work wet on wet rather than wet on dry.

Scan to view a
video tutorial

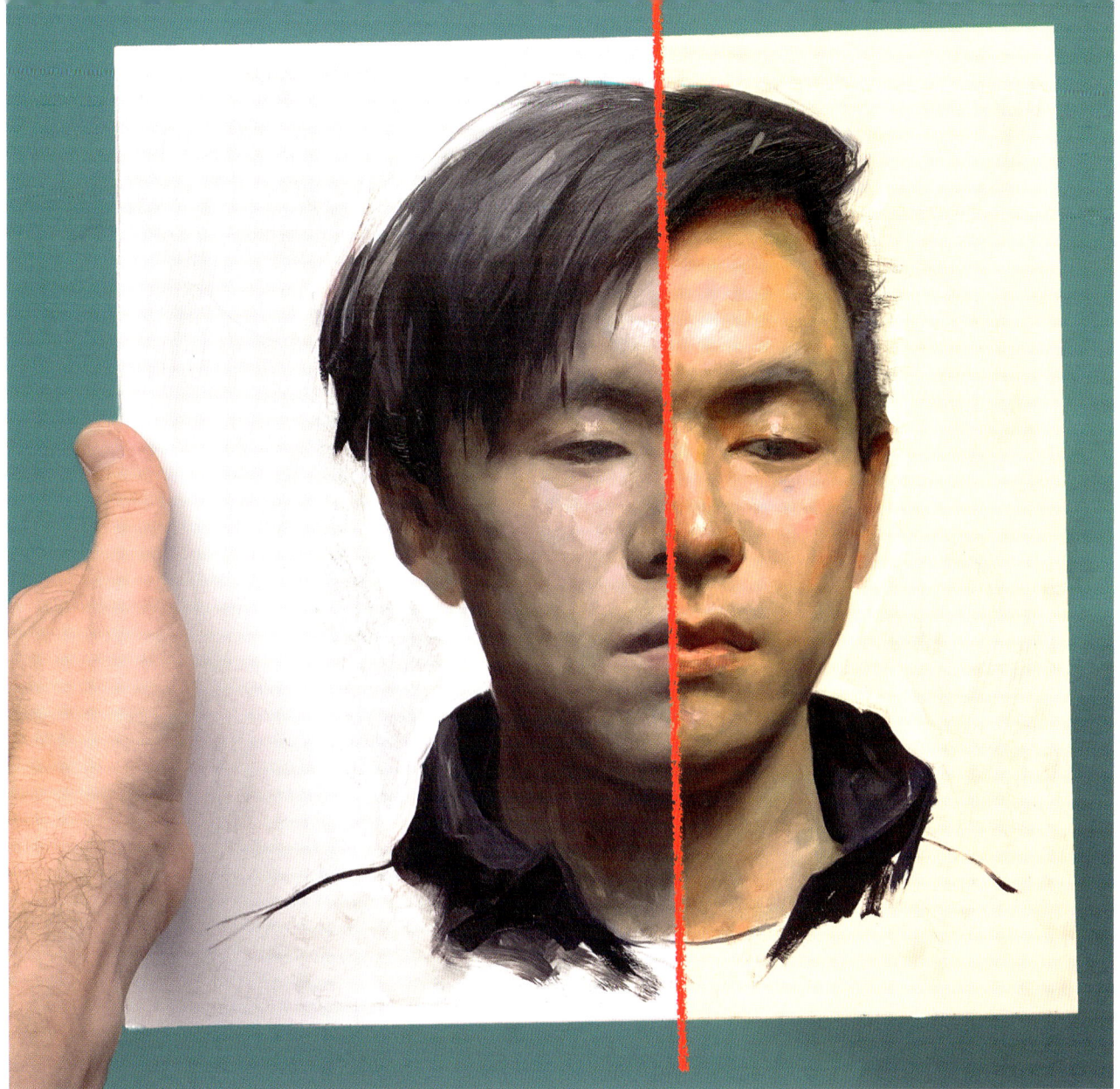

Another variation of this is called *glazing in*. This method is appropriate to apply if after oiling out, the colors are still cold, chalky, and not that vibrant, and the darkness still isn't strong. One way of glazing in is to rub a thin coating of burnt sienna or another warmer tone over the entire section of picture you plan to work on, which will have a universal warming affect over the image (as seen on the right side in above image). Then, into that glazed area, do some spot glazing where certain areas of the face might receive more red or more black or more diversity. These little tiny tweaks will change the overall appearance and color vibe of the picture.

It's easy to become confused when we try to identify what's bothering us about the picture we're making, but often, the color choices and value choices are at the crux of it. We can work all day on a painting and end up in the same spot that we were in last session. The benefit of glazing in like this is that we're able to change the color globally to efficiently reach the effect that we want, and then we're free to continue to work up the drawing and finish the painting. Without glazing in, we might feel obliged to repaint the entire thing, becoming bogged down and discouraged.

A TEST OF CHROMA

Every pigment handles differently. You'd think that most pigments would have similar properties because they're all oil paint, but one of the realities of paint is that some colors that look colorful when you add white to them are not actually very colorful. This is often true of the pigment cobalt blue. It looks like such a wonderful blue, but it becomes weak with the addition of other colors **(A)**. On the other hand, phthalo blue looks dark and it's hard to see what its color will be. When white is added, it's quite chromatic and perhaps the better choice when painting something like a sky or colorful blue clothing **(B)**.

LIGHT-COLORED PAINT DRIES DARKER

Among the many frustrating things that accompanies trying to make a great painting, this one ranks pretty high. You may be unaware of the fact that wet paint dries darker. In Figure **(C)**, we see dry paint, and it has a certain value of darkness. When I take the same exact color from the tube and put a fresh dollop of that color on top of its dry companion, the issue is made clear **(D)**. Figure **(C)** and Figure **(D)** have the exact same pigment, but Figure **(D)** contains a dollop of wet paint, which appears much lighter and brighter. Why does this matter? Because if your painting is dry, and you go to match the color exactly the way that it looks dry, you'll find when you come in the next day that the newer color dried darker and they're no longer the same. Generally speaking, titanium white is one of the worst offenders of this phenomenon of light-colored paint drying darker.

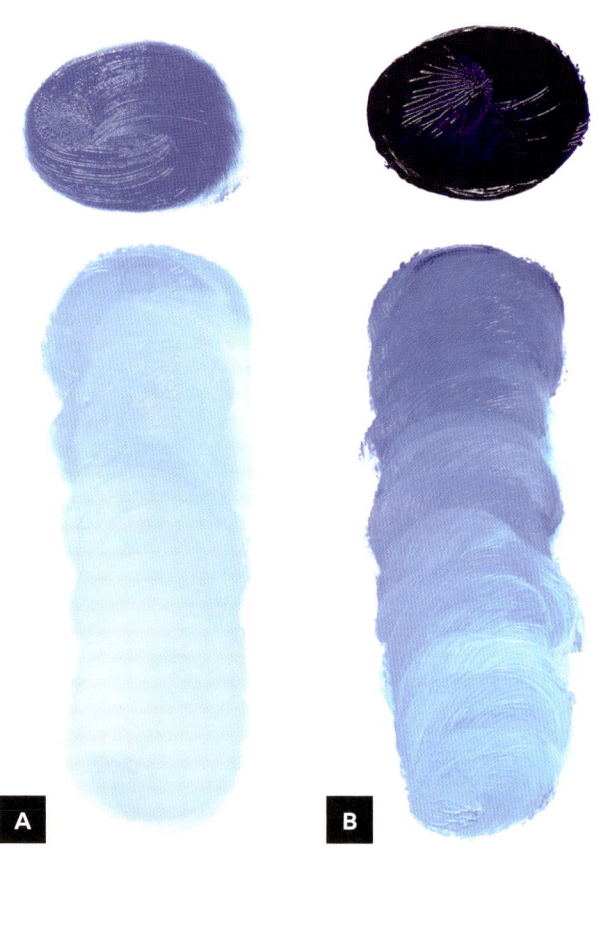

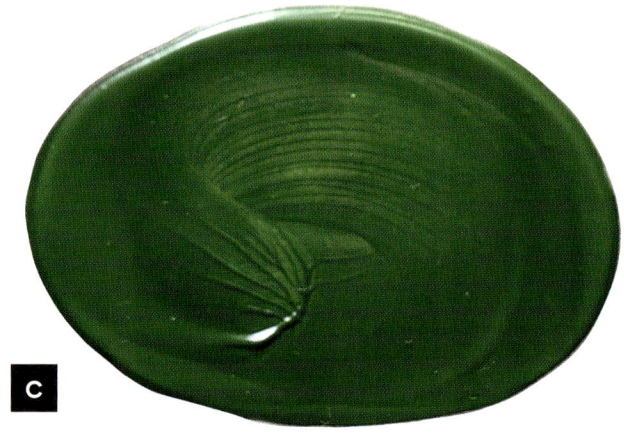

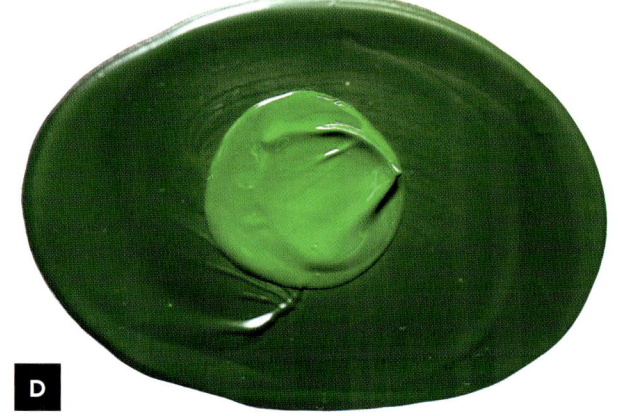

DENSE PAINT VS. THIN PAINT (CHEAP PAINT VS. MORE EXPENSIVE)

Somewhat different than just using thick paint, there's a wide range of densities when it comes to oil paint. Some colors are not really opaque and dense and feel like there's almost a clear liquid inside of them that keeps them from covering the surface well. This is especially true of cheap oil paint, which has many extenders in it to fill the tube up and is lower on pigment content. It's also the property of some naturally found pigments, such as lead white. In the case of lead white, this can actually be beneficial. It's a great pigment to use for glazing and to make slight modifications of the lighter tones in a portrait long after something has been dry. The light airy nature of the thinner pigment of lead white allows it to blend into a dry painting, and it doesn't darken as much as titanium white when it dries. So, this allows you to match the tones and blend them into the surface, more easily than titanium white, which easily covers but in a more brutal way.

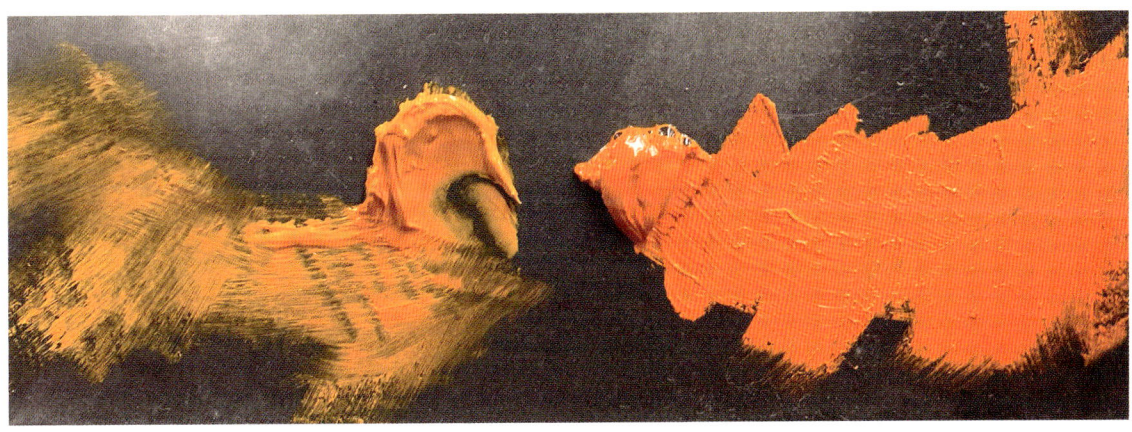

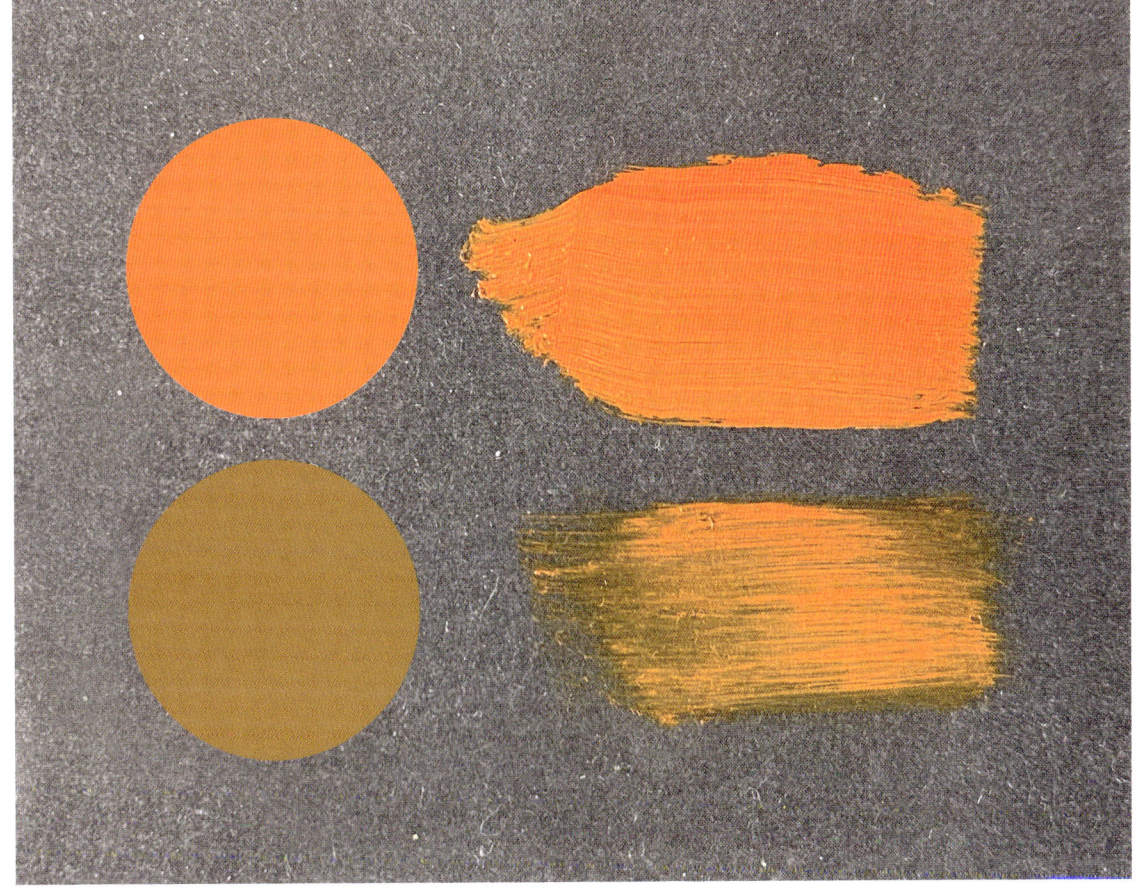

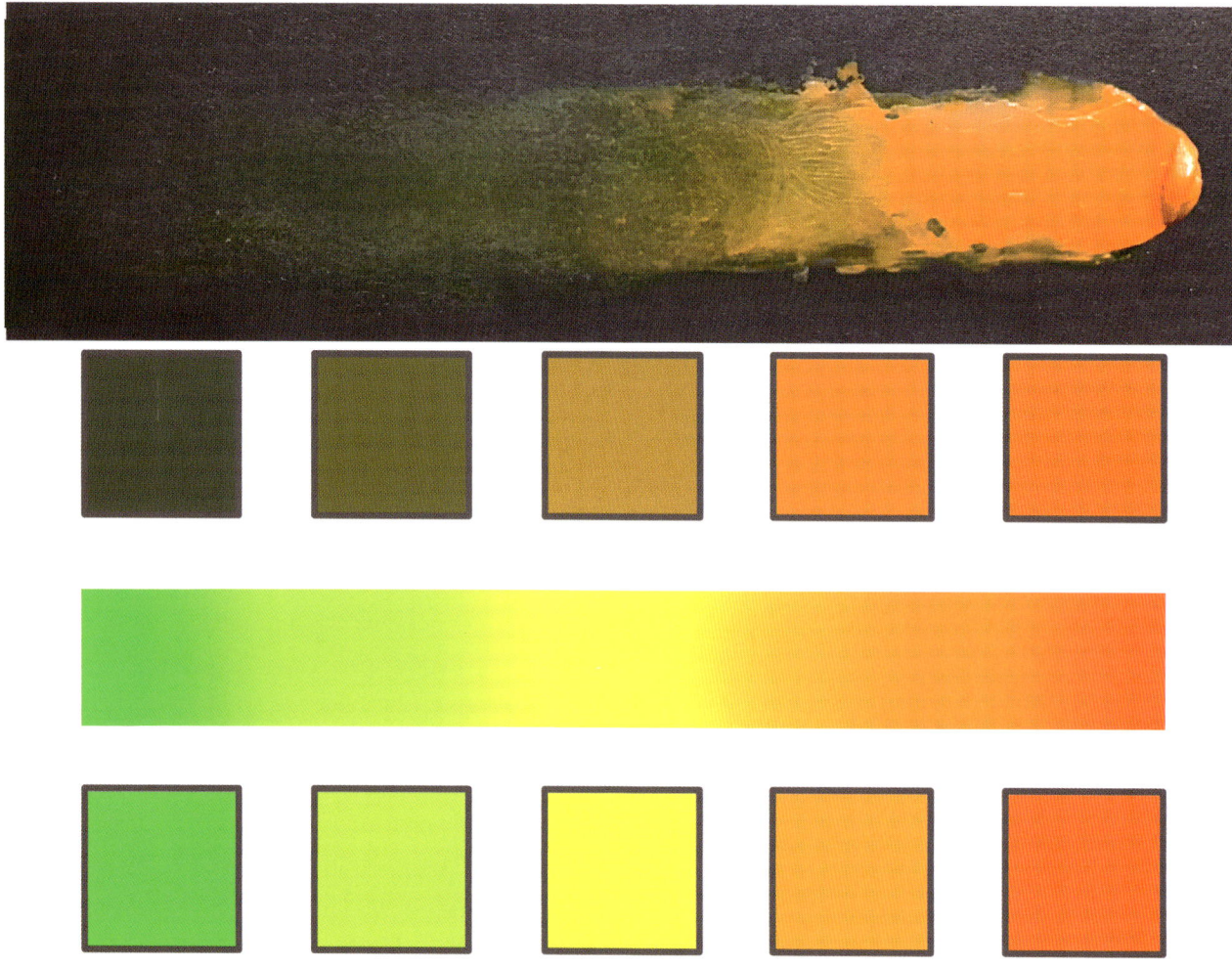

WHY DOES THAT ORANGE LOOK GREEN . . . OR BLUE?

The way that you use the paint affects the ultimate outcome of the color being used. If you're using orange over a dark surface and it becomes transparent, sometimes it appears greenish or even blue if mixed with white. This demonstrates that transparency changes the nature of the color being used by optically mixing with the surface being painted. Thus, the color of the surface, or ground, optically mixes with the color on your brush. This is what's known as a *scumble*, or a *velatura*. Sometimes, it just fits into the generic category of a glaze, but it's a specific phenomenon that when you use a light color over a dark color, when the light color thins out, it has a cooler cast. Why does this matter? Because it bends the color in an undesirable way when you're painting flesh tones.

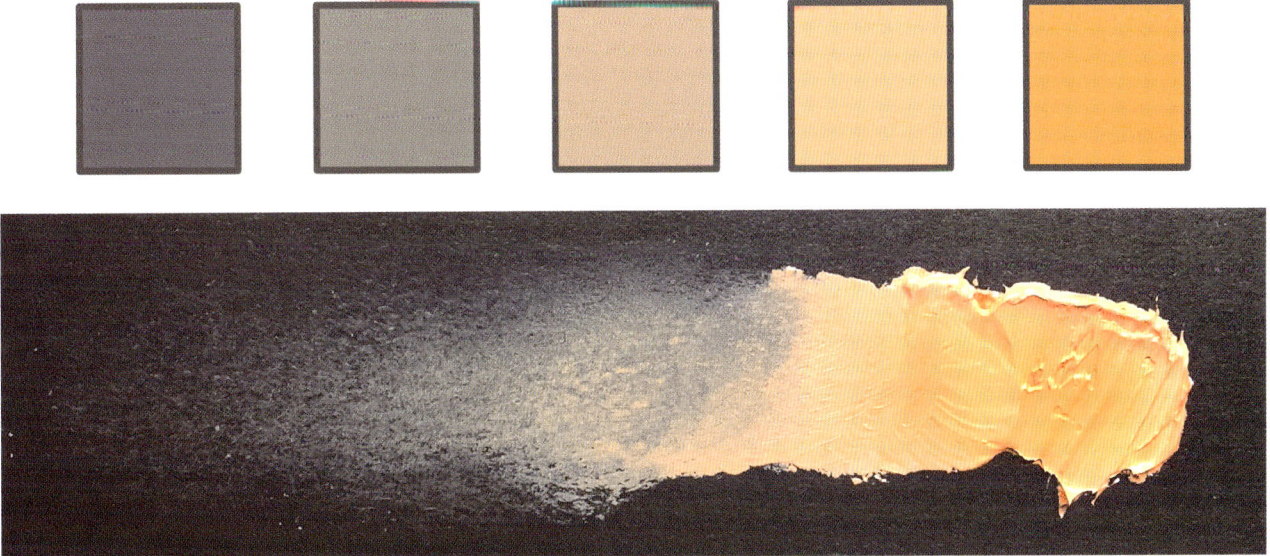

This can be remedied by either letting it dry and glazing it warmer or putting down colorful chromatic paint in those darker regions. This is often a problem when people blend their colors so much and stretch the highlights out too far without painting new colors to keep the warm tone of the face going from light to dark. Sometimes, this is effective when you're trying to create the classical flesh model of making a cool turning right before the shadow, so it really depends upon the situation.

This may be considered esoteric information; however, I do see it as a recurring problem for people who want rich, vibrant flesh tones and keep getting tones that are not what they desire.

COMPETING WITH A MODERN SENSE OF COLOR

Probably more than anything when it comes to color, even for many experienced painters, is that their colors tend to die out in the places where they'd like them to be the most chromatic. As seen in the diagram at right, where there's this range of colors that are really rich, we often settle for something slightly greater and move towards the middle. I don't think the old masters really had questions or frustrations with this because they didn't live in a world that was profoundly colorful in the way that we experience today, with movies, photographs, graphic design, and media where the colors always seem rich and full.

So the pressure that the modern painter feels to be able to compete with media is definitely a challenge for the realist painter, because as we blend our paintings and as paintings dry, the color is modified and becomes grayer. And even if we use some of the most colorful colors, often they fall a little bit short of the color that we experience on glowing screens like our phones and tablets.

One of the things I do in order to compete with this modern sense of color is that I try to do my best with the colors I have and I try to paint with cadmiums and normal strong colors such as the phthalos and other prismatic tones, but then at the end, when I want to reach that ultimate peak of chroma, I glaze in with some neon colors. That little extra push of color and chroma is dramatically effective and can't be overstated, especially when it's applied throughout the whole painting or with subjects like flowers or light shining through skin, creating a strong orange red.

All too often, I see amazing realist paintings that lack a sense of luminosity and colorfulness, and that's why tiny glazes of incredibly chromatic pigments at the end of a painting are so important because they really keep that fresh sense of color. Glazes push this color in a way that most other ways of applying paint can't accomplish.

So if you genuinely want luminous fresh color, this can still happen after everything has been painted. You use the paint, transparently, and extremely strong pigments to create that sense of chroma. And even before the advent of neon colors,

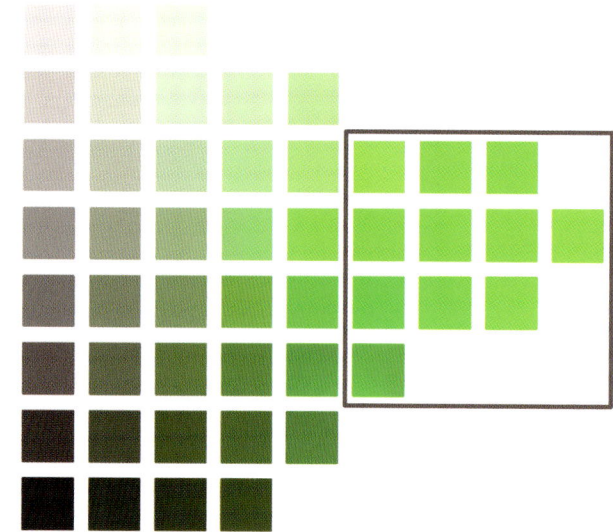

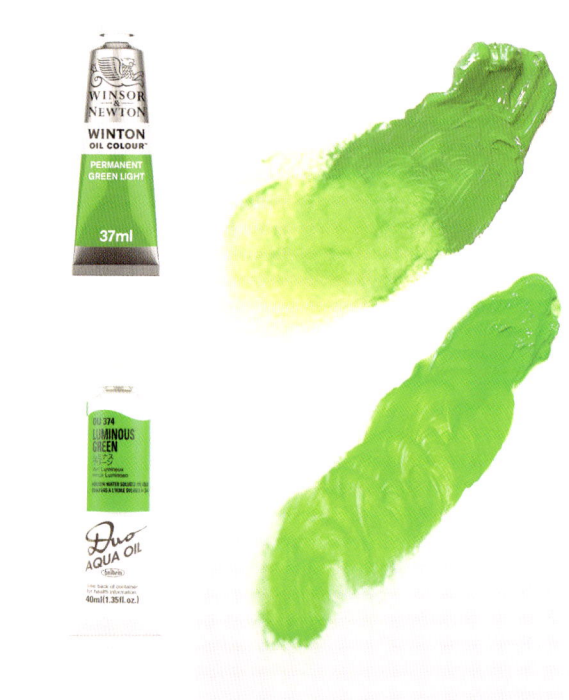

Flemish painters who used strong colored glazes on white panels still have luminous color today, 500 years later. This quality of glazing in strong jewel tone colors at the end is truly the answer for competing with a modern sense of color, and we also have new color options available that allow it to be even richer today.

VALUE AND CHROMA IN SHADOWS

Because chromatic possibilities tend to shrink in the dark region based on the Munsell model, which says that most colors peak in the middle range, maintaining chroma in the darks can be a challenge, especially when things become blended and if you use too many earth colors. So just in the same way that it's somewhat challenging to get your colors to peak and become truly chromatic, the same can be said for in the darks where things often get muddy and homogenized.

Most strong prismatic colors, such as alizarin crimson or ultramarine blue, usually come straight out of the tube quite dark. In order to lighten them to really get a sense of their pigment, you must add a bit of white. Too much white and they're really not dark anymore. So it really requires a lot of control in order to stay dark but also have color in that region. My answer for this is to have a lot of dark color options so that I can control the chroma and hue shifts in the dark. I'd prefer to have an ultramarine blue, an alizarin crimson, a dioxazine purple, a raw umber, and a deep, dark burnt sienna in order to shift around and truly control these tones. Too often, we rely on black and ivory and raw umber to navigate this value space, and that creates a lot of mud. Some professors I've had in the past would recommend using ultramarine blue, alizarin crimson, and burnt sienna as a black, which is called a *chromatic black*, because they'd prefer there to be real thought and choice in what the darks and the shadow colors are in the painting, rather than reaching for the obvious answer of ivory, black, or raw umber. I think this is a good solution and use it frequently to navigate color space on the dark end. I still use black and find it to be an incredibly necessary color, because sometimes by using this method things get a little wacky into colorful, and black can mellow out your tones quickly and effectively.

RESOURCES

BOOKS

Bauman, Stephen. *The Art of Portraiture.* Worcester, UK: 3DTotal Publishing, 2024.

Forster, Steve, and 3DTotal. *Beginner's Guide to Creating Portraits: Learning the Essentials & Developing Your Own Style.* 3DTotal Publishing, 2024.

Fowkes, Nathan. *How to Draw Portraits in Charcoal.* Design Studio Press, 2016.

Gurney, James. *Color and Light: A Guide for the Realist Painter (Volume 2).* Andrews McMeel Publishing, 2010.

Schmid, Richard. *Alla Prima II: Everything I Know about Painting.* 3rd ed. Stove Prairie Press, 2013.

Sin, Oliver. *Drawing the Head for Artists.* Beverly, MA: Quarry Books, 2019.

Sin, Oliver. *Facial Expressions for Artists.* Beverly, MA: Rockport Publishers, 2024.

Wu, Zhaoming. *Famous Classic Sketch Wu Zhaoming.* Guangxi Art Publishing House, 2016.

MAGAZINES

Artists Magazine
artistsnetwork.com

International Artist
internationalartist.com

Portrait Painter
artacademy.com

The Art of the Portrait Journal
portraitsociety.org

APPS

Artstudio Pro

Head Study App

MUSEUMS AND ORGANIZATIONS

National Portrait Gallery (London, UK)
npg.org.uk

National Portrait Gallery (Washington, D.C.)
npg.si.edu

Portrait Society of America
portraitsociety.org

The Royal Society of Portrait Painters
therp.co.uk

STEVE FORSTER

To learn more about Steve Forster, his school, and his classes (both online and in person), visit:

steveforster.net

Instagram: @steveforsterpaintings

Long Island Academy of Fine Art: liafa.com

ACKNOWLEDGMENTS

First and foremost, I would like to express my deepest gratitude to my wife, Rebecca. You have, above everyone else, given me the time, support, and love that it takes to sustain this artist through his creative, messy journey. Thank you for your calm, steady, and faithful approach to life.

I am also deeply grateful to my best friend, who also happens to be an amazing artist and teacher, Stephen Bauman. Your infectious enthusiasm and beautifully curious mind have inspired me for many years, but of course your friendship matters most. I am glad to have had so many artistic journeys and beautiful conversations with you.

I would like to thank The Florence Academy of Art for providing me with the foundational skills and artistic discipline that have shaped my skill set. Thank you to Daniel Graves, who provided for so many of us a school to learn and grow in the traditions of representational art. Without this school, I would never have met my wife, which has added one more marriage to the many that were produced from such an amazing place.

I am also deeply grateful to the New York Academy of Art, where I had the privilege of furthering my studies. Many of the color ideas in this book stem from my experiences there, which are too numerous to mention. Special thanks to Vincent Desiderio, David Kratz, Peter Drake, Mike Smith, John Cichowski, and John Volk.

In addition, I would like to thank the Long Island Academy of Fine Art community. So many beautiful humans have passed through these halls on Long Island, plus those who have joined our community online. You have been a constant support, especially the "Ladies of LIAFA"—you know who you are.

Thank you all for your contributions to this project and to my ongoing development as an artist.

INDEX

ALSO IN ROCKPORT'S
FOR ARTISTS SERIES

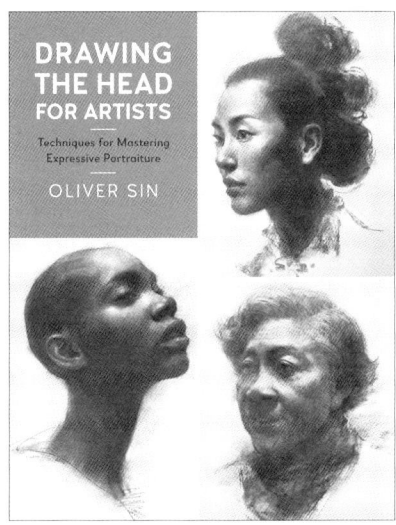

Drawing the Head for Artists
978-1-6315-9692-6

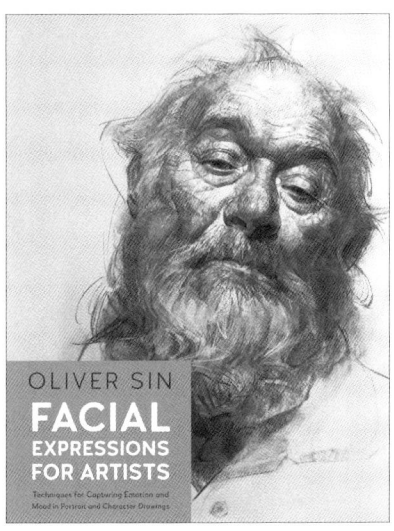

Facial Expressions for Artists
978-0-7603-8240-0

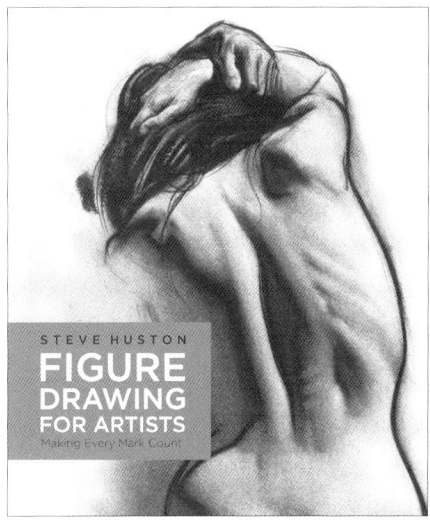

Figure Drawing for Artists
978-1-6315-9065-8

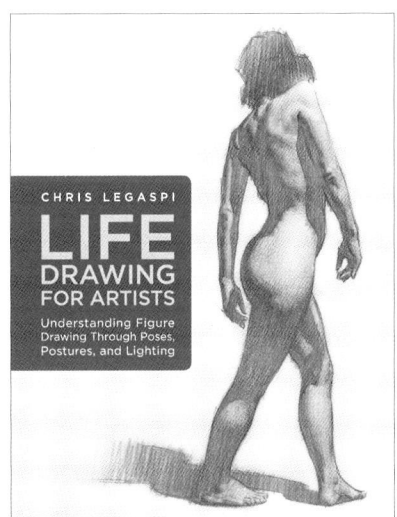

Life Drawing for Artists
978-1-6315-9801-2

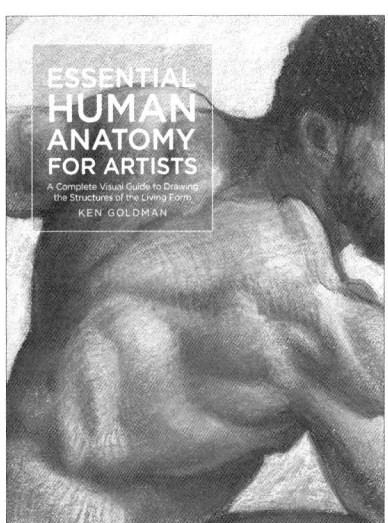

Essential Human Anatomy for Artists
978-1-6315-9959-0

ALSO IN ROCKPORT'S FOR ARTISTS SERIES